SILENT CINEMA
OF SPACE

NEW DIRECTIONS IN NATIONAL CINEMAS

Jacqueline Reich, editor

SILENT CINEMA AND THE POLITICS OF SPACE

Edited by Jennifer M. Bean, Anupama Kapse, and Laura Horak

Indiana University Press

Bloomington and Indianapolis

Taylor,
For the love of
silent cinema!
Laura Isabel Serna
+ the SCPS
team!
May 2014

This book is a publication of

Indiana University Press
Office of Scholarly Publishing
Herman B Wells Library 350
1320 East 10th Street
Bloomington, Indiana 47405 USA

iupress.indiana.edu

Telephone orders 800-842-6796
Fax orders 812-855-7931

∞ The paper used in this publication meets the minimum requirements of the American National Standard for Information Sciences—Permanence of Paper for Printed Library Materials, ANSI Z39.48-1992.

Manufactured in the United States of America

Library of Congress Cataloging-in-Publication Data

Silent film and the politics of space / edited by Jennifer M. Bean, Anupama Kapse, and Laura Horak.
pages cm — (New directions in national cinemas)
Includes bibliographical references.
ISBN 978-0-253-01226-5 (cloth) — ISBN 978-0-253-01230-2 (pbk.)
1. Silent films—History and criticism. 2. Space in motion pictures. I. Bean, Jennifer M., [date]- editor of compilation. II. Kapse, Anupama, editor of compilation. III. Horak, Laura, editor of compilation.
PN1995.75.S557 2014
791.4302′5—dc23

2013043181

1 2 3 4 5 19 18 17 16 15 14

Contents

Acknowledgments

When we first began what became *Silent Cinema and the Politics of Space,* the editors were convinced that early-twentieth-century film and media cultures offered a dynamic site for retroactively assessing the forces and tensions of globalization. As the central concept around which theories of contemporary politics, society, and culture have been organized in the past decade and a half, the term has elicited a vast spectrum of competing analyses and interpretations, a discursive constellation in which new forms of flow (of goods, people, images, ideas), the loss of bounded space, and the transgression of borders prove recurrent, common denominators. While it would be foolish to imagine that economic systems, socio-cultural conditions, or cinema and media formats of the early twentieth century are in any way identical to those of the early twenty-first, it struck us as peculiar that most studies of contemporary globalization and spatial heterogeneity proceed with the "assumption," to follow geographer Doreen Massey, "that once (once upon a time) those boundaries were *im*permeable, that there was no transgression."[1]

For film and media scholars who cling to the Ptolemaic perspective touted in introductory-level survey textbooks, those glossy makers of taste who parse the history of cinema country by country while also writing that history as the exclusive affair of a few "mature" nations and directors, such assumptions about a heavily bordered past may make sense. We discussed as much during conversations shared over the past decade at the annual Giornate del Cinema Muto (Days of Silent Cinema) festival in Pordenone, Italy, murmuring over shots of espresso (and more vociferously, late at night, with grappa in hand) that a Copernican revolution was surely underway. Those conversations assumed particular shape when several of the contributors and editors met at the fourth Women and the Silent Screen (W&SS) symposium hosted by the University of Guadalajara, Mexico, in June 2006. In their plenary address, Ivan Trujillo and Jennifer Bean, respectively representing the Mexican National Film Archive and the U.S. National Film Preservation Foundation, shared their conviction that silent era film history was happening "now." We happily acknowledged the lengthy history of La Fédération Internationale des Archives du Film, while agreeing that the dynamic alliances forged among national archives, international organizations, regional coalitions, local film museums, grassroots preservation societies, and private collectors were now taking place on a scale unimaginable to historians a generation ago.

This investment in historical plurality shaped the conference "Border Crossings: Rethinking Silent Cinema," organized by Anupama Kapse and Laura Horak at the University of California, Berkeley, in February 2008, where several of the essays gathered here were first conceived. The concept grew in intellectual scope as the three of us cemented our commitment to expanding the geopolitical terrain of film and media histories, first as a conference and then as an edited volume with original essays. For their tireless effort in making "Border Crossings" happen, we owe special thanks to Irene Chien, Paul Dobryden, Erica Levin, and Rielle Navitski, who sat on the steering committee while also gracefully negotiating the multiple, indispensable pragmatics necessary for such an event to take place. Ashley White-Stern, in particular, was our "righthand woman"—her ability (and willingness) to coordinate the financial aspects of the conference with style and precision models professionalism at its very best. The Pacific Film Archive partnered with us to present a program of Sessue Hayakawa films. The event was made possible by the generous support of Film Studies and the Townsend Center, Consortium for the Arts, Beatrice Bain Working Group, and the Departments of Rhetoric, Scandinavian, German, East Asian Languages and Cultures, and Gender and Women's Studies at the University of California, Berkeley. We remain deeply grateful to Jackie Reich, who encouraged us to consider a volume on the topics debated at the Berkeley event (even before the proposals were submitted), and whose support has never wavered through the many years in which this collection's contents and conception continued to shift and coalesce.

The contents of this volume also reflect ideas initially presented at the Colonial Film Project Seminar hosted by the British Film Institute in July 2008 and a few developed for (if not delivered at) the Society for Cinema and Media Studies (SCMS) conference scheduled to take place in Tokyo, Japan, in May 2009. Other chapters derive from discussions generated at the W&SS conferences in Guadalajara (June 2006), Stockholm (June 2008), and Bologna (June 2010). Across this same span of six years, many of the contributors and editors also participated in nearly concurrent conferences organized by Domitor: The International Society for the Study of Early Cinema in Michigan (June 2006), Girona and Peripignan (June 2008), and Toronto (June 2010). It would be impossible to enumerate the many colleagues, volunteers, universities, archivists, and cinémathèque programmers throughout the world whose efforts have enabled and sustained these international gatherings, but we would be remiss in not recognizing Monica Dall'Asta, Astrid Söderbergh Widding, Rosanna Maule, Shelley Stamp, Jane Gaines, Mark Cooper, Jennifer Horne, Kathleen Newman, Christine Gledhill, Dan Streible, Scott Curtis, Richard Abel, Lee Grieveson, Abé Mark Nornes, Bryony Dixon, Vanessa Toulmin, Frank Gray, Ravi Vasudevan, André Gaudreault, Paolo Cherchi Usai, and David Robinson as individuals whose passionate commitment to service equals that of their superb scholarship. A hats off as well to

Patrice Petro, whose eight-year term as the far-sighted president of the Society for Cinema and Media Studies (SCMS) parallel the years in which this volume came together, during which time she aggressively mounted initiatives to expand the international reach of that organization.

We consider ourselves especially privileged to have worked with a group of scholars whose linguistic and geographical expertise rests on archival perspectives grounded in ten different countries but whose intellectual investment in "the disorder inherent in every order," to borrow a phrase from Trinh T. Minh-ha, means that each refuses the fixity of any one event, object, or location as the constitutive source of historical meaning.[2] For their outstanding scholarship, and for their patience and goodwill in discussing these many ideas both individually and collectively, we remain deeply indebted to our contributors. We fondly recall Jane Behnken's initial enthusiasm for this project, while acknowledging that its completion would not have been possible without the steadfast support of Raina Polivka, whose resilience and incisive insights buoyed our spirits and ensured this project's integrity. A special shout-out goes to Fran Andersen for shepherding us through the production process and to Christine Gever for her sharp eye and meticulous care in the final editing stages. We are very grateful to our anonymous readers for their enthusiastic support and careful and valuable feedback on this volume. Anders Mellbourn and the Department of Media Studies at Stockholm University provided an extra and welcome boost by liberally supporting production expenses through the Rector's Strategic Fund. Jennifer Lynn Witzke transformed our fuzzy conception for this book's cover into a dazzling visual design, while Joshua Yumibe generously shared images and ideas when we most needed them. Many thanks to the George Eastman House, which supplied the cover images.

The perspective shaping this book emerges from our fascination with loose ends and obscured views in the multifaceted histories we seek to tell, as well as from a restless curiosity with the insufficiency and uncertainty of knowledges already acquired. What remains certain is the simple (albeit marvelous) fact that we maintained our commitment to working as a team—including the tricky task of communicating across three different time zones—while navigating the many stages of this complex project. Jennifer Bean would like to thank Patricia Torres de San Martín for the invitation to serve on the Board of Directors for the fourth Women and Silent Screen symposium in Guadalajara, Mexico, as well as her co-directors (and conspirators) Joanne Hershfield and Jane Gaines for modeling international collaboration on a scale that initially inspired, and continually informed, her efforts here. She offers a hushed nod of respect to Sudhir Mahadevan, Tamara Cooper, Gary Handwerk, Giorgio Bertellini, and Rob King for ongoing intellectual and collegial support, and a hug to Julie Bremer, Frank Alongi, Sara Bankemper, and Stephanie Bean for lessons in balance, introspection, and play.

Words don't quite convey her gratitude to John O'Neal, not only for affording her endless space to roam as she writes, but for the security of knowing he always will be there—grinning—when she gets home. Anupama Kapse is indebted to Richard Maxwell, Jonathan Buchsbaum, Amy Herzog, and Roopali Mukherjee for being extraordinary mentors, colleagues, and friends (or all at once). Linda Williams and Kristen Whissel nurtured this project from its earliest stages. Monika Mehta, Neepa Majumdar, Nitin Govil, Joy Fuqua, and Ellen Scott were much more than compatriots and offered forms of support that one can only dream of having. The days spent on putting this volume together fostered a degree of intellectual camaraderie, feistiness, and intimacy that one can share with only the best of friends and closest of family members. Young Shaunak Kapse waded through drafts only because they were written by his mother but was fearless in pointing out what was wrong with them. Dhananjay Kapse braved the toughest of spatial and temporal hurdles in innumerable conversations across the globe. For their unwavering support, both intellectual and emotional, Laura Horak would like to thank Gunnar Iversen, Ashley White-Stern, Althea Wasow, Nicholas Baer, and Mark Sandberg. To them and to the dedicated individuals who expanded the space of silent cinema through conferences, festivals, archives, departments, and institutions, we express our sincerest thanks.

Jennifer Bean, Anupama Kapse,
and Laura Horak
Seattle, New York, Stockholm
October 1, 2013

Notes

1. See Doreen Massey, *for space* (London: Sage, 2010), 65.
2. The quoted phrase comes from Trinh T. Minh-ha, "Documentary Is/Not a Name," *October* 52 (Summer 1990): 95.

SILENT CINEMA AND THE POLITICS OF SPACE

Introduction

Jennifer M. Bean

Not by chance, the problematics that would intrinsically expose the multicultural and multilinguistic fabric of silent cinema—i.e. cross-national commercialisations and "influences"—have for a long time received scant attention.

Giorgio Bertellini

Spatialising the story of modernity . . . has had effects—it has not left the story the same.

Doreen Masey

It seems prudent to begin with a simple statement: *Silent Cinema and the Politics of Space* offers a cross-cultural history of narrative film and related media objects in the years loosely dating from the early 1910s through the early 1930s. That single sentence sounds sensible, the kind of summary I have tossed around on several occasions when describing this collection and its contents to curious friends. But the stand-alone adjective "cross-cultural" doesn't quite capture the editors' and contributors' shared belief that "film history" marks a constellation of uneven forces (geographical, economical, political, psychological, textual, experiential) that display neither the coherence of an integral entity nor the continuity of a successive lineage that develops over time. We are fascinated by the messiness of cinema's dispersed existence in these years: by the cross-pollination of images in diverse parts of the globe; by the international penchant for piracy (and piracy's cheeky cousins, modification and appropriation); by the recycling of obsolete or junk prints in so-called peripheral markets; and by the refashioning of iconic identities and events as they cross media forms and geographic borders. Such a perspective inevitably shakes things up. It provides methodological entry into unexpected political, social, and aesthetic constellations that just as quickly skitter into alternative pathways, effecting a spatial disorientation of "silent cinema" as we know it.

We find this disorientation extremely stimulating, in part because it expands the geopolitical terrain of English-language film and media histories to encompass non-Western cinemas and cultures. The phrase "in part" is an especially important qualification. There is absolutely no question that the years in which cinema flourished as an international phenomenon corresponded with the political and economic dominance of a few imperialist and capitalist nations. Nor would we quarrel over whether early film and film cultures in France, Germany, Russia, and especially the United States have enjoyed preeminent status in the field. But spinning the globe to face east (rather than west) or south (rather than north) not only artificially bifurcates the world into Western/non-Western spheres; it also sidesteps the task of challenging certain constitutive assumptions in Anglophone film and media studies, including some of the commitments, some of the stages and positions, that may have been historically necessary in order for the field to flourish but to which it can no longer adhere. Many of these commitments have vitalized scholarly debates in recent years and will be addressed in the editors' introductions to the respective sections that follow. But some are harder to name and interrogate than others, belonging as they do to critical controversies not yet fully played out and in some cases not yet posed as a question for thought. They persist in a historicism that revels in the pleasures and delights of temporality at the expense of space and spatiality.

By foregrounding a "politics of space" as its organizing principle, this volume encourages those writing and teaching silent era cinema to ask how and why a lingering historicism constrains or distorts our ability to account for the radical heterogeneity of early film and film cultures for people in diverse sectors and strata of the globe. The problem is not simply that a historicist logic inherited from nineteenth-century European and North American intellectual traditions depends on a conception of time as linear and successive, cyclical and recurrent; it is also that this conceptual legacy obfuscates a view of the rest of the world as anything other than space to be conquered or, emphatically, *developed.* As sociologist Dipesh Chakrabarty put the matter in his ambitious attempt at "Provincializing Europe" (the title of his 2002 study): "It [historicism] was one important form that the ideology of progress or 'development' took from the nineteenth century on. Historicism is what made modernity or capitalism look not simply global but rather something that became global *over time,* by originating in one place (Europe) and then spreading outside it. This 'first in Europe, then elsewhere' structure of global historical time was historicist."[1]

This mode of thinking legitimated the "civilizing" mission of colonial empires beginning in the nineteenth century and underlies the ideology of progress intrinsic to Western capitalist democracies. This mode of thinking allowed Karl Marx to say that the "country that is more developed industrially only shows, to the less developed, the image of its own future."[2] And it is this mode of thinking that informed the first generation of film historians, who wrote what Valentina Vitali and Paul Willemen shrewdly categorize as "biographies of an industrial sector." In their introduction to the fine collection *Theorising National Cinema*

(2006), Vitali and Willemen identify in particular the work of Paul Rotha (1949) in Britain, as well as Georges Charensol (1935) and Georges Sadoul (1949) in France, as studies that privileged industrial rather than cultural factors as developmental engines that drive film history. In so doing, these histories "recounted the birth and growth of an industry that proliferated, radiating outwards from the heartlands of capital—a thrust forward, from advanced societies such as Western Europe and [the] United States to the periphery as an exemplary trajectory of modernization sweeping across the world. In this context, the film industry was a metonym for the industrialization of culture and a metaphor for modernity itself."[3]

However paradoxically, a particularly powerful means of forestalling critical interrogation of this historicist logic emerged as a somewhat oblique and unintended consequence of revisionist approaches to early film history in the late 1970s and 1980s. The legendary thirty-fourth conference of the *Fédération Internationale des Archives du Film* (FIAF), held in Brighton, England, in 1978, is often cited as a moment when Old Film History began transforming into New Film History. Here participants systematically viewed hundreds of films produced prior to 1906, revolutionizing assumptions of the earliest cinema as an embryonic or infantile stage awaiting the maturity bestowed by the innovations of D. W. Griffith, the arrival of the feature film, and a self-sustained narrative form in the second decade of motion picture production. Noël Burch's pivotal address at the conference urged participants to conceive the earliest cinema as modeling a distinct representational system and a relationship between viewer and image that he called the "primitive mode of representation" and which he distinguished from a later "institutional mode of representation." This paradigmatic shift to a pre-institutional (pre-industrial) period of cinema might look from one perspective like a Foucault-inspired reaction against a historicist and Euro-centric perspective inherited from nineteenth-century modernity. But a closer look reveals that the aggressive anti-teleological rhetoric dominating the New Film History movement assumed an alternative critical posture. "The rediscovery of the 'primitive mode,'" to follow Thomas Elsaesser's recent summation, "seemed a vindication of more than fifty years' indefatigable efforts on the part of the avant-garde in both North America and Europe to rethink the basis of 'film language.' It raised the hope of retiring once and for all the notion that the development of cinema towards fictional narrative in the form of representational illusionism had been its pre-ordained destiny."[4]

By shunting "representational illusionism" to the periphery, the wild success of the New Film History somewhat ironically assumed technological and industrial modernity as the medium's explanatory center. Few essays did as much to secure the earliest cinema's axiomatic relation to modernity than Tom Gunning's "The Cinema of Attraction: Early Film, Its Spectator and the Avant-Garde," first published in 1986. Categorically speaking, the "cinema of attractions" model shares much in common with Burch's "primitive mode of representation," including a belief in the earliest cinema's representational integrity, its frontal positioning, its proclivity for acts of overt display, the viewers' awareness of the act of looking, and the pertinence of all of the above to the avant-garde. But it was Gunning who reassessed the predominantly non-narrative moving images popular at the fin de siècle as an aesthetic fully consistent with the kinesthetic shocks and thrills associated with modern technology. More than a vehicle for *representing* modernity, the actualities of the Lumière brothers, the trick films of Georges Méliès, or the many "phantom rides," for instance, initially *attract* as an instance of modern technology itself, thereby recoding and reflecting the very modernity in which they play an integral part. This is not the place to rehearse once again the valuable, even irreplaceable, insights promulgated by the conceptual/historical model of "attractions" and its seismic impact on film and media studies more generally.[5] But this is precisely the place to keep in mind that any heuristic which privileges "phenomenological categories like 'shock,' 'sensation,' and 'force,'" as Rob King writes with characteristic insight, "corresponds term for term with the language with which [Western] modernity was itself described at the turn of the century." "In a very real sense," King urges, "the contemporary historiography of early cinema has, knowingly or not, answered to Henry Adams' already-quoted call for a history focused on the 'dynamics of Forces,' and, to this extent, falls squarely within the parameters of [Western] modernity's own discourse about itself."[6]

How then does early cinema assume significance for audiences in areas peripheral to "modernity's own discourse about itself," or for those viewers inhabiting sectors and strata of the globe where cinema was predominantly an import? It was not until 2000 that Ana López's justly influential essay "Early Cinema and Modernity in Latin America" expanded the geopolitical terrain of New Film History, asking how the constellation of terms linking "cinema" with "modernity," both understood as synchronic and welded together by the phenomenology of technologically produced "sensation," bears meaning for countries like Peru, Argentina, Brazil, and Mexico. There is no simple answer. Indeed, part of what makes López's analysis so compelling is her refusal to posit a simple binary between the modern and the traditional, or between *their* images and *our* culture. While acknowledging that cinema in Latin America was (and in many cases remains) an import, López charts early cinema's reception and subsequent modification relative to the "decentered, fragmented and uneven" processes of modernization in Latin American countries.[7] The quasi-feudal state of Peru, for instance, in which only 5 percent of the population had the right to vote, may explain why screenings of Edison's Vitascope (likely first shown in Lima on January 2, 1897) generated less appeal than the same screening in Argentina six months earlier, in July 1896, a month which also witnessed the premiere of the British Vivomatograph and the Lumière Cinématographe in Buenos Aires. The saturation of cinema in Buenos Aires is commensurate, Lopez argues, with that city's function as the center of national industrial activity, replete with a reliable electrical infrastructure, telephones, and a cosmopolitan population. This does not mean that *Porteños* (Buenos Aires residents) either mimicked or mirrored the responses of viewers in France, Britain, or the United States. "To the degree that the cinema of attractions depended on a highly conscious awareness of the film image as image and of the act of looking itself, it also produced a tremendously self-conscious form of spectatorship . . . almost immediately translated as the need to assert the self as modern but also and, more lastingly, as different, ultimately as a national subject."[8]

In the decade since López's article was first published, a flurry of very good work by scholars of diverse regional, linguistic, and even disciplinary allegiances has expanded our understanding of the earliest cinema's cross-cultural caprice.[9] The publication which perhaps has done most to disquiet the categorical interaction of terms like "modernity" and "nationality" is Richard Abel, Giorgio Bertellini, and Rob King's *Early Cinema and the "National."* Based on the proceedings of the ninth biannual conference of Domitor: The International Association for the Study of Early Cinema, held in Ann Arbor, Michigan, in 2006, the book's thirty-four essays are by necessity short, occasionally sporadic, and decidedly provocative.[10] The dynamic handful of essays that roam outside the Northwestern Hemisphere of the globe, in particular, chart diverse processes of adaptation, contestation, and innovation as the machines that made images move spread rapidly through the international marketplace. Daniel Sánchaz Salas, for instance, also recovers a distinctive national identity produced by way of the machine's arrival in Spain, although viewers' conscious awareness of the act of looking, a feature important to López's analysis, transforms into an act of *listening* in the context of early-twentieth-century Spanish culture. More specifically, he recovers the "performative function" of local lecturers who relocated or interpreted events depicted on screen, changed characters' names, and spoke in local dialects; these human performances "made the early film show part of the dominant national popular culture."[11]

While López and Sánchaz Salas have good reason for perceiving nationalism as a response to the importation of cinematic devices, countervailing perspectives emerge. Notwithstanding Benedict Anderson's proclamation that "nationalism" became the "international norm" in the early part of the twentieth century, a European nation-state model is not translatable to Italy, for instance, nor to the territories of the erstwhile Ottoman Empire.[12] As historian Palmira Brummet elaborates in another context, identity for Ottoman "citizens" residing anywhere from Macedonia to Arabia until World War I "was never merely a question linking one's destiny to an Ottomanist or nationalist program. Nowhere has it ever been demonstrated that any but a few of the sultan's subjects ever identified themselves primarily as Osmanli (Ottoman)."[13] Building from this premise, Canan Balan argues that any consideration of cinema's "arrival" in Istanbul must refuse a national framework, especially given the cosmopolitan nature of entertainment districts such as Pera where some of the first screenings took place in 1896, and where Muslim, Jewish, Armenian, and Greek families coexisted with European businessmen, sailors, tramps, dandies, and so on.[14] By conceiving cinema's reception in Istanbul relative to the region's pre-cinematic visual culture, and by demonstrating its rapid assimilation in popular *meddah* storyteller performances and popular shadow plays known as *Karagöz,* Balan's study shares a surprisingly powerful resonance with Aaron Gerow's reconstruction of the discourse surrounding the moving-image machine's initial reception in Japan in his chapter in part 3 of this volume. Although Gerow's analysis attends primarily to the "problem" engendered by the later importation of the French crime serial *Zigomar* (1911), he begins by sketching the cinematograph's seamless assimilation in a nineteenth-century tradition of *misenomo,* including hand-crafted dolls, lifelike performances, X-rays, and magic lantern demonstrations by skilled Japanese artists. Skilled Italian writers such as Vincenzo Cecchetti, however, who wrote a sonnet in 1897 titled "The Lumière Cinematographe," rejected the machine's assimilation to existing traditions. As John P. Welle observes, the fact that Cecchetti's sonnet was written in the distinctive regional dialect of Rome, *romanesco,* and published in a popular Roman newspaper, gains importance relative to its description of the cinématographe as emblematic of a chimerical international identity; the poem likens the itinerant Lumière projectionist to a "mysterious man" who wears a "French hat," sports "Abbruzzese side-whiskers," and drives "a carriage as the English do." That carriage also resembles a "Japanese see-saw." The machine's promiscuous identity renders it a bad object, Welle argues, a corrupting element relative to the imagined stability of a regional—albeit emphatically not national—identity.[15]

In the most general and obvious way, these multifarious responses to early cinema's "arrival" in diverse regions and nations challenge a historicist imagination in which technology plays the role of seductive protagonist in a tale about an unceasing movement from local, distinct, traditional cultures to an ever more industrialized, globalized, and modernized world. More specifically, what is at stake in some of the most remarkable work in film historical studies of recent years, including the eleven chapters in the present volume, are variations on what I will call the "eruption of the local" into the presumed deterritorialization effected by the Lumière brothers' globe-trotting personnel in the late nineteenth century, the imperial spread of the French giant Pathé Frères in the years prior to World War I, or the U.S. film industry's assumed hegemony as transnational puppeteer in the mid- to late silent era—the period most at stake in the pages that follow. I use the term "eruption" to suggest an activity, a sort of breaking forth of locality constituted in relation to Western modernity's global campaign (of which "Hollywood" continues to serve as an altogether simplistic emblem in contemporary film and media studies). Locality, in other words, means something other than the commonsensical conception of a pre-existent community held together by common habits, shared histories, and geographical as well as imagined borders capable of identifying and excluding non-locals or foreign others. Rather, locality as it has been conceived (if not always named) in recent film-historical work shares with thinkers as diverse as Arjun Appadurai, T. S. Oakes, Doreen Massey, and Eric Wolf, among others, a basic understanding that locality is never pre-existent, internally generated, or isolated.[16] It is, rather, context dependent. As Oakes puts the matter in his study of place in pre-modern and modern China, "Distinctive cultural spaces [have always been] maintained . . . through connections rather than disjunctions. . . . 'Locality' is simply a contingent component of that 'space of flows' rather than its antithesis."[17]

Ultimately, by casting the history of popular narrative cinema from the early 1910s through the early 1930s in primarily spatial terms, this volume indicates the urgency of responding to Giorgio Bertellini's call to engage "the problematics that would intrinsically expose the multi-linguistic and multi-cultural fabric of silent cinema—i.e. its cross-national commercialization and 'influences.'"[18] As Bertellini observes in his introduction to a special issue of *Film History* (2000) on "Early Italian Cinema," there is a reason why these "problematics . . . have received scant attention."[19] The delay results in part from economic agendas that constitute and regulate, often in complicit ways, archival and academic work. On one hand, state-sponsored funding for the majority of the world's film archives marshals an imperative to organize, preserve, and assess cinema under the rubric of nationality and nationhood. On the other hand, the location of film and media scholars in traditional humanities and area studies departments ensures, and often demands, a scholarly and curricular commitment to nation- or region-specific cultures and traditions. These reasons help explain why our scholarship often suffers from what Bertellini diagnoses as "cultural monoglottism," and why collections based on conference proceedings at Domitor such as *Early Cinema and the "National"* detailed above, or those derived from Women and the Silent Screen international conferences of the past decade offer an exception to the rule.[20] The general rule for even the most sophisticated English-language collections dedicated to the period, most notably Lee Grieveson and Peter Krämer's *The Silent Cinema Reader* (2004), is to organize chapters pertinent to narrative cinema after 1910 country by country while also writing film history and geography as an exclusively Euro-Russian-American affair. By way of explanation, as Grieveson and Krämer clarify in their introduction, the book's organization follows "major *developments* in silent cinema" (my emphasis).[21] More precisely, they write: "The principal thread of our narrative is the *development* of American cinema. . . . *Developments* in America were to some extent representative of general *developments* in Western filmmaking; what happened in the U.S. also happened—and for similar reasons—in other countries. At the same time, U.S. *developments* no doubt influenced international filmmaking due to Hollywood's preeminent role in exporting films from the 1910s onwards" (my emphasis).[22]

To say that this organizational paradigm is symptomatic of the persistence and power of a fundamentally underspatialized historicism does not mean that the editors of *The Silent Cinema Reader* are either wicked or ignorant.[23] To the contrary, I foreground their volume precisely because they are so very, very good at what they do, choosing to represent even the most canonical of U.S. films, *Birth of a Nation* (1915), for instance, with a smart chapter by Linda Williams that situates D. W. Griffith's grandiose multi-reel phenomenon as part of a melodramatic tradition in American culture that mobilizes suffering as a means of codifying racial antipathy. Other cultural anxieties pertaining to shifting ethnic or gender norms in the United States during these years inform important chapters by Gaylyn Studlar, Sumiko Higashi, and Shelley Stamp, while the complex business strategies through which the American film industry sought to secure and maintain a position in the global marketplace, which have been the focus of several notable studies, are shrewdly included by way of an excerpt from Ruth Vasey's *The World According to Hollywood, 1919–1939*.[24] Indeed, the volume more generally thwarts totalizing claims to the meaning of any one industrial transition, film format, or audience experience in the major film-producing countries. An essay on Russian film culture between 1908 and 1919 by Yuri Tsivian (also a contributor here) exemplifies some of the most ambitious recent work in national film studies of the period, what might be called a sort of teleology in reverse that refuses the fetish for the 1920s (Soviet montage, German expressionism, French impressionism) so prevalent in canonical litanies elsewhere, while Joseph Garnacz charts the robust growth of a popular German cinema in the 1920s as absolutely irreducible to the haunting and oblique stylizations associated with "expressionism."

It should be clear by now that the organization of the present volume differs significantly from that of *The Silent Cinema Reader* and that it intends to provide an introduction to some of the efforts to lay the groundwork for a philosophical and methodological shift in the writing of film history and geography. Since the majority of the contributors to this volume currently reside and teach in the United States (with two exceptions, both based in Stockholm), certain commonalities and blind spots inevitably are shared. We also share an explicit interest in fostering the teaching of films that may no longer exist, as well as introducing students and scholars to archival perspectives and materials drawn from Mexico, Iran, China, Sweden, India, Denmark, Japan, Germany, and Russia, among others. Taken together, these chapters map "a distinctly centrifugal logic for the field," a phrase I borrow from Ravi Vasduvan's shrewd summation of emerging work on early film history and cultures in South Asia. In a short essay published in *Cinema Journal* in 2010, at the very moment the editors had finalized the selection of authors for this collection, Vasudevan articulated one of the methodological principles informing our endeavor: to wit, "history is intelligible as distributed into various elements, which in turn, implies several histories; this means that an understanding of the object, cinema, can only emerge from its dispersal."[25]

A dynamic dispersal of that peculiar "object" commonly known as "Hollywood" also informs this volume's sources, aims and goals. Sweeping generalizations regarding the American film industry's rapid and unhindered ascension to the status of transnational puppeteer in the years immediately following the First World War have been particularly pervasive in scholarship on contemporary "world cinema," as Lúcia Nagib demonstrates in a deft survey. She also wages a compelling polemic, arguing that relentless iterations of the truism regarding Hollywood's longstanding global dominance means that "world cinema" can only be defined "negatively"—defined, that is, by what American/Hollywood cinema is not.[26] In the spirit of loosening the hold this truism has on our thinking, many of the chapters included in this volume study the constellation of effects reflecting and disorienting "American" cinema's surfeit in international markets. Far from privileging U.S. cinema as a reified presence or entity, much less an industrial engine driving the development of film history, these investigations map the dispersal of certain (often canonical) films and figures within a transnational context of contestation, transformation, exchange, collaboration, travel, and appropriation. In every case, the organizational principle involves a "dialectical confrontation," and hence an approach that follows anthropologist Johannes Fabian's insistence that historicist conceptions of space and time are central to the construction of a particular form of knowledge/power that is very much alive today and that refuses to acknowledge what he calls "coevalness." As he writes, "Coevalness aims at recognizing cotemporality as the condition for a truly dialectical confrontation" in which "what are opposed . . . are not the same societies at different stages of development, but different societies facing each other at the same Time."[27]

In this respect, the four parts that follow (each of which comprises several chapters), "Picturing Space," "Prints in Motion," "Impertinent Appropriations," and "Cosmopolitan Sexualities and Female Stars," could just as easily be placed in any other order. And while the editors offer alternative heuristic frameworks for thinking about each of the sections individually, we encourage the reader to experience these framing devices as a series of flashes that "zoom in" on a particular set of issues condensed in (but not corralled by) the respective section, and then "rack out" to other spaces, including those available on the many websites included as links throughout the pages that follow. It is not unlikely that the reader who visits the home page for the Permanent Seminar on the History of Film Theories (http://filmtheories.org) will be distracted by the list of early Italian film critics slated for translation, if not the detailed abstracts for over fifty papers presented at the Histories of East Asian Film Theory Conference held at the University of Michigan in September 2012. Others may lose track of time while browsing the panoply of amateur, documentary, fictional, and missionary films related to Great Britain's erstwhile colonial territories, recently streamed and now freely accessible on the Colonial Film Project site (www.colonialfilm/uk.org), or while surfing the literally thousands of print-based documents from the period uploaded on the recently launched Media History Digital Library (http://mediahistoryproject.org/). Such wandering is neither peripheral nor incidental to the goals of this volume. It is not simply that online sites such as these offer fundamentally new vantage points and perspectives for a field that, until quite recently, stubbornly clung to a venerable legacy of canonical figures and films; it is also that new media formats and their overlapping "windows"—to stress Anne Friedberg's incisive use of the term—produce a fundamentally new spatial-temporal syntax through which moving images and texts no longer assume a temporality understood as exclusively sequential, nor a perspective anchored or fixed to a single window or frame.[28]

Indeed, it may very well be that the propinquity and spatial heterogeneity fostered by the overlapping windows of the electronic age will enable at long last an attitude, an imaginative space of engagement, for entertaining situations of actually existing multiplicity. We proceed with the conviction that "spatializing the story of modernity," to paraphrase geographer Doreen Massey, will have its effects.[29] It will not leave the story the same.

Notes

1. Dipesh Chakrabarty, *Provincializing Europe: Postcolonial Thought and Historical Difference* (Princeton, NJ: Princeton University Press, 2000), 7.

2. "Preface to the First Edition," in Karl Marx, *Capital: A Critique of Political Economy*, vol. 1, translated by Ben Fowkes (Harmondsworth, UK: Penguin Books, 1990), 91.

3. Valentina Vitali and Paul Willemen, Introduction to *Theorising National Cinema* (London: British Film Institute, 2006), 2.

4. Thomas Elsaesser, "The New Film History as Media Archaeology," *Cinemas* 14.2–3 (2004): 81.

5. Although Gunning overtly limits his study to pre-1906 cinema (and implicitly to those films manufactured and received in Western, imperial countries), his suggestion that attractions do not "disappear" with the later turn toward a predominantly narrative cinema, but rather go "underground" and resurface in various genres like the musical, animated a wide-scale resuscitation of many "lowbrow" genre traditions, including the crucial genealogies of

slapstick comedy, pornography, and adventure serials. The quoted phrases are taken from Gunning's initial essay on the cinema of attractions, titled "The Cinema of Attraction: Early Film, Its Spectator and the Avant-Garde," first published in *Wide Angle* 8.3–4 (1986): 63–70. It has been republished most recently in Wanda Strauven, ed., *The Cinema of Attractions Reloaded* (Amsterdam: University of Amsterdam Press, 2006), 381–388, a collection designed as a tribute honoring (and debating) the impact of "attractions" on contemporary as well as historical approaches to film and media studies over the past twenty years.

6. See Rob King, "Uproarious Inventions: The Keystone Film Company, Modernity, and the Art of the Motor," in *Slapstick Comedy*, ed. Tom Paulus and Rob King (New York: Routledge, 2010), 132. I quote King in particular insofar as this collection shares his belief that it is impossible to understand cinema without considering the cultural context of Western modernity; the point is that any assessment of this cultural context must seek out and critique, rather than replicate, the blind spots intrinsic to Western modernity's "own discourse about itself." From this perspective, our endeavor shares kinship with a methodological legacy pursued most prominently in English-language film and media studies by scholars attuned to the tensions of gender, race, and class *internal* to various Western nations and regions. Patrice Petro (also a contributor to this volume) arguably pioneered this approach to the conjunction of the terms "cinema" and "modernity" in her *Joyless Streets: Women and Melodramatic Representation in Weimar Germany* (Princeton, NJ: Princeton University Press, 1989), inaugurating an intellectual/disciplinary genealogy that stretches through important studies by Lynne Kirby, *Parallel Tracks: The Railroad and Silent Cinema* (Durham, NC: Duke University Press, 1997); Jacqueline Najuma Stewart, *Migrating to the Movies: Cinema and Black Urban Modernity* (Berkeley: University of California Press, 2005); Angela Dalle Vacche, *Diva: Defiance and Passion in Early Italian Cinema* (Austin: University of Texas Press, 2008); Kristen Whissel, *Picturing American Modernity: Traffic, Technology, and the Silent Cinema* (Durham, NC: Duke University Press, 2008); and Giorgio Bertellini, *Italy in Early American Cinema: Race, Landscape, and the Picturesque* (Bloomington: Indiana University Press, 2010), among others.

7. Ana M. López, "Early Cinema and Modernity in Latin America," *Cinema Journal* 40.1 (2000): 48–78.

8. Ibid., 53.

9. For particularly significant studies published in the twenty-first century that focus on silent era film and film cultures in China, Japan, and Iran, respectively, see Zhen Zhang, *An Amorous History of the Silver Screen: Shanghai Cinema, 1896–1937* (Chicago: University of Chicago Press, 2005); Aaron Gerow, *Visions of Japanese Modernity: Articulations of Cinema, Nation, and Spectatorship, 1895–1925* (Berkeley: University of California Press, 2010); and Hamid Naficy, *A Social History of Iranian Cinema*, vol. 1, *The Artisanal Era, 1897–1941* (Durham, NC: Duke University Press, 2011).

10. See Richard Abel, Giorgio Bertellini, and Rob King, eds., *Early Cinema and the "National"* (New Barnet, UK: John Libbey, 2008).

11. Daniel Sánchaz Salas, "Spanish Lecturers and Their Relations with the National," in Abel, Bertellini, and King, *Early Cinema and the "National,"* 199–206. It is particularly interesting to consider the role of these Spanish lecturers in relation to the film culture that developed in Iran throughout the silent era, for instance, where filmgoers listened to what Hamid Naficy describes as the "intervention of interpreters," some professionals but many of them students, who functioned as "intermediaries" between "the apparent intention of the filmmakers" and viewers' reception and understanding of the film. When "translat[ing] the intertitles, the subtitles, or the foreign language dialog in real time," Naficy observes, "they often resorted to colorful Persian phrases and expressions, thereby indigenizing and enriching the film experience." See Naficy, "Theorizing 'Third-World' Spectatorship," *Wide Angle* 18.4 (1996), 6.

12. See Benedict Anderson, *Imagined Communities: Reflections on the Origin and Spread of Nationalism* (New York: Verso, 1991), 4. Italy's belated unification (1861) and the prominent position of the Catholic Church on the peninsula have long been understood as factors prohibiting the imagination of a national community in Anderson's sense. Less understood has been Italy's rich cinematic heritage and critical/popular film cultures in the silent era, a lacuna redressed by Giorgio Bertellini's fine new collection, *Italian Silent Cinema: A Reader* (Bloomington: Indiana University Press, 2013). See also John P. Welle below.

13. Palmira Brummet, *Image and Imperialism in the Ottoman Revolutionary Press, 1908–1911* (Albany: SUNY Press, 2000), 11.

14. Canan Balan, "Wondrous Pictures in Istanbul: From Cosmopolitanism to Nationalism," in Abel, Bertellini, and King, *Early Cinema and the "National,"* 172–184.

15. Those "Abbruzzese side-whiskers" sported by the itinerant showman in the sonnet once again point to the fervent regionalism dominating Italy's "imagination" of what constitutes community. John P. Welle, "The Cinema Arrives in Italy: City, Region and Nation in Early Film Discourse," in Abel, Bertellini, and King, *Early Cinema and the "National,"* 164–171.

16. See Arjun Appadurai, *Modernity at Large: Cultural Dimensions of Globalization* (Minneapolis: University of Minnesota Press, 1996), esp. chap. 9, "The Production of Locality"; T. S. Oakes, "Ethnic Tourism and Place Identity in China," *Environment and Planning D: Society and Space* 11 (1993): 47–66; Doreen Massey, *for space* (London: Sage, 2010); and Eric Wolf, *Europe and the People without History* (Berkeley: University of California Press, 1982).

17. Oakes, "Ethnic Tourism," 63.

18. Giorgio Bertellini, "Introduction," in "Early Italian Cinema," special issue, *Film History* 12.3 (2000): 235.

19. Ibid.

20. For instance, "New Women of the Silent Screen: China, Japan, Hollywood," a special issue of *Camera Obscura* edited by Catherine Russell, presents materials initially delivered at the 2004 Women and the Silent Screen conference in Montreal, Canada. See also Sofia Bull and Astrid Söderbergh Widding, eds., *Not So Silent: Women in Cinema before Sound* (Stockholm: Acta Universitatis Stockholmiensis, 2010), based on the proceedings of the Women and Silent Screen conference held at the University of Stockholm in 2008. For more on the Women and Film History International Association, an organization formed through the scholarly coalitions promoted by these events, see http://www.wfhi.org/.

21. Lee Grieveson and Peter Krämer, introduction to *The Silent Cinema Reader* (London: Routledge, 2004), 2.

22. Ibid., 6.

23. Nor does it mean that *The Silent Cinema Reader* assumes a *teleological* stance. Grieveson and Krämer fruitfully clarify that a teleological account "assumes an inherent goal, or telos, for historical developments" and adamantly oppose an approach that selects from the past only those elements that illuminate or foreshadow later cinematic forms or cultural forces (5). It is important to stress in this regard that "historicism" does not necessarily entail an assumption of teleology. Rather, as Dipesh Chakrabarty summarizes when referring to a historicist logic that persists in the craft of academic historians today:

> Historicism tells us that in order to understand anything in this world we must see it as an historically developing entity, that is, first, as an individual and unique whole—as some kind of unity at least in potentia—and, second, as something that develops over time. Historicism typically can allow for complexities and zigzags in this development . . . but the idea of development and the assumption that a certain amount of time elapses in the very process of development are crucial to this understanding. . . . Ideas, old and new, about discontinuities, ruptures, and shifts in the historical process have

> from time to time challenged the dominance of historicism, but much written history still remains deeply historicist. . . . This is particularly true—for all their differences with classical historicism—of historical narratives underpinned by Marxist or liberal views of the world, and is what underlies descriptions/explanations in the genre "history of"—capitalism, industrialization, nationalism, and so on. (Chakrabarty, *Provincializing Europe*, 23)

24. See, for example, Kristin Thompson, *Exporting Entertainment: America in the World Film Market, 1907–1934* (London: British Film Institute, 1985); Ian Jarvie, *Hollywood's Overseas Campaign: The North Atlantic Movie Trade, 1920–1950* (Cambridge, UK: Cambridge University Press, 1992); Ruth Vasey, *The World According to Hollywood, 1918–1939* (Madison: University of Wisconsin Press, 1997); Andrew Higson and Richard Maltby, eds., *"Film Europe" and "Film America": Cinema, Commerce and Cultural Exchange, 1920–1939* (Exeter, UK: University of Exeter Press, 1999); and John Trumpbour, *Selling Hollywood to the World: U.S. and European Struggles for Mastery of the Global Film Industry, 1920–1950* (Cambridge, UK: Cambridge University Press, 2002).

25. Ravi Vasudevan, "In the Centrifuge of History," *Cinema Journal* 50.1 (Fall 2010): 136.

26. See Lúcia Nagib, "Towards a Positive Definition of World Cinema," in *Remapping World Cinema*, ed. Stephanie Dennison and Song Hwee Lim (London: Wallflower Press, 2006), 30–37.

27. Johannes Fabian, *Time and the Other: How Anthropology Makes Its Object* (New York: Columbia University Press, 1983), 155.

28. In her astounding study of the history of Western perspective, *The Virtual Window: From Alberti to Microsoft* (Cambridge, MA: MIT Press, 2006), Anne Friedberg argues that the surfeit of computer, cell phone, iPad, and other web-interface screens in twenty-first-century daily life have produced a new "vernacular visual syntax" determined by the abundance of spatial relationships (above, below, beside, behind) through which "a text or image in one 'window' meets other texts or images in other 'windows' on the same screen" (2).

29. Massey, *for space*, 64.

PART I
Picturing Space

Introduction

Anupama Kapse

> The mirror is, after all, a utopia, since it reflects a placeless place.
>
> Michel Foucault, "Of Other Spaces"

One of the most useful insights of scholarship that considers the conversion of 35mm films to 3D is the reminder that the latter's appearance is not a mere novelty. Such revivals are not, as Kristen Whissel points out, a way of rescuing a seemingly threatened (U.S.) film industry in view of the coming of newer and more profitable technologies of viewing and consuming visual media. Rather, 3D is better approached as a practice that "has migrated across a broad range of platforms and media, including television, smart phones, photography, tablets, video games, and live theatrical performances."[1] Which is to say that the spatial vision of 3D—its direct, tactile address to the spectator, its mutations of time and space, its loosening of the film frame—is not a phenomenon that emerged in the crisis of the fifties, as is commonly believed. Rather, such attempts need to be understood within an archaeology of media forms that have, since the late nineteenth and early twentieth century, continued to relay moving images in a variety of spatial formats which include the history of binocular and stereoscopic vision.

Nor can we assume that such frank play with time and space is restricted to silent films made before World War I. Indeed, both *Hugo* (Martin Scorcese, 2011) and *The Artist* (Michel Hazanavicius, 2011) unhinge the very idea of the material stability (or endurance) of celluloid by restaging film itself as the fiction now resident in digital or 3D formats. In the words of Thomas Elsaesser, such transformations have made their reappearance "as only one part of an emerging set of new default values—about how to locate ourselves [and the medium of film] in simultaneous spaces [and] multiple temporalities."[2] If both *Hugo* and

The Artist reconceptualize the ontology of silent film by inserting its history into a seamless, invisible continuum of time and space, then the essays in this section make silent film history visible at the disciplinary level in several different ways. In the most basic sense, they intervene in the existing historiography of silent cinema by expanding its time and place to manifestly include the present. Still more, they shift the critical object away from the United States to include what were, in the days of the silent era, "small" nations like Denmark and India. Seen this way, the critical space of what can no longer simply be called early cinemas invites approaches that can encompass a range of not only media forms but also other places and periods. What happens, then, if we turn to what can only provisionally be called early cinemas elsewhere in Europe and Asia? While the focus here comes from neither stereoscopy nor 3D vision, "Picturing Space" takes stock of location as an exemplary film practice that could radically destablize the early film viewer's experience of and interaction with lived space. Take, for example, the Danish film *Løvejagten* (The lion hunt; 1907), which was marketed as a film about an African lion hunt but was shot in a Hamburg zoo. Then again, what happens if we shift the focus to a one-reel Edison film, *The Relief of Lucknow* (1912; henceforth *Relief*) which was made in the United States, set in the India of 1857, but shot in the Bermuda of 1912? While it is reasonably safe to assume that both *Løvejagten* and *Relief* were addressed to local spectators in Denmark and the United States, respectively, it is also clear that both films depend on fictions of an Africa and India that immediately broaden the rhetoric of how cinema can "reach" out to the spectator in direct and often unexpected ways.

Mark B. Sandberg shows how Danish locations could be passed off as sites in New York, while Priya Jaikumar reveals just how small physical knowledge of Lucknow could be in a larger geopolitical space: so small that Bermuda could be passed off as Lucknow. Still more, rather than starting with the work of Denmark's Nordisk film company, Sandberg begins with the recent example of *The Kite Runner* (2007), drawing attention to the paradoxical implications of "location" shooting in this transnational production: a film like *The Kite Runner* makes us believe that we are seeing a Kabul situated in Afghanistan, although the film was actually shot in a town named Kashgar, located in China. Moreover, information about the fakeness of the location is not hidden but made explicit through special features on a DVD that can be viewed on demand with the main feature. By acknowledging the gap between actual place and filmic space, such information throws the unmappable quality of cinematic place (China or Afghanistan?) into stark relief: as Sandberg puts it, "the possibilities for substitution and misidentification are endless." The deeper implications of altering place emerge sharply when he delineates a rhetoric of place substitution whereby he himself translocates the instance of *The Kite Runner* to the Nordisk Film Company in silent-era Denmark.

The results of such an inquiry are extraordinary: location emerges as the productive force which allowed Nordisk to capture an international market by *erasing* Denmark's local landmarks from its cinematic topography. In other words, Denmark literally expanded its position as a national cinema in the global mediascape by mobilizing apparently distant, inaccessible locations which included both Africa and the United States. Displacement and dispersal abound here: even makeup, or the dressing up of a location (not necessarily of people), emerges as a metaphor for the trickery of cinematic placelessness, one that converts known places into formidable, Other spaces. Sandberg lists a number of ways in which cinematic sites can be not merely simulated but openly enhanced, even replaced or substituted, like the Copenhagen zoo, which can be passed off as sub-Saharan Africa. While both theater and cinema have always had the ability to mask the actual place, set, or site of shooting by using of painted backdrops, fake locations, or clever camera angles that block, reconstruct or even fabricate film space—such a move insists that we be alert to cinema's deterritorialization of national maps by virtue of its hypermobile staging of location. Put differently, location emerges as the governing principle of a "façade aesthetics": a cinematic drive that is always already fraught with deceptions, strategies of overcompensation, and "sleights of location" that pervade a majority of genres in Danish silent cinema—hunt films, erotic melodramas, and science fiction—spilling over into a vast, related domain of film production which comprises set design, location photography, publicity material, and "how it was done" fan discourse. Here the problematization of cinematic place enables glimpses into a "smaller" or distinctive mode of production that proves to be the exception when seen in relation to U.S. silent cinema, one that can by turn controvert, imitate, or, as we will see again and again in this volume, appropriate American strategies of filmmaking in order to compete with that "large" nation.[3] Although Nordisk came from what Sandberg characterizes as the "small" nation of Denmark, it could compete in the European market by deploying—even preempting—the same tactics that eventually made American cinema so successful. Concomitantly, we may think of the subsequent return of the national as characterized by an insistence on the authenticity of location (for example, in the films of Carl Dreyer and the Dogme 95 Manifesto), as a turn that explicitly fetishizes the local over the global. Above all, Sandberg argues that the incompleteness and imminent failure of place substitution could well be its most compelling feature. To this end, he points out those moments when the "here" of the actual place supplants the "there" of the imagined and the fictional: moments when made-up locations betray their origins (a resident of Denmark knows instantly when he or she sees it and looks right through the cinematic fiction).

As such, this chapter is particularly noteworthy in its articulation of what Edward Soja calls "a geographical or spatial imagination" that can break critical silence about "milieu, immediate locales and provocative emplacements" and intervene in modes of historicism that privilege the authenticity and representational illusionism of cinematic space.[4] Michel de Certeau's distinction between place (*lieu*) and space (*espace*) is also instructive here: "The law of the proper rules 'place'—the elements taken into consideration are *beside* one another, each situated in its proper and distinct location, a location it defines"; while space "is composed of intersections and mobile elements. . . . Space occurs as the effect that is produced by the operations that orient it, situate it, temporalize it. . . . In contradistinction to the place, it has none of the univocity or stability of a 'proper.'"[5] Collectively, Sandberg and Jaikumar dismantle the "proper" elements of place to reveal cinema's *spatial* practices, which are shown to be contingent on competing economies of production, variable temporalities, ideologies of power, local sensoria, and individualized modes of spectatorship. Furthermore, this "spatial turn," defined by Soja as "an unprecedented diffusion of critical spatial thinking across an unusually broad spectrum of subject areas," uncovers the silences of older modes of film historicism of which Euro- or U.S.-centrism is only one example.[6]

Edward Said's well-known formulation about the imperial control of space immediately comes to mind: "The actual, geographical possession of land is what empire in the final analysis is all about."[7] Within this formulation, geography, or the geographical sense, is geared toward "projections—imaginative, cartographic" in a tussle that locks colonizer and colonized in an endless quest for power, control, and ownership. However, it is worth noting that Said was speaking of the tightly demarcated "narrative space" of the novel here, a form deeply imbricated in the bourgeois control of marriage and private property. Projections of power collapse easily when the viewer who lives in Lucknow confronts it on film and personal memories of lived space, whether British or Indian, intrude upon the narrative and space of representation. In a dazzling reconceptualization, Jaikumar turns away from both the logic of representation in film theory and the issue of represented space in cinema to focus instead on what Henri Lefebvre describes as a "trial by space," by which he means an analysis that "embraces production and reproduction . . . the particular locations of each social formation . . . representations of space, *and* representational space" (my emphasis).[8] Rather than situating *The Relief of Lucknow* as a product of the Edison film company, Jaikumar approaches it as a film that unveils Lucknow's spatial unconscious; that is, it activates, in the space that falls *outside* the logic of representation, *repressed* memories of a city that launched India's first rebellion against British rule in 1857. Such memories are usually obscured in British accounts (official and novelistic) of what came to be known as "the Indian mutiny" and not as the first war of independence. Not surprisingly, the insurgency fired the imagination of British novelists, who exploited its intrigue and sensational violence to crank out narratives of kidnapped Englishwomen, "brown-faced" Englishmen, and double-crossing Indian spies.

Soon, the tight master narrative of betrayal would be loosened in an outbreak of photographs, personal albums, and letters. With the coming of photography, the British public could, for the first time, capture and share the images of an empire ruined in stunning detail. The proliferation of the telegraph and its instantaneous circuits of communication simply aided the rapid circulation of this exciting news. Drawing attention to a remarkable perceptual shift, Jaikumar writes, "Unlike literature, location shooting is a medium-specific industrial and aesthetic practice with its own history in cinema." Taking an altogether different approach to space, she goes well beyond a strident—and long overdue—revision of Saidian notions of spatial control. For Jaikumar, space, understood as a destabilizing mechanism produced by shooting on location, loosens the notion of place as something narrowly tied to territory and dominion. In the case of Lucknow, pre-cinematic media such as the photographic album document a perceived rather than secondhand sense of Lucknow—as a space rather than a place, mobilizing the affective value of location for both colonizer and colonized and straddling a competing set of demands. To be sure, the Italian photographer Felice Beato transformed Lucknow into a sensational global site of disaster tourism. However, the flurry of personal photographs collected over a period of time in family albums or the subsequent emergence of postcards would interrupt the smooth manifestation of disastrous effects, foregrounding a plethora of intimately observed sensations and details. Here personal memory and the immediacy of photographic capture accumulate meanings that overlay the touristic, anticipating cinema's play with received history and thereby rupturing the precise idea of place as a knowable entity. In skirting the *diktats* of representational illusionism, the photographic album shows how these smaller, more *moffusil* media could defy the very notion of historical truth. Thus the album *produces space* as a series of views, rather than as a singular image of the city of Lucknow: it becomes part of an ongoing historical chain that is suffused with the contradictory optics of local remembrance.

The Reverend Thomas Moore's album *Cawnpore and Lucknow during the Mutiny of 1857* is a case in point. Jaikumar contrasts the album's dynamic imagery with the imposing still photographs of the so-called mutiny of official accounts which were "massive in scale and newsworthiness" yet "not capable of yielding answers outside the text's ideological containment." Here photographer Felice Beato's "masculine" pictures of the Chutter Munzil palace (an imposing structure central to the imagery of revolt) appear with "feminine" materials such as Moore's letters to his wife and are accompanied by newspaper cuttings of a monument of love, to produce a "rival geography" of an intimately experienced Lucknow, located, at least in the eyes of Thomas Moore, in the land of the Taj Mahal. Similarly, *The Lucknow Album* (1874) predicates its photographic collection on the shared memory of a city-space frequented by British soldiers and educated

Indian men alike. These images unfold in a sequential form, like a montage of stills in a moving image, calling attention to a syncretism that amalgamated Gothic and Islamicate architectural influences to fuse rival geographies which destabilize the visual rhetoric of empire while leaving the official story of insurgency intact.

If the album disturbs the fixity of Lucknow as the de facto setting of what eventually became the first war of independence, *Chaudhvin ka Chand* (Moon of the fourteenth day / Full moon; M. Sadiq, 1960), a film set in free India, recharges the city with the aura of a sacred memory. As Jaikumar points out, Edison's *Relief* was not shot in India but in Bermuda. The idea was to create the *impression* of a Lucknow brutalized in a globally legible register of "authenticity." Made a hundred years after 1857 and nearly fifty years since Edison's *Relief, Chaudhvin* was shot on location *in Lucknow.* Tellingly, it simply refuses to remember the narrative of the rebellion as its female protagonist wanders restlessly through the city streets. The Lucknow of *Chaudhvin* is thoroughly displaced as the film unfolds from the point of view of a female subject (and a veiled Muslim one at that) who has been doubly barred from seeing or inhabiting the history of the British—or for that matter, "Indian" Lucknow. "To which temporal and spatial axis does she belong?" asks Jaikumar. Dislocating the Lucknow of the present, *Chaudhvin* refuses to remember the Lucknow of the past. Effectively, the film privileges a placeless view that is embodied in the inscrutable yet penetrating gaze of a woman in a burqa who fights for visibility, against chronicles written and organized by men. Such, then, are the benefits of studying cinematic location as an arena cut loose from the boundaries of time and place: *Chaudhvin*'s Lucknow is abstract and only partially visible; it is disorienting as a place and yet entirely seductive as a space. Nor is this space strictly about 1857; it is one that extends through 1960 into a present that disperses Lucknow into multiple points located in differing moments of spatial and ideological retrieval.

Put simply, the chapters in this section engage with the concept of space as a dynamic element in silent cinema's destabilization of place. Cinemas that are at points of emergence seem particularly predisposed to a variety of spatial maneuvers: paradoxically, Denmark iterates its smallness through its globally expansive use of locations, while India expresses the empire's reduction of place by projecting Lucknow into an expansive space recovered from the overarching frame of the rebellion. Going beyond the old dynamic of center and periphery, power and knowledge, or real and imagined place, both contributions gesture toward what Michel Foucault would call "other spaces" or heterotopias.[9] Foucault defines the heterotopia as a forbidden place that turns into a privileged or sacred space in modern societies, like a brothel or cemetery. Though vitiated by ruin, these marginalized sites are reinvested with new meanings during contested periods in history in order to defy the norm and reflect "a space that is other, another real space, as perfect, as meticulous, as well arranged as ours is messy, ill-constructed and jumbled."[10] As Foucault had rightly suspected, colonized and immobilized places transform themselves into heterotopic spots during moments of intense upheaval in order to forge access to forbidden or lost spaces, whether it is a refabricated Finse or a vitiated, resacralized Lucknow. "The heterotopia is capable of juxtaposing in a single real space several spaces, several sites that are in themselves incompatible," writes Foucault.[11]

"Picturing Space" demonstrates cinema's resounding capacity for violating protocols of place, as Africa and Denmark, Lucknow and Bermuda bleed into each other, as areas that juxtapose varying orders of space and time that are somehow rendered *more real* in their life and time as cinematic locations. In other words, Sandberg and Jaikumar "do" film history in a spatial rather than textual or teleological sense. Treating space as a fertile playground, their chapters convey a heady sense of cinema's portable materials—its ability to disguise place in order to picture space. Seen this way, silent cinema resonates as a heterotopia of the unmapped space of film history, picturing both paths not taken, or tussling paths taken at once—critical and everyday—to insist that "space matters."[12]

Notes

1. Kristen Whissel, "Guest Editor's Introduction: Genealogical and Archaeological Approaches to 3-D," *Film Criticism* 37/38.3/1 (Spring/Fall 2013): 7.
2. Thomas Elsaesser, "The 'Return' of 3-D: On Some of the Logics and Genealogies of the Image in the Twenty-First Century," *Critical Inquiry*, no. 39 (Winter 2013): 228.
3. See David Cook, *A History of Narrative Film* (New York: W. W. Norton, 2008), particularly chapter 2, "International Expansion," which considers France and Italy as the main competitors of the United States in the years between 1907 and 1918. Sandberg turns to Denmark and considers the same period, addressing an important omission in the global history of silent cinema.
4. Edward Soja, *Postmodern Geographies: The Reassertion of Space in Postmodern Local Geographies* (London: Verso, 1989), 14.
5. Michel de Certeau, *The Practice of Everyday Life*, trans. Steven Rendall (Berkeley: University of California Press, 1984), 117.
6. Edward Soja, *Seeking Spatial Justice* (Minneapolis: University of Minnesota Press, 2010), 1.
7. Edward Said, *Culture and Imperialism* (London: Vintage, 1994), 93.
8. Henri Lefebvre, *The Production of Space*, trans. Donald Nicholson-Smith (Malden, MA: Blackwell, 1991), 216, 33.
9. Michel Foucault, "Of Other Spaces," trans. Jay Miskowiec, *Diacritics* 16 (1986): 22.
10. Ibid., 27.
11. Ibid., 25.
12. The quoted phrase is from Soja, *Seeking Spatial Justice*, 2.

1 Location, "Location"

On the Plausibility of Place Substitution

Mark B. Sandberg

HIDDEN BEHIND THE casual use of studio terms such as "location scout" and "shot on location" are histories of film practice that reveal ongoing, productive tensions inherent in the idea of cinematic place. On the one hand, the filmic medium conveys a strong impression of specific location because of the photographic image's indexical properties, which inspire confidence in the verifiability of an original shooting location. On the other hand, the inherent mobility and portability of the camera and cinema editing's powers of formal juxtaposition combine to untether the image from any securely specific sense of originary place. One might sum up this contradiction by saying that although we can be confident that we are seeing *some place* filmed by the camera, the cinematic image itself can never make us completely sure of the *actual* place; the possibilities for substitution and misidentification are endless. The commoditization and interchangeability of shooting locations are a direct result of this central ambiguity. Add to that the convincing impressions of fictional location made possible by an array of cinematic sleights of hand (animation, miniature models, and increasingly, digital imaging), and one quickly sees the need for an approach to cinematic place that acknowledges the wide variability of the concept.

Thinking carefully about such issues might help to open up the habitual terminology of cinematic location to more genealogical perspectives. The questions that arise from the recognition of the historical contingency of current practices include: At what points in film history have audiences cared about the actual location of filming? When did it become a mentionable, promotional asset for studios to claim that a film was shot "on location," and what contrastive prior practices gave that claim its value? When does the identification of actual shooting locations become an expected piece of information in the end credits of films, and why? At what point does the investigation of location discrepancy (the disparity between actual and ostensible locations) become a pleasurable form of fan discourse in its own right? What is the history of these geographical-analytic modes of film spectating?

A recent example will help set the stage. In the 2007 film *The Kite Runner*, there are two diegetic locations established for the film, one of which happens to be very remote from my current writing location (Kabul, Afghanistan) and one that is quite close (the San Francisco Bay Area). As each of the two locations is introduced in the film, a conventionally superimposed title locates the image in the usual authoritative way. As it turns out, however, the scenes marked "Kabul, Afghanistan 1978" were not actually filmed there, but were shot on location in three different filming locations in China instead. Here is what a *New York Times* reporter wrote about one of the location choices while the film was still in production in December of 2006:

> The production team spent three months researching locations, giving little thought to Afghanistan itself, for obvious reasons, as they drew up an initial list of 20 countries and deliberated on which one would get them closest to Afghanistan's look. The possibilities ranged from India to Morocco to South Africa, but E. Bennett Walsh, who oversaw the search, said the conversations kept returning to Kashgar, a place that few people in Hollywood had ever heard of and where no Western film had ever been made.[1]

Kashgar is a small city in far western China, actually not far from the Afghanistan border, which partially explains its potential to duplicate "Afghanistan's look," as the reporter puts it. While the substitution of China for Afghanistan might initially sound quite incongruous, when one sees this relationship on a map the differences seem less stark. Both of the cities in question are actually in the foothills of the Pamir mountain range (Kabul to the west, Kashgar to the east). The distinction between the two places, in other words, might not be so much geographically essential as it is politically arbitrary, since topographically speaking, there might not be much of a "substitution" at work here at all. Since Kashgar is culturally speaking also a Muslim community like Kabul, the discrepancy between the real and ostensible locations has more to do with preconceptions of "China" than with anything else.

One of the film's producers, Rebecca Yeldham, revealed the complexity of the location simulation in commentary included on the DVD:

> We filmed in China, but where we filmed in China isn't really China . . . and the old town of Kashgar feels like a city, as we were told, a city in Afghanistan that is now long forgotten, so it was a perfect place for filming. In fact many of the Afghans who again traveled through the Xinjiang-Kashgar portion of our filming felt like they were home, and it was a very surreal experience in the movie through their eyes because the cities that we shot in are strangely locked in time.[2]

Her observation helps to isolate a central issue about location shooting: what constitutes substitution? If two places belong to a continuous landscape or some other larger entity, does it make sense to use the word "substitution" at all? Or does using the term "substitution" only come into play because of the existence of a perceived border or boundary, a clash of some sort that must be ignored or covered over in order for the process to be successful? And further: does the image itself betray that difference? How much can one rely on something resistant in the image itself, some visual ontological tie to actual location, and to what degree is this instead a function of supplementary labeling and the viewer's verification abilities?

The *Times* reporter continues his description of *The Kite Runner*'s location shooting in this way:

> Beyond the cooperation of authorities and the availability of highly skilled filmmakers in China, Kashgar was always the best fit in terms of appearance, beginning with a diverse but overwhelmingly Muslim population and a countryside that plausibly resembles Afghanistan. "In some locations you are limited to working small, little corners, whereas here you can shoot 100 yards down the road," Mr. Walsh said. "The streets of this city are just dripping with production value. All you have to do is change the signs."[3]

The phrase "dripping with production value" reveals the economic calculation involved in place substitution—the bet that the visual similarities of the substitute will help cut corners on either set building or travel, or perhaps circumvent political obstacles to filming in the place the fiction is located. The reporter's final claim is also interesting, since it reinforces a definition of cinematic location as nonessential; his implication is that for the purposes of filming, the distinctiveness of place is assumed to reside in a thin, superficially visual layer of culture that can be taken on and off like clothing. In this case, it seems that film's long-standing exploitation of façade aesthetics has colored assumptions about cinematic location as well.

All of these considerations become more resonant, of course, when seen against the central metaphor of the film: the "kite runner" is a young boy with an inerrant sense of location, a living GPS system really—he is the one who can run down a kite when the string breaks and arrive first at the spot of its landing. At the same time, the film production itself was forced off location by the political realities in contemporary Afghanistan, presumably because it was too difficult to film there. Like the unmoored kite, the production's affiliations with place were quite untethered. As screenwriter David Benioff puts it at one point in the DVD commentary:

> So you have a book written by an Afghan-American, adapted by a New Yorker, directed by a Swiss man, one of the producers is Australian, being shot in Beijing with the kids from Kabul, Baba from Iran, other actors from England and France, incredibly international, all gathered together to shoot

> this movie set in Afghanistan. It's just kind of bizarre, but . . . but you know, and, it . . . it worked.[4]

Since "no Western film had ever been made" in Kashgar, and since the Afghanistan imagined in 1978 might be assumed to be a lost place anyway, there was probably a calculation that the substitution of Kashgar for Kabul would not be noticed by the likely audience of the film. And in fact, although I am told by friends who have traveled in Afghanistan that they did notice something slightly "off" in these location shots, for me Kashgar made an unproblematic Kabul. I suspect the same was true for a majority of those who saw the film. Benioff even boasts:

> One of the really gratifying things that we've heard just recently was that the movie was shown to the Afghan diplomats including the ambassador, I think, to the United Nations and, you know, several officials, all of whom grew up in Kabul, all of whom lived there during the seventies, and they couldn't believe that [director] Marc [Forster] was Swiss, you know, they thought it was so accurate—first of all they couldn't believe it wasn't shot in Kabul because it looked exactly the way they remembered it.[5]

From this comment we see that place substitution is a kind of calculated risk for the film producers about the degree of specific geographic knowledge resident in the audience and about how much that will matter to the reception of the film, a wager that paid off well in this case since even some viewers with insider knowledge found the substitution plausible.

The film's other location suggests the possibility of alternative reactions. When I see the opening scene identified as "San Francisco, California 2000," I recognize the actual location to be a particular grassy hill down at César Chávez Park near the Berkeley Marina where the annual kite festival is held. Those of us who know that place well enough and intimately enough—that is to say, *locally* enough—might even object to the caption here, since for us this is not San Francisco at all, but more precisely the Berkeley Marina with a view of San Francisco. To those who have never been to Berkeley or experienced the distinctions between the city and the East Bay, this will likely matter as little as the relationship between Kashgar and Kabul, since the image performs adequately as the visual invocation of "San Francisco," just as Kashgar did for Kabul. It is the deictic aspect of this location recovery, however—encapsulated in the shock of recognition that reveals the "there" of the film to be the "here" of my daily life—that is worth emphasizing. The free substitution of shooting locations for fictional locations by film producers will inevitably collide at times with local site-specific knowledge, but if it does so within an acceptable range of plausibility for most viewers, it will pass unnoticed.

Of course, our current viewing culture of DVD special features and PIP (Picture-in-Picture) bonus views creates a niche for those spectators who want their location-recovery information delivered in tandem with the fiction itself.[6] In effect, the availability of these features can potentially turn all viewers into "kite runners" able to recover the specific shooting locations of films cut loose by the practice of place substitution and international distribution. Although DVD commentaries have proliferated only recently, the analytic function of the behind-the-scenes, on-location peek into the filming process belongs to a much-older analytic fan discourse that has long taken pleasure in uncovering the "truth" of the filmmaking process. Early on, we can find that impulse in photographs of film sets that reveal façade-like architectural structures, or the actual way that a stunt was created, or the unstaged physical environment just beyond the framed image. The existence of these "revealing" perspectives as a parallel pleasure to that of immersive viewing was an early fact of film spectatorship. The impulse continued with the proliferation of fan magazines, the eventual rise of "making-of" documentaries as a genre, and more recently, with the analytic apparatus that makes up the special features of today's DVDs. Tellingly, this kind of viewing pleasure is now also fostered by sites such as the Internet Movie Database (IMDb), which provide in their "trivia" section this kind of detailed information about real production locations as well, though derived in many cases from a symbiotic relationship with the DVD commentary, the source of much of the insider location information.[7] Although various desires motivate fans to look behind the curtain of the film production process, one recurring attraction throughout film history has involved the sorting of real from fictional location: the pleasure in finding out that although it *looks like* it was shot in Afghanistan, it was *really* shot in China. We might call this "kite-runner spectatorship."

This geographic settling of accounts does not appeal to all viewers, of course, and it is certainly reasonable to assume that public interest in location discrepancies would wax and wane throughout cinema's history. Today, for example, it is easy to think of many factors in the current media landscape that might motivate public interest in knowing more about cinematic practices of place substitution, including the explosion of virtual geographic access online through various kinds of mapping software and the general proliferation of GPS technology (including the ability to geo-tag photos and videos). These and other media developments have arguably created a particular consciousness of the location and dislocation of the image, not only in contemporary films but in those of the past as well.

I readily acknowledge that the questions that interest me in what follows are driven in large part by my own current cultural context of early-twenty-first-century place sensitivity. Current questions make it possible to see new things about the past, however, and it is in this spirit that I turn now to a case study of the use of location in early Danish silent film. The gaps between then and now, between there and here, present themselves as an interesting challenge for reconstructing what mattered to the Danish producers and their European audiences of the early 1910s. Some of the questions I have posed can only be answered through suggestive, fragmentary evidence or when triangulated from surviving textual materials, but it seems to me that the only way to answer questions about shifting historical horizons and audience expectations is in fact through the accumulation of specific case studies. The one offered here is both significant and evocative, but will eventually be most useful in comparison with others.

My reasons for choosing this material are several. First, the Danish film industry was unusually precocious in the years before World War I, so it gives us an early example of successful studio production at a time when some of the initial shifts in thinking about location are particularly visible. The Nordisk Film Company, founded in 1906, became one of the world's leading studios by 1913, in that year second only to the French company Pathé Frères in terms of film production.[8] But the size and output of the company were not so large as to make the trends unobservable. The Danish film industry also played a leading role internationally in the development of the multi-reel feature film around 1910–1911,[9] so the development of a sustained sense of fictional place proves acutely interesting in this cinematic tradition from an early stage. Furthermore, the entrepreneur behind the Nordisk Film Company, Ole Olsen, was a clever businessman who came to own a vast distribution and cinema network, not just in Denmark but throughout Germany as well.[10] His savvy international marketing strategy included a calculation that prewar audiences would prefer a placeless product, one that traveled freely between markets, unburdened by obvious cultural signifiers. In the time and place of early Danish cinema, this was accomplished through a combination of place substitution and the erasure of site specificity from the fictional worlds of the films.

What I am calling the "erasure" of "site specificity" counters recent thinking about "small-nation filmmaking," as theorized by Mette Hjort in her analysis of contemporary global cinema. Her analysis of the "small nation" as a category of film production includes a common set of strategies that are necessarily deployed today in countries with small domestic markets.[11] One of the primary strategies of small-nation filmmaking, according to Hjort, is to make a virtue of locality, to sell cultural and geographic difference in an appealing way to a niche market. This allows small-scale production to compete in the larger distribution networks with a unique product. The early Danish studio, with the flamboyant Ole Olsen at its head, initially pursued quite a different strategy: namely, to compete from a small-nation position on the same turf as larger film-producing countries like France, Britain, Italy, and the United States by creating a "placeless" product. In the years before World War I, it should be emphasized, none of Nordisk's competitors had yet developed to the degree that Hollywood would later do, so in this period before 1914, there were possibilities for Danish cinema that would be closed off after the war. The reasons suggested for that sudden decline have included both aesthetic and economic causal factors, but one of its effects included a shift in thinking about cinematic location.[12]

A look at the earliest history of Danish film, before the rise of Olsen's studio, can give a background indication of the initial currency of locality. The most prominent and influential of the early Danish actuality filmmakers, Peter Elfelt, set the tone. He was an established photographer in his own right—the royal photographer, actually—before branching out into filmmaking as well.[13] He has the distinction of having filmed the first actualities in Denmark and of creating that country's first "fiction" film.[14] A good number of Elfelt's early films focused on the kind of official event that would naturally interest a court photographer: the arrival of foreign officials to Denmark and other public gatherings. Although he also included views of Copenhagen and its immediate surroundings, Peter Elfelt was not the photographic tourist that many other early cameramen were. A look through his catalogue reveals that he primarily documented the outside world when it came to him, unlike many of his contemporaries in the first years of the twentieth century.[15]

It was within this context of the relatively place-bound Danish actuality film that Ole Olsen founded the first Danish film production company, Nordisk Films Kompagni, in 1906. One of the effects of the advances in Danish film production was the availability of studio resources for filming foreign travelogues in a way that the court photographer would not be able or inclined to do. Of course, there were increasingly many other non-Danish travel films shown to Copenhagen film audiences as well—views of other localities around the world, filmed by cameramen there but distributed internationally to Denmark.[16] The Nordisk studio did start sending its own cameramen abroad to film actuality footage of foreign sites as early as 1906, according to Ole Olsen,[17] but in the first instance this concerned mainly trips to nearby locations in Norway, Sweden, and Germany. In the years 1908–1910, the geographic range would increase significantly, with Nordisk cameramen obtaining actuality footage from Russia, Thailand, Egypt, Sudan, and Argentina, among other locations.[18]

Olsen was already something of a charlatan promoter when he got into the film business.[19] Along with his fairground ethos came the idea that feigning a sense of place on film might be both possible and profitable. The idea of fooling the audience is, of course, a departure from the dislocation effects of the travelogue film, which still rest on an assumption of documentary truth, of seeing real images from *there* while nevertheless sitting *here*. The idea of place substitution, by contrast, involves a level of sleight of hand essential to the idea of fiction film. Olsen explored both of these possibilities in tandem; while Nordisk photographers went out to fetch their visual samples of the world, Olsen also found it advantageous to attempt the substitution of near for far when shooting at home in Denmark.

The test case that emerged from Olsen's early film practice was a film from 1907 called *Løvejagten* (The lion hunt). This breakthrough film pretended to depict a lion hunt in Africa, but was actually filmed mostly on a shallow sandbar in the Roskilde Fjord in Denmark. Olsen describes the choice of location in this way: "I had the idea that everyone around the world would be interested to see how a lion hunt happens. Not everyone can travel to Africa, of course, to see it in reality, but with two lions, exploited in the right way, one could perhaps create an illusion."[20] To create the effect of an African landscape, palm fronds were stuck in the ground here and there on a shallow slip of land shot from high angle. For the lion hunt itself, two lions were purchased from Carl Hagenbeck's Hamburg zoo, let loose on the island, and shot down by hunters dressed in safari costumes.[21] The reaction to the film was a mixture of outrage and enthusiasm, inspiring censorship, indignant letters to the editor, official fines, plagiarized film copies, and caricatures in print.[22] Most interesting for the present argument, however, is Figure 1.1, a contemporary caricature of the filming process. Here we have clearly crossed over to a new conception of cinematic place, when even the lions have to attend makeup calls and the location needs to be prepped and costumed before it can be filmed. In one sense, this drawing catches place substitution in the act and foregrounds it as a central characteristic of fiction filmmaking: place now needs *makeup* in order to appear on film. This introduces into early Danish cinema the distinction between apparent and actual location that would later become so productive for film more generally.

When one sees the images from the film itself, it is hard not to be amused by this early use of cinematic place—it seems so pathetic (see Figure 1.2). The establishing shots in the film are obviously not shot in Africa—the fictional aspects of the place (the palm fronds) are purely decorative, clearly an overlay on a real place whose true characteristics shine through. The image here both conceals and reveals the actual characteristics of the place at the same time, with a now-amusing sense of discrepancy. The subsequent sequences are slightly more convincing, taking better advantage of the film frame's ability to conceal. For instance, there is a montage of various African animals shown darting across the screen. However, these animals were not actually filmed in the African wild either—they were residents of the Copenhagen zoo. The unusually high angle of most of these shots was necessary so as to avoid filming the bars of the cage.[23]

As one can see from the index of Danish films from this time, it was presumably possible for a Nordisk cameraman to travel to Africa and film a lion hunt. For example, two years later, Olsen's employee Ludvig Lippert would travel to the Sudan to take actuality footage of folklife there. Further, Engberg notes that an Italian company actually did film a lion hunt in Africa in 1908.[24] The choice to stay at home in Denmark in 1907 and do one's best with the Roskilde Fjord may have been a choice determined by early financial constraints on the company,

Figure 1.1 Contemporaneous caricature imagining the dressing of the filming location for *The Lion Hunt* (Nordisk, 1907). Color version by Alfred Schmidt in *Blæksprutten,* 1907.

Figure 1.2 A Danish sandbar dressed as Africa. Frame enlargement from *The Lion Hunt* (Nordisk, 1907). Photo courtesy of the Danish Film Institute / Stills & Poster Archive.

but it is more interesting to see this as an alternative conception of cinematic location based on place substitution. This reading is strengthened by the fact that two other, now-lost Nordisk hunting films apparently performed the same kind of substitution. One of them, *Isbjørnejagt* (Polar bear hunt; 1907), preceded the lion hunt film. Its ostensible location was the Arctic, but it was actually filmed in Amager, an area just south of Copenhagen. Olsen describes the shooting location in his memoir: "The ice and snow lay so thick and the landscape was so desolate that it looked completely as it should in the image."[25] The third film came after the success of *The Lion Hunt,* and was entitled *Bjørnejagt* (Bear hunt; 1908), with the alternative title *Bjørnejagt i Rusland* (Bear hunt in Russia). The addition of this geographic detail is important, because the film was not shot in Russia but in Skåne, the area of southern Sweden across the sound from Copenhagen. In short, there were three Nordisk hunting films in 1907–1908 whose production formula was predicated on the feigning of location.

This strategy would of course eventually flourish in Hollywood in the late 1910s and 1920s. Hollywood's eventual dominance was due in part to the rich array of settings conveniently at hand in California's varied geography, which made location shooting both economical and evocative. A map produced by Paramount Studios for publicity purposes provides an amusingly graphic representation of the possibilities, with distant locations replacing the usual ones on a map of California: the Mojave Desert has become the "Sahara" instead, the Lake Tahoe region the "French Alps," and the Sacramento River delta area the "Mississippi River."[26] This is place substitution at its most confident, even hubristic, perhaps because the Hollywood studios had by that time been fictionalizing place successfully for many years (see Figure 1.3).

The charm of the earlier attempt at tropical Denmark for us today is precisely that we are not fooled in the slightest by that landscape. The image is so wonderfully hybrid; all of the seams are showing. We might even have our own reasons to prefer the failure of this early attempt at location cosmetics, reasons that for some might have to do with the waning sense of authentic location today and attendant worries about loss of leverage on "place": there might be something retrospectively satisfying about seeing this early example in which the actual place trumps the ostensible one. For us today, it might provide reassurance that there are limits to substitution.

It is more difficult to gauge the reaction of the original audiences in 1907. The film was a popular success, but that may have been more a function of the animal-cruelty controversy and initial censorship of the film in Denmark than an indication that viewers found the location shooting convincing. Certainly, it would have been difficult for anyone seeing the film in 1907 *not* to know at some conscious level that the scenes presented were filmed at the Danish location of Elleore in the Roskilde Fjord, because the public controversy about the shooting (in

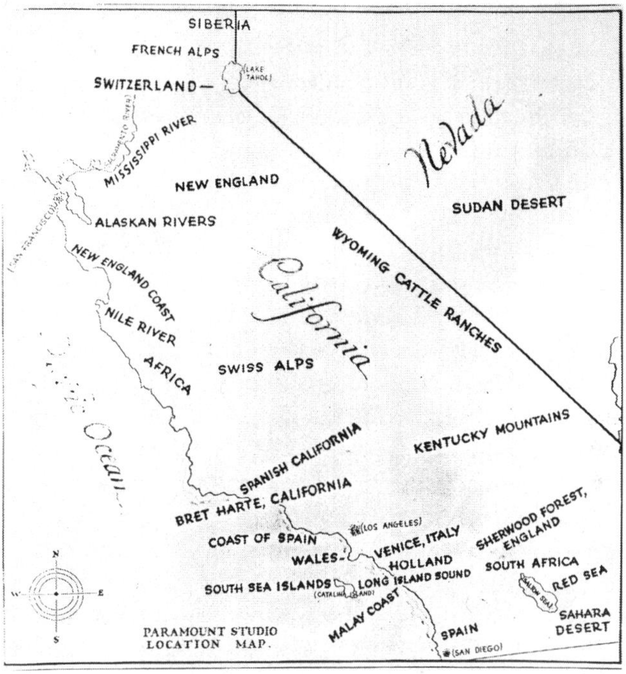

Figure 1.3 Promotional location map released to the press by Paramount Studios as early as 1930 (this version is from 1937). Image courtesy of Marc Wanamaker / Bison Archives.

both senses of the word) preceded the screening. One should thus resist the retrospective temptation to see a clumsy place substitution and assume that the audience was as naïve as the image seems to be; more likely it was an audience that was in part amused by the audacity of Olsen's geographic substitution, in part attracted to the controversy, and in part curious to see the lions shot on screen.

The eventual style of the Nordisk studio at its peak was more like *The Lion Hunt*'s carefully framed shots of the exotic wildlife at the Copenhagen zoo than the visual discrepancies of the "African" fjord, because the tendency was increasingly to eliminate conspicuous cultural idiosyncrasies or settings that might function as a barrier to international appeal. Place identifiers in an image would thus be the equivalent of the bars on the cage at the zoo, betraying an original location that would compete with the fictional claims. Essentially, Olsen's wager at the time was that cultural specificity and identifiable location would hinder success. One can see this tendency at work in the way Nordisk formalized its requirements for freelance script submissions. The rules include this statement: "The plot shall take place in the present and be played out in high society. Stories that play out among people of humble means or among farmers will not be accepted. The same goes for chivalric, historical, or nationalist stories."[27] One can quickly see that the prohibited cultural-historical themes and settings include all those that would not only require insider national knowledge, but might betray the cinematic place as specifically Danish. But this expressed desire to depict an unidentifiable elsewhere, taken together with the limited resources of the Danish studio, committed Nordisk to one of two strategies: either to depict the non-place of international "high society" or to undertake a systematic project of place substitution. But how does one scrub a place clean of its native cultural signifiers? And conversely, when a foreign scene had to be shot at home, what signifiers could one add to the scene to evoke that sense of cultural difference? When working with a relatively homogeneous Danish landscape, it was not true that "all you have to do is change the signs"—or was it?

We can see evidence of these questions in one of the leading genres of pre–World War I Danish cinema, the so-called "erotic melodrama," which was built on that premise.[28] These risqué romantic-triangle films were also sometimes called "count-and-countess" films, since their action was centered in an unlocatable upper-class milieu, with the erotic complications usually arising from some female performer or shopgirl from the lower classes. The effect of placelessness could be maintained easily by sticking mostly to the interiors of casinos, clubs, and apartments, with only brief glimpses of exteriors, which minimized (but of course ultimately did not eliminate) traces of cultural specificity. One example from the heart of that genre is the film *Ved Fængslets Port* (*Temptations of a Great City* / At prison's gate; 1911). In the film, a playboy count, up to his ears in debt, is working on a new romantic conquest—a young shopgirl. The film consists mostly of generic interior scenes, with only three very short exterior shots in the entire film. Exterior views, of course, probably risk more in revealing specificities of place—details like architectural style, flora, and climate—since the move from inside to outside entails the shift from a built to a given environment. The streets in this film, though, have few, if any, recognizably Danish signifiers, appearing strangely void. In other words, the scenes seem to have been shot precisely from the kind of "small corners" referred to by the producer of *The Kite Runner*—viewing angles are controlled, passersby avoided, and so forth. The English translation of the film's title underscores this point, since the Danish original translates quite simply as "At Prison's Gate." Nordisk's international marketing strategy is clear in the distribution title, *Temptations of a Great City,* which refers to place in the most generic sense. Depiction of this "great city" of empty streets and intercultural upper-class interiors was the aspiration of Nordisk's location policy for many of its feature films before the war.

A subgenre of the erotic melodrama, the series of white-slavery films produced in Denmark between 1910 and 1913, shows how Nordisk handled the related scenario of feigning specific foreign places while filming in Denmark. The very premise of each of these stock narratives—abduction into forced prostitution in a foreign land—would seem to require filming abroad. In *Den hvide Slavehandel* (The white slave trade; 1910) the ostensible location of the slavers' brothel is London, but the geographic effects are quite superficial. When the young victim says goodbye to her family, it takes place at a generic boat dock. She thinks she is off to employment in a foreign city, but then comes the sudden intertitle ("Deceived"), followed by a shot of her trapped inside a brothel in her nightgown. The clock painted unconvincingly on a backdrop visible through the brothel window serves as the sole signifier of the foreign place. A later intertitle in the same film ("In London") confirms that the clock was probably meant to be Big Ben. In the few exterior scenes depicting the rescue by her fiancé, there are few local identifiers on the streets, and certainly nothing that looks particularly British. Of course, there would have been a risk in turning Danish locations into London, since some in the film's intended European audience would surely have the specific geographic knowledge that would make the visual discrepancies obvious. Instead, the scene is left visually nondescript, leaving most of the location effect to the intertitle. This strategy recalls Tom Conley's argument that the appearance of a map in a film—or any other overdetermined claim of place—is the surest sign of an underlying dislocation and placelessness.[29]

One of the other white-slavery films that followed *The White Slave Trade* is especially interesting because it exploited the opposite situation—namely, the vagueness of the intended audience's mental geography—to make its geographic compromises. Titled *Mormonens Offer* (*The Victims of the Mormon* / A victim of the Mormons; 1911), the film depicts a young woman from Denmark who is kidnapped into polygamy instead of white slavery and spirited off to Utah. The plot premise would make it difficult not to attempt at least some exterior scenes of Salt Lake City to capitalize on public curiosity about the Mormons (another simple cut directly to a nondescript "Salt Lake City" interior would not do), but traveling to Utah with actors, equipment, and a film crew was clearly not part of the production model for Nordisk at the time. It was simply more complicated and costly for acting troupes to go on location than it was for actuality cameramen to travel. The film thus has many exterior scenes shot in Denmark, including a car chase meant to take place in Salt Lake City (see Figure 1.4).

This frame enlargement shows a pursuit on a bridge with a cityscape in the background, and a later shot shows the car chase ending near a body of water that seems intended to represent the Great Salt Lake. Never mind that the buildings in the background of the bridge look strikingly European, or that there would be no bridges whatsoever within Salt Lake City itself, or that there are no mountains or desert visible in the scene by the lake. Anyone with even a passing acquaintance with Salt Lake City would probably not say that these particular location choices in Denmark were "dripping with production value" for their intended purpose;

Figure 1.4 Copenhagen as stand-in for Salt Lake City. Frame enlargement from *Mormonens offer* (Nordisk, 1911). Used by permission from the Danish Film Institute / Nordisk Film.

Copenhagen and Salt Lake City seem even less substitutable than Kashgar and Kabul in many respects, at least from our perspective. For the original audience, however, the license taken would likely have been perfectly plausible, since the look of Salt Lake City was probably visually unverifiable for most viewers in the European audiences Nordisk was targeting. For most viewers, the idea of "Salt Lake City" was simply not part of their mental geography.

It is also worth thinking about the original Danish viewers, however, the ones who almost certainly recognized that bridge in Copenhagen as quickly as I did the Berkeley Marina in *The Kite Runner.* As it turns out, Ole Olsen didn't actually care much about those with local geographic knowledge—he had already ceded the small domestic Danish market to a rival company by that time as the legal settlement of a plagiarism case with Nordisk's rival company Fotorama.[30] If we can assume that the geographic shortcuts of place substitution in *A Victim of the Mormons* were in fact given some thought and are not just the result of hasty production decisions, we can conclude that the film's director, August Blom, made a calculation that most of the eventual viewers in Nordisk's international audience would not likely have been able to verify either Salt Lake City or Copenhagen, and that a local cityscape would thus suit their purposes. The film was a moderate sales success for Nordisk, so the location discrepancies do not seem to have been a liability.[31]

Nordisk's prestige project prior to World War I was a film adaptation in 1913 of the Gerhart Hauptmann novel *Atlantis*. This film attempted more authentic location shooting than the previous Danish melodramas, with the narrative material from the novel indicating locations in Berlin, Paris, Southampton, New York City, and Meriden, Connecticut, a rural area north of New Haven. For the film's narrative, the urban locations were retained, but with fictional locations serving as the origin ("Henschener" in Germany) and the final destination on the main character's journey ("Handon" instead of Meriden). For the urban locations, only one of them (Berlin) resulted in the filming of the main actor, Olaf Fønss, on location in the image, including scenes showing him walking through streets with recognizable landmarks and buildings in the background and an extended, attractively mobile shot showing Fønss riding through Berlin in the back of an automobile. According to Engberg, the director, August Blom, was interested in doing something more than the simple intercutting of generic actuality footage for the Berlin scenes, emphasizing the importance of sending Fønss personally for the shooting there.[32] By contrast, the Parisian scenes with Fønss were all interiors filmed in Denmark, and the embarkation in Southampton was also likely done at a Danish dock. The required New York City scenes exceeded the limits of Nordisk's location shooting calculations, however, because for these, Blom requested that the Nordisk representative at its American affiliate, Ingvald Aas, engage a capable photographer to obtain footage of specified locations in New York City. These were shot actuality style without the presence of the film's fictional characters and inserted into the segment of *Atlantis* that takes place there.[33] The final location of the film at the snowy, remote mountain cabin is purported to be a rural location somewhere to the north of New York City, but it was actually shot in the interior upland area of Finse, Norway.

Several perspectives emerge from this mix of location practices in *Atlantis*. One is that this film makes a real attempt at authentic location shooting, both with and without the fictional characters present, even if the intentions could not all be realized. For example, Blom requested of Aas that he find a music-hall location in New York with an exterior crowd that could be filmed outside the ticket office, noting that they would send a poster advertising the performance by Mr. Unthan, the Armless Wonder, the images of which would directly follow the exterior shot.[34] The plan, in other words, was to use a real found location and equip it temporarily with a superficial fictional layer of "clothing"—the poster from the narrative of the film ("all you have to do is change the signs"). What seems to have happened was a further compromise, however, judging from the final version included in the film. The film's actors, including Fønss, show up in this scene buying tickets outside a theater with the "Armless Wonder" poster, but since Fønss was never sent to the United States for the filming, the exterior must be a built set instead. Indeed, if one inspects the image closely, one can see that the exterior wall in this scene is in fact a painted canvas. The filmic image thus indicates that at some point Blom changed his plans, perhaps because the New York photographer was unable in the end to find suitable footage. This kind of compromise can also be seen in the exterior scene at the New York artist colony (actually filmed outside of Copenhagen) when a cab with Danish license plates drops off the main character.

These issues come to a head in the Nordisk film that better than any other allegorizes these issues of location substitution and film production. The film was *Himmelskibet* (*A Trip to Mars* / The spaceship; 1917).[35] This science fiction film was one of a string of pacifist films made in Denmark during and after the war.[36] It concerns the building of a rocket ship to travel to Mars to find solutions for humanity's problems. Relevant to the present argument, the film raises the question: How does the choice of a fundamentally alien fictional landscape put pressure on the practice of location substitution? One might on the one hand follow the strategy of the Soviet film *Aelita: Queen of Mars*, from 1924, later in the silent period, which depicts Mars as a fascinating Constructivist environment, with no attempt to represent a Martian exterior landscape whatsoever. The Mars of that film is a planet of Caligari-like interiors, with a love story that is used to play out allegories of revolution from Soviet society back home.

Nordisk's film *A Trip to Mars* is also performing a kind of political allegory—the rocket ship leaves Earth in order to find alternatives to the current international strife. In a kind of wartime fantasy of cooperation, the rocket crew thus includes "Europeans," an American, and a man "from the East" (who seems to be Russian). The issues specific to World War I are displaced to the interface between Earth and Mars. In a long scene depicting the arrival of the rocket ship to Mars, we get a classic border crossing when the crew meets the Martian natives. Although the earthlings expect to have trouble breathing on Mars, they discover instead that the atmosphere is actually just like Earth's. Similarly, we find that these highly evolved Martians can communicate telepathically across language barriers. As it turns out, this Mars is in fact a utopia of wisdom, pacifism, chastity, and vegetarianism, whose advanced wisdom might yet persuade the Earth to renounce war.

But there is a sophisticated allegorization of Nordisk's film production at stake here as well. The "mutual language, understandable for all souls" is also the language of silent film, as Miriam Hansen has discussed in her treatment of D. W. Griffith's *Intolerance*.[37] Up until World War I, silent films had in fact crossed borders almost "telepathically," since all one had to do was rephotograph translations of intertitles (although these translations become increasingly fraught in the late 1910s and 1920s, as Laura Serna discusses in her essay for this

Figure 1.5 Imagining world peace and open markets during World War I. Frame enlargement from *A Trip to Mars* (Nordisk, 1917).

volume). The resurgence of those borders through trade embargos during the war proved to be the undoing of Nordisk Films Kompagni and its successful international production model, so there is something more at stake in preaching pacifism; for Nordisk Film, it is most surely also a desire to return to the open markets it had enjoyed before the war. In this way, there is a particular resonance in the moment when the Martian leaders hand the globe of Earth to the space travelers. It is not just giving back a peaceful world to representatives of the war-torn human societies; it is also giving back a cooperative global market to the Nordisk Films Kompagni (see Figure 1.5). This becomes even clearer when one remembers that the famous Nordisk logo is in fact a polar bear on top of the globe. The fantasy just under the surface here is the Nordisk polar bear's reconquest of a world market with reopened borders.

But I would also like to dwell on the first part of this sequence a bit longer, the part that claims an interchangeability of atmospheres. This is a very useful idea for a Danish production company that not only faced significant financial pressures during the war, but also the attendant wartime political barriers to filming abroad, not unlike those that made present-day Afghanistan unsuitable for filming *The Kite Runner*. (*A Trip to Mars* was shot during the war in 1917 and

Figure 1.6 Martian pastoral scene, with bonus Nordic birch trees. Frame enlargement from *A Trip to Mars* (Nordisk, 1917).

released in 1918.) By claiming that the atmosphere—and by extension, the rest of the natural world on Mars—is surprisingly like its own, Nordisk could motivate shooting on location in Denmark. But just barely. For here is what the alien planet looks like in *A Trip to Mars:* remarkably Nordic (see Figure 1.6). Granted, there is a portion of the film that looks more strange and foreboding, something more like the usual topography of alien planets in science fiction films. But that location turns out to be fairly local as well—it was filmed at a limestone quarry south of Copenhagen, the Faxe Kalkbrud, whose proximity to Copenhagen made it an excellent, economically viable Mars.

There is one more sequence of interest in this film—a love scene between the two lead characters in the Martian "Forest of Love." As the explorer from Earth confesses his love to the Martian woman, they wander through a forest strewn with illuminated paper flowers (see Figure 1.7). The scenery looks as if it were the precise referent of a paragraph in a Danish film treatise published one year later. This work (*Film: Dens Midler og Maal*) has not been translated into English, but its title would read *Film: Its Means and Goals.* It was written by Urban Gad, the important early director in both Denmark and Germany who is most famous

Figure 1.7 Paper flowers saving a love scene. Frame enlargement from *A Trip to Mars* (Nordisk, 1917).

for his work with Asta Nielsen. The purpose of the book was to give practical instruction in filmmaking; here is Gad's advice about exterior location shooting:

> The basic element, common vegetation, is fairly similar all over the world, and a simple transplanted palm or banana plant can contribute a lot to a sense of local color; accompanying paper flowers, when placed on the bushes, also seem completely convincing and have saved the atmosphere of more than one love scene. If one has to create impressions of distant regions, it is fairly easy to add decorative elements depicted on wood and canvas and get them to melt completely into the landscape.[38]

It is not possible to know if Gad is referring directly to *A Trip to Mars,* but he might well have been doing so. Mars would certainly count as a "distant region," even if the Martian flowers have not exactly "melted into the landscape" in this particular scene. Gad is of course mistaken when he says that vegetation is basically the same all over the world (and by extension, throughout the solar system), because in fact it is very easy to see the typically Nordic meadows, forests, and lakes that are peeking through this trip to Mars; flora is in fact one of the most insurmountable localizing factors. Today we probably experience a discrepancy in these images that veers quickly into a kind of camp appreciation for failed production values. What Gad's comments reveal about attitudes at the time, however, is the assumption that the specificity of location could and should be overcome. In this sense, Gad continues the attitude Ole Olsen adopted in *The Lion Hunt,* with the paper flowers performing the function of the palm fronds on the island in the fjord. For Danish small-nation filmmaking to work at that time, place had to be regarded as a superficial, cosmetic effect rather than as an ontological truth of the image.

Interestingly, elsewhere in his book Gad tries to distinguish his stance toward location shooting from that of the U.S. film industry, which at the time of his writing was poised to carry out its conquest of the European market. Gad admits that it certainly doesn't make any sense to travel all the way to India simply to catch a scene or two on film (note how that assumption has disappeared today). But even so, he finds it arrogant for Hollywood to claim that it can substitute something local for any distant landscape it chooses:

> One should not cut corners on authenticity when the fundamental tone of the drama is at stake. Still, this kind of artistic error is committed all the time, particularly by the American studios, who despite their abundant financial resources subscribe to the fallacy that one can film everything in California—everything without exception.[39]

This statement pre-dates the Paramount Studio location map discussed earlier in this essay; we might see it as an early European criticism of Hollywood's developing place promiscuity. Gad is not exactly lobbying for a rigorous site specificity; when he emphasizes the purely decorative aspects of film location, one sees the persistence of the initial Danish marketing strategy. When he expresses concern, however, about the encroachment of the California studios, which are able to substitute landscapes more plausibly and efficiently, we perceive the seeds of the Danish strategy's decline. It was at this juncture in the development of the notion of film location that Denmark was forced to give up its global aspirations, because the limits of a small-nation model of filmmaking necessarily reasserted themselves when Nordisk was forced to compete with California's more extensive imaginary geography and the superior financial resources of the American film studios. Denmark might be able to provide a simulacrum of Mars by using a limestone quarry—at one point it even attempted Egypt, with a sphinx built in the sand dunes of Northern Jutland in the film *Sfinxens Hemmelighed* (*The Secret of the Desert* / The sphinx's secret; 1918). But Denmark has no mountains, no pine forests; it cannot aspire to a universal geography, even if one can find something like a huge sand dune in the middle of the countryside. Its actual climate and topography make it a more limited, specific kind of place. When Gad pivots away from the fully developed practice of American place substitution and back to values of place authenticity in his book, we can see the realities of small-nation filmmaking reemerging.

Interestingly, this is exactly the strategy that allowed Swedish silent film to flower into a golden age after World War I—an intense focus on Nordic landscapes, narratives set in rural farming milieus, and nationally specific material. Note that these are the very things Nordisk had banned from its scripts in 1912. The point is that assumptions about place had shifted dramatically in the intervening years. The appeal of a Nordic landscape untouched by the trench warfare that had scarred much of Europe made site specificity a viable commodity instead of a potential hindrance to the free flow of films between countries. For the early Danish industry, the specificity of location had been a market barrier that needed to be overcome; after the war, it became possible to regard locality both as a philosophical virtue and a valuable visual commodity. Swedish film was successful for reasons almost exactly opposite those for Danish film's earlier success.

And if we then scan the rest of Danish film history for breakout phases of international recognition similar to the early Nordisk studio success, we find two prominent examples. One would be the high-art films of Carl Theodor Dreyer, and the other would be the more recent Dogme 95 films. Interestingly, both of these examples are famous for extreme forms of site specificity. Dreyer was fanatical about creating inhabitable sets or using found locations—that was one of the reasons he made relatively few films.[40] And of the famous ten rules in Dogme 95's "vow of chastity," the rule that heads the list reads: "Shooting must be done on location. Props and sets must not be brought in (if a particular prop is necessary for the story, a location must be chosen where this prop is to be found)."[41] In other words, this kind of filmmaking requires a completely uncosmetic use of location and adopts the "givenness" of place as a productive artistic constraint by forbidding substitution. A sense of locality is one of the few bits of leverage a small film industry has on the global market today.

This look back at the early days of Nordisk, in other words, reveals a trajectory never completed, a location practice that was unlikely to succeed in a national film industry the size of Denmark's. For a time the polar bear did rule the globe by playing fast and loose with geography, but the fact that it no longer does so is perhaps even more instructive, because it shows us the contingency of attitudes toward place. Those early experiments with place substitution and location simulation, however, also create an inadvertent historical appeal. As I have worked with this material, I have found myself consistently drawn to what one might call the "failed" locations—those that substitute poorly. We might call these the "African fjord," the "Mormon cityscape," and the "Martian meadow." It seems likely that the attraction of these images now, in our own historically contingent time and location, is precisely that they resonate with our experience of "incompatible" places forced together by global flow. Perhaps it is a relief to us to see that not every place can be substituted smoothly, that places can in fact still matter.

Notes

1. Howard W. French, "Where to Shoot an Epic about Afghanistan? China, Where Else?" *New York Times,* December 31, 2006.

2. Rebecca Yeldham, "Images from 'The Kite Runner,'" Blu-ray DVD special feature directed by Laurent Bouzereau (*The Kite Runner,* dir. Marc Forster [Glendale, CA: Dreamworks Video, 2009], DVD).

3. French, "Where to Shoot."

4. David Benioff, "Images from 'The Kite Runner,'" Blu-ray DVD special feature directed by Laurent Bouzereau (*The Kite Runner,* dir. Marc Forster [Glendale, CA: Dreamworks Video, 2009], DVD).

5. Ibid.

6. For instance, the Picture-in-Picture feature of some Blu-ray discs allows more than audio commentary while watching the feature; the PIP window can also provide competing analytic visual material as well. For instance, the PIP might show how a digital effect was created in the shooting. The film *Vantage Point* (2008) reveals another possibility: the scrambled chronology and limited vantage points of the film's plot fragments motivates the availability of a PIP window that tracks all the character movements in overview on a map while each individual sequence is taking place.

7. For this film, for example, a look at the trivia section reveals these facts: "The scenes ostensibly taking place in Afghanistan were mainly shot in the cities of Kashgar and Tashkurgan in the Xinjiang region of China (officially the Xinjiang Uygur Autonomous Region). The DVD commentary mentions that scenes shot in Kashgar include the kite tournament (at 24:15), the mosque where Amir prays (110:40), and Rahim Khan's apartment in Peshawar, Pakistan (76:11). Scenes shot in Tashkurgan include the opening scenes of a kite duel and the boys running the kite (06:00), the pomegranate tree (19:04), and the Taliban compound where Amir meets Sohrab (101:00). Scenes shot in or outside of Beijing include the wedding (72:41) and the soccer match (96:53). The San Francisco bar scene (55:07) was also shot in China." See "Trivia for *The Kite Runner,*" Internet Movie Database, http://www.imdb.com/title/tt0419887/trivia.

8. Marguerite Engberg, *Dansk Stumfilm: De Store År* (Copenhagen: Rhodos, 1977), 2:619.

9. Mark B. Sandberg, "Multiple-Reel Feature Films: Europe," in *Encyclopedia of Early Cinema,* ed. Richard Abel (New York: Routledge, 2005), 452–456; and Sandberg, "Pocket Movies: Souvenir Cinema Programs and the Danish Silent Cinema," *Film History* 13.1 (Fall 2001): 6–22.

10. For an overview in English of the early history of Nordisk Film, see Isak Thorsen, "The Rise and Fall of the Polar Bear," in *100 Years of Nordisk Film,* ed. Lisbeth Richter Larsen and Dan Nissen (Copenhagen: Danish Film Institute, 2006), 53–71.

11. Mette Hjort and Duncan Petrie, eds., *The Cinema of Small Nations* (Bloomington: Indiana University Press, 2007), 2.

12. For an overview of these explanations and an argument for the priority of the economic causal factors, see Thomas G. Christensen, "Nordisk Films Kompagni and the First World War," in *Nordic Explorations: Film before 1930,* ed. John Fullerton and Jan Olsson (Sydney: John Libbey, 1999), 12–18.

13. For a sample of Elfelt's work as a still photographer, see Ib Rønne Kejlbo, *Kongelig Hoffotograf Peter Elfelt: En billedkavalkade* (Copenhagen: Det Kongelige Bibliotek, 1989).

14. The brief fiction film *Henrettelsen* (The execution, 1903) restaged the famous execution of a Frenchwoman who had killed her children.

15. A thorough catalogue of Elfelt's approximately two hundred films can be found in Marguerite Engberg, *Registrant over Danske Film 1896–1914*, vol. 1 (Copenhagen: Institut for Filmvidenskab, 1977). Information about much of Elfelt's early film work is also available in the National Filmography on the Danish Film Institute's website, where one can find facts about the films and in many cases view video clips of the films themselves. See "Nationalfilmografien," Danish Film Institute, http://www.dfi.dk/FaktaOmFilm/Nationalfilmografien.aspx.

16. For an overview of the travelogue in cinema history, see Jennifer Lynn Peterson, "World Pictures: Travelogue Films and the Lure of the Exotic, 1890–1920" (PhD dissertation, University of Chicago, 1999); and "Travelogues," in *Encyclopedia of Early Cinema*, ed. Richard Abel (New York: Routledge, 2005), 640–643. See also Jeffrey Ruoff, ed., *Virtual Voyages: Cinema and Travel* (Durham, NC: Duke University Press, 2006), a useful anthology dealing with travel and cinema history more broadly.

17. Ole Olsen, *Filmens Eventyr og Mit Eget* (Copenhagen: Jespersen og Pios Forlag, 1940), 51.

18. Engberg, *Registrant over Danske Film*.

19. The best biography of Olsen in Danish is Poul Malmkjær, *Gøgler og Generaldirektør: Ole Olsen, grundleggeren af Nordisk Film* (Copenhagen: Gyldendals Bogklubber, 1997).

20. Olsen, *Filmens Eventyr*, 56; my translation here and in subsequent citations from Danish originals.

21. For a thorough discussion of the film and its connection to Hagenbeck, see Eric Ames, *Carl Hagenbeck's Empire of Entertainments* (Seattle: University of Washington Press, 2008), 200–206.

22. Engberg, *Dansk Stumfilm*, 136–146.

23. Ibid., 145.

24. Ibid., 143.

25. Olsen, *Filmens Eventyr*, 72.

26. The map is included in Tino Balio, ed., *The American Film Industry* (Madison: University of Wisconsin Press, 1985), 202. It can also be found on various websites, including "465: Scene to Be Believed: California as the World," Strange Maps, http://strangemaps.wordpress.com/2010/05/21/465-scene-to-be-believed-california-as-the-world/. An early published source for the map is "Paramount 'Location Map' Plays Odd Trick on World," *Washington Post*, March 2, 1930, A2. My thanks go to Patrick Ellis for calling this to my attention.

27. Quoted in Malmkjær, *Gøgler og Generaldirektør*, 186. The context immediately before and after this quotation is also interesting: "There must be a max. of 1–3 main characters around whom the plot revolves, and the author should always make sure that there is always at least one person the audience can sympathize with. A simple, straightforward plot without too many digressions is preferable. Crimes such as murder, theft, forgery etc. must absolutely not be shown, but only hinted at. . . . It is not permitted to write anything disrespectful about royalty, public officers, priests, or the military. Nihilism, anarchism, and the like must not appear. In every film there should be some spectacular—and above all original—trick that can form the film's main attraction" (185–186).

28. Engberg, *Dansk Stumfilm*, 439–441. For her overview of all of the various genres of Danish dramatic film during the period 1910–1914, see 405–519.

29. Tom Conley, *Cartographic Cinema* (Minneapolis: University of Minnesota Press, 2007), 4.

30. Marguerite Engberg, "Plagiarism and the Birth of the Danish Multi-Reel Film," in *100 Years of Nordisk Film*, ed. Lisbeth Richter Larsen and Dan Nissen (Copenhagen: Danish Film Institute, 2006), 73–79.

31. Engberg, *Dansk Stumfilm,* 416. The film sold 137 copies, which is an above-average sales total for Nordisk in 1911 (the highest seller that year was *The White Slave Trade* at 250 copies sold; the lowest was *Freslserpigen* at 24).

32. Engberg, *Dansk Stumfilm,* 493.

33. Ibid., 493–494.

34. Ibid., 494.

35. This film is available on an excellent DVD produced by the Danish Film Institute from a restored version of the film in 2006: *Himmelskibet,* Danish Silent Classics (Copenhagen: Danish Film Institute, 2006).

36. Other films in this genre include *Ned med Vaabnene!* (Lay down arms!, 1914), *Pro Patria* (1916), and *Pax Æterna* (1917).

37. Miriam Hansen, *Babel and Babylon: Spectatorship in American Silent Film* (Cambridge, MA: Harvard University Press, 1991), 173–187.

38. Urban Gad, *Filmen: Dens Midler og Maal* (Copenhagen: Gyldendal, 1918), 216.

39. Ibid., 230.

40. For an in-depth look at one such Dreyer film, see Mark B. Sandberg, "Mastering the House: Performative Inhabitation in Carl Th. Dreyer's *The Parson's Widow,*" in *Northern Constellations: New Readings in Nordic Cinema,* ed. C. Claire Thompson (Norwich, UK: Norvik Press, 2006), 23–42.

41. The entire Dogme 95 vow of chastity, along with other founding documents and manifestos, is reproduced in Mette Hjort and Scott MacKenzie, eds., *Purity and Provocation: Dogma 95* (London: British Film Institute, 2003).

2 Insurgent Place as Visual Space

Location Shots and Rival Geographies of 1857 Lucknow

Priya Jaikumar

This soil of Lucknow.
This orchard of color or country
of heady love and beautiful forms,
where Awadh's setting sun
seeks its destination.
This place of bewitchment.
This place of youth.
This land of Lucknow.

Yeh Lucknow ki sarzameen, yeh Lucknow ki sarzameen.
Yeh rang-roop ka chaman, yeh husnon-ishq ka watan,
Yehi to woh maqaam hai, jahaan Awadh ki shaam hai.
Jawaan-Jawaan Haseen-Haseen, yeh Lucknow ki sarzami.

Shakeel Badayuni

Film not only depicted movement in space and space in movement, it also unpacked the modern subject's spatial unconscious and its layers of (repressed) memories.

Anthony Vidler

Introduction: Colonial Socio-Spatiality and the Visual

How do we historicize *film space,* understanding the term to refer to the space within a film frame and the interregnum between frames? The spatial tropes of *The Relief of Lucknow* (1912; henceforth *The Relief*), directed by Serle J. Dawley for the U.S. Edison Company, will be recognizable to anyone familiar with American westerns.[1] In this single-reel fiction film, Englishmen save their women and children from a colonial city besieged by hostile Indian natives. Thematically and formally, the text is transportable across context through its abstractions of space, achieved by what Ella Shohat and Robert Stam refer to as an "imagery of encirclement" menacing both the camera and the audience.[2] The authors are discussing images from American westerns that invert history to make Native Americans intruders in their own land, by visualizing them as threatening the domestic spaces of white settlers, within which the camera remains nested. In this formulation, the film's politically motivated spatial design is in an inverse relationship with the context of historical events, like a camera obscura image of reality. Consequently, grasping social history through filmic space becomes an exercise in tracking the film's textual affiliations to the dominant ideologies of its period. Such an interpretive move is easy to make in relation to the Edison film, because its tense, internally coherent conflicts, produced by contrasting frame compositions and brisk edits, create a hermetic world that usurps the socio-spatial conflicts of 1857 Lucknow.

I take the hyphen between those two words—social and spatial—seriously, following Edward Soja in his assessment that society is simultaneously space forming and space contingent.[3] Colonial social *and* spatial relations were violently reordered in Lucknow, a North Indian city in the province of Awadh (now Uttar Pradesh), when Indian sepoys (soldiers) massacred British and loyalist members of the British East India Company in June 1857. In this rebellion, Awadh was like numerous Indian cities such as Meerut, Delhi, Mathura, Kanpur, Agra, and Gwalior where there were anti-British uprisings. Partially as a response to the British usurpation of Awadh from Nawab Wajid Ali Shah, over eight thousand rebelling Indian sepoys besieged women, children, officers, and allies of Sir Henry Lawrence's administration in Lucknow. The ranks of insurgents swelled, as did the number of deaths in the British camp, which rose to two thousand. The Mutiny of 1857, as it was referred to, was part of a historic rebellion that radically altered the nature of the British presence in India and the form of its empire worldwide, ending the East India Company's economic monopoly over South Asia and initiating the administrative rationalities of Crown rule.

But this brief narrative about the rebellion impedes, rather than serves, my attempt at using an early film's spatial structure to launch a historiographic analysis. It does little to clarify whether the cataclysmic social and spatial reorganization of India during and after 1857 bore any relevance to the spatiality of a film like *The Relief.* And a chronicle of events alone conveys little of its political or historical context. The events of 1857 Lucknow were under erasure almost as soon as they began, expressed in their contested definition as a "mutiny" as opposed to a "rebellion" or "the first war of independence," as a sign of their unstable assimilation within historiographic narratives.[4] Was the rebellion a cause, or on a continuum of consequences, of shifts in imperial policies in British India? Was it a tragic but necessary destruction of pre-capitalist India, or an articulation of the colonized as agents of their own history?[5] Historiography was precisely the problem for narratives of the Indian rebellion. Ranajit Guha notes in his classic text on peasant revolts that insurgencies, as violent reversals of habitual codes of power, provoke a radical crisis in knowledge and narrativization. Identifying causes for insurgencies demands a critical dismantling of prevalent paradigms of power, provoking explanatory frameworks to resolve more easily into attributions of spontaneous or congenital violence in a subject people. The rupture of knowledge produced by the Indian rebellion has been managed in master narratives of British imperialism (through counterinsurgent archives that erase rationales for rebel actions) and Indian nationalism (which assimilates rebels into self-affirming narratives of predetermined national genesis). The archive's rhetorical and ideological management of 1857 is the focus of much of the scholarship about the rebellion so far.[6]

In visual studies as well, we witness similar analyses of the rebellion as a site for counterinsurgent rhetorical closure. Discussing photographer Felice Beato's shocking image of the interior of the walled garden of Sekunderbagh in Lucknow after it was retaken by the British, Zahid Chaudhary argues that the rebellion was formative not only of British imperial history, but also of ways of looking at colonial bodies. Beato arrived in Lucknow five months after the suppression of the insurgency, having just photographed the Crimean War. As Chaudhary notes, "Not content with mere architectural ruins, Beato ordered full exhumation of the only half-buried corpses and posed them in the courtyard of Sekunderbagh."[7] The result is an image of a grand, pitted façade in the background with a litter of the skeletal remains of Indian sepoys in the foreground, viewed by four Indian men and a horse, arranged to convey little regard for the macabre sight facing them. This photograph, with its excavation of bodies and its contention with the camera's slow exposure time, gives ghoulish evidence to the danger of historical representations becoming a restaged frieze. Chaudhary focuses on the management of perception in the photograph, linked to what he develops as a phantasmagoric aesthetic through which visible, physical colonial violence was transformed into an invisible power permeating British India, fragmenting and rearranging native lives and deaths through new technologies of statistical surveys, factory clocks, and above all, photography.

Undeniably, photographs of insurgencies controlled (in that they managed the horizon of meanings of) colonial bodies, particularly the marauding, slaughtered bodies of the insurgents. But there were other, equally significant functions to such photographs, particularly in a context where details of deaths found their way to print but visuals of dead insurgents remained rare. Photographs of ruins and devastated land predominated over photographs of bodies, of particular relevance given the post-revolt British policy to level to the ground all Indian cities that supported the insurgency or that neighbored insurgent cities. Administrators, writers, and the public alike wanted to take visual measure of the insurgent place, with its shifting boundaries of control and photogenic architectures of ruin, whether to comprehend the events, to officiate, to decimate, or to spectate with thrill and horror. Visuality was central to the transformation of an insurgent place into perceived space, and it is in this context that we can begin to link the city of Lucknow to *The Relief of Lucknow*.[8]

In 1858, the *Calcutta Review* reported that Britain's apathy toward India was radically jolted after "the *electric shock* of the mutiny."[9] Electricity was an appropriate metaphor to convey the speed and violence of the rebellion's news, which traveled via the recently invented telegraph and resulted in more current reportage of distant events than previously possible. This was still a precarious task, as telegraphed news could be either validated or reversed in clarifications arriving by slower, more reliable mail. According to Karl Marx in the *New-York Tribune* of August 1857: "On the arrival at London of the voluminous reports conveyed by the last Indian mail, the meager outlines of which had been anticipated by the electric telegraph, the rumor of the capture of Delhi [from the insurgents] was rapidly spreading and winning so much consistency as to influence the transactions of the Stock Exchange."[10] Rumors of events, their implications, and the thrust and parry of insurgents and counterinsurgents across unknown terrain were imagined and reacted to in a relatively condensed period of time.[11] The unfamiliar geography of Lucknow, Agra, Rohulcund, and Jumna unfolded before the British public even as its spatial boundaries were erased and rewritten by a spreading insurgency and its suppression, and by constellated channels of information about it.

The Indian Rebellion of 1857 should be treated as an early indication of the centrality of technologies of visual reproduction in the surfacing of local sites of violence in a national and imperial imaginary. Photographs and early films that depicted sites of a revolt, massive in scale and newsworthiness, popularized through news reportage and novels, consciously produced unfamiliar regions for cosmopolitan subjects of consumption through a conclave of texts, images, and narratives about it. Lucknow emerged on the world stage, or indeed called into existence a global performative arena, through its part in a hitherto unimagined kind of violence. Like comparable locations—most recently, Fallujah and Tikrit in Iraq, or Kabul in Afghanistan—Lucknow was as much a construct of multiple imaginings as it was a referent. The place became globally familiar at the same time that a spectacular and violent suppression of its sovereignty implanted a local sense of alienation and unhousing. Photography played a crucial part in the incursion of world history into Lucknow's intimate spaces, creating visceral distances for the geographically proximate and a visceral proximity for the geographically distant. This was not a singular dynamic to be understood primarily for its imperial containment, but one with multiple implications for several constituencies with varying kinds of investments in Lucknow. How subsequent visual reproductions of this place dealt with its entrapment in the moment of insurgency, which definitively altered its temporality, is a question best answered by *interrogating* rather than accepting the analytic framework of rhetorical and ideological closures.

The question of Lucknow's representation in a given film (such as *The Relief*) or a photograph (such as Beato's Sekunderbagh interior) is not capable of yielding answers outside the terms of the text's ideological containment. Of equal significance are questions related to the context of circulation of such photographs and films; questions dealing with how artists in India, Britain, or the United States used visual technologies to depict sites of insurgency; and questions about the potential encounters such images could stage by transporting spectators to the site of destruction virtually. These questions pertain to the visually mediated circulation, spectation, and production of colonial space.

The difference between thinking about visual representations of a place and the visual production of space bears further explanation. Scholars of early cinema talk of cinema's coincidence with new technologies of travel, such as the steamship, the railways, and the automobile, significant for their novelty in creating a mobile perspective for accessing and consuming the world.[12] Virtual travel is not equivalent to physical mobility, but both can empathetically transport people out of their spheres of comfort, and both are deeply contaminated by commercial industries driven by the imperative to generate profit. Visual accounts of the 1857 insurgency were created with administrative *and* commercial rationales, and intertwined principles of commerce and the state were precisely characteristic of modern, rationalizing empire. So an exclusive focus on state power in fixing the meaning of an image detracts from the realities of how images of destruction and death circulated among emergent modern publics and markets in the nexus of Britain and India.[13] It also disregards the ongoing negotiations that people had to make with the memory of violence, when forced to habituate themselves to ruined lives and surroundings. Evaluating *The Relief* in relation to the multiple affective territorialities of Lucknow unleashed by an anti-colonial insurgency demands enlarging our field of investigation beyond the film's representation (or textualization) of a colonial people or place. Though important, questions of representation remain framed by the terms of the film text under scrutiny. In addition to importing a literary mode of analysis to visual media in a manner that may not be appropriate, the investigation remains caught in the impasse of using a racist text against itself by seeking internal aporias.

Following Henri Lefebvre, the question to ask is not how a silent film represents a colonial place, but how a colonial place was multiply (commercially, administratively, socially, culturally) produced as space at a particular historical time, and what role the visual played within this dynamic. Rather than using the film narrative or image as an interpretive launching point for its history, starting the analysis with a focus on historical and social productive forces returns us to the visual with greater vehemence and insight. Whereas space as an exclusively textual function of film may throw us off the scent of its context, an assessment of visual media in relation to the materiality (physical production) and immateriality (memory traces) of social space returns us to a wide-ranging critical historiographic practice. With this in mind, I reinitiate my essay.

Colonial cityscapes and architectures were driven by the dual imperatives to maintain a nostalgic memorialization of the colonizer's homeland and to perpetuate a physical/psychic segregation between the occupiers and the occupied.[14] These two foundational aspects of colonial socio-spatiality were enhanced by insurgencies, which resulted in a further enforcement of spatial divisions. However, the colonizer/colonized divide was complicated by the popularization of photography and the invention of cinema. The spatial crisis produced by visual technologies is clear if we consider photographs not as static images in isolation, but as visual records of an event dynamically circulating among a consuming and meaning-making public, thereby destabilizing political hierarchies through a more expansive spectatorial address, mixed exhibitions sites, and a commercially driven logic of circulation, to be negotiated anew by the state. One of the most popular modes for circulating photographs of the insurgency was the album. Photographic "mutiny memorial" albums served as a visual precedent for films about Indian "mutiny sites," revealing a popular audience for images of the violent events that would preoccupy British literary imagination until the first decade of the twentieth century.[15] Photographic reproductions of a mutiny site constituted iconic and indexical visual renditions of an Indian city whose architectonics had been forcefully reconfigured by the insurgency and its suppression. As Ben Lifson notes, the practical decision of where to place a camera in a city deprived of strategic vantage points by its systematic leveling by British forces made the city's terrain an unavoidable reality of photographic renditions. Each visual iteration interpreted, activated, or suppressed the historical remapping of a colony in ways revealing the sympathies and desires of its creator and presumed audiences.[16] *The Relief* must be considered in relation to these layered and varied productions of Lucknow's "rival geographies."[17] An album of Lucknow's mutiny sites forms a precursor to my analysis of the film, not only for its precedence as a representational and memorializing form but also for a rival cinematicity against which I evaluate the spatial design of the subsequent short narrative film.

The Lucknow Album (1874)

A transitional artifact of the mid- to late nineteenth century, photographic albums were increasingly confined to domestic spaces after art moved into public, museological arenas regulated by the prohibition of tactility.[18] In the 1800s, "albums" referred to personal collages by Victorian women who pasted together paintings, poems, and mechanically reproduced images to peruse in living rooms as a sign of their gentility. Additionally, they were the domain of British amateur and professional male photographers, who used albums to sample their work. Victorian men also used albums to display their world travels; thus it would appear that, more often than not, photographs exhibited the Victorian woman's experience by proxy and the Victorian man's claim to professionalism and experiential immediacy.[19] As a crafted commodity of one's professional expertise and world travels, the masculine photographic album soon overshadowed feminine decoupage of visual ephemera. Felice Beato's photographs of the Indian "mutiny," like most mutiny memorial photographs, circulated in such masculine pastiches.

One such instance is Reverend Thomas Moore's album of materials related to Kanpur and Lucknow during the Mutiny of 1857.[20] The album shares with its feminine counterparts the format of a personal journal, composed of heterogeneous found materials ranging from sketches, newspaper cuttings, transcribed letters, quoted poetry, and commercial photographs relating directly or indirectly to the revolt. Moore's album was notably not just a journal recording places of interest, but a memoir of his travels combining varying modes of address and registers of (historical and fictional) time. He underlines his presence at the hospitals and funerals of Kanpur and Lucknow during the "mutiny" by transcribing copies of his letters to his wife, exhorting her not to join him in an India made unsafe by the "lickering we have received."[21] These personal letters are embedded in an album that begins with a transcribed verse from Thomas Babington Macaulay's *Lays of Ancient Rome* which offers an ode to heroic men who die "facing fearful odd [*sic*]," followed by newspaper cuttings about the Taj Mahal as the world's most expensive monument, a painting of the steamer *Brahmaputra,* a handwritten account of the brutal massacre of fifty Christian Europeans and Eurasians in Delhi, detailed transcriptions of angry letters between Colonel Neill and General Henry Havelock, who were involved in the Lucknow garrison and relief attempts, along with photographs of Lucknow's Chutter Munzil palace and Bailie Guard archway by Felice Beato.[22]

The heteroglossia of the album is our first clue to what exceeds a monocular management of perceptions of violence and to the larger context of the circulation of images of Lucknow. The album stages its status as solemn witness to the revolt through evidentiary texts such as the letters of dispute between British officers and a rebuttal of "The Mythical Story of Jessie Brown," wife of a soldier who claims to have heard the Highlanders' bagpipes play during the relief of Lucknow's garrison. Alongside such deflating narratives that refuse to mythologize British counterinsurgency are paeans to British heroism, such as Alfred Lord

Tennyson's poem "The Defence of Lucknow." In other words, the album combines the "somber discourse" of witnessing history with the intimate discourse of personal epistolary and the commercial discourses of popular tourism.[23] In this register, Reverend Moore offers the appeal of his being in the land of the Taj Mahal, in addition to narrating the risks of imminent attack.

Insurgency albums reveal a kind of colonial disaster tourism that informed early consumptions of visual violence, and complicated visual modes of state power. A particularly nuanced mode of this spectatorial address appears in *The Lucknow Album,* a photographic album of Lucknow's buildings published by the Baptist Mission Press in Calcutta in 1874 and authored by the Indian engineer and photographer Darogha Ubbas Ali. This album offers a proto-cinematic text by binding together fifty albumen prints of Lucknow's architectural landmarks, accompanied by a text presumably authored by Ubbas Ali. *The Lucknow Album* prefigures the structure of an early travelogue slide show or film, addressing its viewer by using a kinetic sense of movement across pitted buildings with deep historical residue. It begins with these words:

> Ruins, ancient and modern, bearing marks of oriental splendour and extravagance . . . shattered and shot-battered walls, scathed monuments, telling of the horrors of war, rebellion and siege . . . dismantled palaces, fast falling into decay, are all objects of interest and curiosity to the tourist, the antiquary, the historian, the archeologist and the lover of art. The City of Lucknow . . . abounds with objects of this description in all the intense sublimity of ruin . . . that, but for the present volume, would have ruthlessly consigned them to everlasting oblivion.[24]

Aligned with Victorian women's albums in its questionable legitimacy given its Indian authorship, this album's self-conscious deployment of the trope of a "ruin" can be read as a labored self-legitimation designed to increase its purchase. The book addresses "survivors of the Garrison." Equally, it describes itself as an "illustrated guide" that will "succeed in fostering the spirit of enquiry, to which the histories of objects afore mentioned [railways and ruins] have so manifestly given birth, and to which *the educated Native of India and the traveling public of all nations throughout the civilized world* are so much attached."[25] The emotional appeal of the album exists alongside promises of an "intellectual treat," so that it draws upon a contemplative mode of perception celebrated by the use of space in the English picturesque, while simultaneously interrupting it with a Benjaminian dialectic about a past open to the restless inquiry of the present. Shifts between reverential commemoration and sociable gossip are present throughout the album's text, saving its images from the fixity of a frieze. The equivalent of an early limited-edition book, and more seamless than a personal pastiche, Ubbas Ali's *Lucknow Album* carries a multi-tonality that I wish to convey by the term "colonial disaster tourism."

Figure 2.1 Bailie Guard gate at Lucknow. Courtesy the Getty Research Institute, Los Angeles (92-B22782).

The album proves to be less a commemoration of counterinsurgency than an incorporation of the city's buildings into narrative accounts of ongoing life. Each monument comes with a surplus of information that exceeds the text's mournful attitude and counters the stunning evacuation of life from the visuals by placing the deaths on a continuum with other points of significance, approximating to a discourse of disaster tourism that is as much about consumption as it is about grief.[26] The text frequently lists the names and titles of the British dead, as at the infamous Bailie Guard gate (Figure 2.1), but it is quick to suggest that the "consecrated ground" is "prettily laid out" with "floral walks," and "without these pleasant additions to such a mournful spot, the ruins themselves are more than sufficient to repay the visit of the most indifferent tourist" (Figure 2.2).[27] The Moti Mahal (Figure 2.3) is described as the site of many British deaths during the revolt, and the text lists the names of the British officials killed. It is *also* described as a seraglio (*zenana khana*), from which the nawabs (rulers of Lucknow) witnessed wild sport such as tiger combats or fights between an elephant and a rhinoceros. It is at the indifferent tourist, perhaps at the potential distractability of *every* tourist, that the combination of mournful, incidental, and salacious details are aimed: details about how much money was plundered by trustees of the Husainabad Imambara; or how the Gomati River provided pure and drinkable

Figure 2.2 Inside the Bailie Guard. Courtesy the Getty Research Institute, Los Angeles (92-B22782).

Figure 2.3 Moti Mahal in Lucknow. Courtesy the Getty Research Institute, Los Angeles (92-B22782).

water despite the English poet William Wordsworth's condemnation that it was poisoned by "the number of dead bodies thrown in it."[28]

Here we catch fleeting subversions of the imperial regime and a refusal to strike one single emotional tone regarding Lucknow's recent past. In her essay on this album, Sophie Gordon points out the multilayered nature of mourning conveyed by the album's organization of the photographs. While the album follows the east-to-westerly path taken by British troops in 1857, Gordon notes that the final three images of the book are geographically incongruous. The album shifts directionality to conclude with images of three of Lucknow's mosques, which were not destinations for British tourists commemorating sites of British deaths but rather culminations of Shi'ite processions. Lucknow's architecture was in significant part defined by its role as a leading Shi'ite city, attracting mourners from all over the region to move through the streets and its religious sites during Muharram.[29]

By its own proclamation, however, the album also intends to follow a route to the city "by rail from Cawnpore, commencing from a southerly direction."[30] The "talismanic power" of photography (using the album's words) that grants the ruins enduring power derives its aura not only from traditions of sacred mourning, but from new habits of curious looking as well. A secular perspective attuned to the trivia of architectural and industrial history only tangentially related to the history of the rebellion inflects this layered portrayal of a mourning claimed for the British tourist and the Shi'ite viewer. The album negotiates among diverse modes of perceiving place on account of its own historical location at the cusp of a technological transition, where distant, sacred places could become consumable sites through photography, endowing the image rather than the monument with talismanic powers. The photograph destroys the aura of the place and makes it available to every reader, but the text describing the place invests the photograph with those very attributes: "This Album will bear a sacred interest, and many a tear will fall at the contemplation of some well-remembered spot, over which a sort of holy radiance will appear to linger."[31]

If travel films display a modern mode of perception, as Charles Musser and Tom Gunning argue,[32] colonial tourism is confronted with the challenge of creating compatible sympathies between the "educated," "civilized" publics among colonizers *and* the colonized, cutting across fundamental antagonisms between those two subject positions. Efforts to incorporate expanding notions of new publics and competing perceptions of sites of destruction account for the emotional variegations of the pre-cinematic travel album. We are shown places such as Chutter Manzil (Figure 2.4), an extravagant *nawabi* seraglio that becomes a United Service Club in Lucknow, rivaling "the clubs of Pall Mall" in England.[33] An architectural form is presented in transition, transforming from a house of women owned by nawabs into a club for the British, at a distance yet at the same

Figure 2.4 Chutter Manzil on the banks of the Gomati River. Courtesy the Getty Research Institute, Los Angeles (92-B22782).

time comparable to the classed spaces of Britain. With the acknowledgment of the resilience of Lucknow's pre-colonial pasts alongside an affirmation of British alterations to this landscape that render it bureaucratic, replete with banks, schools, and clubs reminiscent of Britain, the album struggles to fabricate a perspective that may be shared by the British and the Indian traveler ("the educated Native of India and the traveling public of all nations"), *despite* the dividing chasm of an insurgency.

An important element in the manufacture of this Anglo-Indian perspective is the active submergence of the feminine as a precondition to articulating mass appeals based on soldierly grief, salacious violence, feats of architectural antiquity, and engineering modernity. The female subject position is excluded from the mixed-racial address of colonial spectatorship in this album. But much in it that I have noted thus far—the presence of seraglios, the stunning absence of men *and* women in visuals accompanying vivid accounts of masculine activity described in the text, the acknowledgment of multiple temporalities of an event (of insurgency) or place (of Lucknow)—points to a complex mode of spectation, which allows what is repressed in explicit narration to nevertheless be present ephemerally. I will return later to the absence/presence of a feminine mode of spectation within the album's variegated address. For now, I want to consider how the photographic album produces the space of Lucknow by engaging the potentially mixed racial composition of colonial spectatorship, which *The Relief* evades in all but formal terms.

The Relief of Lucknow (1912)

Literary historian Gautam Chakravarty finds that the revolt of 1857 was by far the most popular theme of British novels, producing a greater "literary yield" than any other conflict of the nineteenth century. The popularity of this literature parallels the political and cultural ascendancy of the British middle class. Two key icons of rebellion novels validated middle-class values: that of the treacherous native spy and that of a British officer in disguise, who penetrates native masses. Chakravarty suggests that both figures offer "a fantasy of mastery that sutured actual intelligence failures during the rebellion" and the "underlying anxieties of a colonial regime . . . exiled . . . from . . . the indigenous world."[34] These figures are prominent in the Edison film as well, where they help unfold a narrative about surveillance and conspiracy.

As the film opens, we cut from the exterior of a fort with British troops and Indian sepoys to a living room with a piano, two Englishmen, and a woman. A spying native and a letter warning of a rebellion disrupt their peace ("Meerot, May 12, 1857. 'Dear Helen, The native troops here have revolted . . .'"). The film's ensuing drama is articulated through a combination of dynamic outdoor shots and interiors, rapidly transforming under the siege. In an exterior shot of a home framed on one side by lush trees, we see Indians running toward the house and away from the camera into off-screen space. Soon Englishwomen, children, and a man run toward the camera out of the house, followed by reemerging Indians who open gunfire on the fleeing group. Outdoor action is typically shot at an acute angle to the horizontal planes of the camera frame, giving it a sense of urgency, while interiors are framed frontally. In the sequence titled "The Death of Sir Henry Lawrence," for instance, Lawrence sits at a table facing the camera when a cannonball slams through a painting on the wall and kills him.

Unlike *The Lucknow Album,* "place" is no longer out *there,* as a series of sites to be visited, commemorated, and consumed, but *here,* in the intimate surroundings of sympathetic figures onscreen. The effect is to create an ideological narrative about the sanctity of British inner space, the threat of an outer space, the violent ingress of that threat, and its deflection by the liminal body of an Englishman in disguise. Narratively, the film adapts a factual episode involving volunteer Thomas Kavanagh, who assisted in an attempt to relieve the garrison. An Englishman's escape from the garrison in the guise of a native to guide back relieving troops forges associative links between the radically antagonistic spaces of inside and outside and victoriously ends the spatial drama of encirclement. This volunteer is also romancing a woman in the garrison, which additionally lends the film's historical ambition a personal dimension appreciated by reviewers. "We may say at once that this is quite one of the finest pictures the Edison Company have yet produced. They have taken a great historical theme . . . inspired it with the glow and the tumult of real life and action, and at the same time closely adhered to recorded fact. . . . Into the web of famous historical happenings, which, of course, forms the subject matter of the film, there has been woven a pleasant little love story, just sufficient to give the requisite touch of more personal human interest."[35]

Released in Britain on the fifty-fifth anniversary of the Indian Rebellion of 1857, *The Relief* traded on discourses of mimesis and authenticity to be marketed as a "historical picture."[36] In notes on the production of this film, director Dawley writes that nonagenarians who had survived the Lucknow rebellion were driven down for a screening of the film in 1912, one of whom was so impressed by its realism that he stood up and shouted at the screen, "That's him, that 'Arry' my old buddy."[37] Alongside this promised sense of communion with the past played up in the film's exhibition was the danger of a rebellion absorbed from the safety of distance. In an advertisement in *Bioscope* aimed at British exhibitors, they are exhorted to book the film with a playful pun: "If you want your Show besieged do not fail to show THE RELIEF OF LUCKNOW . . . BECAUSE it is an actual page from the actual history of the past and is historically correct as regards soldiers' uniforms, the fighting, the various wild rushes and mad repulses."[38] The U.S. film garnered critical praise for its authentic replication of place and time, in a review which noted that "the suggestion of Indian scenery is quite perfect, tropical foliage, glittering buildings and burning sunshine all complete."[39]

In fact, *The Relief* was shot on location in Bermuda, and not in Lucknow. With its fictional interweaving of inner and outer space through edits, the film suppresses the materiality of its own landscape. This omission becomes available to our analytic view after a consideration of the pre-cinematic *Lucknow Album,* which moves place from an "unconscious optic" to a foregrounded terrain. *The Lucknow Album* is an album of photographs of Lucknow; by definition, its images make mimetic claims to the city. In contrast, fiction film's mimesis is complex in that it has numerous devices to "bear away" spectatorial faith, in the Bazinian sense.[40]

As a film shot on location, *The Relief* had to creatively adapt a place to its fictional space. Following the thread of location shooting in film *literally* foregrounds the visual medium's abilities and constraints in producing and abstracting space. It also underscores the fact that, unlike literature, location shooting is a medium-specific industrial and aesthetic practice with its own history in cinema.[41] Following the production rather than the representation of place leads to a second turn, the first having dealt with the crisis posed to colonial sociospatiality by the expanding circulation and address of visual technologies.

Location films seek an apparently authentic place or territorial access to a proximate region where their fiction can unfold. The incorporation of a real place into a filmic narrative and the production of a film's imagined space from available cityscapes and landscapes bring questions of territoriality into the circumstance of every location-based film production. *The Relief* made use of Bermuda, a British colony yet a satellite island of the United States. Bermuda had played an active part in domestic U.S. politics and housed the Queen's Own Regiment, a regiment that had been involved in suppressing the rebellion in India. It was also the perfect answer to the problem of location shooting in faraway India, given its sunshine, relative proximity to Edison's studios in New Jersey, and the presence of real British troops.

From 1911 onwards, Edison began to produce films on historically British themes for British audiences. Shooting in foreign locales increased at this time, with Edison's Serle J. Dawley shooting films in Cuba and Canada, and Ashley Miller taking crews to London.[42] Bermuda became a popular British, Canadian, and U.S. tourist destination after Princess Louise, Queen Victoria's daughter, visited the islands in 1883. Wife of the governor general of Canada, Princess Louise connected the old and new empires of Britain and North America in her matrimony. Edison's paths of access were opened up by the increasing numbers of steamers filled with neobourgeoisie crossing North America to Bermuda, pursuing leisure and warm weather in imitation of the aristocracy. The film's reality claims depended on a myth enabled by the convenient availability of commensurate subject places and races that could support an ideology of territorial dominance in Britain and the United States, especially as the latter wrestled domestically with debates on imperialism in relation to the Philippine-American war ending in 1913. In the growing sphere of publics implicated in each other's political events and economic markets, the Edison film about Lucknow exhibited structures of sympathy linking Britain and the United States.

The Relief is premised on substituting one place for another to facilitate the mass consumption of a violent history and politics through an architectonic visual. Thus the substitution of Bermuda for Lucknow has implications for the cinematic visualization of destruction. Insurgencies register changes on the surface of a site, and in this sense the visualization of an insurgent site is rendered cinematic in the manner of time-lapse photographs, where the thrill lies in the transformations of buildings moving from structural integrity to fragmentation over a short span of time. The album and the film convey alterations to the site's buildings in remarkably different ways. St. George and the Thomas Moore Tavern in Bermuda play the roles of Lucknow's streets and forts in the film, with staged sets registering destruction to their surfaces and interiors. The film attempts to make its location cinematic through edits and explosions showing visible alterations to buildings in a steady progression to the climax.

The Lucknow Album, on the other hand, allows the intrinsic cinematicity of Lucknow's monuments to emerge through its interplay of visual perspective and text. In the Eisensteinian sense of the term, Lucknow's architecture was already "cinematic." If, as Eisenstein argued, sequentiality and montage are two essential conditions of cinema, and all arts tend toward the cinematic, then montage computation was already present in Lucknow's architectural ensemble in a manner deeply colonial. Rosie Llewellyn-Jones offers rich details on how Lucknow's nawabs, aspiring to British models of structure and notions of the modern, employed British architects.[43] They combined hybrid influences, incorporating the neoclassical and Graeco-Roman revival popular in England with more environmentally friendly local styles. In the city's architecture was a sedimented sense of time (and significance), and in the construction of city space a diachrony that is activated in *The Lucknow Album*. Describing Chutter Munzil as a "mixture of the Oriental geometrical, the Italian, and the French Chateaus," the album constructs Lucknow as a city of multiple, coexistent pasts. With its subtle celebration of the syncretism of city space, the album allows itself to become an ensemble of perspectives in a manner that displaces more linear historiographies of the place and the insurgency (see Figure 2.4).

The instant of the photograph is in dialogue with the duration of the buildings within the album, when emotional affect crowds into the architecture's silences and absences through the album's written text, which provides an idiosyncratic architectural biography. This was a bold stance in the post-1857 environment, when Britain reviled Lucknow's architectural hybridity as excessive, wasteful, and worthy of imperial destruction, a sign of the degenerate luxury of the nawabs. Lucknow's cultural syncretism promoted by its nawabs, such as the art-loving Wajid Ali Shah, was condemned as a sign of their powerless effeminacy in the face of the aggressively masculine incursions of the British.

Film Space, Film Time

The gendering of power relations between Britain and India after the 1857 rebellion, thematically depicted on film by Satyajit Ray's *Chess Players* (1977), provides an occasion to step back from the thickness of analysis to examine the hidden politics of representational tropes. In my essay, to counter the montage of *The Relief*, I have offered an analytic montage of my own. Eisenstein suggests that architectural ensembles reveal their montage computations as we move through the structures, but for a stationary viewer, the author needs to juxtapose "in one unique point the elements of that which is dispersed in reality, unseizable to a single gaze." Cinematic montage is thus a "means to 'link' in one point—the screen—various elements (fragments) of a phenomenon filmed in diverse dimensions, from diverse points of view and sides."[44] In my more linear essay here, two disparate examples dealing with the ruination of the same site are viewed simultaneously to convey differential perspectives of a place, with the intention of undercutting the singularity of each textual gaze, or indeed of showing how each text produced space through the management of *other* potential relations between time and place, memory and history, society and subject. The challenge of thematizing colonial modernity's splintering temporalities within its spatially leveling political forces, which brought the revenues, narratives, and images of Lucknow to audiences in London, may be conveyed by this analysis. Unfortunately, an analytic montage is more successful in pointing to the dialectical difference between visual media objects, and less so in revealing their collusions.

Photography's and cinema's coincidence with colonialism points to the paradox that the cosmopolitan visual knowledge of locations worldwide emerged alongside a deeply splintered subjective sense of time and place, when imperial regimes violently appropriated land and alienated it from its people. At stake in comprehending this de-linking of space and time, simultaneous with notations of time-space compression under colonial modernity, is an ambition to disrupt the universalizing presumptions of colonial and neocolonial socio-spatiality. As I have argued, *The Lucknow Album* disrupted the demarcating narrative of Lucknow's buildings as pre- or post-1857, by placing them in an ongoing narrative of secular tourism, which subtly commended Lucknow's past as much as its present. In fact, the production of its secular perspective rested equally on a masculinization of time and a consignment of the feminine to the past. Much as *The Relief* contains its Englishwomen within domestic interiors, *The Lucknow Album* spectrally relegates Indian women to the unseen historic recesses of Lucknow's architectural landmarks.

At the figural level, Muslim women are a shadowy presence in *The Lucknow Album,* present through their absence in seraglios once built for them. Absence, nevertheless, plays a profound role in an album that is the impress of a city remarkable for its ruins. Some structures survive the passage to the present, while others, such as private hospitals and state banks, are reconstructed from older monuments built by the nawabs. The remaindered city lacks access to temporal progression and is of interest for its association with a lost past. The feminine is relegated to *this* past, in a move that feminizes the space of history as time progresses forward through technologies of civil engineering, industrial architecture, and photography, each of which signify a triumph over the ephemerality of time and the threat of obsolescence.

Is it possible to write the history of a city as imagined on film and photography when time itself is troped and split in its visual archive, between monuments feminized as accretions of the past and perspectives masculinized as their mobile, presentist counterparts? With his reference to Paul Klee's "Angelus Novus," Walter Benjamin suggests a path for historical writing that refuses to think of the past as complete or of movement as singular. This writing is swept by a vertiginous temporality like the forward-moving angel whose eyes are prized open by recursive visions. Perhaps a critical historiography is born from the active dismantling of gendered spatial tropes premised on a linear temporality. So perhaps it is not incongruous, or just incongruous enough, that a Hindi-Urdu sound film shot on location in Lucknow in 1960 should be allowed to undercut the tropic affiliations between an early photographic album and a silent film about Lucknow.

The complex referential web spun between image, lyrics, land, and monument in the credit sequence of *Chaudhvin ka Chand* (Moon of the fourteenth day / Full moon; M. Sadiq, 1960) unravels the feminization of ruin and masculination of progress.[45] The film was a commercially successful tragicomic love story produced by India's critically acclaimed filmmaker Guru Dutt. Set in Lucknow, *Chaudhvin* depicts a range of characters from the feudal Muslim aristocracy preoccupied with the pursuit of love, poetry, music, artful conversation, and courtship. The film's prologue is shot on location in Lucknow and takes us to some of the city's landmark buildings, such as the Husainabad Bazaar Gateway and the Asafi Mosque in the Bara Imambara complex. The landmarks belong to the space of syncretic culture and architecture criticized for symbolizing the decadent and impractical lifestyle of nawabs. These were sites reviled by the British as a living monument to the degenerate lifestyle of rulers incapable of just governance, providing the rationale for usurpation of the Indian domain. Caught in the rupture of this cataclysmic event, the city itself is left with no easy passage to the present. In 1960, the Lucknow of Hindi cinema still lives with that which *The Relief* rewrote in 1912.[46]

The credit sequence of *Chaudhvin* opens with a brief tour. Soon we realize that the camera is shadowing the ghostly figure of a woman in a burqa (a full-body veil). The tour is accompanied by Shakeel Badayuni's lyrics, sung by Mohammad Rafi and quoted in the epigraph to this essay: "*This soil of Lucknow. This orchard of color or country of heady love and beautiful forms, where Awadh's setting sun seeks its destination. This place of bewitchment. This place of youth. This land of Lucknow.*"[47] The city is presented to us through an oblique range of conflicting lyrical registers. The song has the pathos of a paean to a fallen city that was once an epitome of exquisite beauty. The buildings reproduce the grandeur and hide the marks of violence. The burqa-clad woman—a restricted denizen of Lucknow's public spaces during the city's *nawabi* and British past, as well as its nationalist present—guides us. The combination of her attire, her solitude, and her touristic visitations make her difficult to read. To which temporal and spatial axis does *she* belong? Is she of Mughal India, partitioned India, or a unified India? How does she see the architecture? Why do we hear a male vocalist as the background for a female figure? She becomes more inscrutable as the film's narrative unfolds. The narrative opens with a man at a fair falling in love with a glimpse of Jameela, a woman in a burqa. Jameela's veil is the start of several erroneous attempts at identifying and wooing her, so that in the confusing events that follow, Jameela is unwittingly caught in a love triangle between two male friends who must balance their desire for her against their loyalties to each other. In contrast to Jameela's imprisonment in a mesh of male priorities in the film's narrative, the unidentified woman in the prologue is a lone traveler in public places of mourning (at the Imambaras) and pleasure (promised by the lyrics). This figure offers an unsettling sensibility that disturbs previous iterations of the city space.

Theorists of visuality persuasively point to links between cinema and travel culture. Foundationally, modernity was defined by changing relations between the body and spatial perception through technologies of motion, of which cinema and travel were equally a part. As Giuliana Bruno shows, understanding cinematics as a new form of mobility allows us to see its modes embedded in evolving architectures of an urban space conducive to habits of *flânerie*. Cinematic spectatorship opened avenues of exploration for the female *flâneuse*, traditionally restrained from the perambulatory freedom available to a man.[48]

What is gripping about Lucknow, or indeed any site of anti-colonial insurgency, is the emergence of place as visual commodity and subject of travel literature and imagery *after* acts of violence rewrite its rules of mobility. The event and its representation introduce new spatial mobilities and immobilities, defining who can travel, who can participate in its virtual and visceral pleasures or horrors, who can access the cosmopolitanism of consuming place through the visual, and who is consumed as topography.

In the two colonial texts discussed previously, the subaltern female remains topographic. *Chaudhvin*'s fleeting retrieval of the topographic feminine produces the shock of a new perspective, redefining the gendered troping of time, monumental landscape, and spectatorship. The feminine is situated neither within nor outside the lost time of a destroyed city. She is not *of* the ruins, but she is not, given the lyric's nostalgic register, entirely of the modern world. She is a tourist in her own land and of her own past. In the cloaked woman's tour through city space, the sequence animates the strange intimacies and distances with respect to place and time produced by political rupture, hinting at the temporal residues of the past in the present and at the impossibility of a return. By articulating the immediacy of the real (shot location) with a spectral distancing (through a restless perspective following the ghostly female figure), this sequence produces a dialectical image of the city's past which is embedded in its present, without reconciling the two.

Referring to "Muslim socials" in Indian cinema, a loosely defined genre of films depicting Muslim families and lives, Moinak Biswas rightly notes that they have "always been marked with nostalgia."[49] *Chaudhvin* is a Muslim social, and its narrative is nostalgic in the sense that it transports us to a timeless Islamic world by erasing all traces of colonial as well as contemporary (post-partition) India. But if history is evacuated from the narrative's undated Islamic milieu, this prologue stages another kind of nostalgia. Its lyrics accompany the journey of a veiled, solitary woman through Lucknow's past that comes alive through her perambulation across the city's architecture, which promises pleasures that have never heretofore been addressed to her. The prologue is powerful because it fills us with a sense of losing something that was never in our possession. The woman offers spectators a way to experience the uncanny or "unhomely" in a Lucknow where "recesses of the domestic space [have] become sites for history's most intricate invasions."[50]

After the suppression of the 1857 rebellion, there could be no unmediated local access to Lucknow's surroundings. Yearning for a retrieval strained against the enforced distance of multiple abstractions of place, as the past itself became a construct filtered through those abstractions. I have asked how we may thread a location back to its translation into a sensibility and spectatorial space, particularly when this location achieves instantaneous global familiarity as a site of violent insurgency. An expanding public became familiar with a place when it was reconfigured as an example of imperial vulnerability and retribution. At this time, the place irreparably diverged in its sense of significance to various publics.

The dispersal of affective and spectatorial relations to place, which makes place "auratic" through technological mediation, is also the story of the circulation of visual media practices. The challenge is to consider the politicization of territory that accompanied its shared familiarity—that made place an object of consumption or a memorialized space for some and a prison-house of time for others. By unfixing a ruined city from its role as locational backdrop, I have used a history of produced space against the idea of universal time.

Notes

This essay is for Tom Gunning. I am grateful to Anupama Kapse, Alex Lykidis, Sudhir Mahadevan, Christopher Pinney, Vanessa Schwartz, and the editors of this anthology for their valuable suggestions and comments. The ideas contained in this article were presented at several different forums, and I benefited greatly from the engagement of my audience. In particular, I thank Shelley Stamp and the Film and Digital Media Department at the University of California, Santa Cruz; Romita Ray, Steve Cohan, and the English Department at Syracuse University; and David Rodowick, Eric Rentschler, and Tom Conley at Harvard University's Department of Visual and Environmental Studies.

1. A complete print of *The Relief of Lucknow* is currently available for online viewing at: http://www.colonialfilm.org.uk/node/1836.

2. Ella Shohat and Robert Stam, *Unthinking Eurocentrism: Multiculturalism and the Media* (London: Routledge, 1994), 119.

3. Edward Soja, *Postmodern Geographies: The Reassertion of Space in Critical Social Theory* (London: Verso, 1989).

4. It was telling when, during my visit to Lucknow in November 2009, a travel guide who showed us Lucknow's architectural sites that are frozen in time to bear the scars of 1857 drew a blank when I asked him about "the mutiny," using the English phrase. His reference was to "Azadi ki pehli jung," or the first war of independence.

5. For an analysis of these competing ways of making sense of the rebellion and Karl Marx's controversial stance in the debates, see Pranav Jani, "Karl Marx, Eurocentrism, and the 1857 Revolt in British India," in *Marxism, Modernity and Postcolonial Studies,* ed. Crystal Bartolovich and Neil Lazarus (Cambridge, UK: Cambridge University Press,, 2002), 81–97.

6. Ranajit Guha's "The Prose of Counter-Insurgency," in *Selected Subaltern Studies,* ed. Ranajit Guha and Gayatri Spivak (New York: Oxford University Press, 1988), 45–86, is foundational to this critique of the archive (and for initiating a mode of historiography characteristic of subaltern studies, which reads the archive against its political grain). Gautam Chakravarty's *The Indian Mutiny and the British Imagination* (Cambridge, UK: Cambridge University Press, 2005) extends the discussion beyond imperial historiography to demonstrate the Indian rebellion's formative role in the cultural production of Britain's popular imagination, through an exhaustive study of fiction, memoirs, and autobiographies dealing with it. Anjali Arondekar questions the tendency to see popular discourse concerning the rebellion as an extension of the discursive tropes of imperial historiography. Against this, she reads the mutiny/rebellion as a fundamentally non-narratable experience, threatening the literary archive by its recalcitrance. See Anjali Arondekar, *For the Record: On Sexuality and the Colonial Archive in India* (Durham, NC: Duke University Press, 2009), particularly chap. 4.

7. Zahid Chaudhary, "Phantasmagoric Aesthetics: Colonial Violence and the Management of Perception," *Cultural Critique* 59 (Winter 2005): 63–119.

8. I deliberately echo Michel de Certeau's formulation that "space is a practiced place" (*The Practice of Everyday Life,* trans. Steven Rendall [Berkeley: University of California Press, 1984], 117). Perception is key to the consumption and narration of a place.

9. Harriet Martineau, "Suggestions towards the Future Government of India," *Calcutta Review* 30 (January–June 1858): 358.

10. Karl Marx, "State of the Indian Insurrection," *New-York Tribune,* August 18, 1857, http://www.marxist.org/archive/marx/works/1857/08/18.htm.

11. News from India arrived in Britain within a month to two months of its occurrence through a combination of the telegraph, military dispatches, and mail carried by steamers.

12. In addition to essays on travel and early cinema mentioned later in this article, consult Lynne Kirby, *Parallel Tracks: The Railroad and Silent Cinema* (Durham, NC: Duke University Press, 1997); the anthology edited by Jeffrey Ruoff, *Virtual Voyages: Cinema and Travel* (Durham, NC: Duke University Press, 2006); Peter Bloom, *French Colonial Documentary: Mythologies of Humanitarianism* (Minneapolis: University of Minnesota Press, 2008); and Wolfgang Schivelbusch, *The Railway Journey: The Industrialization of Time and Space in the 19th Century* (Berkeley: University of California Press, 1986), which is frequently referenced in scholarship on early film.

13. The argument to take circulation seriously in this context is also made by Saloni Mathur, *India by Design: Colonial History and Cultural Display* (Berkeley: University of California Press, 2009). Mathur studies how the circulation of commodities defined India in the imperial world's arenas of display, such as museums, exhibitions, department stores, and art.

14. For studies of Lucknow's city space and architecture, see Rosie Llewellyn-Jones, *A Fatal Friendship: The Nawabs, the British and the City of Lucknow,* and Veena Talwar Oldenberg, *The Making of Colonial Lucknow: 1856–1877,* both published in *The Lucknow Omnibus,* ed. Abdul Halim Sharar, Rosie Llewellyn-Jones, and Veena Talwar Oldenberg (New Delhi: Oxford University Press, 2001).

15. Chakravarty finds that "mutiny narratives" were the most popular theme in British literature in the early twentieth century (*The Indian Mutiny*, 8). Photographic albums on India, in addition to the mutiny albums cited in this essay, are too numerous to be listed. For a recent exhaustive study, consult Christopher Pinney, *The Coming of Photography in India* (London: British Library, 2008). Based on surviving fragments and reports of films, it appears that mutiny films of the early 1900s were documentary travelogues as well as fiction films. See, for instance, *Historic Mutiny Sites* (c. 1916) at the British Film Institute, a short 35mm silent produced in Great Britain (production company unknown); a note to Selig London recommending a film titled *A Visit to Lucknow* (c. 1913), in Document #14, Folder 501 (Correspondence: India), William Selig Collection, AMPAS, Fairbanks Center for Motion Picture Study, Margaret Herrick Library (henceforth MHL); and a fiction film called *A Sepoy's Wife* (Vitagraph Fiction Films, 1910) at the British Film Institute.

16. Ben Lifson, "Beato in Lucknow," *Artforum* (May 1988): 99–103. "The strategic demolition of the town had left him few high places to look out from, and only wasteland to look onto from the palaces that were spared" (101). For the function of this kind of devastated landscape in cinema in another national context, see Noa Steimatsky, *Italian Locations: Reinhabiting the Past in Postwar Cinema* (Minneapolis: University of Minnesota Press, 2008).

17. The term "rival geographies" here and in my title is borrowed from Edward Said, *Culture and Imperialism* (New York: Vintage, 1993), xx.

18. Patrizia Di Bello, *Women's Albums and Photography in Victorian England: Ladies, Mothers and Flirts* (Aldershot, UK: Ashgate, 2007).

19. Englishwomen in India during the 1857 rebellion did leave extensive written accounts of their experiences. See Claudia Klaver, "Domesticity under Siege: British Women and Imperial Crisis at the Siege of Lucknow, 1857," *Women's Writing: The Elizabethan to Victorian Period* 8.1 (2001): 21–58. There are a few examples of female mutiny albums, though less numerous than their male counterparts (see Lifson, "Beato in Lucknow").

20. Reverend Thomas Moore, *Cawnpore and Lucknow during the Mutiny of 1857: Diary, Sketches, Photographs, Maps, and Plans by Reverend T. Moore, 1958*, Add. 37151–37153, Manuscript Department, British Library, London.

21. Ibid., 26–28.

22. Looking at albums that similarly intermingle Beato's photographs with later images of "British officers, military camps, [and] the rebuilt city" taken by an assortment of photographers, Ben Lifson ("Beato in Lucknow," 100) notes two presences: that of Beato and that of unknown album makers, each competing to create a different narrative about violence. Reframed in this context, place emerges as the site of mass destruction through complex modes of visuality, exceeding colonial/governmental perceptual regimes.

23. I am paraphrasing Bill Nichols's well-known description of the institutional discourses of medicine, science, and educational policies as "discourses of sobriety," in which documentary films participate. History, when treated as a documentation of the real, becomes central to the authorization of such discourses. Bill Nichols, *Introduction to Documentary* (Bloomington: Indiana University Press, 2001), 39.

24. *The Lucknow Album* (Baptist Mission Press, 1874). For a recently uploaded version of the full album, see http://archive.org/stream/gri_00003312500 8608313#page/n173/mode/2up.

25. Ibid., 2 (my emphasis).

26. For a detailed argument about links between consumer culture, memory, and mourning in the contemporary United States, see Marita Sturken, *Tourists of History: Memory, Kitsch, and Consumerism from Oklahoma City to Ground Zero* (Durham, NC: Duke University Press), 2007.

27. *Lucknow Album*, 45.

28. Ibid., 52–54, 47–48.

29. Sophie Gordon, "A City of Mourning: The Representation of Lucknow, India in Nineteenth-Century Photography," *History of Photography* 30.1 (Spring 2006): 80–91.

30. *Lucknow Album,* 6. Through its embrace of a technological modernity that parallels its evocation of multiple architectural pasts, the album launches equally subtle critiques of the imperial administration. Appearing immediately after the image and text about the Iron Bridge, sent out in sections from England in 1816 but left incomplete, is that of the Stone Bridge, built in 1780 by Nawab Asaf-Ud-Daula, which is described as durable through time and catastrophe (48).

31. Ibid., 2.

32. Charles Musser, "The Travel Genre in 1903–1904: Moving towards Fictional Narrative," in *Early Cinema: Space, Frame and Narrative,* ed. Thomas Elsaesser (London: British Film Institute, 1990), 123–132; Tom Gunning, "The Whole World within Reach: Travel Images without Borders," in Ruoff, *Virtual Voyages,* 25–41.

33. *Lucknow Album,* 31.

34. Chakravarty, *The Indian Mutiny,* 7.

35. *Bioscope* 16.307 (August 29, 1912), 664.

36. Ibid., 664.

37. Notebook #2 (*The Relief of Lucknow*), 204, Dawley Collection, AMPAS, Fairbanks Center for Motion Picture Study, MHL.

38. *Bioscope* 16.307 (August 29, 1912), 652–653.

39. Ibid., 663.

40. "A very faithful drawing . . . will never have the irrational power of the photograph to bear away our faith." Andre Bazin, *What Is Cinema?,* vol. 1, trans. Hugh Gray (Berkeley: University of California Press, 1967).

41. This is a genealogy that Mark B. Sandberg also traces through the location-shooting policies of the Nordisk Film Company in the 1910s. See chapter 1 in this volume. See also John David Rhodes and Elena Gorfinkel, eds. *Taking Place: Location and the Moving Image* (Minneapolis: University of Minnesota Press, 2011).

42. Charles Musser, *Thomas A. Edison and His Kinetographic Motion Pictures* (New Brunswick, NJ: Rutgers University Press, 1995), 48–50. Another example of location shooting aimed at British audiences is J. Searle Dawley's *Charge of the Light Brigade* (1912), which uses Alfred Lord Tennyson's poem to depict the Battle of Balaclava, in which Lord Lucan misunderstood military directions and sent Lord Cardigan's brigade directly into Russian fire. Shot in Cheyenne, Wyoming, with the cooperation of eight hundred troopers of the U.S. Cavalry, the short film imparts a positive message to a distressing episode, creating a palatable narrative for cinema's growing middle-class audiences (location details from BFI's NFA catalogue, http://ftvdb.bfi.org.uk/sift/title/25522?view=synopsis). Where in reality the two British aristocrats were feuding brothers-in-law caught in a confusing and contested military maneuver, in fiction it becomes a tale of loyalty within the military chain of command. As the intertitles remind us, echoing Tennyson, "Theirs not to make reply / Theirs not to reason why / Theirs but to do and die." The appeal of British military hierarchy, courage, and masculine code of honor are repeated in *The Relief,* which, as suggested by its title, emphasizes the relief rather than the rout of the British garrison. In reality, there was more than one failed attempt at the "relief" of Lucknow.

43. Llewellyn-Jones, *A Fatal Friendship.*

44. Yve-Alain Bois, "Introduction. Sergei Eisenstein: Montage and Architecture," trans. Michael Glenny, *Assemblage,* no. 10 (December 1989), 111.

45. This film was produced by Guru Dutt, who is also believed to have directed the film without credit.

46. As a thematic, 1857 continues to resonate in Hindi/Urdu films from India. Most recently, *Mangal Pandey* (Ketan Mehta, 2005) is about a central figure of the revolt. Others such as *Umrao Jaan* (Muzaffar Ali, 1981) refer to the revolt as a shaping influence in the life of the protagonist (the city of Lucknow still conserves monuments that served as shooting locations for the film). Yet I find that the brief prologue to *Chaudhvin ka Chand,* which is not about 1857 at all, offers the most compelling expression of the suppressed links between history, location, and the feminine through its filmic production and spatial design. Shyam Benegal's *Junoon* (1978), which depicts a cross-racial love triangle during the revolt, does this overtly as a theme, but does not always use actual location as its provocation.

47. The translation is mine, but I am indebted to Iftekhar Dadi and Shohini Ghosh for their assistance. The original lyrics are Shakeel Badayuni's composition for *Chaudhvin ka Chand* (Urdu/Hindi, 1960).

48. Giuliana Bruno, *Atlas of Emotion: Journeys in Art, Architecture and Film* (London: Verso, 2007); Anne Friedberg, "The Mobilized and Virtual Gaze of Modernity: Flâneur/Flâneuse," in *Window Shopping: Cinema and the Postmodern* (Berkeley: University of California Press, 1993), 15–32.

49. Moinak Biswas, "Mourning and Blood Ties: Macbeth in Mumbai," *Journal of the Moving Image,* no. 5 (December 2006): 78–85.

50. Homi Bhabha, *The Location of Culture* (London: Routledge, 2004), 33.

Part II
Prints in Motion

Introduction

Jennifer M. Bean

The experience of watching a good film is often described as *moving.* This is because narrative texts, at their best, take us elsewhere, hastening a passage or transition from one psychic or physiological space to another, from one thought, term, or concept to another. While scholarship of the past decade has been profoundly successful in demonstrating how imported films generate competing affective and psychological responses from active viewers and cultural agencies in different parts of the globe (a set of debates elaborated in part 3), the formal and material instability of the textual object itself has hardly been voiced as a question. This section models an alternative to standard historiographies of silent era cinema by showing what people in different places did with filmic prints as those objects moved across space and time and were themselves put *in motion,* transforming from one material or textual state of existence to another.

Each of the three contributors to this section assumes the task of tracking specific films as they are imported and reshaped—recycled, re-edited, retitled—at different scales and in different markets, respectively in the Middle East, the Soviet Union, and Latin America between the late 1910s and late 1920s. Since the primary focus of each chapter is how films produced in the United States (and a few from Western Europe) become a de-standardized product, a different text or "thing," through contact with intermediary agents or agencies, they collectively open a zone for assessing American cinema's global sprawl in these years without prematurely reinforcing Western industrialism's cultural imperialism. They urge us to grasp importation as something other than the "bringing in" and regulated circulation of a pre-formed, stable, homogeneous object. While the analyses differ as a matter of course, the chapters share a series of linked questions. The most obvious, perhaps, concerns the mechanisms of transfer: which local exhibitor, "foreign" office, national bureau, entrepreneurial company, regional distributor, or "cranky" projectionist transformed the print? Through what routes, alternately contentious or clandestine, did the film travel as it moved from the geographical locus of production to site of exhibition? Who promoted or suppressed it? Who "owned" or profited from it as its material and textual composition shifted over time? What might these material transfigurations tell us about transnational realignments of meaning and power? Beyond that, how are we to delineate temporal and spatial frameworks for film history once the material status of "the text" is understood to be in flux, scattered and realigned with different materials and meanings as it is reconstructed (not mechanically *reproduced*) in different regions, territories, and markets?

By way of contextualizing these questions, a brief detour through 1918 Tokyo may prove useful. This was the time and place that Japanese author Tanizaki Jun'ichirō published his "Jinmenso" (1918), a fantastical short story concerning an exceptionally powerful film known in English as *The Tumor with a Human Face* but which is circulating in the suburbs outside of Tokyo under the title of *Vengeance* as the story begins.[1] Strangely enough, the opening credits list only the name of an internationally acclaimed actress, Utagawa Yuri, who had recently returned to Japan after working "four or five years" for the "Globe Company in Los Angeles." Stranger still, after several "ardent fans" describe the film to her (a plot Tanizaki lingers over in exquisite detail), she cannot remember appearing in any such production. She cannot recall performing in the kinds of costumes described, nor in specific scenes. While she wishes to see the film herself, "it was playing far out in the suburbs, and because it moved from day to day, from Aoyama to Shinagawa and so forth, and because she was working incessantly, the opportunity always passed her by."[2] The situation rouses her curiosity: "*When* had it been imported into Japan? Also, *where* had it been released, and under the direction of what company? *What* circuitous route had it traveled before it appeared in the Tokyo suburbs?" (my emphasis).[3] Although these questions motivate the actress-turned-detective to interrogate others who had worked for the same company—initially clerks and some of the crew—the plot heeds American author Gertrude Stein's dictum that "in written crime stories knowing the answer spoils it." Better put, "Jinmenso" heeds Stein's caveat that the answer is a "let down of interest . . . unless another mystery crops up during the crime and that mystery remains.[4]

Of particular interest in this mysterious tale is the way that Tanizaki's story incorporates innumerable formal details of the film in question, including elaborate scene-by-scene synopses of the five-reel film and lavish descriptions of individual shots and shot sequences. But these details never eventuate in explanatory power, never disclose the time and place of the film's origins. When Yuri finally tracks down a "high-ranking officer" from the film's Tokyo distributor, "a certain H" who managed the company's foreign business, he cautiously outlines a history of the film's circulation: "It wasn't bought directly from Globe," H recounts; "a certain Frenchman in Yokohama came and sold it. The Frenchman said that he had acquired it along with many other films in Shanghai and had long used it for pleasure at home. Apparently, before he bought it, it was used throughout the colonies in China and the South Seas, where it probably sustained much harm and damage."[5] Flaunting Tanizaki's fascination with what Thomas LaMarre calls "the cinematic erasure of geographical origins," this passage hints that the successive dislocations of the filmic object—circulating initially among Japan's colonial territories, passed on to Shanghai theaters, purchased for private use by a Frenchman, then sold to the Nitto Company, who lease it to another company for screening in the suburbs—shatter any direct link with the alleged locus of production, the Globe Company in Los Angeles.[6] At the same time, the print itself has shattered, having "sustained much harm and damage," moving further and further away from any semblance to an original as it skitters, leaps, and crawls across multiple borders.[7] "It seemed most likely," the characters ultimately agree, "that someone had spliced together a number of other films for this Globe imitation, deftly altering footage and using double-exposure in order to fabricate a new picture."[8]

This is "most likely" the case. But any interpretive gesture that pinpoints a specific site of origin or singular raison d'être for this filmic object misses the compelling ambivalence of Tanizaki's story, which calls into question any reading practice that would pronounce certitudes and identify origins. It calls us to imagine the historical experience of global viewers in a period when the material and textual structure of any given film moved as it traveled across space and time, often becoming localized to the point of no longer resembling the text it once was. "Needless to say," writes LaMarre when summarizing Tanizaki's conception of the new geopolitical realities that cinema's inherent instability engenders, "linear movement from West to the Rest, or from center to periphery, is no longer the exclusive or primary form of movement."[9] Contributors here undoubtedly agree, but if saying as much seems "needless," then why would Dudley Andrew, one of the most gifted of our contemporary critics, misread this story as illustrating Tanizaki's "paranoia about Hollywood"? "In its opening passages," Andrew inveighs, referring in particular to the passage quoted above, "*Jinmenso* imagines an immediate international comradeship of enthusiasts, adventurous men . . . all on the lookout for risqué and even dangerous amusements issuing from Los Angeles, and purveyed by a company with a likely name, 'Globe Films.'"[10] Insofar as the story adamantly refuses to locate "Los Angeles" as the source or origin of the film in question, Andrew's interpretation proves puzzling at first glance. At second glance, however, his assessment reveals the persistence and power of the oft-stated truism regarding Hollywood's hegemony over the world's film markets at the time, and a critical sensibility that repeatedly reifies (even when laboring to displace or challenge) the American film industry as the "center" of global film production.

More specifically, there are two interlocking "centers" at stake in traditional historiographies—bounded at once by the geographical locus of production and by the boundedness of the text per se. In Nataša Ďurovičová's brief rehearsal of this historical development, the earliest cinema's fascination with the act of looking, and hence viewers' awareness of their spatial emplotment in a specific locale where the screening took place, was offset—even "dialectically countered"—by the rise of the fiction film and the construction of a filmic space that absorbed the viewer in a self-contained, hermetically sealed fictional world. The boundedness of this filmic space was then doubly bound, "respatialized," Ďurovičová writes, and "put in the service of the paradigm of the nation. This nationalizing turn has been seen as a rhetorical strategy in the battle for control of markets—a battle which acquired a more explicitly political goal in the course of World War I."[11]

The oft-cited truism that attributes preeminent political and economic power to the U.S. film industry and its textual production in the years immediately following World War I encounters severe discrepancies when we recognize that the literal transfiguration of cinematic objects arguably characterizes the circulation of commercial films in the 1910s and 1920s, to such a degree that the marketplace was isomorphic with the "mutilation" of prints, as Abram Myers put it in 1927. As presiding commissioner of the U.S. Motion Picture Trade Practice Conference, Myers had reason for concern. That same year the MPPDA (Motion Picture Producers and Distributors of America), the U.S. industry's central trade association, estimated that 80 percent of its total business would be mechanically modified at regional as well as municipal levels in domestic distribution, while virtually *every* exported film (a hefty 30 percent of the industry's total business) would be subject to alteration. As Ruth Vasey explains in a significant study, *The World According to Hollywood,* the practice of altering prints at the site of exhibition was so common in the United States that it became a subject of debate between producer-distributors and exhibitors at the 1927 *Trade Practice Conference for the Motion Picture Industry.* A resolution was passed that "the changing by exhibitors of motion pictures or the cutting by exhibitors of motion pictures with no other purpose than to shorten their length, is an unfair trade practice." Whether or not the distributors found this resolution satisfactory is questionable. As Vasey neatly quips: "It allowed the exhibitors to do as they wished with the movies on any pretext *except* shortening the length."[12]

Moral and political pretexts for modifying prints proved especially ubiquitous in the context of the U.S. industry's export business. The brash snip of the censor's shears could rearrange or cut entire scenes. They could transform or delete intertitles, characters, and close-ups. They could even reduce "eight and nine reel pictures" to "five reels," a sizeable cut by anyone's tally, and one that so stunned Rowland V. Lee, a director for the Fox Company, that he appealed to the industrial giants and trade organizations gathered at the Academy of Motion Picture Arts and Sciences conference in July 1927 following his return from an extended trip to "eighteen different countries" in Europe:

> Now to my knowledge, what happens to a picture after it leaves the director never comes back to the director. There is no way in which he can find out what happens to his picture. . . . It seems to me that every picture should have a history, a production history, and that production history should be a part and parcel of the knowledge that goes to the director and a part of the director's duties should be to find out why his picture didn't do well in the South, why his picture didn't do well in England, why his picture could not be shown in Germany. We have not the slightest idea what happens to our pictures.[13]

It does not take much to see that Lee, like the actress in "Jinmenso," is haunted by uncertainty ("we have not the slightest idea what happens"; "there is no way in which he can find out what happens"). And like his fictional counterpart, Lee recognizes that knowing more means tracking a print's geopolitical routes of travel. What strikes me as particularly apposite, however, is Lee's use of the phrase "production history," a term generally associated with the linear processes of pre-production (planning), production (shooting), or post-production (editing). "Production" in this context takes place elsewhere, potentially anywhere, transforming the international marketplace into a force field of ongoing activity that, in the multiple etymological senses of the term, generates or *produces:* it begets and begins things; it gives them being, form, or shape; it enables their existence.

Or, as Yuri Tsivian puts the matter in his chapter on the Soviet re-editing bureau that opens this section, it gives them "life." Significantly, the re-editing bureau, established in Moscow in 1924 (followed shortly by its counterpart in Leningrad), was not a censorship board. Rather, the censors reviewed imported films (from all countries, especially Germany, as well as the United States) after they had passed through the hands of the re-editors, an artistically inclined group that initially included the likes of Sergei Eisenstein, Esfir Shub, Veniamin Boitler, and the Vasiliev brothers (Sergei and Georgi), among others. As this list suggests, the generative act of re-editing imported films also generated, Tsivian argues, "much of what would later be known as Soviet montage theory and practice."

This point is worth lingering over momentarily. Scholars have regularly traced montage debates in the Soviet golden age of the 1920s through an array of modern experimentations, some of them theatrical, others quasi-scientific, but all of them in one way or another resulting in editing as the de facto generative principle of filmic form and art. Eisenstein in particular believed that neither the image nor the individual shot has any inherent semiotic power. The shot, he wrote, in his oft-cited and anthologized 1929 essay "The Dramaturgy of Film Form," is a "montage cell"; it attains aesthetic force only when placed in relation to other shots that together create a meaning larger than—and different from—the individual elements.[14] To demonstrate the efficacy of his theory in this essay, Eisenstein draws from very specific sequences in his own films, including *Battleship Potemkin,* thus generating a habit of reading in which the integrity of the individual director's filmic form and the theory of form are, if not mistaken for one another, then understood as mirroring one another. But underlying this mirroring effect is another, cannily revealed in a lesser-known essay, "Through Theater to Cinema," that Eisenstein wrote in 1934. Here he recalls how "the wise and wicked art of reediting the work of others" illustrated in no uncertain terms that the process of joining one piece of film with another, even when that piece belonged to a previously completed film, "suddenly acquires and conveys a sharper and quite different meaning than *that planned for it at the time of filming*" (10; my emphasis).

The "quite different meaning" that D. W. Griffith's *Orphans of the Storm* (1921) obtains in the Soviet 1920s might have rendered Rowland Lee speechless at the very least. In Tsivian's culturally sensitive account, the transformation makes perfect sense. Set during the French Revolution of the late eighteenth century and recounting the overthrow of an aristocratic government by the proletariat, *Orphans* replays a historical event of undeniable interest to Soviet filmgoers in the 1920s. Indeed, Lenin commissioned a statue of French revolutionary leader Maximilien Robespierre to be hastily built and erected in Moscow in 1918 (one of several dozen short-lived statues that Tsivian discusses).[15] But Griffith's version of *Orphans* associates Robespierre with the iconic guillotine as a tool of uncontrolled and intolerable terror, and beyond that with a revolutionary "fanaticism" that the opening titles of his film directly link to the Bolsheviks. Soviet re-editors (most likely the Vasiliev brothers) in turn considered this representation intolerable, so they cut Robespierre out of the film altogether—along with the opening titles, of course. Curiously enough, the deletion of a central character is, in Tsivian's opinion, only a "minor surgery." Other, more complex "operations" took place at the editing bureau, including a wholesale transformation of Henriette's aristocratic lover, Chevalier de Vaudrey. This feat was achieved in part by relocating footage from the beginning of the film (designed as an introduction to Louise's character) and splicing it into a later courtroom scene, where it functions as a first-person flashback explaining the chevalier's (rather than Louise's) humble birth. Far from mutilating, bastardizing, or damaging this filmic text, the re-editors performed what Tsivian calls an "organ transplant operation," while noting that the term "surgery" was often used in re-editing related discussions at the bureau.

Did Griffith care? Did he adopt the demeanor of Rowland Lee and express unease at his film's transplantation into Russian theaters? The absence of specific records leaves the answer to this question potentially uncertain. But extrapolating from Vasey's study *The World According to Hollywood,* which persuasively demonstrates that U.S. production policies and business strategies in the period were determined in every instance by a concern for profit, it is possible to speculate with some degree of accuracy that neither Griffith nor American distributors and producers more generally cared much about the surgical niceties performed on U.S. films in Moscow and Leningrad. As Vasey glosses, the Soviet "market was never a lucrative one for the American industry. According to the *Film Daily Year Book,* the total value of the U.S. films sold to Russia in 1925 was only $10,500, although the fact that most American films were sold to the USSR via German agents renders such figures unreliable."[16] Moreover, the "Soviets did not recognize international copyright conventions, and although Hollywood distributors took the precaution of sending them positive prints rather than negatives, unauthorized duplication was always a problem."[17]

It is not at all surprising that this "problem" inscribes within itself a broader history of cinema's transnational circulation that plunges headlong off the edge of any map that places the "American" film industry as its organizing center. The duplication of U.S. and other "foreign" prints by the Soviets, for instance, which they sold to territories in the Caspian Sea region (including markets in the Middle East that proved especially frustrating to the U.S. industry), generated funds that they utilized to boom their own domestic industry. In turn, as Kaveh Askari recalls, the film culture developing in countries such as Iran during the 1910s and 1920s was strongly tied to the flow of films (and talent and entrepreneurs) from Russia. By the late 1920s, statistical tallies of film titles screened in Tehran might suggest that the U.S. industry had managed, at long last, to successfully market its products to exhibitors in Iran and edge out Soviet control over those territories. But Askari's research reveals a very different rationale, the perhaps ironic result of spiraling cultural-political tensions between Iran and the USSR near the end of the Qajar dynasty (when Reza Khan came to power, becoming Reza Shah in 1925), which encouraged the shah's administration to place severe restrictions on imported Soviet products. As political routes tightened, however, Moscow agents continued to flood the Caspian Sea region with films—not Soviet *produced* films, but rather those of U.S. and French origin which the shah's government admitted as imports.

Once imported, local exhibitors' capacity to reconfigure filmic meanings apparently equaled that of the Soviets, although Tehran did not host a re-editing bureau akin to those in Moscow and Leningrad. But Askari's research in Persian-language dailies reveals that exhibitors in Tehran dusted off prints of "The Fall of Babylon" section of D. W. Griffith's *Intolerance* (1916), which they screened under the title *Cyrus the Great* for annual celebrations such as the Persian New Year. As Askari stresses, one could hardly imagine a meaning that diverges so sharply from Griffith's presumed intention to represent the Persian army as the bellicose intolerants of an era and to provide a lesson about its "fall." By contrast, Persian exhibitors "reconstructed the story as a historical memory of 'conquest,'" emphasizing "the growth of civilization rather than the lessons of catastrophe, so resolutely that Reza Shah could be connected to the film's representation of Cyrus." While a copy of the Iranian version of *Cyrus the Great* is no longer extant, dates alone clarify that this "new" meaning stems from old, worn, tarnished, or scratched prints, part of an aggregate of "junk" prints (including many U.S. and French produced adventure serials) revivified in Askari's terms as "classics" in late-1920s Tehran. Significantly, Askari's conjunction of the terms "junk" and "classic" innovates a historical model that enthusiastically upends scholarly accounts of what mattered to major film production centers such as Los Angeles. It is not simply that Iranian exhibitors recycled the waste, trash, and refuse of Western industries that took pride in the endless production of the new and developed a lucrative local market predicated on relatively cheap prints. It is more precisely that local exhibitors trumpeted the aged status of these material objects, drawing attention to blurred images or missing reels, a creative phenomenon that recalls one etymological sense of the word "classic"—that which has endured over time—where meaning in fact stems from visible signs of aging and previous use.

The recycling and creative repurposing of filmic "junk" constitutes an amazing chapter in transnational histories of silent era cinema. The value of old or apparently obsolete prints for audiences in many sectors of the globe soars geometrically when critical attention shifts away from "modernizing" urban centers and the building of permanent theaters in New York, London, Berlin, Cairo, Mexico City, or Bombay, to rural or small-town markets and practices in these same regions and nations. In North Africa, for instance, settler regions such as Cairo supported high-end picture palaces and a bustling film culture, while theaters in Beirut, Damascus, and Tripoli apparently showed films that had traveled extensively, "amortized," as Askari puts it, and forgotten by producers by the time of their projection. A similar set of distinctions obtains for colonial India. In a remarkable recent essay that shares a sort of lateral kinship with the concerns of this section, Sudhir Mahadevan reveals that U.S. prints routed to India through the UK in the 1910s and 1920s were often illegally duplicated by London exhibitors who had a "legitimate arrangement to exhibit a motion picture by contract with the original suppliers or their Agents." But, as one Indian entrepreneur explained in 1927, "while this film is in his possession he causes to be made a photographic duplicate. . . .The copies or reprints from the wrongfully made film are placed on the market and sold. Such unauthorized copies are called pirated films."[18] The cheaper price of these pirated films, combined with the affordability of "obsolete" prints (as well as secondhand projectors and other technologies), enabled the robust growth of over thirty-six "touring cinemas" that catered to small-town and rural markets in eastern India, predominantly Bengal, by the late 1920s. What Mahadevan describes as the "ceaseless revivification" of materials "deemed unfit for consumption by an anxious colonial state" neither diminishes nor eclipses the historical importance of a burgeoning domestic industry in other areas of the country, particularly Bombay, at the same time.[19] But his assessment of these traveling cinemas and their practices in Bengal, much like those that Askari traces in Tehran, disorient clearly delineated spatial and temporal frameworks for film history, the likes of which Euro-American historiographies invariably measure according to a given film's "original" date of release, its individual author/director, and its national or geographical locus of production.

It should be clear that measuring film history and geography by a few exemplary films authored by exemplary directors, by center-periphery protocols emanating from a few production capitals, or by distribution and exhibition patterns established as industrial norms demands radical revision. So does our conception of what counts as significant formal elements of silent era cinema, as Laura Serna argues in the chapter that closes this section. Whereas editing techniques form a central point of inquiry for contemporary discussions of silent era cinema's meaning-making economies (a status thickly interrelated with the canonical prominence of both Eisenstein and Griffith), Serna draws our attention to intertitles (or titles, as they were often called at the time) as a "crucial element, both material and figurative, in the transnational circulation of silent cinema." Significantly, titles also proved to be an especially labile textual element, acutely visible in the flurry of retitled films moving back and forth across the U.S./Mexico border, the territory that Serna takes as her case study. Given the tense diplomatic disputes generated by imported American films in the early 1920s—disputes that led to the Mexican government's brief embargo on U.S. film imports altogether—it makes sense that American studios responded by supplying translated Spanish-language titles that often directly opposed, and presumably neutralized or tamed, the meanings implied by the image on the screen. But Serna's careful scrutiny of both English and Spanish-language trade journals reveals that prints bearing the linguistic niceties (and resulting aesthetic ironies) generated by in-house translation offices competed with those products offered by a constellation of intermediary agencies dedicated to the translation of titles, ranging from independent distribution companies that specialized in international trade to entrepreneurial Latin Americans. The panoply of versions available for any given filmic text did not circulate randomly. Local exhibitors selected differently titled prints with an eye toward the preference of their audience, often a class-based distinction between those who demanded "proper Spanish" and those who elected the more vernacular and local idioms in which several border-based translation companies specialized.

Taken together, the histories that emerge in this section collectively reveal how silent era films were re-edited, retitled, and recycled into some new form or shape in local and regional cultures, thus conferring on mass-produced objects a "misuse value" (to borrow Theodor Adorno's phrase from a different context), meaning a value that circulates outside of, or in direct defiance of, capitalist and colonialist dictates of use and exchange.[20] While the editors hope that this section fosters further research on the literal modification and transnational *production* of prints as they move across space and time in the silent era, a subordinate purpose travels back to the present: one cannot help but perceive a corollary of such "misuse value" in our contemporary era, a time when the singularity of any "original" or self-contained text is subject to tremendous fraying, digital remixing, media piracy, and at least potential dissolution via electronic representational technologies and their global users.

Notes

1. I refer throughout to the translated version of "Jinmenso" found in Thomas LaMarre, *Shadows on the Screen: Tanizaki Jun'ichirō on Cinema and "Oriental" Aesthetics,* Michigan Monograph Series in Japanese Studies 53 (Ann Arbor: Center for Japanese Studies, University of Michigan, 2005), 86–101.
2. Ibid., 94.
3. Ibid.
4. Gertrude Stein, *Narration: Four Lectures,* intro. Thornton Wilder (Chicago: University of Chicago Press, 1993), 59.
5. Lamarre, "Jinmenso," 96.
6. The quoted phrase comes from p. 114 of Lamarre's "Cinematic Shock and the Collapse of Geopolitical Distance," an analysis which follows his translation of "Jinmenso" in *Shadows on the Screen,* 103–116.
7. Lamarre, "Jinmenso," 98. In fact, by the end of the story the question of who made the film and where remains uncertain. The Globe Studios in Los Angeles cannot locate any record of such a production, the actress who appears in it cannot recall ever making such a film, and when she secures a strip of celluloid from the fifth reel of the film and peers at the tiny frames, the image of the man who plays the eponymous "human tumor" is entirely unknown to her.
8. It also seems likely that the "ghastly" effects of the "spliced-together" film (which generates a feeling of blood-chilling fear in Tokyo executives but not in rural viewers) suggest a sort of phenomenology of colonial insurgency. The Japanese title of the film in question is, after all, *Vengeance,* and the office manager notes in his itinerary of the print that it "sustained much harm and damage" specifically when it circulated "throughout the colonies in China and the South Seas."
9. LaMarre, "Cinematic Shock and the Collapse of Geopolitical Distance," 115.
10. Dudley Andrew, "Time Zones and Jet Lag: The Flows and Phases of World Cinema," in *World Cinemas, Transnational Perspectives,* ed. Nataša Ďurovičová and Kathleen Newman (New York: Routledge, 2010), 64.
11. Nataša Ďurovičová, "Vector, Flow, Zone: Towards a History of Cinematic *Translatio,*" in Ďurovičová and Newman, *World Cinema, Transnational Perspectives,* 91.
12. Ruth Vasey, *The World According to Hollywood, 1918–1939* (Madison: University of Wisconsin Press, 1997), 66.
13. Quoted in ibid., 73. In the most general and obvious way, Lee's concern has to do with the fact that the director's control over "his [de facto] picture" ends the moment the film enters the international marketplace. So, too, ends the controlling hand of the industry. As Vasey notes, this problem was so endemic that the Social Relations Committee (SRC), a subsidiary

of the MPPDA, assumed the task of organizing dossiers on "each foreign country with which we usually have trouble, on each group representing a section of public opinion, and on each subject of picture material usually objected to" with the aim of forestalling external alterations by adjusting internal production and distribution practices in advance (73). The failure of the SRC to coherently organize the overwhelming mass of information and enable studios to act accordingly is of particular interest to the concerns of this section, as it speaks to the absolute irreducibility of the world to any totalizing perspective, "universal" norm, or singular generic product.

14. Current film theory anthologies that include this particular essay often introduce Eisenstein's theories by describing an eclectic list of influences, ranging from Hegelian dialectics and Pavlovian psychology through Japanese kabuki theater and Chinese ideograms to American films, especially serial adventure films with their explosive action stunts and the suspense editing techniques associated with D. W. Griffith.

15. In doing so, Lenin surely had in mind the version of Robespierre's vision for France summarized by contemporary historian Ruth Scurr. As she puts it, Robespierre wanted a "democracy for the people, who are intrinsically good and pure of heart; a democracy in which poverty is honorable, power innocuous, and the vulnerable safe from oppression; a democracy that worships nature—not nature as it really is, cruel and disgusting, but nature sanitized, majestic, and, above all, good." Ruth Scurr, *Fatal Purity: Robespierre and the French Revolution* (New York: Henry Holt, 2006), 358.

16. Vasey, *The World According to Hollywood*, 53.

17. Ibid.

18. Sudhir Mahadevan, "Traveling Showmen, Makeshift Cinemas: The *Bioscopewallah* and Early Cinema History in India," *Bioscope: South Asian Screen Studies* 1.1 (January 2010): 38.

19. Ibid., 36.

20. Theodor Adorno, *Minima Moralia: Reflections from Damaged Life*, trans. E. F. N. Jephcott (New York: Verso, 1978), 227–228. For Adorno, children's propensity to play and interact with objects for purposes other than those of the given product's prescribed function or capitalist "use value" emblematizes what he calls a "misuse value." My extrapolation of this term from Adorno is inspired by literary historian Bill Brown, who explores and tracks the values of "misuse" in his "How to Do Things with Things (A Toy Story)," *Critical Inquiry* 24 (Summer 1998): 935–964.

3 Robespierre Has Been Lost

D. W. Griffith's Movies and the Soviet Twenties

Yuri Tsivian

The monument to Robespierre erected a few days ago in the Aleksandrovsky park has been destroyed by "unidentified criminals."

Anatolii Mariengof, *The Cynics* (1928)

STREET VENDOR: Fur-trimmed brassieres, fur-trimmed brassieres!

(Enter Prisypkin, Rozalia Pavlovna and Bayan).

VENDOR: Fur-trimmed . . .

PRISYPKIN (IN EXULTATION): What an aristocratic pair of bonnets!

ROZALIA PAVLOVNA: What do you mean bonnets, these are . . .

PRISYPKIN: Do you think I have no eyes? What if we have twins? This one will be for Dorothy, and this one for Lillian . . . Decided: I'll give my twins these aristocratic-cinematic names . . . they'll walk side by side. See? My home must be a horn of plenty. Buy them, Rozalia Pavlovna!

Vladimir Mayakovsky, *The Bedbug* (1929)

WHAT D. W. Griffith's films did for Soviet editing is widely known. We learn this from Sergei Eisenstein, Leonid Trauberg, and Dziga Vertov, each of whom used kind words to repay their debt to *Intolerance* (1916)—Vertov in two sentences,[1] Trauberg in a paragraph,[2] Eisenstein in the space of a sizeable treatise.[3] It is less widely known, however, what Soviet editing did to Griffith's films—and it is this other side of the coin that my essay will address.

I am talking about re-editing, of course—the practice of cutting import films to fit the Soviet screen. They did re-edit them heavily in the twenties. This was done, it was said, to preclude foreign films from spreading what was seen as capitalist ills and bourgeois virtues—the ills and virtues the Bolshevist Party claimed it was its goal to weed out. Apparently, Soviet leaders believed that as long as evil was kept off movie screens, it would be easy to hold it at bay in real life. While most modern observers will categorize this as magical rather than logical thinking, one has to admit that this line of reasoning still serves to buttress many an uplift campaign—including some science-based ones, such as the Harvard School of Public Health study on the perils of onscreen smoking in Hollywood films.[4]

I have written about re-editing at length.[5] The present essay is the case study of a print, namely, a Soviet re-edit of Griffith's *Orphans of the Storm* (1921)—the film David Mayer and I have previously addressed in *The Griffith Project*.[6] The film, let's recall, is about two orphaned stepsisters caught in the middle of the great French Revolution. That revolution, Griffith tells us, was yet another historical lesson on intolerance. In *Orphans of the Storm* the symbol of intolerance is the guillotine, which starts by punishing the enemies of the Revolution and ends up devouring its leaders.

Like any melodrama, those about revolutions need to have heroes and villains. In Griffith's *Orphans,* Danton is the hero and Robespierre the villain. Danton fights for freedom, Robespierre for power. Danton's gift is for speech, Robespierre's for intrigue. When Lillian Gish as Henriette befriends Danton, the "pussy-footed" Robespierre becomes envious. When, eager to spite his more popular rival, the evil Robespierre sends Henriette to the guillotine, it is the good Danton who rushes to her rescue.

Through titles more than through action, Griffith ties Robespierre's villainy to his uncompromising political stance. The conflict between him and Danton, Griffith explains, is not only about the girl but also about the fate of the revolution they had won together. Robespierre calls for blood, Danton stands for mercy. The film ends happily for the orphans, yet as far as history is concerned, Griffith warns us, intolerance will prevail. As the reign of terror spirals out of control, Danton's head will fall, soon followed by Robespierre's own. Revolution is only good as long as it does not entrust its power to the guillotine. When it does, the guillotine is the only winner. Such, more or less, was the train of thought Griffith wanted his film to prompt for his fellow Americans—or those of them who, like him, took pride in the fact that their own revolution had been made by the likes of Danton and succeeded.

He could hardly expect this view to resonate with the Soviets, however. Nor did he count on this. On the contrary, the introductory title that opens *Orphans of the Storm* noisily announces the fact that this film, after all, was made in the wake of the period in the history of the United States that was later labeled the Red Scare:

> The lesson—the French revolution RIGHTLY overthrew a BAD government. But we in America should be careful lest we with a GOOD government

mistake fanatics for leaders and exchange our decent law and order for Anarchy and Bolshevism.

We will return to Griffith's movie momentarily. Meanwhile, let us take a look at Russia.

* * *

To see how these matters looked from the Bolshevist side of the fence, allow me to put films aside for a moment and look at some monuments instead. We know how much Lenin valued cinema for its propaganda potential. What was, for him, the second most important art after film?

Had Lenin been asked this question, he might have pointed to sculpture. As early as April 12, 1918 (only six months after the October revolution), the Soviet government issued a decree on monumental propaganda whose aim was to rewrite past history from the standpoint of the present. History, as Marx saw it, was made by rebels, not Caesars, and it was their names that deserved to be written in stone. Accordingly, Lenin's decree mandated the removal of monuments to the tsars and their ministers and the erection of new ones, from Spartacus and Brutus to the more recent Bakunin and Tolstoy. All in all, the number of names to be commemorated by monuments was sixty-nine.

None of these statues remain intact today, nor were they meant to. Patience not being Lenin's greatest virtue, he wanted the monuments to be unveiled within six months of their commission, a date marking the first anniversary of the Great October Socialist Revolution. The deadline (and meager funds) reduced sculptors to using cheap and easy materials—for the most part plaster and concrete. The duration of each particular monument depended on the weather, but permanence appeared to be of little concern to the new government. All the monuments were needed for was to provide an occasion for inaugural speeches, some delivered by Lenin, some by lesser figures.

It is hardly surprising that the first name on Lenin's list of monuments was that of Karl Marx, who happened to be turning one hundred in 1918. Marx was awarded three monuments that year: one in Penza, one in Petrograd, and another one (in tandem with Friedrich Engels) in Moscow. The monument unveiled in Petrograd had been commissioned from Aleksandr Matveev, a sculptor known for his symbolist and neoclassicist sympathies. His standing Marx, made of plaster and wearing a double-breasted frock coat, is shown resting on his right leg while the other is slightly advanced; his right hand is buried under the coat's lapel, the left one hidden behind his back (see Figure 3.1). One does not need to be an expert in *contrapposto* to recognize that the pose Matveev had chosen for his quickie was borrowed from the famous sculpture of Sophocles (Roman copy of a Greek sculpture circa 400 BC) in the Lateran Museum in Rome (see Figure 3.2).

Figure 3.1 Aleksandr Matveev's monument to Karl Marx, 1920s Petrograd. From the author's collection.

Marx had a point when he said that "history *repeats itself*, first as *tragedy*, then as *farce*."

Elsewhere, the Latvian artist Karlis Zale sculpted in plaster the Italian rebel Garibaldi; of the French rebels, Marat, Robespierre, and Danton each received a monument. Footage showing one Comrade Mostavenko as he reveals the Moscow monument to Danton survives in one of the 1918 issues of Vertov's *Kino-Nedelia* (*Kino-Week*)—films do outlive monuments at times (see Figure 3.3).

Unlike the Petrograd Marx, the Moscow Danton (plaster, again) is not a standing figure, nor even a bust, but a giant head mounted on a tall, bar-like

Figure 3.2 Aleksandr Matveev borrowed the pose for his Marx from the famous sculpture of Sophocles (Roman copy of a Greek sculpture circa 400 BC) housed in the Lateran Museum in Rome.

pedestal (see Figure 3.4). It looks almost as if its maker, sculptor Nikolai Andreev, did so in response to the famous last wish Danton is said to have addressed to his executioner: "The main thing is, don't forget to show my head to the people: it deserves it." (N'oublie pas surtout, n'oublie pas de montrer ma tête au peuple: elle en vaut la peine.)

The same month elsewhere in Moscow a statue of Robespierre was solemnly unveiled. The 1928 novel I quote in my epigraph to this essay says that

Figure 3.3 Footage showing Comrade Mostavenko as he reveals the Moscow monument to Danton survives in one of the 1918 issues of Dziga Vertov's *Kino-nedelia (Kino-Week).*

Figure 3.4 Nikolai Andreev's plaster sculpture of Danton in Moscow is not a standing figure, not even a bust, but a giant head mounted on a tall barlike pedestal. From the author's collection.

the monument was soon after destroyed. This is fact, not fiction. A 1918 source, the Moscow daily *Znamia trudovoi kommuny* (Banner of the labor commune), describes the destruction in more detail:

> The monument to Robespierre unveiled a week ago in the Aleksandrovsky Park met its end at the hand of a criminal during the night of November 6/7. Our correspondent who visited the scene of the crime came back fully convinced that the monument had been blown up. The figure of Robespierre was made of concrete, with many hollow pipes inside. Now all that remains is a heap of small fragments scattered around. The pedestal remained intact.[7]

Anyone who has dabbled in history is familiar with the itch to try to solve the puzzle of a ninety-year-old crime. The choice of target, weapon, and date provides one with enough clues to lead to the perpetrators. November 7, of course, is the Western-style calendar date for the October Revolution. The bomb and the Browning were two time-honored weapons used by the right-wing SR (Socialist-Revolutionary) Party terrorists against the tsar and his ministers before October 1917 and against Lenin and high-ranking Bolshevists after the date.

As to the target, its message is as clear as that of the horse's head in Francis Ford Coppola's *The Godfather* (1972). Early on, the Bolshevist Party proudly called themselves Russian Jacobins. While denouncing individual terrorism as ineffective, Lenin, like Robespierre, strongly believed in the efficacy of state-sponsored violence. The Red Terror announced in Russia in 1918 was seen by many as a modern version of Robespierre's *La Terreur.* Seasoned political idealists, the SR Party saw Lenin and his political precursor as two legitimate reasons for their Brownings to fire and their bombs to fly.

* * *

We return from statues to films and from 1918 to the early 1920s. With the civil war now largely over, the NEP (New Economic Policy) was announced, which many expected to become Lenin's Termidor—some with hope, others with a sense of frustration. The second quotation I use as an epigraph for this essay—a few lines from Mayakovsky's wonderful anti-NEP satire—summarizes two of a handful of new freedoms the country now enjoyed: according to the NEP, it was all right to trade in small goods and to watch foreign movies. The fine print attached to both freedoms, however, implied that there was a price for each: those who chose to trade should be ready to lose certain civil rights, and those who distributed foreign films must be careful not to distribute bourgeois ideology, which foreign films were believed to be steeped in.

This brings us back to where we began. In 1924 a re-editing bureau (*biuro montazha*) was founded in Moscow, soon followed by another one in Leningrad. Contrary to what one might expect, re-editing was not done furtively. Critics discussed its multiple failures in the press, and there were newspaper campaigns condemning the practice as bringing more harm than good; but there were enough people who found re-editing useful for both political *and* artistic reasons.

Significantly, the re-editing bureau was the site where much of what would later be known as Soviet montage theory and practice emerged. As future directors were quick to discover, cutting movies made by others was a way of learning how to make their own. Officially, the bureau was a place where films were censored; unofficially, it functioned as a workshop. Here Eisenstein and Esfir Shub took apart Fritz Lang's *Dr. Mabuse, der Spieler* (*Dr. Mabuse the Gambler*; 1922) and put it together again as a different film; and, as we learn from an interview with the Vasiliev brothers, there would be no *Chapaev* (1934) had they not worked as re-editors for years.[8]

For others, re-editing was more of a theoretical experience. In his 1927 book *The Editing Table,* Formalist scholar Viktor Shklovsky summarized what he learned as he worked in the bureau:

> Now I know how loosely the precise meaning of an action in cinema is anchored in this action. . . . The variety of human movements is not that large. The variety of facial expressions is even smaller. Changes made to intertitles and plot construction can completely re-cue our perception of the film hero. . . . The thing is, for the professional re-editor the man in the shot does not laugh or cry or mourn, he only opens and shuts his eyes and his mouth in a specific way. He is raw material. The meaning of a word depends on the phrase I place it in. If I place the word properly in another phrase it will acquire a different meaning, while the viewer believes that he is searching for some kind of true, original meaning of the word, for a lexical meaning of actors' emotions.[9]

To illustrate his point Shklovsky draws an example from the work of a fellow editor. The first thing a re-editor was expected to do with a foreign film was to remove its happy ending. Fat and virtuous people, as with the world and the values they stood for, deserved to be dead, not happy.

> I think one of Vasiliev's inventions is a masterpiece of cinematic thinking. He needed a man to die but the man would not die. He chose a moment when the proposed victim was yawning, printed the same frame over and over again, and the movement stopped. The man froze with his mouth open: it remained to add the title: "death by heart attack." This device was so unexpected that no one protested.[10]

There was one voice that protested, however. Soon after Shklovsky's book came out, a refutation signed by the very man whom Shklovsky credits appeared in the Moscow newspaper *Kino*. Here it is, quoted in full:

> Dear Comrades,
>
> V. Shklovsky's book *The Editing Table* released by "Kinopechat" mentions a freeze-frame experiment allegedly staged by re-editor Vasiliev.
>
> In the interests of truth I hereby assert that I never performed a trick like this, and that the authorship of this trick belongs to Comrade Boitler.
>
> S. Vasiliev.[11]

This coy retort provides excellent evidence of the atmosphere that prevailed in the re-editing bureau. With minds as sharp as Shklovsky's and Eisenstein's around, to say nothing of the legendary Boitler, the place designed to censor films quickly turned into a club for wits.

* * *

Let's now cut back to Danton and Robespierre—this time as film characters rather than as statues. Both figures were highly regarded in Russia, but as Marxists liked to see revolutions, past or present, through the gray lens of class interests and motive forces, they resented the two Frenchmen being painted this way: one as a humorless villain, the other his colorful victim. And this was exactly how movies from the West painted Danton and Robespierre.

One such movie was Dimitri Buchowetzki's mediocre *Danton* (1921), which featured Werner Krauss as Robespierre and Emil Jannings as Danton. The casting alone tells us who is a good guy and who isn't. And Buchowetzki's Robespierre was not just bad, he was vicious—a problem re-editors had to deal with if (against all odds) this film were to be allowed to be shown in Soviet Russia.

It was—in 1924, Buchowetzki's movie was released under the title *Guillotine.* We obtain a glimpse into how it was re-edited from a passage in one of Eisenstein's essays about montage. Montage is truly at work, Eisenstein says, only when, spliced together, two shots change their initial meanings—sometimes to their opposite.

> This is what the wise and wicked art of re-editing was based on. At those moments, of course, when re-editing was really an "art"—and not a patchy potboiler. What gallons of wit used to go into this game! In those glorious days at the dawn of our cinema when, learning to cut, E. Shub, the Vasiliev "brothers," Birrois and Veniamin Boitler worked in this field.[12]

As we read on, we learn what one member of this glorious team did to correct a climactic scene of Buchowetzki's movie:

> I cannot resist the pleasure of citing here one montage *tour de force* executed by Boitler, the last name I mentioned on this list. One film bought from Germany was *Danton,* with Emil Jannings. As released on our screens, this scene

> was shown: Camille Desmoulins is condemned to the guillotine. Greatly agitated, Danton rushes to Robespierre, who turns aside and slowly wipes away a tear. The intertitle said, approximately, "In the name of freedom I had to sacrifice a friend . . ." Fine.
>
> But who could have guessed that in the German original, Danton, represented as an idler, a petticoat-chaser, a splendid chap and the only positive figure in the midst of evil characters, that this Danton ran to the evil Robespierre and . . . spat in his face? And that it was this spit that Robespierre wiped from his face with a handkerchief? And that the title indicated Robespierre's hatred of Danton, a hate that at the end of the film motivates the condemnation of Jannings-Danton to the guillotine?!
>
> Two tiny cuts eliminated a short piece of film, from the moment when Danton spits to the moment when the spit reaches its aim. And the insult is turned into a tear of remorse . . .[13]

Unfortunately, Boitler's re-edited version of *Danton* does not survive. But the original does, and indeed contains the spitting and the wiping. In case someone is interested in repeating Boitler's experiment, this can be done.

* * *

Now let us return to Griffith's *Orphans,* whose treatment of Robespierre (Sydney Herbert) and Danton (Monte Blue) was, in the eyes of the Soviets, as inadmissible as in Buchowetzki's film. The surviving (not in good shape) Russian re-edit of Griffith's movie does not give the name of the re-editor (as was normally the rule), but press discussions encourage us to assume that it was Sergei Vasiliev, most likely in collaboration with his partner and namesake Georgi. Let me rehearse some changes they made in order to clean up Griffith's pictures and improve on what he had done.

That Soviet filmmakers, re-editors included, regarded Griffith as the ultimate authority in the field does not mean they never looked at him critically. Ideology was the most obvious drawback, but they also regretted that the young ladies played by Griffith's actresses so well were such slaves to petit-bourgeois virtues. Moreover, they were surprised that such a great master of editing could be such a bad writer of intertitles.[14]

The following example illustrates what the Vasilievs thought was wrong with Griffith's titling style in *Orphans of the Storm.* The tipping point of the French Revolution (as of the Russian one) is generally taken to be the moment when, convinced by Danton, the military took the side of the people. Griffith lets action speak for itself, helped only by a typically curt intertitle: "Danton wins the guards that bar his way." The Soviet re-editors, who preferred exclamation marks to full stops and spoken words to descriptive phrases, sliced the scene up in order to splice in three titles instead of one:

Forward! Time to throw down the hateful tyranny!
Soldiers! Are you going to attack unarmed people?
No! We will not shoot at those like us![15]

Clearly, Griffith was not paying enough attention to the historical part of his story, which the Vasilievs decided to spell out—just as Russians did in Russian films.

The way in which the young Soviet re-editors dealt with Griffith's old-fashioned petit-bourgeois virtues deserves mention as well. Keep in mind that in *Orphans of the Storm* Griffith brings history—the Storm—and private destinies together. At a certain point one of the orphans, played by Lillian Gish, gives shelter to Danton, who, his arm slightly wounded, is pursued by a Royalist squad. This happens quite early in the film, well before the success of the revolution brings Danton and Robespierre to power, but we already see in the latter the signs of rivalry and envy which will undermine their power in the end.

All this happens on a rainy night. Danton has barely escaped, and having pushed open the first door he passes, he finds himself in a house one of whose tenants happens to be Lillian Gish's Henriette. The Royalist guards being after him, the young lady hides Danton in her room. Having searched the house in vain, the guards leave. In the morning Robespierre ("The original pussy-footer, a splendid regulator of other people's morals and affairs," says the title) knocks at Henriette's door suspecting this may be where his friend is hiding. But having looked at Robespierre's untrustworthy face, Henriette slams the door on him. "A little door slam—yet later it shall shadow Henriette at the door of death," says the title.

Before we look at the way in which this sequence was re-edited in Russia, let me explain how the Vasilievs dealt with the Robespierre problem in general. Unlike Buchowetzki's Robespierre, whom Boitler kept in the film, making him a stern yet compassionate leader, Griffith's Robespierre was simply cut out of the picture. There is Danton, there is Henriette, there is her kidnapped, blind stepsister played by Dorothy Gish, but Robespierre is never mentioned. The revolution is made by Danton alone.

True, two or three times Sydney Herbert's tiptoeing figure does appear briefly on screen, but again, the Russian print never tells us who he is: at one point he is an anonymous orator, at another we take him for a Royalist spy. This is exactly what we take him for when in the morning the erstwhile Robespierre shows up at the place where Henriette lives—to check if Danton has spent a night there or not. Now, we know he did, but Griffith leaves us in no doubt about the chastity of this night. We see the brave, self-sacrificial Henriette lock her room from inside so that Danton cannot leave, for he is wounded and may be caught. "You can't go—Better a little gossip about me than for you to lose your life."

Of course, whatever the gossip, it will be totally groundless. Tired, Griffith's Danton sinks into a chair, and after the title "The Morning" we see him asleep in an improvised bed, all alone. The door of an adjacent room opens and we see Lillian Gish's lovely, innocent face peep in at Danton. There is a brief lyrical pause before Danton's departure, her hand in his, both looking at each other. Clearly, there is more than courtesy to this, but no laws of propriety or of genre are broken. He has his French people to take care of; she, her kidnapped sister to find and a young, handsome aristocrat to marry in the end. History and melodrama may occasionally meet, but they are highly unlikely to get married.

To the young Soviet re-editors all these maneuvers must have looked rather silly. And they had a point. Drafted by that remarkable apostle of free love, Aleksandra Kollontai, Soviet marital laws of the twenties were more liberal than ever before or after in Russia, as were codes of pre- and extramarital behavior that Kollontai hoped would be rebuilt on the basis of "natural spontaneity" instead of cultural prejudice.[16] If you like him so much as to risk your life for his, why not share your bed with this hardened rebel almost twice your size and only twice your age? Not many filmgoers in the Soviet Union would really mind. On the contrary, in their eyes this would give Griffith's pretty orphan a nice romantic secret. So, they cut from the shot which shows Danton staying at Henriette's straight to that parting scene by the open bed. It is up to the viewer to decide what happened in between.

These are all minor surgeries, however. A major one is what the Vasilievs did to Chevalier de Vaudrey, Henriette's aristocratic fiancé played by the young and handsome Joseph Schildkraut, as well as to his unfortunate aunt.

Let's recall two main lines of Griffith's complex plot. The film begins with a murder. We see a man being pierced by two rapiers at the door to a richly decorated bedroom. In the bedroom, there is a woman with a newborn baby. Her husband's aristocratic murderers rush in, determined to take the baby away. The only thing the young mother is able to do is to hide on the baby a note with its name and some money for those who adopt it.

This scene is a prologue, from which we learn the birth story of poor, blind Louise, Henriette's stepsister, played by Dorothy Gish. She is the biological daughter of a high-born lady who suffered the misfortune of falling in love with and secretly marrying a man well below her social rank. We just saw what happened to the husband—he was killed by her relatives, who had learned about the disgrace and decided to take care of it before the secret could be divulged.

We also learn that little Louise (who is not blind at birth but who loses her sight years later when her foster parents die) was found and adopted by a couple who happened to have a daughter of their own of the same age—Henriette, of course. A little later we learn that Louise's mother had been given a second chance. The man she has married this time is the Count de Linieres, a powerful figure at the king's court. They have no children of their own, but they have a young relative whom they love like a son.

Early on in the film, the young relative is introduced by this title: "The young Chevalier de Vaudrey, nephew of the Countess, a descendant of the world's proudest and oldest nobility." This good, carefree chap, it soon turns out, also has a noble heart. He helps the poor, saves Henriette from a near rape, risks his head as he comes to revolutionary Paris to look for her, is indeed caught and condemned to the guillotine, and, when the time comes for the happy ending, marries Henriette, who loves him, too.

All ends happily for Louise as well. A good doctor restores her sight, and her unfortunate mother (whose secret thoughts all these years were about the fate and whereabouts of the daughter she had been forced to abandon) regains her child. Now that Louise is able to see, we are positive she will fall in love with a man worthy of her and marry him before long.

No one will be surprised to learn that the Soviet re-editors did not care for this outcome at all. Even the stoutest Dantonist among us will agree: Griffith's ending is too good to be true. Not that Sergei and Georgi Vasiliev wished Henriette to be killed—if they had they could easily have done so, for at one point in the film her delicate neck is already in the grip of the guillotine, and one brief intertitle would have been enough for Lillian Gish's bonneted head to be in the basket. The problem they had was not with Henriette, but with her beau.

It was not clear to them why Griffith needed a nobleman, and beyond that "a descendant of the world's proudest and oldest nobility," to be loved and married by Henriette, who comes, one should add, from a very humble family. In the Soviet Union of the 1920s, the notions of noble and humble underwent a curious reversal. Passports, for instance, declared each person's social origin, and any citizen labeled as "worker" or "peasant" enjoyed substantial rights and privileges in terms of housing, education, taxes, and even voting rights. Mayakovsky's satirical play *Bedbug,* from which I quote in the second epigraph to this essay, wittily plays with these newly instituted conceptions of social status. Indeed, the play could be described as a Soviet version of the *bourgeois gentilhomme* situation. In it, a family of NEP men (their small business is a beauty salon in Moscow) marry their daughter *up* to a proletarian. For them and for him, this is a marriage of convenience: now they will be able to enjoy all the perks reserved for workers, while he in turn will swim in their money.

To return to *Orphans,* then, in the Soviet Union of the twenties it was not a good thing for a movie to have an aristocrat as a positive hero, particularly if he is going to marry a girl of good proletarian origins. It would, of course, be easy enough to get rid of him in the end, by means of the same guillotine, for instance, since he has been convicted by the revolutionary tribunal anyway, but this would hardly solve the problem. Somehow Griffith makes the Chevalier de Vaudrey so lovable from the outset that, call him a chevalier as many times as you wish, viewers would nevertheless be upset by his death. And there is no way to lie about his origins, either, for his wig, his clothes, and the way he fences and moves (this is the eighteenth century, remember) will betray him right away.

The solution the Vasilievs found was truly brilliant. The line of defense taken by the chevalier in the Russian print when facing the tribunal judges is to say that he is not an enemy of the people, because he is not an aristocrat by birth. "I am the son of a person who was as poor as you are. My mother fell in love with a peasant and planned to elope, but her husband Count de Linieres found out and killed my father." These words are followed by a flashback. We see a man being pierced by two rapiers at the door to a richly decorated bedroom. In the bedroom, there is a woman with a newborn baby. This baby is me, Chevalier de Vaudrey explains to the judges. My mother pleaded with her husband to spare me. He forgave her. They raised me as their own child. I did not know then, but now I know, and so on. For a second, the judges look impressed, but only for a second. They must have heard too many melodramatic stories like this, as must their Russian successors during the Red Terror years. They don't believe de Vaudrey, but the viewers do—we all tend to believe what flashbacks show us. De Vaudrey is sent to the guillotine, as is Henriette for trying to hide him in her room from revolutionary guards.

It will be Danton, who recognizes in Henriette the girl who some time ago had saved him in exactly the same way, who rescues both Henriette and the chevalier at the last moment. His Russian plea to the judges sounds like a quotation from Lenin: "Listen to me! The Tribunal must not be soft but it must be just! I know: magnanimity shown to the enemies of Revolution may often cost us hundreds of its friends' heads; but I also know: these two are not enemies at all." Unlike Griffith's Danton, his Soviet double is not against the Terror; he only wants one exemption from it. He is Danton and Robespierre in one.

Many said that re-editors crippled movies. One of the scenes in *Orphans* shows Henriette unwittingly caught in a maelstrom of drunken revolutionary canaille dancing "La Carmagnole." Of all Griffith's orgies this one is by far the best. It is so good that Vsevolod Pudovkin, one of Griffith's greatest admirers, admitted in a 1926 interview that even though he understood the ideological reason why the scene was cut from the Soviet version of the film, he thought it should have been left in. "Wouldn't it be a more honest thing to do if they left the scene as it was created by the great master adding a title that warns that it is ideologically harmful—instead of showing us the re-editors' clumsy exercises?" Pudovkin asks.[17]

On the other hand, knowing the system of Soviet film censorship, one could argue the opposite way and say that by crippling movies the re-editors actually were saving them. It was not up to re-editors to decide whether this or that film might or might not be admitted to the screen. Only professional ideologists from a Party-staffed institution known as the Glavrepertkom (Chief Repertory Committee) could green-light or shelve a film. Before films were sent to the real censors, they went through the hands of re-editors. Sometimes pictures were sent back for additional re-editing. By cutting Griffith's movie, whether clumsily or cleverly, re-editors saved its life on the Soviet screen.

It is for this reason that the word "surgery" was sometimes used in discussions about re-editing. If we take up this metaphor and apply it to the Vasilievs' work on Griffith's *Orphans,* we can compare their work to an organ transplant. They removed Griffith's footage from the beginning of the film and spliced it inside the courtroom scene; from being a prologue it was turned into a first-person flashback spoken by an accused man who renounces his title. By so doing, our transplant surgeons turned the baby girl of the prologue into the baby boy of the flashback—and poor Louise lost her mother again.

The happy ending reads like this: Griffith's movie was saved and could be seen again and again by so many people that Mayakovsky's mocking reference to the "aristocratic-cinematic" names Lillian and Dorothy, together with their proverbial twin bonnets, could bring down, as it did in 1928, the walls of Meyerhold's theater with laughter.

Notes

1. "After a while Griffith's *Intolerance* arrived. It then became easier to talk" (Dziga Vertov, *Kino-Eye: The Writings of Dziga Vertov,* ed. Annette Michelson [Berkeley: University of California Press, 1984], 94).

2. In his book about Leonid Trauberg, Theodor van Houten writes: "On July 12, Trauberg sent everybody away near him, and asked for me. He had started to make his will on a piece of paper. He said: 'I know I can have another heart attack. But I am not afraid of death. I will be there (he raised his arms to the ceiling), not with God, but . . . some power. I will be there . . . with Eisenstein and Griffith'" (Theodor van Houten, *"Eisenstein Was Great Eater": In Memory of Leonid Trauberg* [Buren, Netherlands: A&R/GP, 1991], 72).

3. Sergei Eisenstein, "Dickens, Griffith and Ourselves," in *S. M. Eisenstein: Selected Works,* vol. 3, *Writings 1934–47,* trans. and ed. Richard Taylor (London: British Film Institute; Bloomington: Indiana University Press, 1996), 193–239.

4. Jeffrey Kluger, "Hollywood's Smoke Alarm," *Time,* April 12, 2007, http://www.time.com/time/magazine/article/0,9171,1609773,00.html.

5. Yuri Tsivian, "The Wise and Wicked Game: Re-Editing and Soviet Film Culture of the 1920s," *Film History* 8.3 (1996): 327–343.

6. Yuri Tsivian and David Mayer, "*Orphans of the Storm,*" in *The Griffith Project,* vol. 10, *Films Produced in 1919–46,* ed. Paolo Cherchi Usai (London: British Film Institute; Pordenone, Italy: Le Giornate del Cinema Muto, 2006), 116–137.

7. "The Destruction of the Robespierre Monument," *Znamia trudovoi kommuny* [Banner of the labor commune], November 9, 1918.

8. "How I Became a Director," in *Bratia Vasilievy. Sobranie sochinenii v trekh tomakh* [The Vasiliev brothers. Collected works in three volumes] (Moscow: Iskusstvo, 1981), 103–112.

9. Viktor Shklovsky, "The Work of the Re-Editor," in *The Film Factory: Russian and Soviet Cinema in Documents 1896–1939*, ed. Richard Taylor and Ian Christie (London: Routledge and Kegan Paul, 1988), 168–169. I have made some changes to the translation in order to bring it closer to the original.

10. Ibid.

11. Sergei Vasiliev, [Refutation], *Kino*, April 19, 1927.

12. Sergei Eisenstein, *Film Form*, ed. and trans. Jay Leyda (New York: Harcourt, Brace and World, 1949), 10–11. I have made changes to the translation in order to bring it closer to the original.

13. Ibid.

14. Sergei Vasiliev, "*V chem sut spora?*" [What is the essence of the discussion?], in *Bratia Vasilievy. Sobranie sochinenii v trekh tomakh* [The Vasiliev brothers. Collected works in three volumes] (Moscow: Iskusstvo, 1981), 143.

15. The Soviet distribution print of *Danton* has been preserved at the Gosfilmofond (the Russian state film archive in Moscow). Title translations are my own.

16. An English-speaking reader can learn more about this in Richard Stites's *Revolutionary Dreams: Utopian Vision in the Russian Revolution* (New York: Oxford University Press, 1989), 115–119.

17. "Vsevolod Pudovkin on Re-Editing" [interview], *Krasnaya gazeta (vechernii vypusk)* [Red newspaper, evening edition], no. 249, October 22, 1926, 1253.

4 An Afterlife for Junk Prints

Serials and Other "Classics" in Late-1920s Tehran

Kaveh Askari

Volumes like this one underscore how rapidly film historians have been revising the maps of silent film culture in recent years. Not only is there a growing body of research on emergent cinemas outside of Europe and the United States, but the increasingly fine-grained maps of film cultures within European and North American towns have revealed their own overlooked peripheries.[1] In either case, whether researching urban Shanghai or rural Ontario, a consistent corollary emerges: engaging the complexity of silent cinema's geographies necessarily complicates its chronologies.[2] It would make for a much simpler history had each newly released feature or serial film circulated provincially and globally with speed and uniformity. But the physical realities of film prints moving across trade borders and through intermediary institutions, such as international exchanges and government censorship bureaus, create messy periodizations. Quite frankly, the boundaries between early cinema and later film cultures are far more permeable than we have assumed. Their characteristics overlap in ways that warrant more focused attention. In a very general sense any study of distribution attends to the intermediary life of film, but the speed and directness of film circulation vary enormously from region to region. In places that differ widely from general trends, the effect is not so much a local film culture lagging behind the production centers as a film culture out of synch.

Rather than thinking about the interruptions to circulation and damage to prints negatively, as incomplete steps toward more developed national film cultures, I want to consider how silent film's cultural translation can be shaped by the conditions of its physical translation.[3] In this regard silent cinema in the Middle East and North Africa offers standout cases. The strategies of global distribution of films established in the 1910s suffered greatly diminished successes in many cities across the Middle East and North Africa. With some important exceptions, many Western film export businesses considered markets in the Middle East as less accessible or as failed opportunities by the late 1910s. American firms in particular expressed disappointment at failing to establish profitable offices in the region. These failures were all the more conspicuous as American firms' decreasing dependence on intermediary distributors in London and elsewhere boosted efficiency and profitability in other parts of the world.[4]

American trade press articles and letters in distributor archives illustrate a weakening of optimism as the basic situation failed to change through the 1910s and 1920s. In an article in *Motography* in 1912, the consul general in Beirut optimistically tried to tip off American companies to a potential market. He suggested that American firms route their films for the region through Cairo and Alexandria and claimed there is "no reason why a large business cannot be immediately developed."[5] The relatively meager communications with Middle East and North African contacts in the Selig Polyscope collection of letters from the London office in the 1910s suggest some interest in potential markets in Cairo, Tunis, and Istanbul, but not necessarily a realization of that potential.[6] In the following several years, trade articles about the region reported similarly frustrating film import situations, but attributed the continuing inaccessibility to larger cultural obstacles, such as the Muslim ban on images or the difficulty of setting up gender-divided screening spaces. Locations with better film distribution, such as Cairo or settler communities throughout the region, were cited as the exceptions that proved the rule.[7] As one journalist emphasized, "Arabia, therefore promises to be a difficult market, with the exception of the British administered Aden Protectorate, and the rather liberal Sultan of Mokalla."[8]

As the trade articles expressed hope for future business, they also frequently noted the age and poor condition of the prints. The films shown in Aden, for instance, were described as "an exceeding common or archaic type . . . weekly exhibitions of pictures several years old."[9] An article regaling readers with descriptions of the high-fashion picture palaces in Egypt ends with a discussion of other, more rural and far from opulent, theatrical sites: "When the films have been the round of the various picture palaces . . . they are bought up cheap by enterprising Greeks [who] make quite a thriving business out of dilapidated old films" by exhibiting them in the villages.[10] The U.S. consulate reported that theaters in Beirut, Damascus, and Tripoli were supplied by films that "would reach there only after having been used in a number of other towns and were often in bad condition and out of date."[11] These accounts of the troubled and interrupted circulation of worn and incomplete prints depict the diverse kinds of exhibition and reception of a considerable portion of the films screened throughout the region. These films were junk prints, forgotten by producers and amortized long before their arrival. Their life, a kind of afterlife, invites analysis as such.

As a term of reverence, not dismissal, "junk prints" organizes a rich set of associations. If "orphan" has proven useful as a contemporary preservation term for peripheral celluloid material, then "junk" has a compelling historical resonance.[12] The term emerges in tandem with the growing circulation of goods in industrial modernity. It evokes a range of productive secondhand cultures dependent upon obsolescence, like the modern junk shop, but its associations with re-use date back much further. In the seventeenth century, "junk" described the re-usable scrap line on sailing ships. This early definition might seem fitting for anyone who has worked with film fragments in an archive, in a projection booth, or on an optical printer. Someone with a reverent (and admittedly fetishistic) attitude toward junk film would likely notice how the practice of saving and mending frayed marine line oddly recalls the modern labor of mending, saving, splicing, and threading old celluloid.

To refer to film as a kind of junk is nothing new. Importantly, the term described the circulation of secondhand prints in the silent era, and this usage noticeably features as the first modern example in the *Oxford English Dictionary*'s definition of "junk." The OED entry cites Valentia Steer's 1913 study *The Romance of Cinema,* where the term is placed in quotes to note industry jargon.

> The life of a film is very short. It is "first run" today and "junk" a few short weeks hence. What is now 4d. a foot, to be handled like a newborn babe, will, three months later on, be so much scrap, fit only for working up into varnish. Yet millions of feet of this worn-out rubbish are being reeled off daily at fourth[-] and fifth-rate picture theatres.[13]

By *The Romance of Cinema*'s own coincidences of circulation, secondhand film has helped to define modern junk. Steer's revulsion for "worn-out rubbish" notwithstanding, this coincidence indicates the importance of "junk" as a historiographical imperative in film and media studies.

Like garbage and trash, junk is associated with waste, an annoying byproduct, a slur upon the otherwise pristine efficiency associated with modern industrialism. Junk's visibility offends because it is nonsynchronous material.[14] It refers at once to matter out of date, out of place, and to matter that piles up over time.[15] To stress these aspects of modern junk, Rem Koolhaas has tendered the concept of "junkspace." He uses the term to describe the "orphaned," "authorless" spaces created out of the unplanned, incongruous, and wasteful conditions of global exchange.[16] Despite Koolhaas's emphasis on recent decades for his examples, he offers a compelling way to frame questions about the history of silent film exhibition wherever there are elaborate impediments to circulation. A positive conception of junkspace can radically interrupt one-dimensional conceptions of media history, which too often depend on a narrative of development and progress that overlooks out-of-place historical material. These one-dimensional conceptions become even more dubious when tracing the histories of film's global circulation, as they tend to assume a kind of simple delay from one place to another. The notion of a simply delayed film culture (as opposed to an incongruous one) comes too close to the touristic fantasy that one (peripheral) place represents the past of another (central) place.[17] A historiography that places junk in the foreground confronts these assumptions, as junkspaces combine fragments of different historical periods in unplanned ways.

"Junk" augments the conceptions of "archaeology" that have influenced much post-1960s historiography. Archaeology has proven an especially fruitful metaphor in film study, from classic work by C. W. Ceram to the authoritative recent history by Laurent Mannoni, to experimental work by filmmakers such as Gustav Deutsch.[18] Archaeology and junk are intimately related, whether acknowledged or not.[19] Recent criticism on archaeology and modernity by Michael Shanks, David Platt, and William Rathje has pointed out how researchers have historically tried to disavow archaeology's dependence on junk.[20] For them, a modern archaeology acknowledges the redundancy of a phrase like "archaeology of junk." It aligns itself not with what the Futurists condemned as "the chronic necrophilia" of the archaeologists who fetishize antiquity, but rather attends to the "perfume of garbage," to the modernist interest in the material culture of the everyday and its surprising revelations.[21] A modern everyday medium, periodically relegated to and rescued from junk heaps, with its own sour perfumes of decay, cinema proves an easier fit for this approach than most other media.[22]

To consider junk film's afterlife makes clear that the life of a film, while still painfully short to the preservationist, turns out to be nowhere near as short as Valentia Steer assumed. From a transnational perspective, Steer's "fifth-rate picture theaters" only begin the stories of the films' afterlives. The description of film as "worn-out rubbish" could be taken now as a testimony to the longevity and adaptability of these prints. It could draw attention to how the films' object-lives help to shape the translations that occur in new exhibition contexts. Case studies of the prints' age and the intermediary stages of their circulation in the region reveal inventive and often counterintuitive re-uses of junk cinema. Tehran in the 1920s and 1930s provides such a test case for examining some of the geopolitical stakes of out-of-synch and overlapping chronologies of early cinemas.

Film Traffic, Monarchs, and Regional Modernities

Iranian cinema scholarship has had the opportunity to establish itself in recent years, thanks in large part to the film festival successes of a handful of auteurs such as members of the Makhmalbaf family and Abbas Kiarostami and his protégés. While the lion's share of this critical work has focused on the past forty years, there have also been some important efforts to return to original source material and open up the established narratives and assumptions about the silent era as well.

In several essays and in the first volume of his recent social history of Iranian cinema, Hamid Naficy details multiple registers of silent film reception. In his analysis of early imported film screenings, using Iran as a case study, Naficy identifies not only the (Althusserian) "hailing" effects of film technology in the early period, but also the tactics of "haggling" that took place within the diverse ethnic, political, and religious circumstances surrounding these screenings.[23] If "hailing" describes a kind of self-othering in early contacts with moving-image technology, "haggling" describes the adaptations and appropriations to which local film communities subjected these technologies. Since secondhand culture is in some sense always a culture of appropriation, a cultural analysis of junk-print cinema would seem well suited to uncovering the transformative instances of "haggling."

While exploring some of these affinities between secondhand cinema and cultural recontextualization, I want to stay clear of a perhaps too-optimistic assumption that these appropriations imply a separation from official culture. Secondhand films and film technologies served monarchs or absolute rulers just as easily as they served everyday moderns. In a recent essay, Negar Mottahedeh situates early cinema in Iran as one of many recording technologies that were appropriated by the institution of the shah's court and thus aided in the formation of official national discourse.[24] Likewise, some historians have recently re-examined early cinema's often-overlooked role as a royal court recorder or aristocratic diversion in many parts of the world, instances that provide a rather striking contrast to cinema's emergence on the fairground elsewhere.[25] When looking at specific cases from these reception contexts, the political stakes of film's re-use can undergo surprising contortions.

The best-known story of cinematic first contact in the region, mythologized by contemporary Iranian filmmakers, occurred during the visit of the ruling Qajar monarch, Mozaffar ad-din Shah, to the Paris World Exposition in 1900. There was already an established tradition of photography in the Qajar court, and the shah's new cinematograph purchase was simply added to the equipment under the control of the court photographers. They used the cinematograph to film local court entertainments and to make records of the shah's activities (like his use of the gramophone to record his speeches).[26] Stephen Bottomore describes the Persian shah as being more discreet with his new technology than other regional monarchs such as Sultan Abdul Aziz in Morocco. Where the shah kept his cameras and gramophones out of the public eye, the sultan's extravagant public fascination with Western technologies like cinema contributed to his reputation as a "Nero of Today."[27] Perhaps owing in part to the shah's discretion, cinema's role as a commercial entertainment during the last years of the Qajar dynasty in the 1910s grew only in very small increments—much to the frustration of distribution firms in Europe and the United States.

While I am primarily looking at the records of film exhibition in Tehran from the 1920s and early 1930s, the associations of the city's earliest motion pictures with royal privilege offer a vantage point from which to view the following generation. When the British government helped Reza Khan overtake the Qajar dynasty and much of the power of the recently formed constitutional government in the early 1920s (officially in 1925), cinema experienced what we might call a "second wave" of "royalist" film reception in Iran. Cinema's early steps toward viable commercial exhibition of foreign films converged with the official culture, this time a secular nationalist one. Still, this new local viability was of relatively meager interest to distributors in the United States and Western Europe, whose bottom line was better served elsewhere.

International commerce statistics provide the first clues about the films shown on commercial screens in Tehran. There were around thirty cinemas operating in Iran in the late 1920s, with just under half of these located in the capital.[28] These cinemas subsisted on a steady stream of imports accounted for in one report by the U.S. Department of Commerce (see Table 4.1). These statistics confirm that American and French productions far exceed those of any other country, and their share of the market remains fairly stable despite taking an obvious hit from the economic crisis. The low numbers overall and the decreased numbers in 1930 mark disappointment over what the commerce department hoped would be "a promising field for exploitation."[29] But the origins and number of these imported films do not tell the whole story.

The exhibitor advertisements from the 1920s and 1930s in the Persian-language daily *Ettela'at* provide more information about the films represented by the import figures. Launched in 1926, the paper is one of the best sources for evidence about the films from this period. Cinemas advertised in *Ettela'at* from the beginning. In the first few years of the paper's run the only regular film advertisements came from the Grand Cinema operated by Ali Vakili in conjunction with the Grand Hotel on Lalezar Street (Figure 4.1). Beginning around 1929, the film ads become more diverse, with Cinemas Sepah, Zardoshtian (both also owned by Vakili), Pars, Tehran, and Baharestan among the frequent advertisers. These cinemas do not present a comprehensive view of film exhibition in Tehran,

Table 4.1. Imports of motion-picture films into Persia

	YEAR		
Country of origin	1928	1929	1930
United States	133	227	145
France	100	110	94
Germany	30	47	60
Russia	32	57	42
Other countries	10	19	6

Figure 4.1 The Grand Hotel accommodated travelers and traveling films. Its café served as an important gathering place in the changing urban geography of Tehran. Ali Vakili established the Grand Cinema in the auditorium here.

but the regularity of advertisements and continual experiments with tie-in stunts offer a glimpse into exhibition practices and policies at an array of major theaters in the city.

The *Ettela'at* ads confirm the basic numbers indicated in the *Commerce Reports* article, but they also indicate that these numbers are interesting for what they conceal as much as for what they reveal. The films that I have been able to identify were typically eight to ten years old, and they were almost all serials. The gap between the original release date and local screening date common throughout the region is substantial in this case. Notable also is the silent serials' prolonged popularity, which extended well into the early sound period. Some lag in exhibition chronology can be expected in any peripheral market (including, as noted above, the suburbs of major Western cities), but here the lag is particularly dramatic compared with markets in China or major port cities in Latin America, where established exchange offices ensured rapid distribution. To say that the emergence of cinema was simply postponed in Tehran would neglect the most noteworthy aspects of this lag time—how elements of early cinema culture overlapped with 1920s modernity, how intermediary film exchanges exerted their own influence, and how mile markers of exhibition that were experienced elsewhere as continual sequence (the very premise of serialized stories) were often experienced in Tehran as simultaneity.

Because of its natural resources, strategic location, and the fact that it was never colonized by a single Western power, modern Iran experienced intense friction between versions of modernity competing for influence within its borders. Some of this competition manifested itself in the often-complex geopolitical lives of circulating film prints. A cursory glance at the *Commerce Reports* article might suggest that American film dominates the market—followed relatively closely by France and distantly by Germany and Russia. But the circuitous trade routes and geographical intermediaries for these junk prints form as important a part of their story as their places of origin. Films and film culture routed through Istanbul or British-controlled Baghdad seem to easily fit official culture in an Iran governed by a leader who would borrow many of his ideas about nationalist modernization from Atatürk and whose power was enabled by the British government. Intermediaries like Moscow, on the other hand, created more complicated situations in the late 1920s.[30] The film exhibition scene in Iran during the constitutional revolution and end of the Qajar dynasty was strongly tied to Russia. Many of the fledgling early exhibitors in Iran either had ties to Russia or were Russian immigrants themselves. As Reza Khan came to power (becoming Reza Shah in 1925), the dynamic shifted between competing versions of modernity. The shah's government heavily restricted Soviet cultural products, but American and French serials routed through Russia were imported more easily. That serials could circulate so freely is all the more significant when seen alongside the effort of cultural agencies in Moscow to flood the Caspian Sea region with Soviet productions as part of an effort, as Michael Smith puts it, to "civilize the Soviet East."[31]

However free they were from a certain kind of political influence, the junk prints that made it to Tehran by way of Russia were nevertheless physical reminders of a regional mania for serials. The early Soviet mania for adventure serials has been well documented, even as its stakes continue to be explored. Russian and Soviet film historians such as Yuri Tsivian and Denise Youngblood have shown how, by 1916, American films had become the main foreign import and the serial reigned.[32] Tsivian describes how pioneers of the Soviet montage cinema such as Lev Kuleshov turned to American films—to the editing and staging of the Hollywood feature as well as to the anti-realist trick-based structure of the adventure serial—in the development of their own film practice.[33] While Kuleshov's serial-inspired films, such as his kitchen-sink adventure film *The Death Ray* (1925), would have been less available in Tehran, the films that inspired him were part of the weekly program. Despite Reza Shah's resistance to Soviet cultural and political influence, some Tehran cinemas in the 1920s seem to have contracted a strain of "Americanitis" owing at least in part to the films' intermediary homes in Russia. Part of the story of the films' relay between Hollywood and Tehran is the story of their triangulation by significant third parties like this one.

This particular distribution channel and its peripatetic cultural influence can also enrich an understanding of the early attempts to make films in Iran. The politics of serial circulation provide some of the context needed to help position these early attempts, not necessarily at the beginning of a trajectory of Iranian film production that ends with the B movies of the 1950s, but rather at the end of a tradition of exhibition and reception of early cinema's afterlife. The only surviving silent feature made in Iran, *Haji Aqa, Aktor-e Sinema* (Mr. Haji, the movie actor; Ovaness Oganians, 1933), stands as one particularly relevant example. Indeed, only a reading of *Haji Aqa* as belonging to a tradition of cultural reception of cinema could adequately account for how greedily the film appropriates early cinema. Reflexive from the start, the eight-reel comedy tells a conversion story about a religious man who learns to love the cinema after seeing a film that featured him as its unwitting star. The film basically follows the approach of early films like *Uncle Josh at the Moving Picture Show* (Porter, 1902). It satirizes a naïve film spectator in order to simultaneously address the social anxieties surrounding the medium and create a comfortable position from which to understand these anxieties. Throughout his process of conversion, Mr. Haji (a naïve spectator, but not entirely a rube insofar as he represents religious authority) encounters a range of characters from early cinema. These include a Méliès-like magician who makes people and animals disappear, a Luchiano Albertini–like strongman whose strength is necessary to operate an absurdly large winch for removing teeth, and several slapstick characters who chase Mr. Haji around the streets of Tehran. More than a coherent narrative, the film functions as a collage of elements ranging from cinema-of-attractions-type interludes through 1910s-style stunt performances.

Haji Aqa is illustrative here because its all-inclusive, reflexive composition parallels the larger channel of circulation I have been tracing. Its assemblage of dancing, acrobatic stunts, and slapstick gags do recall the Hollywood genre films dominating the nearby cinemas, but equally important are the film's connections to the similar filmmaking efforts to the north. A filmmaker of Armenian origin, Oganians trained in Russia and, upon arrival in Tehran in 1930, he opened the school for acrobatics and film acting featured in *Haji Aqa*'s story. When Oganians shows acrobats flying onto horizontal bars in reverse motion, Dziga Vertov's *Kino-Eye* (1924) footage of athletes seems not far in the background. When Oganians presents as a rapid montage sequence the final screening in which Mr. Haji sees himself in a filmed performance, the influence is clear. The stunts and editing in the film seem to nod to Hollywood action films and to Soviet cinema at the same time.

There were certainly other distribution channels in addition to the one explored here, but the case of American and French films traveling through Russia and then to Iran over the span of a decade highlights the importance of regional circulation in questions of silent film's transnational influence.[34] Indeed, the imperative to reconsider film history in regional, rather than strictly national, terms can more directly address the political nuances and ironies of local cinemas characterized less by the stability of their industries than by their cultures of erratic but vigorous appropriation.

Serials Out of Synch

In its heyday (in the West) in the mid-1910s the silent serial was a blockbuster genre developed by many of the same American and French firms that dominated the world film market. I have been arguing thus far that serial film "junk prints" played a key role in Tehran's silent movie–going culture. Tracing the afterlife of a single serial, *The Tiger's Trail* (Astra/Pathé, 1919), will provide a more detailed picture of the innovations of local exhibitors and the far-reaching flexibility of the serial form. But to clearly grasp these innovations means backing up a moment to understand current assessments of the serial film's form and its reception at home and abroad.

With their episodic format, serials remained amenable to the variety format of early cinema exhibition while also allowing for greater standardization. They followed a proven path (in literature) toward managing repeat business. Nicholas Dulac describes the effects of serial form as synchronizing the spectator with its regularity of content, just as its "to be continued" structure created a desire for more.[35] Hence, in the early and mid-1910s, when feature films were beginning to offer an alternative model of standardizing motion-picture entertainment, the serial's multi-reel format offered a compromise. Medium-length episodes suited the increasing trend toward longer films, but they allowed for standard repetitions from one multi-title program to the next. They could be promoted at great expense, like features, while still remaining flexible for exhibitors' purposes. As a result, serials were far less self-contained as texts. Regularly released episodes benefited in the 1910s from intermedial promotions including public stunts, star discourse, write-in contests, and most importantly, tie-in stories printed in newspapers to complement the film screenings. In many cases these tie-ins supported the aims of standardized management of film reception.

The serial's modern, sensational character continues to motivate a particularly active area of inquiry into its reception. Derived from sensational melodrama, silent serials rejected dramatic realism and instead exploited stunts, suspense, and action (usually in pursuit of a coveted object such as the parcel famously stolen by a human chain formed atop a moving train in *The Tiger's Trail*). As action spectacles, they stood at a charged division of lowbrow and middlebrow entertainments and form a prominent component of the cultural study of modernity in the 1910s.[36] And most important in the present context, these sensational melodramas had an extensive international reach. Adventure serials proved to be highly exportable commodities, fueling local manias for serials around the world, like the Russian "serialitis" noted earlier.

Current investigations of the serial's transcultural circulation have led film historians to a sustained focus on the female star. In her discussion of the "technologies of stardom" Jennifer M. Bean points out the implicit transcultural dimension to the star discourse that made U.S. serial stars like Pearl White such important modern archetypes.[37] Weihong Bao and Rosie Thomas, respectively, have analyzed these translations of Pearl White's stardom, showing how her star persona and the character types she embodied proved highly adaptable to local character types such as the *virangana* warrior woman in India and the *nüxia* female knight-errant in China.[38] While not exactly my focus here, I've chosen to look at *The Tiger's Trail,* a Ruth Roland vehicle, in part because it adds another local variant to this recent scholarship. Roland, like White, worked in the United States for the Pathé company. She had, by 1919, succeeded White as the company's principal serial star. Her success on Tehran screens points to the growing relevance of transnational studies of the serial star. The broader cultural implications of this success deserve more attention than the scope of this essay will allow.

The records of *The Tiger's Trail*'s exhibition mark it as a significant, but not atypical, film event in Tehran. In terms of the number of episodes screened, the diligence of the advertisements, and the tie-in material, *The Tiger's Trail* was among the more complete serials promoted in *Ettela'at.* The newspaper provides a wealth of material about which individual episodes screened, and where. It had a long run at the Grand Cinema, and then screened shortly after at Vakili's Cinema Zardoshtian for women on the north side of the city.[39] *Ettela'at*'s premiere announcement for *The Tiger's Trail* signals the importance of its acrobatic star, its cost, and its international success.

> Grand Cinema, Lalezar
> Friday, Saturday, and Sunday Evening.
> The 1st through the 3rd of the month of Dey [December 23rd–25th 1927].
> Famous and unparalleled serial—*The Tiger's Face* [*The Tiger's Trail*]
> In six episodes
> One of the most celebrated masterpieces by American artists.
> With astonishing acrobatic action—by Ruth Roland, the famous actor.
> This serial cost millions, and has a cast of thousands. Seeing this story of a brave hearted young girl, who is fighting for what is rightfully hers, you will sympathize with her sensational courage.
> This serial has been shown all over Europe and America numerous times. Each day it attracts more and more viewers.[40]

As one of the more extensively promoted serials, *The Tiger's Trail* might seem better suited than most serials in Tehran to the strategies of synchronizing audiences, printed texts, and images with the organized release of each episode. But the tie-in material in this case actually undercuts this assumption. If studies of other reception contexts highlight the serial's connection to planned efficiency and emerging mass marketing, this case highlights its less examined affinity for improvised, creative presentation in local markets. The *Ettela'at* ads offer evidence of the attempt to replicate foreign serial promotion, but the physical changes to the available footage, the damaged or otherwise missing reels, subjected the mechanisms of serial exhibition to continuous redesign. The modular format and tie-in promotion may have been designed to manage a certain type of relationship between film and spectator, but in the films' afterlife these modules and their tie-in stories proved much more pliable.

The Tiger's Trail had undergone multiple transformations even before reaching Tehran. It was made in the United States and distributed by Pathé, but it came to Iran by way of the French Pathé release. The French Pathé version, *Le tigre sacré,* had twelve episodes, as compared with the American version's fifteen, and it appeared on French screens seven months after the completion of the American release. Seven years after the Paris premiere, the film began its Tehran run at the Grand Cinema as *The Holy Tiger,* a translation of the French title, and occasionally as *The Tiger's Face,* a title derived from one of the episodes. The episodes were promoted with tie-in stories as well as advertisements. These also came from France (although the advertisements describe the serial as an "American" masterpiece). The novelist Guy de Téramond had published feuilleton tie-in stories in *L'Avenir* concurrent with Pathé's release of each episode. These were compiled shortly after as a *ciné-roman.*[41] *Ettela'at* published 1,000–2,000-word translations of all twelve of de Téramond's chapters over a three-week period beginning December 20, 1927.[42]

Exhibitors in Iran partly replicated the promotion strategies that accompanied serial episodes when they were first released nearly a decade prior, but a combination of intentional and unavoidable changes to the programs radically altered the outcomes. *Ettela'at* published feuilletons that were often not in synch with the corresponding film episodes, and patrons of the movie theaters further down the chain of distribution would see the films long after the newspaper printed the tie-in story. *The Tiger's Trail* was no exception. Since only about half of the series made it from the original distribution centers to screens in Tehran, the exhibitors had to modify the timing of the releases. The gaps in the film program offer some indication of the modifications necessary for such a spotty program. Feuilleton episodes five, six, seven, and eleven appear to fill in for missing footage. They are accompanied only by general ads promoting the Grand Cinema, while other story episodes carry announcements that the corresponding film episode will be screened at the cinema that evening. Like many of the serials that played at the Grand Cinema, the episodes were then given a second run at Vakili's Cinema Zardoshtian. Here they fell further out of synch with the printed stories.

These serialized story versions of the films, as a result of their loose fit with the film programs, often exceeded the function of clarifying plot points for filmgoers.[43] While exhibitors did utilize printed plot summaries in many cases, live narration was still the most effective way to ensure that the audience engaged with the films' stories. Even with the translations of de Téramond's chapters, *The Tiger's Face* screenings were preceded by "an oral introduction for the gentlemen who have missed some of the episodes."[44] The translations of de Téramond's work could not really substitute for on-site narration. Low literacy rates aside, his story episodes often spanned wide and erratic gaps in the film programming. Live narrators could always improvise. The printed stories' regularity and completeness set them apart from the irregularly sequenced films. The printed stories had a definite value, but it was not primarily as a substitute for live narration.

During the intervening decade between production and exhibition, reels, scenes, and titles inevitably went missing and were re-edited. The shipments must have been a programmer's nightmare, with odd reels, unreliable labeling, and translation issues. In many instances, the films were shaped more by the intermediary distributors' scissors than by the original production company. In *Esquisse d'une psychologie du cinéma,* André Malraux offers a rare account of these kinds of transformations:

> In Persia, I once saw a film that does not exist. It was called *The Life of Charlie.* Persian cinemas show their films in the open air, while black cats look on from the walls surrounding the audience. The Armenian exhibitors had artfully compiled Chaplin's shorts into a single film. The resulting feature film was surprising: the myth of Chaplin appeared in its pure state.[45]

In explaining how Chaplin transcends the physical manipulations of his films internationally, Malraux indicates how extensive these manipulations could be. The film he describes seems closer to a Soviet compilation film than to a program of shorts. It is likely that distributors frequently gave serial episodes a similar treatment.

The *Ettela'at* advertisements give little indication of modifications to individual episodes of *The Tiger's Trail,* but if the missing and re-edited footage within reels was comparable to the percentage of missing episodes, then the divergences between the *ciné-roman* (itself a double translation) and the films were considerable. Mistakes in the programming schedule offer some clues about this state of the films upon arrival in Tehran. At the outset of the Grand Cinema screening of *The Tiger's Face,* the advertisements announce repeatedly that the cinema will show six episodes.[46] By mid-January 1928, eight episodes of the series had screened. The eighth episode corresponded to the twelfth and final feuilleton episode. These mistakes in counting the episodes were repeated in different ads. The exhibitor may have tracked down another two episodes elsewhere, or he may have eventually discovered them within the shipment. Whether these specific mistakes in the program resulted from assessments of the prints or the printing of the advertisements, shipments containing half of the original footage would have made these kinds of revisions difficult to completely avoid.

All of these factors worked in concert to disrupt the timing that had made the serial such an efficient organizer of mass audiences across other national borders. As Paul Moore has shown in a detailed study of exhibition history in Toronto in the 1910s, the serial format helped to consolidate multiple episodes, promotional materials, and screening locations and thus to synchronize a mass audience across North America.[47] Since it enabled many episodes to play "at once" in multiple locations, accompanied by tie-ins in the daily papers, the serial form fashioned an integrated network of multiple texts. One essential feature of this network was a tiered hierarchy based on first- and second-run theater locations. Moore's systematic analyses of these effects on imported films in Toronto cast the serial's diversity in Tehran into sharp relief. Whereas brief planned delays reinforced synchronization and mass organization in Toronto, extended unplanned delays, missing reels, and unpredictable tie-ins undermined or even reversed these effects, even as Tehran exhibitors partially imitated strategies of synchronized promotion.

One aim of this planned organization of the serial was to engage a wider public with a sensational genre often considered more narrowly as lowbrow entertainment. And just as serials did not foster mass culture in the Middle East the way they began to in North America, the association of serial melodrama with lowbrow culture does not exactly fit their reception in Tehran either. The class associations of the films and their tie-in stories could vary widely. For a newspaper made up of only a few pages per issue, it is remarkable that the translations of tie-in stories for each serial episode sometimes spread over multiple pages. *Ettela'at* likely devoted so much space to the film stories because serialized stories (often translated work by foreign authors) already formed an important component of the Iranian periodical press. The translated serial story's elite status in some papers, combined with the arrhythmic pairing of *ciné-roman* and serial, mark these stories as special features, as amusements in themselves for a reading public that primarily represented the educated class far from the lowbrow.

Because the serials in Tehran were undeniably out of date, exhibitors faced a challenge in marketing these films as legitimate works. The blurbs in the ads would of course not want to give any sense of the film programs as being obsolete, so it might seem counterintuitive to make note of a film's age and intermediary life. But rather than attempting to conceal the reality of their films' age, exhibitors often embraced it as an asset for promotion. The last line of the *Tiger's*

Trail advertisement cited above, about "attracting new viewers daily," is one example among many. Other advertisements, such as those for *The Secrets of an Invisible Woman* (probably episodes from Pathé's *La femme inconnue*), are billed as having more cultural merit because they played in the United States for many years.[48] The promotional line for an American serial with the Persian title *The Invisible Protector* boasts: "The film has screened around the world."[49] These ads express a cosmopolitan sentiment that turns the films' road-worn status on its head through a rhetoric of world travel. Exhibitors used their long trade life, the same trade life that rendered these scratched, warped, and heavily spliced prints little more than the waste products of yesterday's business, as a way to elevate their films' status to something like "classics" of the international screen. The trickier it was to promote junk prints as of-the-moment fashions, the easier it was to creatively promote them as modern "classics."

These "classics" endured, even as they lost legitimacy to dramatic realist forms and feature films in other parts of the world. Some of the established accounts of early Iranian film history, which frequently return to pioneering work by Farrokh Ghaffary, argue that the serial form lost prestige after the introduction of *The Thief of Bagdad* and *The Count of Monte Cristo* in the late 1920s.[50] This is already an extension of the serial's longevity, but the screening notices indicate that there is even more to the story. By the early 1930s the advertisements do reflect an increased concentration of feature films, but they also show how serials continued to maintain a strong presence by adapting to the increase in feature exhibition. One discernible trend involved "featurizing" the serials by projecting two or three episodes at a single screening. The serials do not appear to be any more complete in the early 1930s than they were in the mid-1920s (still not much more than half the number of original episodes), so this adaptation would have served the exhibitors' practical need to assemble a program out of odd reels while also serving a demand for longer-format evening entertainment. *The 2000 Year-Old Woman, The Brass Bullet* ("with the famous Juanita [Hansen]"; 1918), *The Fast Express* (retitled *Death Train;* 1924), Louis Feuillade's *Barrabas* (in only six of the original twelve episodes; 1919), and *The Iron Man* ("the international serial with Luciano Albertini"; 1924) each screened two or three episodes at a time.[51] On occasion, perhaps because of the familiarity of this screening format, the exhibitors mistakenly (or creatively) billed feature films as screening in two-episode segments. The early-1930s notices for Jean Epstein's *Mauprat* (1926) and Harry Piel's *The False Verdict* (1924) make this mistake, even as they provide details concerning the actors in the features.[52] The act structure in features and the episode structure in serials appear to be to some extent interchangeable in the film descriptions. Like *The Tiger's Trail,* with its imported tie-in story and well-traveled reputation, these examples indicate how widely serials' cultural legitimacy could vary depending on the exhibition context. Positing sharp class distinctions between the serial and the full feature format might in this case belie the ways in which cultural capital could be imaginatively constructed through shrewd programming and promotion.

Ironies of Appropriation

I want to follow up these observations with a final non-serial example of a reconfigured "classic." The Tehran exhibition of D. W. Griffith's *The Fall of Babylon* shows just how counterintuitive and politically significant the afterlives of these silent-film prints could be. Long before its wide global circulation, the film had already endured one of the most famous re-editions in the silent era. In an effort to salvage something more marketable out of his epic *Intolerance* (1916), Griffith extracted its Babylonian story for release as a stand-alone feature in 1919. In this form, the film did prove marketable in Tehran, enough to reappear with some frequency in the early years of *Ettela'at.* Notices for the screenings as celebrations of Iranian history were listed on the front page of the paper as well as in the advertisements section. They indicate that the reels of *The Fall of Babylon* were dusted off regularly for screenings promoted as special events.

The film proved well suited to local and official appropriation, where its import status and the draw of its stars worked in concert with its local appeal. The acting talent of Constance Talmadge competed for space in the advertisements with the historical interest of the setting.[53] In some cases the exhibitors adapted Griffith's own famous gestures toward historical authenticity for this end. Their advertisements paraphrased the film's intertitles that footnote the historical sources for the film's images. A 1926 screening notice for the Grand Cinema invites viewers "who have read the history of Iran . . . to get acquainted with the forefathers of your country personally" by seeing "the great historical city of Babylon, its buildings, gardens, and towers, with your own eyes."[54] A 1930 screening notice at the Cinema Sepah explains: "For this glorious film the filmmakers built an accurate replica of Belshazzar's famous fortress walls."[55] The advertisements borrow wholesale the rhetoric of moving-picture re-creations as guaranteeing historical accuracy, a rhetoric that Griffith had honed in *The Birth of a Nation* (1915). As accurate replicas the architectural details enabled the film to function as a kind of local, place-specific tourism while remaining recognizable as a featured import in which "one scene alone cost millions to make."[56]

The greatest irony of this afterlife of *Intolerance* lies in its mistranslatability. The film regularly screened as part of celebrations like the Persian New Year. Its claims to historical accuracy, transparency, and universal appeal were freely borrowed, but the film's message was not.

> New Year's Festivities
> —Grand Cinema—

> On Wednesday and Thursday, the first two evenings of spring
> Film—*Cyrus the Great*—Conquering Babylon
> The Grand Cinema, the preeminent film exhibition hall, has organized an event to honor our customers and celebrate our Iranian history on this special occasion of the New Year. We will show the famous film—*Cyrus the Great*—about the conqueror, whose name is the pride of Iran and Iranians. No one who is interested in this story should delay seeing the film.[57]

It is tempting to speculate how many times this print may have been re-edited prior to this screening, especially after reading Yuri Tsivian's essay in this volume on the Soviet re-edit of one of Griffith's other classics. But scissors are only one tool among many. Radically recut or not, this film clearly conveys a new message. A story about a fall has become a story about a conquest. The narrative of *Intolerance* and *The Fall of Babylon,* in which the Persian army represents the bellicose intolerance of the era, is aggressively misread in *Cyrus the Great.* The advertisements for the screenings of this film emphasize the growth of a civilization rather than the lessons of catastrophe, so resolutely that Reza Shah could be connected to the film's representation of Cyrus. Sidestepping Griffith's aims of realizing film's potential as a universal language, Reza Shah's supporters constructed an alternate epic narrative, one that obscures the historical contingencies of his very recent rise to power by creating an image of this modern regime as a continuation of the ancient Persian Empire. In other words, these special-event screenings enabled local misreadings of a film famous for its ambition to eliminate local misreadings.

In *The Fall of Babylon* and in each of the examples outlined here, these inventive promotions challenge simplistic conceptions of periphery and center. An interpretation would be lacking if it framed the liberally translated tie-in stories one-dimensionally as fostering progressive variations on film fandom without recognizing how they also functioned as special features imported by a savvy promoter for a small, mandarin reading public. In searching a cinema culture for adaptations to dislocated films, it is just as important to identify how cinema's modern vernacular often intertwined with nationalist discourses.[58] Everyday language was heavily politicized under Reza Shah. He banned theater in Armenian in 1927 and soon after launched a massive language reform campaign.[59] Imported, translated silent era films adapted to this environment. Their exhibitions could integrate with a regime in which sovereignty relied more on the centralized spectacle of modernization than on its sustainability. The advertisements and tie-in publicity, developed during an earlier period in these films' history and creatively misused to promote the films as modern classics, could overlap with the cosmopolitan modernity aggressively promoted by Reza Shah. If the publicity helped to localize the reception of the films, the relation between a bottom-up reflective reception and the official government's "modernization from above" remained complicated and unresolved.[60]

Whether in service of progressive improvisation or demagogic appropriation, these uses of junk serials and other "masterpieces" betray second-hand film as a kind of conspicuous living artifact. Even if the 1920s readership of *Ettela'at*'s tie-in publicity was limited, the "world travel" rhetoric was commercially motivated, and the modernity of these films was appropriated as a spectacle of authority, there is also the possibility that the film-going public in Tehran, because of the various adaptations to the serials' age, wear, and missing reels, could experience these films as objects with histories in a way that resonates with other re-viewing cultures. The increase in scholarly work on the institutions that redefined films as historical objects after their commercial viability had waned speaks, albeit in an oblique way, to the types of film culture I have been tracing here.[61] It is certainly important not to overstate affinities in placing these local appropriations in some relation to the well-known second-hand cinema clubs in, say, London or Paris that famously fostered an early historical awareness of cinema in the silent era. A wide gap will always remain between the deliberately out-of-date programs at 1920s European film clubs and the necessarily out-of-date programs pieced together in 1920s Tehran. But the motivations and methods used to understand and evaluate each of these practices might reveal something compelling about the other. Just as film historians like Malte Hagener have worked to show how avant-garde second-hand screening practices, which he associates with "the birth of film history," were more eclectic, mainstream, and improvisational than the participants' writings would lead one to assume, research into the eclectic, mainstream screenings at cinemas in Tehran can begin to show how these events generated another sense of film's historical value through their creative adaptation to "obsolete" footage.[62]

I make these assertions tentatively here with the intention of inviting more discussion about the kinds of historical reflection available in emergent, second-hand exhibition contexts. The question of the connection between a film culture's historical awareness and the awareness of celluloid as material is not a geographically limited question, nor does its relevance end in the silent era. A generation later in Iran, the practice of collecting fragments of celluloid from Hollywood films became a widespread practice among preadolescent boys. Stories of these film-notebook collections and the inventive attempts to project still film frames (in need of oral histories) are well known among the children of those who grew up shortly after World War II in cities across Iran.[63] These broken pieces of junk prints lovingly gleaned from the floors of projection booths stand as reminders of the extended life of celluloid and its importance in the history of the material awareness of film. Perhaps an attention to the morphology of the print in early commercial film culture in Tehran will draw attention to the urgent relevance of the material that remains.

Notes

I would like to thank the editors of *Silent Cinema and the Politics of Space*, together with Cloé Drieu, Alyssa Gabbay, Hamid Naficy, and Jaleh Pirnazar, for their invaluable feedback on earlier versions of this essay. Thanks also to Sahar Rastakhiz for her skilled research assistance at UC Berkeley.

1. These expanded maps have appeared at several silent film conferences over the past few years. The presentations and publications surrounding the Women and the Silent Screen conference, for instance, have recovered ephemeral films in Mexico, transnational star discourse between the United States and China, and exhibition practices in Swedish provinces. Participants at the 2008 Domitor conference in Girona and Perpignan explored the idea of early cinema and "the peripheral" in its multiple senses. See François Amy de la Bretèque, Michel Cade, Angel Quintana Morraja, and Jordi Pons I Busquet, eds., *Les cinémas périphériques dans la périod des premiers temps / Peripheral Early Cinemas* (Perpignan, France: University of Perpigan Press, 2010), as well as the proceedings of the 2006 Domitor conference: Richard Abel, Giorgio Bertellini, and Rob King, eds., *Early Cinema and the "National"* (New Barnet, UK: John Libbey, 2008).

2. Zhang Zhen discusses the need to expand early cinema studies' periodization for Shanghai cinema in her *An Amorous History of the Silver Screen: Shanghai Cinema, 1896–1937* (Chicago: University of Chicago Press, 2005).

3. I use the term "translation" here in hopes that it will resonate with Laura Isabel Serna's essay in this volume on the literal translation of intertitles for U.S. films shown in Mexico.

4. See Kristin Thompson, *Exporting Entertainment: America in the World Film Market, 1907–34* (London: British Film Institute, 1985).

5. "Syria's Picture Shows," *Motography* 7.7 (1912).

6. See the William Selig Papers, Margaret Herrick Library Special Collections, Academy of Motion Pictures Arts and Sciences, Los Angeles. The majority of correspondence about global distribution in the collection comes from London intermediaries such as the New Bioscope Trading Company and J. W. Wright and Son. The collection also contains a few letters from exhibitors in major cities in the Middle East and North Africa hoping to establish direct and more exclusive trade in Selig films.

7. Homer Croy, "Shadows of Asia," *Photoplay* 11 (1917): 63.

8. "The Cinematograph in Aden," *Near East and India* 32.862 (1927).

9. Ibid.

10. "Egyptian Picture-Goers," *Near East and India* 30.798 (1926).

11. "Syria's Picture Shows."

12. In linking questions of cultural translation with the physical life of a print, the interest in global secondhand cinema can draw impetus from the shifting interest in the film preservation and archiving community toward orphan films. Characterized recently by Dan Streible as unprotected "unprofitable (an orphan drug) [or] discontinued . . . (an orphan automobile)," the growing interest in orphan films not only marks an increase in the drive to preserve ephemeral films but also reflects increasing critical attention to these films' discontinued, unprofitable, or obsolete character as something worthy of critical attention in itself. See Dan Streible, "The Role of Orphan Films in the 21st Century Archive," *Cinema Journal* 46.3 (2007), 124–128.

13. Valentia Steer, *The Romance of the Cinema: A Short Record of the Development of the Most Popular Form of Amusement of the Day* (London: C. Arthur Pearson, 1913), 40.

14. See Ernst Bloch, "Nonsynchronism and the Obligation to Its Dialectics," *New German Critique*, no. 11 (1977), 22–38.

15. See Nicky Gregson and Louise Crewe, *Second-Hand Cultures* (Oxford: Berg, 2003), and Susan Strasser, *Waste and Want: A Social History of Trash* (New York: Metropolitan Books, 1999).

16. See Rem Koolhaas, "Junkspace," *October* 100 (2002), 175–190.

17. For more on the fantasies of positing one place as the past of another, see Arjun Appadurai, "Disjuncture and Difference in the Global Cultural Economy," *Public Culture* 2.2 (1990), 1–24.

18. Laurent Mannoni, *Le grand art de la lumière et de l'ombre: Archéologie du cinema* (Paris: Nathan, 1995); C. W. Ceram, *Archaeology of the Cinema* (New York: Harcourt Brace, 1965).

19. To be sure, some of the most valuable collections of films have spent the majority of their lives in junk heaps in basements or at the bottom of frozen lakes.

20. Michael Shanks, David Platt, and William Rathje, "The Perfume of Garbage: Modernity and the Archaeological," *Modernism/Modernity* 11.1 (2004), 61–83.

21. On "modernist dreams of an other archaeology," see the introduction to *Modernism/Modernity* 11.1 (2004): 1–16.

22. Shanks et al. remark that humans are one of the only species not attracted to garbage's colors and smells. They derive "the perfume of garbage" from Dominique Laporte's *History of Shit* (Cambridge, MA: MIT Press, 2000), but a better analogy for a film historian would be the olfactory similarities between garbage and decaying nitrate and acetate.

23. Hamid Naficy, "Self-Othering: A Postcolonial Discourse on Cinematic First Contacts," in *The Pre-Occupation of Postcolonial Studies*, ed. Fawzia Afzal-Khan and Kalpana Seshadri-Crooks (Durham, NC: Duke University Press, 2000); Naficy, *A Social History of Iranian Cinema*, vol. 1, *The Artisanal Era, 1897–1941* (Durham, NC: Duke University Press, 2011).

24. Negar Mottahedeh, "Collection and Recollection: On Studying the Early History of Motion Pictures in Iran," *Early Popular Visual Culture* 6.2 (2008): 103–120.

25. See Stephen Bottomore, "'She's Just Like My Granny, Where's Her Crown?' Monarchs and Movies, 1896–1916," in *Celebrating 1895: The Centenary of Cinema*, ed. John Fullerton (Sydney: John Libbey, 1998), 172–181.

26. See Negar Mottahedeh, *Representing the Unrepresentable: Images of Reform from the Qajars to the Islamic Republic of Iran* (Syracuse, NY: Syracuse University Press, 2008).

27. Stephen Bottomore, "The Sultan and the Cinematograph," *Early Popular Visual Culture* 6.2 (2008): 121–144.

28. Mohammad Ali Issari, *Cinema in Iran, 1900–1979* (London: Scarecrow Press, 1989).

29. Henry S. Villard, "Film Importers Face Difficulties in Persia," *Commerce Reports* 14 (1931).

30. On Reza Khan's relation to Atatürk, see Erik Touraj and Zürcher Atabaki, *Men of Order: Authoritarian Modernization under Atatürk and Reza Shah* (London: I. B. Tauris, 2004).

31. Michael Smith, "Cinema for the Soviet East: National Fact and Revolutionary Fiction in Early Azerbaijani Film," *Slavic Review* 56.4 (1997): 645–678.

32. Denise Youngblood, *Movies for the Masses: Popular Cinema and Soviet Society in the 1920s* (Cambridge, UK: Cambridge University Press, 1992).

33. Yuri Tsivian, "Between the Old and the New: Soviet Film Culture in 1918–1924," *Griffithiana* 55/56 (1996): 15–63.

34. On the advantages of "the regional" as a frame for historical analysis, see Hamid Naficy, "For a Theory of Regional Cinemas: Middle Eastern, North African, and Central Asian Cinemas," *Early Popular Visual Culture* 6.2 (2008), 97–102.

35. Nicholas Dulac, "Distribution sérielle et synchronization du spectateur aux premiers temps du cinéma," in *Networks of Entertainment: Early Film Distribution 1895–1915*, ed. Frank Kessler and Nanna Verhoeff (Eastleigh, UK: John Libbey, 2007), 167–179.

36. See Ben Singer, *Melodrama and Modernity: Early Sensational Cinema and Its Contexts* (New York: Columbia University Press, 2001).

37. Jennifer M. Bean, "Technologies of Early Stardom and the Extraordinary Body," *Camera Obscura* 16.3 (2001): 8–57.

38. Weihong Bao, "From Pearl White to White Rose Woo: Tracing the Vernacular Body of *Nüxia* in Chinese Silent Cinema, 1927–1931," *Camera Obscura* 20.3 (2005): 193–231; Rosie Thomas, "Not Quite (Pearl) White: Fearless Nadia, Queen of the Stunts," in *Bollyworld: Popular Indian Cinema through a Transnational Lens,* ed. Raminder Kaur and Ajay Sinha (New Delhi: Sage, 2005), 35–69.

39. Vakili established the Cinema Zardoshtan, or Zoroastrian Cinema, in one of several attempts to provide gender-segregated screening space (a common problem for exhibitors throughout the region). Other solutions included setting up physical divisions in the Grand Cinema space, complete with separate entrances for women and men: one through the main box office and one through the attached Grand Hotel lobby.

40. *Ettela'at,* Mehr 27 [October 20] 1306 [1927]. All translations from *Ettela'at* are my own.

41. Guy de Téramond, *Le tigre sacré* (Paris: Les Romans Cinéma, 1920).

42. *Ettela'at,* Azar 28 [December 20] 1306 [1927].

43. For a discussion of the ways in which tie-in promotion exceeded narrative clarification in the United States, see Shelly Stamp, *Movie-Struck Girls: Women and Motion Picture Culture after the Nickelodeon* (Princeton, NJ: Princeton University Press, 2000), 102–125.

44. *Ettela'at,* Dey 3 [December 25] 1306 [1927].

45. André Malraux, *Esquisse d'une psychologie du cinéma* (Paris: Gallimard, 1946), 34 (translation mine).

46. *Ettela'at,* Azar 28 [December 20] 1306 [1927].

47. Paul Moore, *Now Playing: Early Moviegoing and the Regulation of Fun* (Albany: SUNY Press, 2008).

48. The advertisement for *Secrets of an Invisible Woman* describes the film as having been "shown in America for three consecutive years" (*Ettela'at,* Mehr 27 [October 20], 1307 [1927]).

49. *Ettala'at,* Shahrivar 29 [September 21] 1306 [1927].

50. See Issari, *Cinema in Iran,* 64–65; Hamid Reza Sadr, *Iranian Cinema: A Political History* (London: I. B. Tauris, 2006), 12–26. See also Farrokh Ghaffary, "Cinema I: History of Cinema in Persia," in *Encyclopedia Iranica Online* (2005); and Ghaffary, *Le cinéma en Iran* (Tehran: Conseil de la Culture et des Arts, Centre d'Étude et de la Coordination Culturelle, 1973).

51. *The Brass Bullet* screened at the Grand Cinema three episodes at a time (*Ettela'at,* Shahrivar 5 [August 25] 1307 [1928]). The Cinema Tehran showed *Barrabas* (*Ettela'at,* Farvardin 27 [April 16] 1309 [1930]) and *The Iron Man* (touting Albertini's celebrity). The Cinema Sepah screened *The Fast Express* as *Death Train,* announcing ten episodes (*Ettela'at,* Dey 14 [January 4] 1309 [1931]). The last notice for *Death Train* is listed as the "fourth and final" (*Ettala'at,* Bahman 7 [January 27] 1309 [1931]).

52. *Mauprat* and *The False Verdict* both screened at the Cinema Sepah.

53. *Ettela'at,* Farvardin 27 [April 16] 1309 [1930].

54. *Ettela'at,* Azar 19 [December 11] 1305 [1926].

55. *Ettela'at,* Farvardin 27 [April 16] 1309 [1930].

56. *Ettela'at,* Azar 19 [December 11] 1305 [1926].

57. *Ettela'at,* Esfand 28 [March 19] 1306 [1928].

58. My essay is indebted to Miriam Hansen's conception of 1920s cinema as a global vernacular. The examples of nationalist appropriations of cinema's modernity given here serve to reinforce Hansen's claims about the cinema's role as a modern vernacular while highlighting an extreme local variation in the political uses of discourse surrounding cinema's modernity.

See Miriam Bratu Hansen, "The Mass Production of the Senses: Classical Cinema as Vernacular Modernism," *Modernism/Modernity* 6.2 (1999): 59–77, and Hansen, "Vernacular Modernism: Tracking Cinema on a Global Scale," in *World Cinemas, Transnational Perspectives,* ed. Nataša Ďurovičová and Kathleen Newman (London: Routledge, 2009), 287–314.

59. See Willem Floor, *The History of Theater in Iran* (Washington, DC: Mage, 2005), 259, and John Perry, "Language Reform in Turkey and Iran," *International Journal of Middle East Studies* 17 (1985): 295–311.

60. On Reza Khan's modernization from above, see Nikki Keddie, *Modern Iran: Roots and Results of Revolution,* updated edition (New Haven, CT: Yale University Press, 2006).

61. See Lee Grieveson and Haidee Wasson, eds., *Inventing Film Studies* (Durham, NC: Duke University Press, 2008).

62. Malte Hagener, "Programming Attractions: Avant-Garde Exhibition Practices in the 1920s and 1930s," in *The Cinema of Attractions Reloaded,* ed. Wanda Strauven (Amsterdam: Amsterdam University Press, 2006), 265–279.

63. Hamid Dabashi gives a brief account of his own experience with this practice in the introduction to his book on contemporary Iranian cinema: "We would collect and trade these pairs of slides pretty much as American kids did baseball cards, except that procuring them was far more of an adventure than paying a visit to a local store. We found hours of pleasure in just sitting and viewing these slides against sunlight or a lamp." Hamid Dabashi, *Close-Up: Iranian Cinema, Past, Present and Future* (New York: Verso, 2001), 40. I can personally relate many similar stories. In one instance, after explaining to me how easy it was to build a makeshift film-still projector out of cardboard and scrap lenses, my father tried to convince me to make such a project the center of a fifth-grade science presentation. The projector's design, based on the ones he recalled having made in Tehran in the early 1950s, was elegant but not entirely functional.

5 Translations and Transportation

Toward a Transnational History of the Intertitle

Laura Isabel Serna

Of all the narrative resources of transitional and classical era silent cinema, the intertitle is perhaps the one most taken for granted—taken for granted both in its status as a prerequisite for narrative legibility and, paradoxically, its assumed superfluity. Historians' consistent if passing attention to the intertitle, embodied in sentences that read "then an intertitle appears . . . ," confirms the former, while repeated affirmations of silent cinema's universally legible visual economy attest to the latter.[1] Only recently have scholars begun to reconsider the function of the intertitle in silent cinema as well as the role of subtitling and other translation practices more generally.[2]

This essay approaches the translated intertitle (sometimes referred to in the trade press as a leader or simply a title) as a crucial element both materially and figuratively in the transnational circulation of cinema during the silent era. Its importance was rendered graphically in a 1927 chart of Famous Players–Lasky's Foreign Department (Figure 5.1), in which the Translation Department and the Transportation Department flank the distribution operations that sent films across the globe. To my mind this is a perfect reckoning of the link between translation, in the sense of text being transformed from one language into another, and transportation, a different sort of movement from one condition or place to another.

Here, I examine the intertitle and its translation as evidence of concrete business practices that facilitated the dispersion of U.S. cinema across the globe—the catalyst for debates over language and cultural imperialism—and as a narrative element that vividly demonstrates the ways in which individuals, audiences, or even nations might have contested the meanings produced by those filmic texts. In doing so, I draw on sources related to the distribution of U.S. films in Latin America, which range from the English-language and Spanish-language trade press, archival documents related to negotiations between Mexico and the United States regarding films deemed "offensive" by the Mexican government,

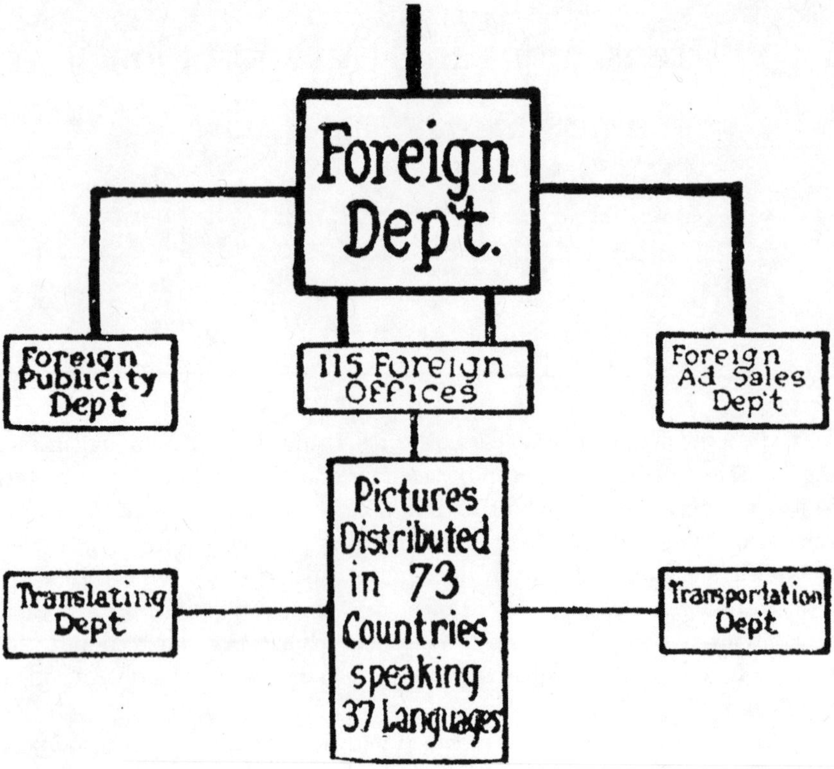

Figure 5.1 A chart shows the role of translation and transportation in the Foreign Department's distribution activities. Reproduced from *The Story of the Films*, edited by Joseph Patrick Kennedy, Cambridge, MA: Harvard University Graduate School of Business Administration, 1927.

and the popular press in Mexico. I focus primarily on Mexico, a case that has its particularities but will, I believe, illustrate a methodology necessary to any consideration of silent cinema's notorious flow across national borders.

Using this case study, I suggest that sustained attention to the practical aspects and cultural politics of intertitle translation can reveal shifts in production and marketing practices, draw our attention to the politics of narrative legibility in particular historical contexts, and deepen our understanding of the way in which interpretive communities formed in motion picture theaters across the globe. While Mexico, like Latin American markets more generally, might have been relatively marginal to the U.S. industry's primary sources of foreign revenue, understanding these practices of translation and their politics is critical to creating a more nuanced account of the development of mass audiences for cinema in Latin America and to thinking through the issue of translation in regard to the "universal art" of silent cinema more generally.[3]

Recent scholarship has made contradictory claims for intertitles, both as signs of "Americanness" and as signs of "international traffic." Most recently Torey Liepa has argued that intertitles, as they were used to convey vernacular speech, functioned as a key mechanism by which American films became American for both domestic and foreign audiences. In his consideration of titles and the international market, Liepa traces initial experiments with intertitle translation before World War I and the "normative commercial procedures of translation" that were established after the war.[4] Strikingly, at the end of this account, Liepa dismisses the far-off markets represented by Asia and Latin America and baldly states that "more often these [foreign] audiences represented smaller communities not yet fully plugged into a global network of commercial capital, but rather on its fringes."[5] Foreign audiences might have been at the outer edges of global commercial networks in a literal, geographic sense—and perhaps from the perspective of the metropole, which consistently created an "other" in order to center itself—but those far-off lands were crucial to the day-to-day functioning of commercial capital insofar as they supplied natural resources, low-wage labor, and potential markets for mass-produced goods, including cinema.

Abé Mark Nornes acknowledges the importance of these peripheral markets when he declares the translated intertitle a sign of "international traffic."[6] He too presents a chronological account of the development of dialogue titles and their translation, but in contrast to Liepa he focuses precisely on those foreign markets, drawing examples from a range of contexts including Cuba, Transylvania, India, South Africa, and Japan. For Nornes, the varied practices he found—bilingual and multilingual titles, loose rather than literal translations, and the minimal use of titles for maximum portability—lead him to conclude that translatability is "built into [the original film's] substance," a claim he makes for sound as well as silent film.[7]

It is worthwhile, at this conceptual juncture between specificity and potential universality, to look back at the position staked out by Ruth Vasey in *The World According to Hollywood, 1918–1939*. There, in preparation for a discussion about the crisis generated by the introduction of sound technology—that crisis being the suddenly immutable nature of cinema—Vasey rehearses the ways in which the silent filmic text could be altered. After considering the snip-snip of the censor's shears, the free-hand with which exhibitors "shaped" their programs to fit time constraints and local tastes, and the wide-ranging musical practices that could give the same film an entirely different feel, she pronounces the intertitle "the principal site of international adaptability in the silent format."[8] Where Liepa claims cultural specificity for silent film intertitles and Nornes sees translated intertitles as just one example of the possibility of linguistic subversion of cinematic texts that continues today, Vasey asserts that silent titles, themselves "vague and euphemistic," served to clarify, though not concretize, an art form characterized by "metaphor and allusion" and opened silent film texts to an infinite number of interpretations that would be foreclosed by the introduction of sound and the standardization of classical Hollywood.[9]

Perhaps what the industry wanted to standardize during the silent period was the notion of universal appeal. As Miriam Hansen has argued, the conceit of film as a "universal language" circulated widely and with varying ideological emphases throughout the silent period.[10] Examples of this rhetorical hubris include the not-so-subtle name of Carl Laemmle's Universal Film Manufacturing Company (later Universal Pictures), whose advertising laboriously conveyed its global aspirations. In like fashion, the American Projecting Company pronounced in 1921 that "pictures have no language" (Figure 5.2), while others, such as Goldwyn-Cosmopolitan, claimed that their films were decidedly polyglot, if not universally legible (Figure 5.3).[11] While, as Hansen elaborates, many prominent figures—such as D. W. Griffith—expressed utopian hopes for this allegedly universal language, silent films more clearly spoke the language of international capitalism. In 1927, then secretary of commerce Herbert Hoover, speaking before the MPPDA (Motion Picture Producers and Distributors of America) and diplomatic corps members from almost all the Latin American nations, proclaimed: "They [films] speak a universal language" that fosters not only the "interchange of intellectual and social ideas," but also "mutual trade and commerce."[12] Hoover's comments can be understood as having two meanings: first, that films foster trade in "tropical produce," "natural resources," and "capital," a concept he elaborates throughout his speech;[13] and second, more implicitly, that film's universality (or translatability) facilitates the transnational film trade itself.

But beyond pointing to the fact that translation facilitated international commerce, how can we approach the cultural work performed by those translated intertitles? Like any other product, films needed to appeal to their audiences—not just convey information—and that appeal had cultural and social significance that extended beyond the walls of the movie theater or studio offices. The relatively recent discovery of an extant print of Oscar Micheaux's *Within Our Gates* (1920), a film previously considered lost, helps make some of these issues clear. Discovered under the title *La negra* in the Filmoteca Española in Madrid in the late 1970s and subsequently restored by the Library of Congress in the early 1990s, this film's journey across the Atlantic and back again has prompted Jane Gaines to declare that the film led "two cultural lives."[14] She asserts that the version of the film found in Madrid, with Spanish intertitles, is inaccessible to monolingual English-language speakers today because the intertitles are crucial to understanding the film's cinematic style, which is marked by Micheaux's "off-centered attitude toward using conventional forms."[15] That is, without titles the

Figure 5.2 According to the American Projecting Company, "pictures have no language." *Moving Picture World,* March 1921.

film would have been incomprehensible to either Spanish-speaking or English-speaking audiences, regardless of the nature of silent cinema. Moreover, Gaines concludes that the Spanish-language intertitles offered viewers crucial information for understanding a narrative far removed from their cultural context, in this case Spanish audiences who were less intimately familiar with the United States' culture of segregation and racism than domestic audiences. That translation, Gaines implies, was crucial to the film's legibility for foreign audiences; it also rendered the film a new text.

Closer to home, Mexican migrants living in the United States lamented the fact that intertitles were seldom translated in theaters outside of major migrant

Figure 5.3 Advertisement for Goldwyn-Cosmopolitan, "Films speak all languages," *Cine-Mundial,* November 1923. Billy Rose Theatre Division, New York Public Library for the Performing Arts, Astor, Lenox and Tilden Foundations.

enclaves like Los Angeles or San Antonio. In an interview conducted by economist Paul J. Taylor in the early 1930s as part of a study about Mexican labor in the United States, the wife of a railroad track worker living in the Midwest reported feeling isolated in part because she could not read the English-language titles at the movies. "My husband knows a little English," she said, "but sometimes we miss the meaning of things and we are lost." Another unnamed informant declared that in the United States "work is hard. Life is more *triste* [sad]. . . . We don't know the language and can't read the titles of the movies."[16] For these interviewees the absence of translation limited their capacity to fully enjoy the experience of moviegoing, a loss that became a figure for immigrant alienation.

These two examples, one drawn from the transnational trade in films and the other from the transnational circulation of movie audiences, suggest that exhibiting silent films to foreign audiences—"universal" language and democratic rhetoric notwithstanding—whether at home or abroad, required translation. Certainly, the trade and fan press in the United States indicates that intertitles were increasingly important to the creation of successful narratives. Take, for example, the discussion "Let's Talk about Titles" in *Wid's Film and Folks* in September 1915. Admitting that some titles were used as filler or to smooth over rough editing, the anonymous author advocated reforming titling practices, rendering them in "language that flows" rather than abandoning them altogether.[17] In 1922, *Moving Picture World* published a short essay by Fred Schaefer on what the editors referred to as "the motion picture subtitle," or the intertitle.[18] According to Schaefer, the intertitle constituted an important narrative element difficult to execute and underrated by many studios in its importance. Poor titles often resulted from the use of "bad" English and the perception that just anyone could title a picture. Schaefer was perhaps trying to secure a privileged position for writers in the industry when he wrote that one must be immersed in "miles of celluloid" in order to grasp the way that titles should be crafted. He makes a strong case for their importance in indicating motive, introducing characters, and "establish[ing] conflict or . . . develop[ing] intrigue, or inspir[ing] expectancy."[19] In other words, Schaefer argued that titles did some of the work that would increasingly be carried by cinematic techniques such as editing. By the early 1920s, regardless of complaints about their quality, intertitles had become an integral narrative and visual element of any given film.[20]

As the importance of intertitles was being remarked upon in the English-language trade press, the industry began to look to Latin America as a potentially rich market. Although Latin America represented only 10.6 percent of the industry's total foreign revenues in 1920, like Asia it was seen as a market with the potential for enormous growth, particularly after World War I.[21] As Kristin Thompson notes, "during the war the American film industry had high hopes for South America as a replacement for the European market."[22] Markets, such as Mexico, that previously had been dominated by European fare were now wide open to American exports. By 1929, Argentina and Brazil would constitute the largest Latin American markets for U.S. films, largely because of the dense urban centers in these regions.[23] After the revolution, Mexico was considered a gateway country central to controlling piracy in the region.[24] By the end of the 1920s, Mexico ranked third after Argentina and Brazil in importance, and when sound was introduced in 1929, Mexico led all of Latin America in the number of theaters wired for sound.[25]

As the U.S. film industry entered Latin America, it became clear to studios and distributors that language mattered. As early as 1916, *Exhibitor's Herald* cautioned those interested in expanding into South America: "Good translation [is] essential. . . . Nothing hurts the susceptibilities of an audience like being 'stared at' by glaring errors of idiom and spelling."[26] In 1922, a brief item in *Moving Picture World* urged film "men" interested in moving into Latin American markets to learn from the experiences of manufacturers whose "manhandling of the Spanish language is causing all sorts of trouble."[27] The year before, *Moving Picture World* publicized a communication from the American consul in Ceiba, Honduras, about film distribution and exhibition in that region. The consul noted that the local sugar and railroad companies (American concerns) sponsored the majority of films shown in the region, but that most of the films were rented from an agency in Guatemala that only dealt in European films. The few American films that had been shown were extremely popular; even so, the consul observed, "the fact that the 'leads' were printed in English . . . was an objection."[28] These reports, which were directed at American cinema entrepreneurs, focused on very practical, material aspects of titles rather than the aesthetic qualities of films or even the genres that might appeal to Latin American audiences. Strikingly, despite the assumption that audiences in countries like Honduras and Guatemala were assumed by some to be uniformly illiterate, the issue of language loomed large.

Indeed, from a Latin American perspective, the translation of intertitles played a determinate role in the U.S. cinema's appeal for Spanish-speaking audiences (remember the Mexican migrants disappointed by monolingual titles). On the one hand, commentators frequently complained about poor translations. Writers for *Cine-Mundial, Moving Picture World*'s Spanish-language counterpart, which began publication in 1916, decried the translations provided by translators who were ill equipped to do their jobs, either because they lacked a basic understanding of the relationship between titles and scenes or because they were not shown the films but merely given a list of titles to translate.[29] Mexican critics likewise protested translations that failed to take into account the linguistic particularities of their target audiences, which varied by country and region. For example, when Rafael Bermúdez Zartrain reviewed the Mary Pickford film *Daddy Long Legs* (1919), which he generally admired, he complained at length about intertitles full of "españolismos" that did not work in an American context—in this case the use of the term "papaito" for "Daddy" when "papacito," "papito," or "viejito" would have been more comprehensible to Mexican and other Latin American audiences.[30]

On the other hand, journalists praised companies that offered what they assessed as "good" translations. For example, in 1916 the editors of *Cine-Mundial* observed approvingly that some film production companies were translating a "good percentage of their production" before offering their product for sale or rent.[31] Companies that made this effort took "pieces of completely Yankee origin in argument and execution" and adapted them to Latin American tastes. If they are "comic and the principal actor is named 'Charles' in English, in Latino countries the name will be transformed into 'Carlos' or 'Carlitos.'"[32] As this comment indicates, not only did foreign audiences perceive themselves as having specific tastes, but Hollywood cinema also required acts of translation that took signifiers such as names and translated them into the affective register of the target language and culture. These translation practices, as the admonishments in the English-language trade press suggest, could generate profits. *Cine-Mundial's* Mexico correspondent lavished praise on the translations—"always correct and appropriate"—provided for Goldwyn comedies, which he also evaluated as the key to their success.[33] The manager of the United Artists' Mexico City office, Harvey Sheahan, reported to the home office in New York that the "translation of pictures of stars other than our own four have only been mediocre," leading to predictably poor box office performance. In contrast, Sheahan continued, "the translation of ROSITA and WOMAN OF PARIS [*sic*]," two United Artists films that did extremely well at the Mexican box office, "are [*sic*] excellent."[34] Thus, companies that provided "good," culturally legible translations would find themselves with an advantage in entering Latin American markets.

Using translated titles rather than a formal lecturer or informal translator (e.g., one's neighbor) demanded that there be some mechanism and a set of practices for creating them. In the above examples, translations were provided by the production companies or by local distributors. Evidence from the Spanish-language trade press indicates that for a certain period of time the translation of intertitles could also take place in a middle space between production and local contexts of distribution and exhibition. Nestled among the back-page advertisements for furnishings, photographs, and other commercial fixtures in *Cine-Mundial,* companies regularly advertised translation services in multiple languages, including German, Dutch, Portuguese, and Spanish. Focusing on the ads that offered services exclusively in Spanish, we can discern a range of businesses involved in this specialized aspect of the industry. There appears to have been a set of independent distributors who focused on the international trade and offered title translation as one among many services. For example, the Commercial Motion Pictures Company, located in midtown Manhattan, made prints, did coloring work, and translated intertitles into Spanish at a rate of eight cents per foot of film.[35] Likewise, the A.B.C. Film Co. offered clients used films for rent or sale in addition to title card translation in multiple languages (see Figure 5.4).[36] A second group, according to their advertisements, dealt exclusively with distribution in Latin America. For example, Francisco Elias ran a multi-service business but focused on trade in the hemisphere. In addition to direct sales, he offered his services as an agent, assuring potential clients that "every film will be selected and supervised by this firm, with the artistic titles in correct and literary Spanish" (see Figure 5.5).[37]

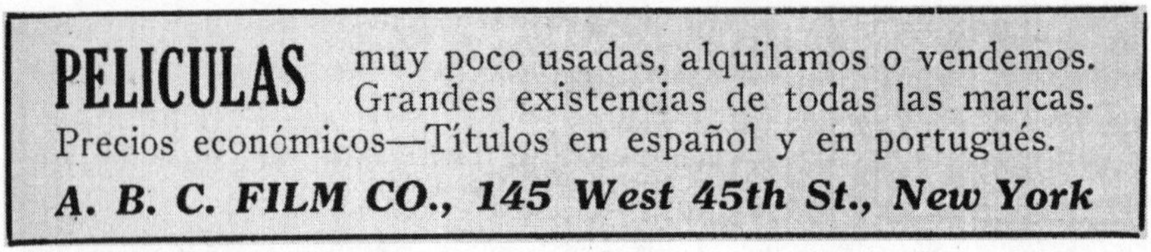
PELICULAS muy poco usadas, alquilamos o vendemos.
Grandes existencias de todas las marcas.
Precios económicos—Títulos en español y en portugués.
A. B. C. FILM CO., 145 West 45th St., New York

Figure 5.4 The A.B.C. Film Co. advertises "Slightly used films from various studios sold or rented cheap, ask for a list and prices. We insert titles in Spanish or Portuguese." *Cine-Mundial,* May 1917. Billy Rose Theatre Division, New York Public Library for the Performing Arts, Astor, Lenox and Tilden Foundations.

Elaine Bowser notes that after 1915 the translation of intertitles became the responsibility of the foreign office staff that managed the distribution of film and advertising materials to studios' distribution branches across the globe.[38] Indeed, in his lecture to students at Harvard Business School in 1927, Paramount–Famous Players–Lasky's general manager Sidney Kent elaborated on the role that translation played in foreign distribution.[39] This period also provided opportunities for smaller specialized companies and notably entrepreneurial Latin Americans to participate in the film trade, which in Latin America had not yet been integrated completely into industry processes and procedures. The tag line of Elias's advertisement—"Take success with you"—hints at the importance of well-translated titles for international distribution. Significantly, these sorts of advertisements did not appear in *Moving Picture World* during the same period; they obviously addressed a very particular segment of the trade that did business in Spanish-speaking parts of the world.

In the early 1920s, even as U.S. studios established a more solid presence in Latin America by opening branch offices in major cities, this pattern of overlapping translation practices continued. Evidence from the Spanish-language trade and daily press indicates that despite studios' shift toward in-house translation, intertitles were often translated at the point of local distribution or exhibition. In Mexico, this was particularly true in areas on the margins of the major distribution networks that fanned out from Mexico City. For example, one film entrepreneur on the U.S.-Mexico border, Juan de la Cruz Alarcón, identified the lack of "snappy" title translations as one of the chief obstacles to introducing American films to the Mexican market. Alarcón was credited, perhaps apocryphally, with developing an early form of subtitling. He would, *Moving Picture World* reported, place the Spanish titles below the English titles by typing the Spanish titles on a strip of celluloid that would be projected at the bottom of the screen with a separate projector. Alarcón kept translators on staff who could translate a five- or six-reel film "within a few minutes."[40] His employees were considered experts in translating American slang into its local equivalent—a critical element,

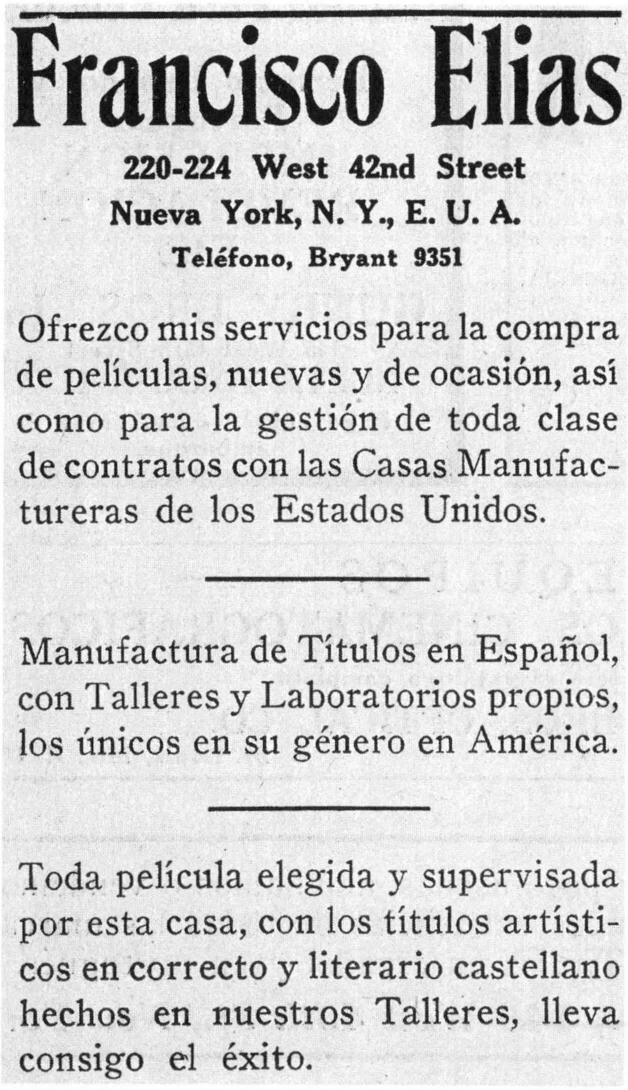

Francisco Elias
220-224 West 42nd Street
Nueva York, N. Y., E. U. A.
Teléfono, Bryant 9351
Ofrezco mis servicios para la compra de películas, nuevas y de ocasión, así como para la gestión de toda clase de contratos con las Casas Manufactureras de los Estados Unidos.
Manufactura de Títulos en Español, con Talleres y Laboratorios propios, los únicos en su género en América.
Toda película elegida y supervisada por esta casa, con los títulos artísticos en correcto y literario castellano hechos en nuestros Talleres, lleva consigo el éxito.

Figure 5.5 Francisco Elias offers his services as a purchasing agent and manufacturer of "artistic in correct and literary Castilian Spanish" intertitles. *Cine-Mundial,* November 1917. Billy Rose Theatre Division, New York Public Library for the Performing Arts, Astor, Lenox and Tilden Foundations.

according to Alarcón, of successful translations and a linguistic feat that studio translators could not provide.[41] Alarcón's focus on his local audience presents a very different perspective on translation from that of the studios, with their focus on efficiency, or even third parties such as Francisco Elias who emphasized "correct and literary Spanish." These diverse practices played a critical role in determining the fate of U.S.-produced films in Latin American markets, themselves marked by linguistic diversity and local cultures.

The Politics of Title Translation

Intertitles and their translation were more than just a strategy for appealing to far-flung audiences; the process of translation also lays bare the political dimensions of the circulation of films produced in the United States within specific contexts of reception and demonstrates the ways in which filmic texts intersected with other discourses such as those on national identity, class, or cultural imperialism. Rick Altman's innovative conceptualization of "cinema as event," a call to resist textual-based (bound) analyses and to consider every film as "constituted by a continuing interchange, neither beginning nor ending at any specific point," proves useful in thinking through the politics of intertitle translation.[42] Each instance of translation was evaluated not only in the context of international trade but also within frameworks of national interest, local struggles for power that fell along class lines, and regionally specific political configurations, as well as the immediate experience of viewing. Or, put another way, the translation of intertitles and its accompanying politics of language constituted another vector along which films intersected with multiple discourses inside and outside the movie theater. This perspective has something in common with Vasey's notion of the silent film text as open to multiple interpretations, but refuses her emphasis on silent film's "metaphoric and allusionistic qualities" in order to locate that interpretability in a broader definition of cinema that takes into account the performative, material, and mediated qualities of filmic texts.[43]

Intertitle translation could, for example, become the stuff of diplomatic negotiations. In 1922, *Her Husband's Trademark,* starring Gloria Swanson and Richard Wayne, was counted among the "denigrating" films—films that portrayed Mexico and Mexicans in a negative manner—that precipitated a brief but effective embargo against American films in Mexico. As originally produced, *Her Husband's Trademark* tells the story of a love triangle in which James Berkeley (Stuart Holmes) and his friend Allan Franklin (Richard Wayne) vie for the hand of Lois Miller (Gloria Swanson). Lois marries James, who keeps her in furs, gowns, and jewels as a visual testament, or "trademark," of an upper-class status even as his business ventures flounder. When Allan obtains an oil concession from the Mexican government, James attempts to get in on the venture. He and

Lois accompany Allan back to Mexico. There, Lois realizes she really loves Allan. In the final reel Mexican bandits try to kidnap Lois. During the battle James is conveniently killed and the two lovers escape danger by fleeing over the Mexican border.[44]

Upon its release the film became the subject of protest by Mexican diplomats and citizens in San Francisco, New York, Philadelphia, Boston, Los Angeles, Albuquerque, Rio de Janeiro, Chicago, and even Tokyo.[45] While the film appears to have been received as a regular program picture in the United States, perhaps notable for Gloria Swanson's numerous costume changes (the *New York Times* acknowledged its release but did not bother to review it, noting only that it starred the popular Gloria Swanson), Mexican spectators took umbrage at what many Anglo audiences might have perceived as merely a "colorful" background for the romantic drama of a modern love triangle. Mexican audiences complained that this film, like so many other American films, portrayed Mexico as a lawless place overrun by bandits, while Mexicans appeared as duplicitous, cowardly, and violent.[46]

Pressured by the Mexican government's embargo against any films produced and distributed by companies that released such "denigrating" films, Famous Players–Lasky attempted to placate the Mexican government by changing specific elements of *Her Husband's Trademark*. In April of 1922, the name of the story's setting was changed from Mexico to "Cristobana." One company executive wrote to the Mexican State Department, stressing "that this is not a simulated change, such as writing the name of Mexico backwards or selecting a name that suggests that of Mexico, but a real and effective change."[47] At the same time, the company agreed to change nineteen of the film's dialogue and expository titles—changes that attempted to alter the way that audiences read the film's visual images.[48]

At first glance the alterations made to the film's titles seem to support the studio's claims of "real and effective change." The words "Cristobana" or "South America" have been substituted for the word "Mexico" wherever it appeared in the continuity script's list of titles. For an industry that noisily proclaimed the power of images, such measures indicate an equally powerful belief in the capacity of words to alter those images' signification. But Famous Players–Lasky went beyond the alteration of signs to insert information in the form of intertitles that would direct viewers to assume that Cristobana was located in South America. For example, the trio's voyage to Mexico, which in the original was accomplished via train and took just four days, was transformed by means of titles into a steamer voyage of two weeks. All of these transformations asked viewers to believe what they read rather than what they saw, seemingly contradicting the logic of cinema. No changes were made to the costuming or other elements of the mise-en-scène, such as the cacti that appear at Allan's ranch. Thus, viewers

Figure 5.6 Ostensibly non-Mexican bandits attack the protagonists of *Her Husband's Trademark* (1922). Courtesy of the Academy of Motion Picture Arts and Sciences.

habituated to specific costumes, sets, and narrative situations indicating Mexico were asked to take all of those textual markers and intertextual references, including the much-publicized controversy over oil territories in Mexico, and assign them a more general "South American" association (Figure 5.6).

The final sequence of the film became the subject of the most radical alteration of meaning. In its original version the film portrayed Lois and Allan fleeing across the U.S.-Mexico border to the safety of a military encampment north of the Rio Grande. The screenplay synopsis summarizes the end of the story: "After a battle, Allan gets Lois safely over the American border, and they find happiness in their love for each other."[49] The continuity script renders this event with a title that reads "Sunrise on the Rio Grande," followed by a series of shots of Lois and Allan fleeing Mexican bandits in hot pursuit on horseback toward a camp of American soldiers. The final shot shows Allan and Lois embracing on the northern side of the Rio Grande.[50] In the list of changes that were made to the film's titles, that final intertitle was altered to read "Al amanecer en Río Blanco" (Sunrise in Rio Blanco). More significantly, the Mexican government asked

Famous Players–Lasky to add a title to the penultimate sequence that depicted the struggle between the Mexican bandits and Allan at his hacienda. That title read: "Si podemos llegar a Río Blanco estamos a salvo. El Gobierno de Cristobana tiene allí un patrol" (If we can get to Rio Blanco we're safe. The government of Cristobana has a patrol there). It was to be inserted at the point when Lois and Allan flee the hacienda. Thus, the revised titles labored to transform American soldiers into Cristobanian soldiers and a geographical marker, the Rio Grande, into just another obstacle to safe haven. The difficulty of this task intensifies when we recall that the U.S.-Mexico border had been used time and time again to indicate the limit between civilization and barbarity in films ranging from documentaries about the Pershing Expedition and military preparedness during the Mexican Revolution such as *Following the Flag into Mexico* (Tropical Films Co., 1916), through westerns such as *Western Blood* (Fox Film Corporation, 1918), to romantic dramas such as *The Grandee's Ring* (Interstate Feature Film Company, 1915). The Mexican government's proposed changes thus contravened the visual logic of not only this particular sequence but also that of a whole series of intertexts, an effort that likely did little to alter either Mexican or Anglo audiences' readings of the film.

The example of *Her Husband's Trademark* demonstrates the politics of titling and translation as they played out on the international, institutional level as the production of meaning was negotiated between the Mexican government and Famous Players–Lasky. These politics could also reflect more local concerns. For example, in Mexico City discussions about titles echoed broader debates about the influence of American culture and the linguistic invasion that manifested itself in advertisements, popular slang, and so on. In February of 1925, the mayor of Mexico City announced, following the recommendations of the Comisión de Diversiones (Commission on Diversions), that all films shown in the capital must have Spanish titles, rather than the bilingual titles that had become common. The local expatriate magazine *The Mexican American* surmised, quite correctly, that "the step is meant to emphasize that Spanish is the official and ruling language of the country."[51] This was, after all, only the latest expression of cultural nationalism in regard to titles. Several years earlier the municipal government of the Federal District (essentially the capital) had attempted to enforce a similar measure requiring either that titles appear in Spanish or, if titles were bilingual, that the Spanish titles appear first. Notably, in the spring of 1923, the Cine Olimpia, an upscale downtown theater owned by a group of American investors, had been fined for announcing and projecting a film in which one found, the cinema inspector on duty reported, titles that read, in English, "Mary Pickford in *Tess of the Storm Country*" (dir. John G. Robertson, 1922). Elsewhere, the Cine Rialto, which was also part of the Olimpia chain but located in a less tony part of town, was reprimanded for showing *Sangre y Arena* (*Blood and Sand;* dir. Fred Niblo, 1922) with

English titles, a transgression of local policies that inspired many members of the public to demand their money back.[52]

Other debates about intertitles reflected conflicting ideas about class and culture within Mexican society. Some film critics took local distributors to task for their overly long translations of titles, created "out of fear that Latino audiences won't understand what they see any other way."[53] Others criticized the poor Spanish that found its way onto the screen or even overly zealous attempts to Mexicanize American films. Critic Marco-Aurelio Galindo (obviously a pseudonym) accused distributor A. Gonzalez y Cia. of "completely removing the exclusively Yankee taste" of the film *Un quijote Americano* (*A Connecticut Yankee in King Arthur's Court;* dir. Emmet J. Flynn, 1921). Too free a translation, Galindo argued, had turned the film's protagonist into a mouthpiece for Mexican nationalism, and one who spoke the urban slang of Mexico City's *pelados*—a lower-class urban type—at that. In their attempts to make the film more appealing to Mexican audiences, Gonzalez's in-house translator had, in Galindo's opinion, ruined a film meant to be "completely American."[54] Too much, too little, not slangy enough, too slangy: the debates about title translation were imbricated in local debates on language and cultural imperialism or class.

Practices of translation could also reflect tensions that animated the movie theater in regions with a history of particular relations with the United States. For example, on the U.S.-Mexico border, Mexican and Anglo audiences often shared viewing spaces but perceived the films they saw quite differently. A rare example of extant exhibition titles presents tantalizing suggestions of the multiple meanings intertitles and their translations conveyed in such contexts. The border compilation film *La venganza de Pancho Villa,* which was produced in the El Paso–Ciudad Juárez region in the late 1920s and early 1930s by small-time exhibitor and aspiring director Félix Padilla, was composed from multiple sources including the serial *Liberty: A Daughter of the U.S.A.* (dir. Jacques Jaccard and Henry McRae, 1916), the feature film *Lieutenant Danny U.S.A.* (dir. Walter Edwards, 1916), Mexican documentary footage from the revolution, a Hearst newsreel depicting "negro" soldiers who had been captured in the 1916 Battle of Carrizal being returned over the U.S.-Mexico border, and some footage Félix and his son, Edmundo, shot themselves. The film went through numerous iterations even as it circulated in the early 1930s in smaller theaters along either side of the border.[55]

In creating a narrative out of disparate sources, the Padillas used intertitles that came from exhibition copies of the films they relied on for their source material, in addition to some titles they created themselves. Some intertitles appear onscreen only in Spanish; others are bilingual. Variations in grammar, spelling, fonts, and idiomatic expression suggest that these titles had multiple authors with a range of literacy in Spanish. The most intriguing title, at least for the purposes of this discussion, appears toward the end of the hour-long film. A heated battle scene showing the film's hero, Pancho Villa, and his men fighting against American forces is followed by a bilingual intertitle that reads in Spanish, "Los villistas acabaron con todo el destacamento Americano" (The Villistas did away with the entire American deployment) (Figure 5.7a). In English the title reads, "The American soldiers died like heroes" (Figure 5.7b). This title was almost certainly produced at the point of exhibition. Border theater owners were sensitive to the need to appeal to both Anglo and Mexican audiences and to the politics of those appeals. The radical difference in the two interpretations of this footage suggests that exhibitors who served border audiences were conscious of the historical and social experiences different publics might bring to their viewings and wanted to please them all.[56] Of course, the bilingual viewer (someone Gaines fails to account for in her assessment of *La negra*) could chuckle or fume, depending on his or her perspective. This one title, which provides a glimpse of a practice for which evidence is often lacking, demonstrates how titles and their translations could lead to alternative interpretations of the same visual images, interpretations whose meanings emerged from broader contexts of racial interactions, history, and local politics.

Conclusion

Notwithstanding our belated attentiveness to the intertitle as a crucial element of silent era cinema, studies concerned with the emergence of sound regularly engage the relationship between language and cinema.[57] Importantly, the potential loss of the Latin American market during the transition to sound technologies motivated one of the longest experiments in multilingual production and stimulated the development of the Mexican national film industry.[58] The controversy in Mexico highlights the fraught politics of language that accompanied this technological shift. In 1929, the year that sound films were first exhibited in Mexico, many cultural observers, including journalists, students, and the intellectual elite, inspired by the fervent cultural and economic nationalism that would characterize Mexico in the 1930s, became agitated over what they predicted would soon be the relentless audibility of spoken American English. They joined their voices to those of cultural nationalists in Argentina, France, and even Britain who feared that sound films would make them cultural vassals of the United States.

In Mexico, arguments against sound film ranged from the economic to the aesthetic. Musicians, who had organized early and been tenacious in their demands for adequate pay and job security, may have cared little about cultural imperialism, having spent years picking out jazz tunes for grateful audiences. But they clearly perceived that sound films threatened their livelihood. Members of Mexico's cosmopolitan cultural elite joined their protesting counterparts

(a)

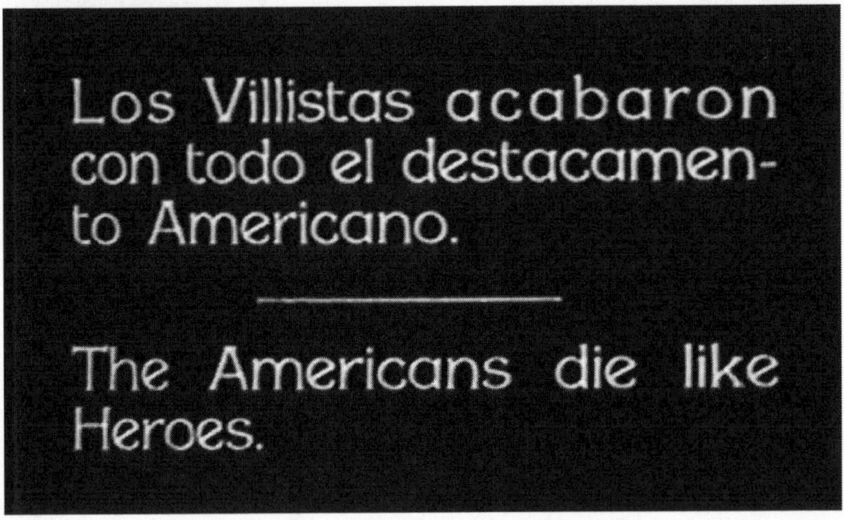
Los Villistas acabaron con todo el destacamento Americano.
The Americans die like Heroes.

(b)

Figure 5.7 Screen shots from *La venganza de Pancho Villa*, showing the American detachment being decimated by Villa's men *or* dying like heroes, depending on one's linguistic perspective.

around the globe, claiming that silent film was a "universal" art form, "a sign of the [modern] age in countries of distinct colors, various languages, and opposing characters."[59] (This argument, ironically, claimed difference as the very stuff of universality.) Cultural nationalists would make quite different sorts of claims about difference. They perceived sound films in English as untranslatable and thus as potentially powerful instruments of U.S. cultural imperialism. In discussing the potential impact of *películas habladas,* many proceeded from the premise that English was already a forceful presence in Mexico. For example, novelist Federico Gamboa began his description of sound film as a "serious threat" with a list of the *yanquismos* (English expressions) that had already invaded Mexico's linguistic sphere.[60] Likewise, journalist Manuel Barajas refers to these additions to Mexican Spanish as a "perversion of our language" before launching into a polemic about Vitaphone's threat to Mexico's struggling film industry.[61] These accounts indicate that sound films represented not an entirely new phenomenon, as many accounts of the transition would have it, but yet another volley in the battle over language and national identity.

During the silent era, that battle played out on international, municipal, regional, and theater-specific levels as intertitle translations were disputed, debated, and assigned meanings beyond their narrative function. In Mexico, a designated professional commentator and/or interpreter of the screen action, such as Japan's *benshi,* never emerged. Descriptions of viewing contexts, however, indicate that both metropolitan and provincial audiences appealed to more literate members of the community for translation, perhaps regardless of the efforts of producers, distributors, and exhibitors. Textual portraits of urban audiences published in popular magazines describe viewers who talked at length to their neighbors: narrating what was happening on the screen, explicating difficult-to-understand bits, and reading intertitles aloud. For example, an anonymous piece published in *Revista de Revistas* described "those girls and young men who read out loud the film's intertitles," which "ends up being bothersome when done in a declamatory voice," and the men who "shout out exclamations and vulgarities" in response to the film.[62] A humorous poem published in *Zig-Zag* included the chatty in its list of characters that one could find at the movie theater:

Tras de mí un viejo gordo no resiste lee todos los letreros en voz alta suelta una carcajada a cada chiste y si hay algún traidor, grita y se exalta.	Behind me an old fat man can't resist; he reads all the intertitles aloud, lets loose a laugh at each joke, and if there's a traitor, yells and gets excited.
Una vieja comenta cada vez, pero entiende las cosas al revés su hija (fea) cada escena se la explica	An old woman comments each time, but understands things backwards; her (ugly) daughter explains each scene to her

y la vieja replica,	and the old woman replies,
nada entiende y se enoja	she understands nothing and gets mad
porque se escapa el de la "Banda Roja."	because the guy from the "Red Band" escapes.[63]

These activities constituted just one element of the movie theater's sonic environment in which neighbors chatted while candy sellers roamed the aisles vending their wares sotto voce. Likewise, recent research into the experiences of provincial audiences suggests that in smaller towns or villages, where the majority of residents were minimally literate or illiterate, certain members of the community assumed the role of commentator. For example, using oral histories Ana María de la O Castellanos describes how, in the 1920s, residents of Zapopan, a small village outside of Guadalajara, remembered the programs offered by Don José (Cervantes), sometime municipal president (mayor), small business owner, and occasional film exhibitor. When they didn't understand the narrative of a particular film, members of the audience would shout "Explain it to us! Explain it to us!" and Cervantes would pause the projection to explain who the characters were and what they were doing.[64] Such ephemeral, context-specific acts of translation co-existed with more formal practices of translation that altered the materiality of the film, creating texts that led multiple cultural lives.

As the global film industry—production, distribution, and exhibition—made the transition to sound, Carlos F. Borosque, the editor of *Cinelandia,* a Spanish-language fan magazine published in Hollywood, wrote regretfully: "A good translator . . . [had been] enough to make Norma Talmadge or Emil Jennings speak Spanish."[65] His lament indicates the central role that intertitle translation played in making Hollywood's wares legible to Spanish-speaking audiences in Mexico and elsewhere in Latin America and suggests that language mattered long before spoken dialogue emerged. Overlapping, often diachronic practices of translation ranged from the institutional to the local. While the material practices of silent film production meant that the translation of titles was neither onerous nor uncommon, the cultural politics of translation gave each act of translation significance in a local, national, or international context. Silent era narratives may indeed have been more legible to audiences across the globe or to immigrant audiences in the United States solely on the basis of their visual content, but producers, exhibitors, audiences, and even the state frequently included intertitles in their readings of filmic texts, demanded that they be translated, and figured them into their calculus of both how to sell films and how to negotiate the political meanings that emerged from those films. Though we have scant evidence of the reactions of individual audience members, the discourse on title translation as expressed by industry representatives, entrepreneurs serving "niche" markets, and local film distributors and exhibitors offers clues to the ways audiences responded to the meanings, pleasures, and politics found in the words and images on the screen.

Considering translated intertitles as a form of context-specific mediation, akin to the sound practices that Altman argues contribute to "cinema as event" rather than a clearly defined, self-contained text, suggests that scholars need to rethink to what extent and how American film functions as a mechanism of cultural imperialism, as Vasey suggests, or acculturation, as Liepa proposes.[66] Indeed, we may need to rethink the category of "American film" per se. Perhaps we can look to other disciplines for models of how to reframe the question of national "texts." For example, in his introduction to *The Multilingual Anthology of American Literature,* literary scholar Werner Sollors asks, "What is American Literature?"[67] His call to include literature written in languages other than English challenges received notions of a national literature. Retraining scholarly attention on multilingual literature produced in the Americas, he asserts, encourages new comparative approaches to American culture in an international context and an understanding of American literature as part of a transnational world. His insight into the way a consideration of linguistic diversity expands our notion of American literature applies, I would argue, to cinema as well. Though a visual medium, it is also a sonic and material medium, one that mobilizes the written word in various ways, whether as intertitles during the silent era or as advertising copy and subtitles today. Rather than seeing those acts of translation as either crass business strategies or the bastardization of an original text, examining the politics of translation as they play out in multiple registers enables us to think about the transnational circulation of cinema beyond the confines of cinematic nationalism that ties filmic texts to nation-states. Instead, we might think about how each act of translation creates a new filmic text, or "cinematic event," whose existence may well be ephemeral, but whose effects radiate out to intersect with other discourses on the politics of language, cultural imperialism, racialization, and the nature of film itself.

Notes

1. This trope, as Miriam Hansen notes, persists in popular film histories and appears with frequency in less specialized writing about the global spread of American mass culture (see Hansen, *Babel and Babylon: Spectatorship in American Silent Film* [Cambridge, MA: Harvard University Press, 1991], 77, 316n52. An example of the latter can be found in Emily Rosenberg, *Spreading the American Dream: American Economic and Cultural Expansion, 1890–1945* (New York: Hill and Wang, 1982), 100.

2. The best examples of this increasing attention include Torey Liepa's recent dissertation on the intertitle as a vehicle for vernacular American Speech, "Figures of Silent Speech: Silent Film Dialogue and the American Vernacular, 1909–1916 (PhD dissertation, New York University, 2008), and Abé Mark Nornes's consideration of subtitling as a potentially subversive

practice in *Cinema Babel: Translating Global Cinema* (Minneapolis: University of Minnesota Press, 2007).

3. By way of illustration, while Mexico represented just 2 percent of the United States' foreign revenue in 1925, American films constituted 90 percent of all the films shown there. The UK and Germany represented 35 percent and 10 percent of the U.S. industry's foreign revenue, respectively. These figures come from William Victor Strauss, "Foreign Distribution of American Motion Pictures," *Harvard Business Review* 8.3 (April 1930): 309.

4. Liepa, "Figures of Silent Speech," 298.

5. Ibid., 391.

6. Nornes, *Cinema Babel*, 108.

7. Ibid.

8. Ruth Vasey, *The World According to Hollywood, 1918–1939* (Madison: University of Wisconsin Press, 1997), 68.

9. Ibid.

10. Miriam Hansen, "Universal Language and Democratic Culture: Myths of Origin in Early American Cinema," in *Myth and Enlightenment in American Literature,* ed. Dieter Miendl and Friedrich W. Horlacher (Erlangen: Erlanger Forschungen, 1985), 321–335.

11. Ibid., 330.

12. Herbert Hoover, "American Relations," *Hispania* 10.3 (May 1927): 132.

13. Ibid., 133–134.

14. Jane M. Gaines, "Micheaux's *Within Our Gates:* Now Available on Videotape," *Oscar Micheaux Society Newsletter* 3 (Summer 1994); Gaines, *Fire and Desire: Mixed-Race Movies in the Silent Era* (Chicago: University of Chicago Press, 2001), 163.

15. Ibid., 181.

16. Paul S. Taylor, *Mexican Labor in the United States: Chicago and the Calumet Region* (Berkeley: University of California Press, 1932), 261, 276.

17. "Let's Talk about Titles," *Wid's Films and Folks,* September 16, 1915.

18. Fred Schaefer, "Uses of the Motion Picture Subtitle," *Moving Picture World,* January 29, 1921, 552. A second essay, "Securing Effect with the Motion Picture Subtitle," was promised but never published.

19. Ibid.

20. In his 1987 essay "Reading Intertitles," Brad Chisolm observes that the linguistic as well as the visual elements of intertitles have been ignored in most close readings of silent era films. According to Chisolm, for a certain period of time titles were integral to the creation of cinematic meaning. The typology he develops for intertitles is remarkably similar to the list generated by Schaefer. Chisolm, "Reading Intertitles," *Journal of Popular Film and Television* 15.3 (1987): 137–142.

21. This figure comes from Gaizka S. de Usabel, *The High Noon of American Films in Latin America* (Ann Arbor, MI: UMI Research Press, 1982), xv.

22. Thompson, *Exporting Entertainment,* 76.

23. In 1929, the Bureau of Foreign and Domestic Commerce, a subagency of the U.S. Department of Commerce, reported that Argentina and Brazil were the second- and third-largest markets for American films and together had 50 percent of the theaters in Latin America. U.S. Department of Commerce, Bureau of Foreign and Domestic Commerce, *Motion Pictures in Argentina and Brazil* (Washington, DC: Government Printing Office, 1929), ii.

24. I make this point about Mexico's role in stemming piracy in my book, *Making Cinelandia: American Films and Mexican Film Culture before the Golden Age, 1896–1936* (Durham, NC: Duke University Press, 2014).

25. U.S. Department of Commerce, Bureau of Foreign and Domestic Commerce, *Motion Pictures in Mexico, Central America, and The Greater Antilles* (Washington, DC: Government Printing Office, 1931), 3.
26. "The Motion Picture Situation in Foreign Countries: Colombia," *Exhibitor's Herald,* June 24, 1916, 27.
27. "Spanish as She Should Not Be Wrote," *Moving Picture World,* November 4, 1922, 42.
28. "Consul Writes North Coast of Honduras Wants U.S. Films with Spanish Titles," *Moving Picture World,* October 1, 1921, 32.
29. "La cuestión de los títulos va de mal en peor," *Cine-Mundial,* May 1919. All translations from the Spanish are mine unless otherwise noted.
30. Rafael Bermúdez Zartrain, "Los estrenos cinematográficos," *El Universal Ilustrado,* June 10, 1920.
31. "Editorial," *Cine-Mundial,* May 1916.
32. Ibid.
33. "Crónica de Méjico," *Cine-Mundial,* May 1921.
34. "Report #1-Mexico," December 29, 1923, US MSS 99AN/2a216.6, O'Brien papers, United Artists Collection, Wisconsin Historical Society, Madison, WI.
35. Advertisement, *Cine-Mundial,* April 1916.
36. Advertisement, *Cine-Mundial,* June 1917, 307.
37. Advertisement, *Cine-Mundial,* November 1917, 584.
38. Elaine Bowser, *The Transformation of Cinema, 1907–1915* (Berkeley: University of California Press, 1990), 37–47.
39. Joseph Kennedy, ed., *The Story of the Films* (Chicago: A. W. Shaw, 1927), 206.
40. "Methods in Mexico," *Moving Picture World,* December 22, 1917, 1796.
41. "Putting Slang into Spanish Is Now a Profession," *El Paso Morning Times,* March 18, 1919, 2.
42. Rick Altman, "General Introduction: Cinema as Event," in *Sound Theory, Sound Practice* (New York: Routledge, 1992), 4.
43. Ibid. Altman actually identifies a dozen discursive aspects of the cinema event; I have chosen to highlight only a few of the most relevant here.
44. This plot summary is drawn from the description of the film in the AFI online catalog: http://www.afi/chadwyck.com.
45. Some of these complaints were merely noted in passing in diplomatic correspondence; others have been preserved in their entirety. See material in the Archivo Histórico de la Secretaría de Relaciones Exteriores, Mexico City (hereafter AHSRE), Fondo Numeración Corrida, legajo 491, folio 19-10-8 (III) 1.
46. See Laura Isabel Serna, "'As a Mexican I Feel It Is My Duty': Citizenship, Censorship, and the Campaign against Derogatory Films in Mexico, 1922–1930," *The Americas: A Quarterly Review of Inter-American Cultural History* 63.2 (October 2006): 225–244.
47. Report, April 1922, AHSRE, Fondo Numeración Corrida, legajo 491, folio 19-10-8 (III) 1.
48. My analysis of these changes is based on a comparison of the list of changes held in the AHSRE in Mexico and a continuity script held at the Margaret Herrick Library in Los Angeles, California (henceforth MHL). The George Eastman House in Rochester, New York, holds a print of the film as it was originally released, but since there is no extant copy of the changed version, a comparison of these two documents provides the most relevant analytic perspective.
49. Clara Berenger, story to *Her Husband's Trademark,* Famous Players–Lasky Corp., n.d., master file 744, p. 6, MHL.

50. Continuity script to *Her Husband's Trademark,* Famous Players–Lasky Corp., n.d., master file 744, p. 23, MHL.

51. "English Banned in Movies," *Mexican American,* February 14, 1925, 35. See also "Los *films* se exhibirán sin títulos en ingles," *El Universal Ilustrado,* February 10, 1925, 1.

52. Juan N. Flores to the Chief of the Department, April 2, 1923, and Carlos Pliego to the Chief of the Department, May 1, 1923, vol. 3951, expediente 25, Departamento de Diversiones Archivo Historico del Distrito Federal, Mexico City.

53. Review of *Confesiones de una reina* [*Confessions of a Queen;* dir. Seastrom, 1925], *Revista de Revistas,* June 12, 1926, 23.

54. Marco-Aurelio Galido, "Los estrenos cinematográficos: Lo que hacen ellos," *El Universal Ilustrado,* October 12, 1922, 45.

55. The extant print of *La venganza de Pancho Villa* was donated to the American Film Institute (AFI) by members of the Padilla family in 2004 and was, until the close of the AFI's restoration unit, slated for restoration. Documentary filmmaker Gregorio Rocha, who was instrumental in the film's transference from a vault at the University of Texas at El Paso to the AFI, was kind enough to share a video copy of the unrestored version with me. My comments refer to this copy, which is unfortunately unavailable to other researchers. For a discussion of the technical aspects of the film, see Gregorio Rocha, "*La venganza de Pancho Villa* (*The Vengeance of Pancho Villa*): A Lost and Found Border Film," *Journal of Film Preservation* 65 (December 2003): 24–31.

56. I expand on these points in my essay "*La venganza de Pancho Villa:* Resistance and Repetition," *Aztlan: A Journal of Chicano Studies* 37.2 (Fall 2012): 11–42.

57. See Donald Crafton, *The Talkies: American Cinema's Transition to Sound, 1926–1931* (Berkeley: University of California Press, 1999), 441–448; Richard Maltby and Ruth Vasey, "The International Language Problem: European Reactions to Hollywood's Conversion to Sound," in *Hollywood in Europe: Experiences of a Cultural Hegemony,* ed. David. W. Ellwood and R. Kroes, European Contributions to American Studies 28 (Amsterdam: VU University Press, 1994), 68–93; Ginette Vincendeau, "Hollywood Babel: The Multiple Language Version," *Screen* 29.2 (1998): 24–39; and Nataša Ďurovičová, "*Los Toquis,* or Urban Babel," in *Global Cities: Cinema, Architecture, and Urbanism in a Digital Age,* ed. Linda Krause and Patrice Petro (New Brunswick, NJ: Rutgers University Press, 2003), 71–86.

58. Spanish multilinguals continued to be produced long after production in other languages had ceased. Juan B. Heinink and Robert G. Dickson provide a filmography that covers the period 1929–1939: Heinink and Dickson, *Cita en Hollywood: Antología de las películas norteamericanas habladas en español* (Bilbao, Spain: Ediciones Mensajero, 1990). On the importance of the transition to sound in the development of Latin American cinema, see Paulo Antonio Paranaguá, *Tradición y modernidad en el cine de América Latina* (Madrid: Fondo de Cultura Económica de España, 2003).

59. "Ruido o silencio," *Excélsior,* June 25, 1929, 7.

60. Federico Gamboa, "Una serie amenaza," *Magazine para Todos,* June 2, 1929, 3.

61. Manuel Barajas, "El vitafono es cuestión de vida o muerte para el arte nacional," *El Nacional Revolucionario,* n.d., clippings file, Fondo Económico, Biblioteca Lerdo de Tejada, Mexico City.

62. "La educación en el cine," *Revista de Revistas,* August 21, 1927, 45.

63. Sanchez Filmador, "El cine y sus admiradores," *Zig-Zag,* February 17, 1921.

64. Ana María de la O Castellanos, "Las vivencias cinematográficas en la memoria de los pueblos de Zapopan y Unión de Tula," in *Microhistorias del cine en México,* ed. Eduardo de la Vega Alfaro (Guadalajara: Universidad de Guadalajara; Mexico City: UNAM / IMCINE / Cineteca Nacional / Instituto Mora, 2000), 159.

65. Carlos F. Borosque, "Se solicitan artistas," *Cinelandia,* February 1931, 43.

66. Recent scholarship on audiences marked by gender, race, or class does not acknowledge Altman's formulation per se, but the relationship between this idea and arguments about the way in which the sonic and performative dimensions of viewing contexts not only change spectators' experience of the film but also foster the formation of ethnic and racial identities is clear. See, for example, Judith Thissen, "Jewish Immigrant Audiences in New York City, 1905–1914," and Giorgio Bertellini, "Italian Imageries, Historical Feature Films, and the Fabrication of Italy's Spectators in Early 1900s New York," both in *American Movie Audiences: From the Turn of the Century to the Early Sound Era,* ed. Richard Maltby and Melvyn Stokes (London: British Film Institute, 1999), 15–28, 29–45. On international contexts, see Richard Maltby and Melvyn Stokes, eds., *Hollywood Abroad: Audiences and Cultural Exchange* (London: British Film Institute, 2004).

67. Werner Sollors, introduction to *The Multilingual Anthology of American: A Reader of Original Texts with English Translations,* ed. Marc Shell and Werner Sollors (New York: NYU Press, 2000), 1.

Part III

Impertinent Appropriations

Introduction

Anupama Kapse

The year was 1897, the film was Edison's *The Kiss,* but the city was Osaka and the audience Japanese. Japanese policemen attempted to forestall its screening, deeming it to be impertinent, but a quick-witted *benshi* assured them that a kiss was like a handshake in America, rather appropriate for the new technology of motion pictures. Mark B. Sandberg and Priya Jaikumar have shown us how cinema played fast and loose with place and location in "Picturing Space"; in this section we turn to some curiously impertinent appropriations of cinema's textual meanings, genres, and stars. Aaron Gerow's account of the initial response to *The Kiss* (1896) shows not only how a change in exhibition venue could stand intended meaning on its head, but also how quickly the spoken word could strike out at early impressions of a "dumb" (the pun is intended) medium imported from the United States. Invoking an originary moment other than that of the Lumière brothers' *Arrival of a Train at a Station* (1896), Gerow redirects us to a scenario where cinema's first audiences responded to it with another kind of horror, marked not by fear and excitement but disdain and suspicion.[1]

The *benshi*'s word saved the day but it was hardly final: *The Kiss* could not sustain the symbolic nod to a handshake between America and Japan. Indeed, Japan's relationship to early cinema, especially imports from the United States or France, remained a fraught one. Instead of celebrating cinema's technological progress, the Japanese intelligentsia bemoaned the coming of what appeared to be an unrefined, upstart technology. Cinema's arrival coincided with the coming of the Meiji Restoration and major constitutional reforms as Japan became highly conscious of its growing political and artistic accomplishments. In addition, the country's ongoing imperial advances in China and Korea positioned it as a growing Asian power vying for a greater portion in the geopolitical space. Not only was Japan, unlike Korea or India, not colonized at this time—as a nation, it aspired to control parts of Asia by competing with other imperial powers like France and Britain. In view of such ambitions, it is hardly surprising that Japan responded to American cinema not as a small nation but as an Asian superpower.

Seen in this light, the *benshi*'s voiceover (already intermedial, falling somewhere between live performance and textually embedded commentary) negotiates between two competing voices, one hostile to the new medium and the other attracted to its exotic potential, where the United States appears in the double-edged role of the foreign Other. On the one hand, one might say that the *benshi* had no choice but to throw in his lot with the institution of the cinema—after all, his very existence depended on it. On the other hand, elite responses were far more constrained by pride in the traditions and arts of a revitalized, modern Japan, which was supposed to protect itself from contamination by Western art forms that had shown up uninvited on its shores. Here the kiss, an expression of intimate contact that portends even more—soon to be banned by the Japanese censors—anticipates seminal discourses that view cinema as a type of threat, an infectious disease.

Indeed, the modern materializes here as a phenomenon that *pre-dates* cinema in Japan. In turn, the kiss mobilizes notions of vulgarity managed differently by the *benshi* and cinema's first viewers in Japan. The gap in their respective reactions shows how quickly early cinema's sensory mechanisms could shift once it was transported to other localities. Even the *benshi*'s account is couched in a playful misrecognition of American mannerisms, for Edison's film conveys erotic messages that exceed any simple notion of a platonic handshake.[2] Nor can we assume that the Japanese audience was so gullible that it accepted the *benshi*'s gloss without hesitation. Perhaps no scholar of early cinema has addressed this conundrum more effectively than Miriam Hansen, who coined the phrase "vernacular modernism" to address American cinema's global presence in the silent era.[3] In its simplest sense, vernacular modernism refers to an "enthusiasm for things American [or Americanism; an enthusiasm for all things American]" that encompasses a variety of film forms and functions that temper enthusiasm with capitalist critique, notably in the case of Soviet cinema's appropriation of American montage.[4] Its more complex meanings address cinema's "engage[ment] with the contradictions of modernity at the level of the senses, a level at which the impact of modern technology on human experience was most palpable and irreversible. . . . The reason slapstick comedy hit home and flourished worldwide was not critical reason but that the films propelled their viewers' bodies into laughter."[5] Unlike high or avant-garde forms of modernism, vernacular modernism allows for a reflexive relationship with the visual image that is free from a cognitive, locally bound reckoning of reality. Simply put, "classical" Hollywood denotes a rigid, hegemonic formal system, while vernacular modernism evokes a critical horizon for delineating silent cinema's play with "hitherto unperceived modes of sensory perception," allowing Hansen to examine a mass culture that is "in excess of and [in] conflict with the regime of production that spawned that mass culture."[6] Hansen conflates the vernacular with the modern in a bid to focus on silent cinema's reflexive dimension, which "may consist precisely in the ways in which [it] allows . . . viewers to confront the constitutive ambivalence of modernity."[7] While this is particularly useful for thinking about the anarchic possibilities of silent film comedy, examples such as Harold Lloyd's *Welcome Danger* (1929)—which is the focus of Yiman Wang's essay in this section—show how national sensibilities can quickly disrupt older, cosmopolitan patterns of reflexivity, favoring sharply defined viewing practices that hinge on a variety of differences which range from the cultural and political to the aesthetic or economic.

To this end, all three essays in this section pay particular attention to the constitution of local modernities while remaining attentive to American cinema's global presence.[8] In Aaron Gerow's words, "Hansen's notion of the vernacular does much to cure us of the notion of an overly monolithic western cinema. . . . Yet by discussing these appropriations as a form of cultural translation, she may be unwittingly reinforcing the idea that Hollywood occupies the center, and that it is the one to be translated."[9] Seen in this light, *The Kiss* is an example of an American film that translated poorly in Japan. That said, Hansen's work has also enabled a critical re-examination of American cinema's standardization and the contradictory nature of its appeal even *within* the United States. Consider Charlie Chaplin—his toothbrush moustache, derby hat, cane, and waddling walk define a globally recognizable star image. It is commonplace to situate his funny antics in a shared community of loving, amused viewers, where he invites, as Hansen might have said, a "mimetic identification that [is] . . . partial and excessive in relation to narrative comprehension."[10] Jennifer Bean has re-examined Chaplin's stardom in the context of inappropriate imitations of his antics: in front of a magistrate, where the accused (a sailor who knocks a young woman down à la Chaplin) defends himself by kicking his foot up in the air and manipulating his pencil-like cane; and young ladies who undermine their beauty by donning baggy pants and drawing moustaches on their faces. She argues that such transgressions destabilize the dominant cinematic apparatus, signifying a rival, "chaotic" system that defies logic or control, approximating "an unsystematic mode of production . . . [that] could be seen as a grotesque interruption of capitalism's rationalized efficiency and systematic coordination of profit."[11] Clearly, Chaplin's global popularity disrupts any straightforward account of his reception in the United States, which in turn remained susceptible to his monumental stature as an international comic icon. The ambiguous and potentially disruptive characteristics of Chaplin's global presence resonate suggestively with Hansen's understanding of the vernacular as an impulse that allows mass culture to be modified *at the site of its reception,* beneath the skin of a powerful mass culture.

Moreover, the articles in "Impertinent Appropriations" address the problem of the vernacular by grappling with the question of how the medium is able to "speak" in spite of its material erasure, particularly in those countries where its development is constrained by or is defined through American cinema's worldwide expansion. Thus, instead of focusing on the absence of early Japanese films, Gerow offers a *discursive* history of early Japanese cinema—examining cinema's presence through home-grown discussions of modernity, modernism, and modernization. Moving away from the question of sensory stimuli, he complicates not only the "spatial borders of early Japanese cinema but also its temporal limits," producing "a history without a beginning" where cinema's origins, if any, fall outside the West.[12] His key example here is *Zigomar* (Victorin Jasset, 1911), drawn from a genre that became popular across the globe: the serial.[13] Though the *benshi* had averted the ban on *The Kiss,* the law successfully banned *Zigomar* because it articulated a clear and present danger: the cinema itself.

This fast-paced detective film was shown in Japan on November 11, 1911, and became "a nationwide sensation [that] came to represent the success of the motion pictures, if not the existence of cinema itself." Followed by a host of Japanese adaptations featuring exciting chases and Westernized patterns of rapid editing, Gerow shows how *Zigomar* became "a complex multi-media phenomenon" that spawned a new genre of Japanese crime fiction, so much so that the word "Zigomar" ingratiated itself into the popular lexicon, signifying a suspicious dandy. In the years between 1897 and 1911, objections went beyond the kiss and extended themselves to the cinema itself. Motion pictures posed no problem as long as they were seen as technological enhancements of *existing* Japanese visual technologies (such as the magic lantern, or fairground amusements such as papier-mâché "living dolls' (*ikiningyō*), which were used to create exotic scenes from foreign lands or historical tableaux. The problem emerges at the precise juncture where the medium transforms from a fairground entertainment (*misemono*) to a moving picture (*katsudo shashin*): into a medium that is key to producing a new mass culture. Gerow discusses a series of media that mimic film technology: *gentō* (literally projection, especially of magic lantern slides), *Seiyō megane* (the Western looking glass), and *shinematekku* (a mix of dioramas and motion pictures) all of which establish continuity between Western and Japanese visual technologies on the basis of a shared sense of realism (*shoutsushi ikiningyō,* or "accurate reflection"). What is so striking here is the idea that cinema does not "arrive" from the West but rather meets its double or predecessor in Japan.

As a global phenomenon, *Zigomar* sets the stage for articulating an epidemic setback, eventually taking shape as a threat that "cause[d] people to lose their mental balance." "It was the alterity of the image, coupled with spectator desires associated with it that helped define the cinema . . . as a threat to a Meiji order that had just seen its leader pass away," writes Gerow. The *benshi*'s interjection heralds a situation that hinges on the problem of how *to speak* about the cinema. Thus the new medium appears "in discourse as a term . . . crucial for identifying [the] problem of modernity" where Western modernity is fixed and peripheral while Japanese modernity is strategically positioned at the center, as the inventor of cinema: the local lingua franca is explicitly mobilized to flag Japanese accomplishment.

Yiman Wang's account of the Grand Theater in Shanghai reveals a similar tussle over the place of American cinema: she reveals a different Shanghai here—not a cosmopolitan one, but a city recast as a vital part of an increasingly nationalizing China. She shows how Shanghai and its cinema are redefined according to new economic, territorial, and ideological impulses that openly challenge Hollywood's standing in the world film market. By the late 1920s, American imports had to contend with a strong local cinema in China. The parallel growth of the Nationalist Party (KMT) and the Communist Party of China (CPC) would lead in turn to internal struggles over power and cultural dominance.[14] It was against this background that the growing presence of the talkies loomed large, as silent cinema came under increasing threat; eventually, speech would become the precondition for complete localization and independence from Hollywood.

The thirties produced some of the most canonical films of the era—*Spring Silkworms* (*Chuncan,* 1933), *Daybreak* (*Tianming,* 1933), and *Goddess* (*Shennii,* 1934) are key examples here. Hansen pays particular attention to these films in her essay "Fallen Women, Rising Stars, New Horizons: Shanghai Silent Film as Vernacular Modernism," arguing that their relationship "to classical Hollywood cinema is neither one of imitation nor one of outright parody; nor does [*Daybreak*] reject the Western model so as to link its revolutionary message to ostensibly more authentic, traditional Chinese values."[15] If Hansen is at pains to show that didactic views such as those advocated by the iconoclastic intellectual Lu Xun (who was at the forefront of nationalist revivalism) did not preclude "multiple readings" of the films in question, Wang's insights complicate any simple understanding of Shanghai as a cosmopolitan center, which emerges as a hotbed of competing discourses about film, with Lu Xun emerging as the upholder of an ambivalent colonial discourse that fluctuates between desire for the plenitude of the West and embarrassment at the East's "lack." Harold Lloyd's *Welcome Danger* (1929, released in Shanghai in 1930) is a doubly interesting film here. First, as a comedy, it should have had an assured audience in China, where the Oriental Pathé had a profitable distribution network, particularly for comedies. Second, although it was dubbed by an anxious Harold Lloyd who did not want to lose out to the newly available sound films, Paramount released the film in China with no sound, marketing it as a silent, ostensibly for an older clientele. Not surprisingly, it failed. Released at the Grand Theater, where international films usually premiered, it sparked off a heated discussion on Chinese stereotypes in American cinema and was banned on the grounds that it was a *ruhua* (China-humiliating) film. The theater closed down after an angry public outcry. Ironically, the ban was lifted after Lloyd tendered an apology. *Welcome Danger* was then shown at the Grand Theater without sound and with no cuts. While official discourse condemned it, exhibitors went on to release the film because, as Lee Grieveson and Peter Krämer put it, in most foreign markets they "ultimately did not care where their films came from and welcomed American films as long as they were popular and/or cheap."[16]

It is worth noting, however, that *Welcome Danger* represents a sort of tipping point in the history of American cinema's life in Shanghai—its circulation hinged on the efficacy of an older distribution network (Paramount and Oriental Pathé) whose monopoly was increasingly threatened. It is clear, too, that locally made films provided a new canvas for drawing a cultural map that put indigenous themes and cultural issues at the forefront. Wang's analysis of the relatively unknown *Song of China* (*Tianlun*, 1935) allows us to situate films such as *Daybreak* and *Goddess* within a domestic context of political agitation and nationalist revival that was an integral part of the experience of modernity in China. Further, *Song of China* provides an early glimpse into an art-house idiom that would later play an important part in marketing Chinese films abroad. Wang argues that such films were made with the specific intent of producing an "authentic" picture of China, with a strong emphasis on Confucian values instead of what was, in local discourse, a globally inflected, detrimental form of Americanism. She examines cinema's nationalization by turning to idealized moments of self-display that are singled out for exhibition in the world market: *Song of China* responded directly to imperialism's racial excesses by foregrounding the most culturally prized elements. However, *Song of China* could achieve only a fraction of the success it had aimed for; if whatever was cosmopolitan was routed through American cinema, then nationalization called for a distinct cultural repertoire of themes, actions, and gestures that did not always translate well in the U.S. market. Such filmic encounters engage American and Asian audiences in a crisscrossed set of conflicts that are undergirded by a need for increased circulation which calls for censorship regulations dictated by new forms of cinematic "contact."

No matter how split, contested, or ambivalent, the urge to mold cinema into a distinct medium that could serve the specific artistic, economic, and political goals of the nation can be discerned across the major Asian silent cinemas of this period: Japan, China, and India. In India, however, American cinema had a relatively small presence in comparison with British cinema of the time, especially because of a quota system that required India to show a percentage of British films in its territory, a rule that unequivocally kept American cinema at bay.[17]

Given this regulation, Britain represented the dominant film industry here; to Indian filmmakers, the American model suggested pathways for loosening British domination. In my own essay in this section, I examine this relationship through Douglas Fairbanks's phenomenal success in India just a decade after the *Relief of Lucknow* (1912) was released. As Fairbanks's most successful film, *The Thief of Bagdad* (1924) came to represent the complex lure of American cinema in India, spawning a host of imitations, none of which can be understood as simple appropriations. The *Oxford English Dictionary* defines appropriation as "the action of taking something for one's own use, typically without the owner's permission." Indeed, references to *Thief* in the wake of its instant ubiquity serve very specific functions in the Indian film industry by defying any straightforward logic of appropriation, functioning instead as quotations that earmark cinema's new amplitude in the late 1920s. These include playful deceptions where women take on masculine identities for greater freedom; seen in this way, Douglas Fairbanks is doubly appropriated—first by the male protagonist of the action drama *Gallant Hearts* (1931) and then again by its cross-dressed female heroine. In both cases, "stealing" from *Thief* calls for elements that "spice up" Fairbanks's existing repertoire of actions with traditional motifs drawn from the *Arabian Nights,* a collection that was already quite popular in India.

While the Indian Cinematograph Committee (1927–1928) dismissed references to *Thief* as cheap imitation, I show how Indian actors, exhibitors, and distributors deployed it by turns as an example of *appropriate* rather than *appropriated* acting and production techniques. Interestingly, the Indian method of production differs sharply from its American counterpart, notably because of its quick turnover, lack of stars, and use of actual locations. While the number of films that borrowed from *Thief* seems staggering, most were made with a fraction of *Thief*'s budget. Quite clearly, such a difference suggests a rather lopsided center-periphery equation (with the United States acting as center and India as periphery), but more importantly, *Thief*'s extraordinary abstraction (already borrowed from the *Arabian Nights* and the ballet *Scheherazade*) allows for an easy transfer that opens it up for infinite modifications which serve specific goals at the Indian end, depending on the time, place, or period. Again, if Fairbanks's *Thief* is primarily a fantastic costume drama, then such a distinction is absent from the contemporary Indian film industry, which found the best use for Fairbanks in the stunt film genre. This genre often poached from other genres described as fantasies, adventure movies, or Muslim spectaculars. It depended on quick bursts of physical action that defied clear conceptions of time and place, favoring historical and spatial abstraction. Such elisions suggest a deliberate effort to stymy neat parallels with *Thief,* revealing a core nationalist impulse that mobilizes appropriation in order to develop an indigenous film industry. Imitating the machinery of American stardom and genre conventions, films such as *Gallant Hearts* catered unapologetically to Indian tastes and audiences, ultimately resisting either British or U.S. monopoly. Together, the three essays collected in this section address American silent cinema's imbrication in types of cultural contact that would play a significant role in developing local film markets geared toward stand-alone national cinemas, which continue to interact dialectically with U.S. cinema in a crisscrossed network of ebb and flow.

Notes

1. As Tom Gunning has shown so persuasively, it would be a mistake to assume that the Lumière brothers' *Arrival of a Train at a Station* scared its first viewers because they "naïvely" assumed that it would crash into them. Nevertheless, the scene at the Grand Café where the film was first screened still serves as a defining image for the Western viewer's first encounter with the moving image, albeit one that stimulates a thrilling sensation of shock rather than fear. For Gunning's discussion of the "cinema of attractions," see "An Aesthetic of Astonishment: Early Film and the (In)credulous Spectator," in *Viewing Positions: Ways of Seeing Film*, ed. Linda Williams (New Brunswick, NJ: Rutgers University Press, 1994), 124–133. For a detailed account of Gunning's response to a critique of attractions and shock as elements of the "modernity thesis," see "Modernity and Cinema: A Culture of Shocks and Flows," in *Cinema and Modernity*, ed. Murray Pomerance (New Brunswick, NJ: Rutgers University Press, 2006), 297–315, esp. 301.

2. Linda Williams argues that *The Kiss* inaugurates a new kind of voyeurism in the history of American cinema. See "Of Kisses and Ellipses: The Long Adolescence of American Movies," *Critical Inquiry* 32 (Winter 2006): 295.

3. Miriam Hansen, "The Mass Production of the Senses: Classical Cinema as Vernacular Modernism," in *Reinventing Film Studies*, ed. Christine Gledhill and Linda Williams (London: Arnold; New York: Oxford University Press, 2000), 332–350.

4. Ibid., 334. Yuri Tsivian analyzes the material transformations of Griffith's work in Russia elsewhere in this volume.

5. Ibid., 342–343.

6. Ibid., 344, 341.

7. Ibid., 341.

8. Hansen first used the term "vernacular modernism" in "Fallen Women, Rising Stars, New Horizons: Shanghai Silent Film as Vernacular Modernism," *Film Quarterly* 54.1 (Fall 2000): 10–22, where she discusses the impact of vernacular modernism on silent cinema in China; see p. 15 for her analysis of *Daybreak*.

9. Aaron Gerow, *Visions of Japanese Modernity: Articulations of Cinema, Nation, and Spectatorship, 1895–1925* (Berkeley: University of California Press, 2010), 23.

10. Hansen, "Mass Production of the Senses," 343.

11. Jennifer M. Bean, "Charles Chaplin: The Object Life of Mass Culture," in *Flickers of Desire: Movie Stars of the 1910s* (New Brunswick, NJ: Rutgers University Press, 2011), 250.

12. Gerow, *Visions of Japanese Modernity*, 25.

13. For another account of the American serial's popularity in Japan, see Mark Garrett Cooper, "Pearl White and Grace Cunard: The Serial Queen's Volatile Present," in Bean, *Flickers of Desire*, 174–195.

14. Yingjn Zhang, *Chinese National Cinema* (London: Routledge, 2004).

15. Hansen, "Fallen Women," 19.

16. Lee Grieveson and Peter Krämer, *The Silent Cinema Reader* (London: Routledge, 2004), 334.

17. For details about the conditions under which the Indian Cinematograph Committee was formed, see Priya Jaikumar, "More Than Morality: The Indian Cinematograph Committee Interviews (1927)," *The Moving Image* 3.1 (Spring 2003): 82–109. For a discussion of racial anxieties that prevailed at the time, see Babli Sinha, "Lowering Our Prestige: American Cinema, Mass Consumerism, and Racial Anxiety in Colonial India," *Comparative Studies of South Asia, Africa and the Middle East* 29.2 (2009): 291–305.

6 From *Misemono* to *Zigomar*

A Discursive History of Early Japanese Cinema

Aaron Gerow

It is one of the bitter tragedies of studying early Japanese film history that only a handful of films before the mid-1920s exist; there are simply not enough extant works to do justice to a history of Japanese film style before 1925. It is thus partly out of necessity that I construct in this chapter a discursive history of early cinema in Japan rather than analyzing many of the filmic texts themselves. But it is also a matter of choice. Remember that Michel Foucault, in *The Archaeology of Knowledge,* argues: "What, in short, we wish to do is dispense with 'things' . . . to substitute for the enigmatic treasure of 'things' anterior to discourse, the regular formation of objects that emerge only in discourse. To define these objects without reference to the *ground,* the *foundation of things,* but by relating them to the body of rules that enable them to form as objects of a discourse and thus constitute the conditions of their historical appearance."[1] Certainly Foucault does not intend a writing of a history without texts, but in a perhaps ironic way his form of discursive history allows us to still talk about early Japanese film history even though many of the "things," the motion pictures themselves, are not present for us to examine and analyze. Maybe it is better this way: until now, it has been the privileging of such works that has led most scholars of later Japanese film history to focus only on the texts and authors, at the expense of understanding either the ways in which they first appear "only in discourse" or the conditions in which they emerged as the objects of people's understanding. That has also led to the downplaying of research on periods like that of early cinema, where there are few films. While certainly not a desirable situation, perhaps the absence of films from the 1910s and early 1920s permits us to pay more attention to the discursive basis on which they would have been created, watched, understood, and discussed.

In the case of many nations, such a discursive history must have a global dimension, considering not only the transnational valences of local film history but also how such factors as borders and global flows of texts and technology are themselves discursively articulated. Especially as a medium whose history is shaped by moments of importation, in terms of the introduction of both the technology and modes of filmmaking, cinema can easily be described through narratives of foreignness, of absence (being outside) changing to presence (being inside Japan) or of starts (when cinema or its modernity "began" in Japan) and stops (when a style of cinema, such as early film or even a more classical cinema, ended or became dominant). Those scholars who, like Isolde Standish, subscribe to a degree of technological determinism, or to a strict ideological profile of certain technologies, tend to write histories that begin with the introduction of such devices.[2] Such boundaries, both temporal and spatial, can play an important role in Japanese film historiography, but I advise caution in constructing similar histories precisely because these boundaries should not be taken as given. They were themselves defined and redefined at crucial conjunctures through the words and meanings attached to them.

A consideration of these discursive struggles complicates narratives of importation, especially any history that spatially divides Japan from the West and states that cinema (and its discourse), being essentially Western, did not exist in Japan before it arrived from abroad. One version of this story features cinema as a carrier of Westernized discourse, invading Japan with foreign modes of seeing and experiencing that begin to spread among the populace through the power of the medium itself. This kind of narrative was utilized in 1930s Japan in complaints about "Americanization," when authorities, beginning to mobilize the citizenry for war, worried about the potential harm that popular foreign films had on the national spirit. This was not merely a question of the content of Hollywood films but of the essence of the medium itself, as even the novelist Tanizaki Jun'ichirō, in wondering in *In'ei raisan* (*In Praise of Shadows*) what the cinema would have been like if Japan had invented it, ascribed a particular Westernized discourse of light and shadow to the existing technology itself.

While such stories of cultural invasion and imperialism cannot be ignored as long as significant imbalances remain between East and West, North and South, or center and periphery, their assumptions often give the nature of discourse and the processes of importation short shrift. If a history of cinema in Japan focuses on the influence of a foreign object, one whose essence to a greater or lesser degree determines its effects (either a Westernized or cinematic essence, or both), then that history assumes that meaning has a univalent quality, which is problematic from the standpoint of poststructuralist semiotic and cultural studies. It also threatens to reproduce such geopolitical imbalances by depriving receivers of the ability to shape, interpret, and appropriate these discourses from abroad. It can also ignore conflicts and inequalities within the local sphere by focusing too much on East/West or domestic/foreign binaries. Even if the technology of cinema was foreign, could one not argue that its articulation or even construction in discourse was at least partly a local affair, if we conceive of the local as porous and crisscrossed by, but never reducible to, the global—if the local itself is conflicted and contradictory, folding within itself a "foreign" discourse as one of a range of unequal and politically charged positions? And can we not also say that some local articulations may pre-date the arrival of this "foreign" technology, establishing the cinema before it arrives?

In approaching the discursive history of the arrival of cinema in Japan, I focus not on the discovery of the essence of cinema or its domestication in an existing Japan but on the ways in which cinema was dialectally accommodated within the uneven field of discourse of post-1890s Japan and helped transform that field. While some of the discursive constructions may be analogous to those found in other situations, it is important to ground them in the historical conjuncture specific to the late Meiji (1868–1912). I argue that a definition of cinema was not created initially; film, while being discussed in then-contemporary journalism within a discernible set of patterns, did not yet exist as a unique problem that demanded a particular discursive solution. It was only around 1910, with a series of debates symbolized by the furor over the French film *Zigomar* (Victorin Jasset, 1911) that cinema, finally defined as an issue requiring a response, began to accumulate a set of meanings that would distinguish it from other media.

Moving Pictures as *Misemono*

Japan is one case in which it is hard to align the history of discourse on film with the arrival of the apparatus from the West. First, long before the cinema's arrival in Japan, books described in rather sensationalistic terms the marvels of Western knowledge, including such proto-cinematic devices as the zoetrope.[3] Then, entering the 1890s, Japanese newspapers, which were always interested in news of the latest trends in Western culture and science, began running articles announcing Thomas Edison's initial work. The film historian and collector Tsukada Yoshinobu painstakingly accumulated over his lifetime most of the newspaper and magazine articles printed in Japan about the motion pictures before and in the first year after the medium was imported into Japan, and he published them in his lifework, *Nihon eigashi no kenkyū* (A study of Japanese film history). Devoted to determining the exact facts and chronology relating to the first year of cinema in Japan (who imported what machine when and how), the book is also a treasure trove of examples of how the Japanese media first approached the motion pictures. According to Tsukada's research, the first article on Edison's new invention was published in the *Fukuoka nichi nichi shinbun* on April 12, 1890, more than a year before Edison even applied for a patent for the Kinetoscope. Several other articles followed over the years, but since one that appeared in the English-language *Japan Weekly Mail* (on July 18, 1891) was reprinted from the *London Times,* it is likely that most of them were translations of pieces that had run in foreign papers. As such, they exemplify the degree to which even the very first discussions of cinema in Japanese crisscrossed whatever boundaries existed between Japan and the West.

As one would expect, the focus of these articles is on the reproduction of movement, emphasizing the new apparatus's ability to represent even the most fleeting and precise transformations, preserving past events so that they could be shown again in the present just as they once were. Underlying these discussions was a conception of realism that praised the machine's ability to present a vision "that is no different than looking at the real thing."[4] The Japanese articles were seemingly not content with describing a new machine that humans could use in their quest to control the natural world. The headline of the first article in the *Fukuoka nichi nichi shinbun* on the Kinetograph (Edison's early attempt to combine motion pictures and the phonograph) is most telling: "Shashin, ensetsu o nasu" (Pictures give a speech). The article goes on to explain that "the pictures can seem as if they are truly moving and giving a speech."[5] Without mentioning that it is the people in the pictures who presumably move and speak, the article focuses attention on technology itself becoming an enunciative subject, spectacularizing the technology by underlining its marvelous qualities. It is this fascination with the apparatus that would dominate discussions of the Kinetoscope, the Cinématographe, and the Vitascope in the year after they were imported to Japan.[6] Yet in attempting to describe the marvels of these new inventions, writers would avail themselves of a variety of existing discourses to connect cinema to known phenomena, discussing it in relation to such discursive categories as *gentō* (the Japanese version of the magic lantern), Westernization, realism, and the wonders of science.

In approaching the technology itself, many availed themselves of *gentō* as a proto-cinematic reference point.[7] The *Yomiuri shinbun* likened the process of projecting the image onto a white screen to that of the *gentō* (in many cases, the term *gentō* itself was used to signify the process of projection),[8] and then went on to describe the motion pictures as "the most evolved version of *utsushi-e*,"[9] thereby creating a history in which the imported cinema was an outgrowth of the Japanese version of the magic lantern. The scientist and film essayist Terada Torahiko reported his first experience of watching film as "the sort of experience of 'not believing until you see it, but once you see it, you are surprised yet at the same time think it's not out of the ordinary.' Anyway, it seems I was not as surprised as the first time I saw *gentō*."[10] A writer with the pen name Dōjin Shiin also wrote in 1903 of a friend who still argued that *gentō*, in addition to being able to show the same "transformations" as the moving pictures, did not suffer from flicker and was certainly richer in entertainment value than the new technology. While Dōjin himself agreed with his colleague on the emotional impact created by a skilled *gentō* performance, he went on to insist that "one cannot show the state of living moving beings without the moving pictures."[11] Although highly praised as an early means of moving image entertainment, the *gentō* in the end was used in most discussions as a difference against which cinema would be defined. The *Fusō shinbun* in Nagoya declared the Vitascope to be "completely different in content from the existing *gentō* in that it looks as if it truly moves."[12] Komada Kōyō, arguably the most prominent of the early motion picture showmen, reproduced a newspaper article in his early pamphlet explaining the Vitascope which declared that the device was "not something like the *gentō* which is made of slipshod imaginary pictures, but directly projects photographs. . . . Since these do not immediately differ from the real thing, . . . they do not move outside of natural laws."[13] The motion pictures were thus valorized over *gentō* on the scale of realism, but only in a field of knowledge in which film was depicted as an extension of the magic lantern. Such is evident in one of the many names given to the cinema in its first few years in Japan: *jidō gentō,* or self-moving magic lantern.[14]

In further explaining the technology, much early discourse on cinema would avail itself of the interest or even faith in scientific knowledge and progress prominent in the Meiji quest to catch up with the West. Early film exhibition was sometimes constructed as a means by which the Japanese could vicariously enter a Western space and overcome the divisions in time and geography to achieve, if only in mind, Fukuzawa Yukichi's call to "leave Asia and join Europe." Yet labeling the cinema a new scientific discovery did not necessarily contain it within a field of knowledge in which its wonders were attributable to human mastery of natural laws. The laws of science themselves, in some ways, were merely some of the inexplicable powers to which the cinema owed its fascinating abilities, a field of mystery and wonder that, by association, paradoxically made the cinema understandable in its marvelousness, fitting easily into the discourse of the fairground entertainments, or *misemono.* This fascination with the technology of cinema ultimately revolved around the apparatus's capacity to reproduce reality. The primary focus of newspaper reports would continue to be on the realism of the motion pictures, as they declared that viewing the new spectacle was "no different from seeing the true thing,"[15] that it gave "the feeling of touching the real thing."[16] In the early discourse on cinema, there was a distinct interest, mixed with a wishful desire, in the motion pictures as a means of revealing all the hidden aspects of reality. The *Osaka asahi shinbun* speculated that, if Edison succeeded in his efforts to add color to this "self-moving means of photography," then "there will not be a single thing under heaven not exposed in front of our eyes."[17] Another paper, already lamenting that the current film technology could only show us limited aspects of things, was hoping that the addition of the newly discovered X-ray photography would allow the apparatus to see everything move.[18]

While this investment in realism and the desire to see may bear some influence from developments in modern visuality in Europe and the United States,[19] that investment must be located within trends in entertainment, both visual and physical, that stretch back to the previous century, especially those embodied in *misemono*. Such trends shape such visuality, rendering it both new and familiar. As art historian Kinoshita Naoyuki repeatedly stresses in his provocative analysis of the role of the *misemono* in modern Japanese art history, *Bijutsu to iu misemono* (The *misemono* called art), a discourse of realism intersected with the *misemono* from the early 1800s, even before the arrival of Commodore Matthew Perry and forms of Western art. As Kinoshita sees it, these ways of speaking not only help define the *misemono* but also elucidate how Western art was introduced into Japan. Kinoshita focuses some attention on *ikiningyō*, the papier-mâché "living dolls" that, when arranged to re-create scenes from history or literature or introduce views of foreign lands, were a popular variety of *misemono* in entertainment districts like Edo's (or Tokyo's) Asakusa in the mid-1800s. When writing of these superbly crafted dolls, especially those molded by the most celebrated master of the art, Matsumoto Kisaburō, contemporary observers noted that viewing them "was like facing living people."[20] Arguing that the *misemono* satisfied desires for realism ignored by other art forms, Kinoshita traces the quest for realism in *misemono* back centuries earlier, but stresses that *ikiningyō* marked a significant shift. Previous *misemono* modes of representation, such as *kago saikō* (baskets woven in the form of people and animals), were enjoyable to the degree that there was a gap between the materials used and the image represented; never forgetting they were viewing baskets, people marveled at how skillfully the materials were made to resemble real people. But everything was done to *ikiningyō* to eliminate the difference between the materials used and real persons, to make viewers forget they were looking at papier-mâché dolls.[21] It is unlikely, of course, that anyone really failed to realize that these were made of paper, and so amid a general shift from stressing the physicality of the object to hiding it, the tension between knowledge of the object and the wonders of technique/technology became a core aspect of the pleasure of *misemono*. Early cinema in Japan would carry on this enjoyable tension.

Ikiningyō were intricately tied to this discourse of realism, the craft itself often being named *shōutsushi ikiningyō*, with a term meaning "accurate reflection" added at the front. It is interesting to note, as Kinoshita does, that the word *shōutsushi* was central to early artistic debates on realism that would eventually give birth to the modern meaning of the term *shashin*, or photography (the ideographic characters *sha* [also read "utsushi"] and *shin* literally meaning "reflecting the truth").[22] As an early mode of "photography," then, *ikiningyō* can be taken as another form of proto-cinema in Japan, along with the *gentō*, satisfying desires to see the unseen (the foreign) or the fantastic (pictures move, dolls "live"). More important for this discussion, the forms for describing *ikiningyō* and later kinds of *misemono* strongly resemble those subsequently used for cinema. The

Western looking glass (*Seiyō megane*), an early Meiji apparatus with numerous lenses through which spectators could see skillfully produced views of the West (usually with a well-lit, three-dimensional effect), was described as "the truly mysterious art of traveling through foreign lands without going to the West"; looking through it was "just like living in the various European countries."[23] The discourse of seeing the unseen was less a property of the cinema than an established way of speaking about visual entertainments in the field of the *misemono.* The term *misemono* literally does mean, after all, "showing something." Imbricated with existing discourses on the *gentō,* science, Westernization, and realism, cinema may have occupied a particular space shaped by the intersections of these discourses, but such a space was not unique and therefore could not define the motion pictures as significantly different from existing forms of *misemono* entertainment. In their first years in Japan, motion pictures were talked about mostly as just the latest attraction, interchangeable with other *misemono* within a common space of exhibition.

Although, in the years following the importation of the motion pictures, *katsudō shashin* (literally, "moving photographs") would become the name of the new medium, discourse on cinema would, for some time, continue to center on the field of the *misemono.* Dōjin Shiin's book *Katsudō shashinjutsu jizai* (All about the moving picture craft) is a good example of the continued prevalence of *misemono* discourse on cinema. Printed in 1903, it came out the year that the first permanent movie theater in Japan, the Denkikan, was established in Tokyo's Asakusa. Cloaked as a technical introduction, the work is basically a fantastic rendition of the wonders of cinema. Dōjin begins by claiming that the cinema was invented by the "anatomist" Lumière in order to show his students the workings of the human heart that could not be sufficiently explained in words or regular pictures. He echoes the first descriptions of cinema offered in Japan, praising it for being able to "continually copy down a state of infinite change without leaving anything out" and for picturing "not the slightest difference from the real thing."[24] Dōjin further pursues the potential of film to capture the motions inside the human body and devotes pages to speculating on whether film can be made to capture the motions of the mind. Citing a report that an Englishman had acquired such a machine from the king of Siam, he even ponders the ethical dilemma of being able to read other people's thoughts. While still focusing attention on the body, Dōjin takes the desire to see the unseen to the extreme, but in a way that again draws on the founding traditions of the *misemono,* where the presentation of deformed creatures, mostly taking place on the grounds of temples and shrines, was used as a means of educating people about the punishments they would receive if they committed sins and accumulated bad karma.[25] That Dōjin's moral lesson, woven in a fantastic and excessive language, was unproblematically combined with both technical explanations of film and photography and a resolute belief in human progress is itself a sign of how inextricably the discourses of science and the motion pictures were still connected with the *misemono* imaginary even in 1903.[26]

The Russo-Japanese War in 1904–1905 provided a boost to the motion pictures, as films treating the war proved box office hits, composing 80 percent of the films shown. Fervently patriotic audiences were eager to see visual evidence that Japan was the first Asian country to defeat a modern European power. But this did not necessarily single the cinema out: as Ueda Manabu has shown, such visual evidence could in some cases, such as Komada Kōyō's *shinematekku* attraction, be a mixture of moving dioramas and motion pictures, in which the latter was actually the less important feature.[27] The discourse of realism did come to the fore again as exhibitors boasted of showing actual scenes from the latest battles and film producers sent cameramen to the front to acquire images that could sell. Yet as Komatsu Hiroshi argues, this version of realism was in no way based on a firm cinematic division between fiction and nonfiction. Fake documentaries, featuring miniature ships and cigar smoke, were just as likely to be classified as "war subjects" as works actually filmed at the front.[28] According to Komatsu, audiences themselves did not seem to mind: "Authenticity on the level of film reception was not that important; all these works were part of a homogenous filmic representation. When spectators got angry that the war images unfolding before their eyes were false, their anger was in no way based on a conceptual opposition of nonfiction to fiction, but was simply directed against the fact the representation was inaccurate."[29]

Whether the representation was seen as real had little to do with a Bazinian perception of the ontological relation of the image to reality; it was merely based on a comparison of known facts with what was presented on the screen. In this logic, panoramas and *ikiningyō,* as long as they were accurate, were equally as real as—and thus interchangeable with—the cinema. According to Komatsu, the modes of film categorization that made fake and real documentaries equal under the rubric "war subjects" were borrowed from nineteenth-century magic lantern catalogues.[30] Abé Mark Nornes takes issue with Komatsu's general claim about a "homogenous cinema," as well as with his tendency to narrate early film history from the position of fiction film. He notes some early actualities, such as *Kankoku Kōtaishi Denka, Itō Daishi Kankoku omiya nyūkyō no kōkei* (Scene of His Imperial Highness the Prince of Korea and Ito Hirobumi entering the Imperial Palace, 1907), that could not have performed their intended functions (such as proving to Koreans that their prince, rumored to be dead, was still alive) had cinema not been recognized as providing truthful evidence.[31] Such films link up with the initial claims about the realism of the new medium, and they point to one way in which it would be distinguished in the coming years, but it would take time before such distinctions were made across the discursive field.

By the end of the first decade of the twentieth century, Japanese intellectuals began recording their observations about the new medium in writing, but it would be several years before they asserted such distinctions. A special collection of such essays, penned by illustrious figures such as the novelists Shimazaki Tōson and Nagai Kafū and the theater director Osanai Kaoru (whose interest in film would later lead him to serve as an advisor to Shōchiku in its early years), appeared in the journal *Shumi* (Taste) in August 1909, one of the first such collections to appear at a time when film magazines did not yet exist. Many of the articles, while focused on the motion pictures as a specific topic, still did not offer a unique definition of the medium. Kafū, like the aficionado of traditional *shitamachi* (downtown Tokyo) culture that he was, merely used the motion pictures as an excuse to grumble about the lack of purity in literature and art in a modernizing age, commenting how, since "the modern is a terrible age," it was "more truly an honor to fail and be buried by the modern."[32] With Kafū helping to establish a pattern of inventing tradition by lamenting the arrival of the modern, cinema served as only one of many unspecified signs of the new that facilitated the creation of the boundaries of old Japan.

Other authors, while more favorable to the motion pictures, mostly treated them as merely a new object of interest. Shimazaki Tōson, in a short piece, remarked that viewing films reminded him of the ever-present difference between East and West.[33] Yoshie Kogan, a scholar of French literature, was still using the language used by the first newspaper articles about film in Japan, commenting on how the device allowed one to preserve the past and witness everyday life in the West. The cinema's interest, to him, remained on the level of the reproduction of simple motion.[34] Finally, the account by the poet and literary critic Kubota Utsubo was largely a skeptical record of his first trip to see the motion pictures earlier that year. Expecting the movies to be of interest only to children, he had been surprised not only because the audience had been mostly adults, but also because the pictures had been worthy of being shown to people of that age. Given that he saw cinema's role as limited only to the introduction of unusual sights, however, he ultimately restricts the motion pictures to the discourse of the *misemono* by claiming they "were the most interesting of the *misemono* of that kind."[35]

In the first years of twentieth century, there was another major field of discourse that made little attempt to define a difference between cinema and other *misemono* entertainments: the law. Starting with Yoshiyama Kyokkō, one of the first film critics in Japan, many have cited the Chosakukenhō (Copyright Law) as the first law to recognize the existence of film: one section declares that reproducing or exhibiting the copyrighted work of another person as a motion picture was to be considered a copyright violation.[36] Such statutes, however, did little to define cinema as a unique object under the law. In fact, Japanese law was very late compared to other nations in clarifying cinema's status as intellectual property.

While Japan, as a signatory to the Berne Convention, technically consented to the provisions in the treaty protecting film, it did nothing to clarify this protection in Japanese law other than establish cinema as a threat to literary copyright. As late as 1929, Yanai Yoshio, legal scholar and former head of film censorship at the Home Ministry, had to devote a major section of his monumental *Katsudō shashin no hogo to torishimari* (Protection and regulation of the moving pictures) to arguing copyright law. He proposed that, while Japanese copyright law did not specifically state that film was subject to protection, the motion pictures were included under the rubric of "other products in the realm of literature, academics, and art," found in Article 1 of the law, and that Japan, by ratifying revisions of the Berne treaty, was obligated to treat domestic films as protected even if this was not specified in its own law.[37] Despite this tacit protection, the film industry would continue asking for some years for more specific provisions in the law. It seems typical of the ironies of early discourse on cinema in Japan that the medium was singled out first only as a threat to an established art like literature, and offered positive legal protection solely as part of an undistinguished, unnamed mass of "other arts."

As a larger potential threat, films were subject to censorship from the very beginning. There is the oft-related anecdote about Edison's film *The Kiss,* in which the police attempted to stop the famous filmed kiss between May Irvin and John C. Rice from being shown in Osaka in 1897, complaining that it harmed public morals. The story goes that the quick-witted *benshi* Ueda Hoteiken apparently convinced the overly prudish police that a kiss was similar to a handshake in the United States and prevented the film from being banned.[38] According to Yoshiyama, the first film to actually be refused permission for exhibition in Japan was one produced by the French company Pathé Frères, *Les martyrs de l'Inquisition* (1905), which was cited for excessive cruelty in 1906.[39] Such cases of police intervention, however, did not take place on the basis of any law that specifically named the motion pictures. Cinema was treated as a *misemono* as much in law as in popular discourse and, thus, initially regulated by the laws that covered those entertainments.[40] In Tokyo during the very first years, this meant either the Regulations for Viewing Establishments—the 1891 statute that covered sports or sideshow entertainments performed in front of public audiences, such as sumō, acrobatics, and panoramas—or, for films shown in regular theaters, possibly also the Theater Regulations from 1890 (overhauled as the Theater Exhibition Regulations of 1900, the first attempt to systematize theater censorship). Such statutes required that exhibitors acquire police permission before presenting entertainments and stipulated that applications deemed to be potentially injurious to public peace and morals would not be approved.

Neither of these regulations, nor the corresponding ones in other localities, specifically cited the motion pictures or contained statutes that called for particular systems of control for film. Cinema certainly existed to the degree that authorities recognized it as an entertainment capable of harming public peace, manners, and morals, but in both the procedures to which it was submitted and the way it was articulated in law, film did not exist independently from other *misemono.* Subject to laws written before the apparatus even appeared on Japanese shores, the motion pictures were merely inserted into a series of longstanding censorship procedures and traditions and treated no differently from Edo era entertainments. According to legal discourse, as well as to many other discourses dealing with film, it was as if cinema either had not yet appeared in Japan or, since it was treated like any other *misemono,* had always already been in Japan and was only assuming a shape not yet its own.

Zigomar and the Problem of Cinema

Cinema would make its appearance in Japan—almost with a vengeance—partly through the incident surrounding the French film *Zigomar,* directed by Victorin Jasset for the Société Française des Films Éclair, which was imported to Japan by Fukuhōdō, a relatively new film company, and opened at their Asakusa theater, the Kinryūkan, on November 11, 1911. The fast-paced detective film, featuring repeated clashes between the debonair criminal mastermind and master of disguise Zigomar and a series of detectives (including one named Nick Carter), proved immensely popular with Japanese fans (see Figure 6.1). The phenomenal success it enjoyed, as well as the authorities' reaction to it, had a major impact on Japanese film culture and created a series of shock waves that would alter the ways in which cinema was discussed and defined. While I do not intend to argue that the *Zigomar* incident was the sole cause of these changes in the way film was defined (there were pointed criticisms of cinema before the series' appearance), it is in many ways a condensation of these transformations.

The Japanese film industry had been enjoying its own small boom starting in about 1909, before the *Zigomar* sensation. With the industry earning vital capital from the success of Russo-Japanese War films—another indication of the important role war has played in the formation of Japanese cinema—the number of permanent motion picture theaters increased, and several companies were formed to regularize production within Japan. Yoshizawa Shōten constructed the first film studio in Tokyo's Meguro district in January 1908, as well as a theme park in Asakusa named after Coney Island's Luna Park; Makino Shōzō began producing immensely popular *kyūgeki* (old style) films starring Onoe Matsunosuke for Yokota Shōkai in 1909; and M. Pathé's Umeya Shōkichi sent cameramen off to the South Pole to record the exploits of a Japanese expedition in one of the industry's first feature documentaries. With Fukuhōdō entering the picture in 1909 with a string of well-built theaters, the number of Tokyo movie houses rose

Figure 6.1 The debonair criminal mastermind and master of disguise, Zigomar. Still courtesy of the Kawakita Memorial Film Institute.

to a total of forty-four by 1912.[41] Film had finally come into its own as a domestic industry, and the papers were replete with comments on how vigorous business was.[42] In July of the same year, the four existing film companies, partly in a belated effort to emulate the monopoly trust formed by the Motion Picture Patents Company in the United States, but also to consolidate the business as a legitimate industry, merged to form the Nihon Katsudō Shashin Kabushiki Kaisha (Japan Moving Picture Company), or Nikkatsu for short. After the Meiji emperor died at the end of July, the Japanese film industry set out on a new path as Japan entered the Taishō era (1912–1926).

At this time, any detective stories featuring chase scenes and criminal masterminds seemed to be a hit with Japanese movie audiences. The first *Zigomar* was followed by a sequel, and other foreign productions were brought in to cash in on the craze. Even Japanese producers began filming their own *Zigomar* imitations, with such works as *Nihon Jigoma* (Japanese Zigomar; Yoshizawa, 1912), *Shin Jigoma daitantei* (New great detective Zigomar; M. Pathé, 1912), and *Jigoma kaishinroku* (The record of Zigomar's reformation; Yoshizawa, 1912) doing much to introduce European techniques such as faster editing into Japanese cinema. The *Tokyo asahi shinbun* reported that four of the major movie theaters in Asakusa were showing *Zigomar* imitations on the night of October 4, 1912.[43] The craze even spread to the publishing industry, which began printing novelizations of these films (or stories based on them), a successful trend that had a definite effect on the development of the Japanese mystery novel.[44] *Zigomar* had become a nationwide sensation and came to represent the success of the motion pictures, if not the existence of cinema itself.[45] Newspapers reported that the name had become part of Japanese slang ("He's a Zigomar!" referred to a dapper, though somewhat suspicious, man), and that children in vacant lots everywhere were enjoying themselves by creating their own versions of the detective Nick Carter chasing the elusive evildoer.

The popularity of *Zigomar*, arguably the first example of a truly mass, modern entertainment fad in Japanese history—if not also, as Nagamine Shigetoshi has argued, of a complex multimedia phenomenon[46]—was not always greeted with favor in public discourse. Education officials began worrying aloud about the potentially harmful effects movies were having on children, prompting a Tokyo school board committee to issue a report in July 1911 warning of the dangers of the medium and its places of exhibition and recommending that the lower schools in the area bar filmgoing by their pupils.[47] As if to verify those worries, rumors spread of minors committing crimes based on what they had learned watching films like *Zigomar*. There arose what Hase Masato has called a kind of "cinemaphobia."[48] Without mentioning the French production, the powerful *Tokyo asahi shinbun* newspaper first ran a ten-part series of articles in February 1912 warning of the dangers of motion pictures to children, and then, on October 4, 1912, began an eight-part series of reports on the *Zigomar* phenomena that characterized these films as "inspiring crime" and roundly criticized the Tokyo Metropolitan Police for not banning the movies before their release. Almost as if directly reacting to these criticisms (the *Asahi* actually took credit in print), the police announced on October 9 that they were banning *Zigomar* and other similar films from Tokyo screens (films that had already started their runs, however, were allowed to be shown until October 20; new films in a similar vein would not be given permission to screen after October 10). Other localities soon followed Tokyo's lead; in this way, Japan's first experience with film as a mass cultural phenomenon was deemed injurious to public morals and effectively stamped out.[49] In this action, and in the discussions surrounding the *Zigomar* craze, one can sense a shift in the way cinema was defined in discourse in Japan.

The *Tokyo asahi* took considerable effort to introduce the *Zigomar* phenomenon to its readership, starting the first article in its series with the inquiring title "Just What Is *Zigomar?*" The subsequent articles attempted to answer this question, explaining that this was "the last phenomenon of the Meiji era"[50] and offering a detailed summary of the plots of the first two French *Zigomar* productions. But this was an *Asahi* that in February had railed that "there are a hundred evils [to the motion pictures] and not one benefit."[51] The series did not stop at objectively describing the craze: in a mixture of reportage and editorializing common to Japanese journalism at the time, it unequivocally stated, "Once you see *Zigomar,* you cannot call it a detective film, but rather a film promoting crime or a film glorifying criminals."[52] Declaring that "the fact that [the *Zigomar* films] have a bad influence on or corrupt audiences is a fact that none can deny,"[53] the *Asahi* proceeded to claim the existence of two or three cases of such corruption. No specifics were given, and the assertion itself seems suspicious when looked at from our point in time. There were virtually no accounts detailing such "corruption" (e.g., examples of crimes being committed because of something the perpetrator had witnessed in a Zigomar film), except, ironically, ones *after* the banning of the film.[54] One may wonder if the claimed ill effect was more a result of the media coverage and police reaction than of the film itself (where cinema was not evil until named so officially), and this problem again prompts us to focus on the role that discourse played in defining cinema in Japan in the early 1910s.

The *Tokyo asahi shinbun* was quick to offer various objects of blame for the *Zigomar* phenomenon. Part of the problem, it said, lay with the film and its producers. In a world of cutthroat competition, companies spared no cost in topping both their competition and previous successes. As a result, works like *Zigomar* were "born of the ferocious competition based in commercialism," exposing the fact that the profit motive was not always consistent with the quest to foster a positive influence on society.[55] Thus, the *Asahi* was introducing a theme that would shape many discussions on film up until World War II: that the problem of cinema lay in part in its nature as an industrial art based on capitalistic practices that did not always support the Neo-Confucian national and social goals central to national ideology from the Meiji on.

At the center of the *Asahi* analysis was a detailed consideration of the uniqueness of cinema as a medium, which began with the fact that films like *Zigomar* were fictional products. Reflecting a Neo-Confucian mistrust of fabrication, the *Asahi* began its series by openly wondering how a fictional creation could have so much power over people. Answering its own question, and thereby underlining its own worries about cinema, the newspaper declared, "Even if one can say that every villain is the product of a serials author's imagination, one cannot neglect the fact that once he appears in a work of the moving pictures, the sense that he is the real thing is more prominent than one's feeling in watching theater. Accordingly, the degree to which film itself exerts a lasting influence on audiences is a problem that cannot be neglected."[56] The fact that cinema could make the fictional seem real was both part of its appeal and a major problem, because "simply and ingeniously flavoring the work with fantasy and fact is itself sufficient to strengthen and spread the film's lasting influence."[57] In emphasizing cinema's unique capacity to turn the imaginary into reality, the *Asahi* was constructing a narrative in which audience influence depended on a difference represented by the cinema. Film was finally beginning to peek out from the shadows of the *misemono,* but ironically, only to the extent that it was a social problem.

At the time, it was felt that not only the realism of the films themselves but also the entire space surrounding cinema distinguished it as a dangerous medium and created a plethora of strong stimuli that left a lasting mark on spectators. In the eighth part of the Zigomar series, the *Asahi* offered a vivid account of the sensory experience of going to the movies in 1912 in the movie theater district of Tokyo's Asakusa (see Figure 6.2):

> Beyond the electric lights that dazzle the eyes and the noise from the bands that tend to stray off-key—both of which lead the minds of passersby astray—the first set of stimuli offered by the moving picture district are the placards painted in strong colors of red, blue, yellow, and purple which incite curious hearts. Men and women who set foot in this area quickly become the prisoners of the moving pictures even before they watch a film, already losing their mental balance.
>
> Audiences stimulated and led on in this way first taste an unpleasant feeling as they enter the darkness from the light. Their state of mind, having lost its balance, eventually falls into an uneasy mood. Here the air inside the theater, inadequately ventilated, assaults people with a kind of unclean humidity and attacks the sense of smell with tobacco smoke, the fragrance of face powder, and the odor of sweat.
>
> In an insecure and unpleasant theater, what is projected into the eyes of people having lost mental tranquility is *Zigomar*. . . . The conditions for extending an evil influence and for causing corruption have all been prepared in these elements.[58]

There were, of course, other entertainments in Asakusa that contributed to this cacophony, but here cinema was being blamed for an entire environment; it was starting to figure in discourse as the core of a new but threatening modern life. Not only the films themselves but also cinema as a modern spatial experience assaulting the senses seemed to contribute to the motion pictures' influence. As the paper had previously stressed, the movie hall represented a dangerous, crass, and almost obscene form of physicality, harming not only the spirits of spectators but also their very bodies (as such, cinema eventually became the object of legal and educational, as well as medical, forms of correction).[59] Carrying on but rendered negative such earlier discourses, cinema was demonized not just for its visuality but also for its physicality. Another example of such medical discourse was the recurring emphasis on film as a form of "stimulation" (*shigeki*), according to which the cinema's influence seemed to bypass the filtering effects

Figure 6.2 Asakusa's moving picture district in 1910, showing the garish banners and ornate facades of the Taishōkan and the Sekaikan. Photo courtesy of the National Diet Library website.

of reason and judgment to affect people's character bodily and directly. Unique not only as a technology, film was identified as a central facet of a new but disorientating culture in which both the boundaries between mind and body and the divisions between social groups were undermined and confused, creating a kind of "heterotopia" in Foucault's sense of the term.[60] Such boundary transgressions were a source of fear for the *Asahi* and cited as the basis of the kind of demolition of normal modes of thought that distinguished the moviegoing experience.

In the *Tokyo asahi*'s vision, conditions of reception were not completely to blame for undermining spectators' processes of reason: moving picture audiences were somehow different from the start. Why, after all, would any normal human being tolerate time and time again the inherently "insecure and unpleasant," the physically damaging conditions of the theater as movie fans did? Implied in the paper's account was a cinema audience almost abnormal in character, made up of fans who possessed addictive personalities that forced them to become "prisoners" of the unpleasant as a perverse necessity. As a whole, the paper characterized movie audiences in less than complimentary terms, stating that those "sucked into this *Zigomar*" were "like ants swarming around a piece of sweet sugar."[61] With the *Asahi* claiming that "sensible-minded people would undoubtedly frown upon this fashion for crime films within the moving picture theaters,"[62] the paper was distancing itself from regular filmgoers, placing them on a lower rung in a hierarchy of right-mindedness and siding itself (and its readers) with the "sensible," who refrained from the mob-like behavior of the movie masses. Reflecting a fear of the modern crowd common in later Japanese intellectual descriptions of mass culture, the discourse established an "us" versus "them" division that defined the medium in class-based terms and placed cinema spectatorship outside the boundaries of right-minded behavior. It was cinema's influence on this other set of people that was of central concern.

A description of the composition of the film audience served in part to justify this hierarchy. According to the *Tokyo asahi,* "the grand majority of the audience is young boys and girls of lower or middle school age,"[63] and such future leaders of society were seemingly vulnerable to the motion pictures' authority.

> With these scenes and props, the film first leads the audience into a field of realistic impression and there shows, putting into motion, various evil deeds. Even adult audiences with good sense and judgment are so impressed they call it "an interesting novelty that works well." The film naturally offers even more intense excitement in the minds of the young, who like both adventure and strong individuals, and who idealize the winner in any situation.
>
> For instance, even if the conclusion results in the death of the villain, just how much does the moral point of view indicated by the death of the villain transmit an authoritative impression to the minds of the young living in today's society? Most of them will only see the success of the elusive onscreen hero, and think in the end how they would like to become a figure onscreen themselves, to act and appear as if on film.[64]

On the one hand, it was believed that children (and other lesser spectators, such as women) did not possess the discernment necessary to both properly read the film's ending and ward off the pernicious stimulations of cinema, especially since the motion pictures offered them modes of identification that were previously unheard of. Given that it is debatable whether the audience was dominated by children as the *Asahi* believed,[65] the problem concerning the film audience was less one of age than of modes of understanding and knowledge.

On the other hand, contemporary discourse was describing a potentially ineluctable historical difference that posed a distinct threat. An editorial in the *Yomiuri shinbun* cited the motion pictures (along with the phonograph) as one of the great modern inventions that had truly penetrated the everyday lives of ordinary people.[66] But to the *Tokyo asahi shinbun,* this modernity served as the background for a new breed of young Japanese who increasingly expressed desires that approved modes of moral discourse could not accommodate. The problem concerned not just a minority of children who were visibly cruel and mischievous by nature, but a majority born with such instincts.[67] The cinema, then, did not simply produce but "conform[ed] to these instincts and tastes," representing a new age that threatened to overturn established orders.[68] Film spectators were not simply undereducated but also fundamentally different in their way of perceiving the world and acting on their desires.

As a problem of knowledge, cinema was considered by many officials an educational issue from the 1910s on.[69] To them, film viewers both young and old required instruction, a mental preparedness that would protect them from the disorienting assault of the cinematic experience and enable them to produce approved meanings from specific film works. But what surfaced in the *Zigomar* incident, and what presented an obstacle not encountered earlier, was the problem of alterity, this time as represented by the question of the image. The *Tokyo asahi* noted, "As expected, the style of explanation of the *benshi* charged with lecturing did not neglect the lesson that good is rewarded and evil punished, . . . but in the minds of audiences who were watching the changes appear before their eyes onscreen, no sense arose of good being rewarded and evil being punished."[70] It was thus felt that spoken language was unable to direct the interpretive processes of cinema audiences; there was something in the image that exceeded or even worked against the word. An official from the Tokyo Metropolitan Police, in explaining their difficulties with the film, also noted the difference between the film summary submitted as part of the censorship procedure and the film itself: "At police headquarters, it was thought, looking at the original story of the French *Zigomar,* that there was nothing much to it. Among works of this kind, you would think they were only a kind of child's play when you inspect the moving picture license. That's why we approved it up until today, thinking it had no effect on public morals. However, looking at the actual film, there is a world of difference from the explanation in both the scenery and the characters."[71]

This was not simply a problem of the accuracy of the plot summary: there was increasing concern that the motion pictures were a medium fundamentally different from existing linguistic arts, one that posed unique problems. The *Tokyo asahi* defined this difference: "Compared to *jōruri* and *naniwa-bushi,*[72] which specialize in the aural, and compared to theater, which attacks using both the visual and the aural, the impression received from the moving pictures is stronger and the influence caused is greater."[73] Working in a register dominated by the visual, cinema was seen as forcing an impact deeper than that of the other arts. With the image seemingly resistant to the restrictions of the spoken or written word, there was no guarantee that the minds of audiences were producing even the desired meanings. It was the alterity of the image, coupled with spectator desires associated with it, that helped define the cinema and mass cultural modernity as a threat to a Meiji order that had just seen its leader pass away.

It is important to emphasize that the problem of the image was not one exclusive to *Zigomar;* in the end, cinema itself was the issue. *Zigomar* was thought to merely represent a dangerous trend in motion picture culture that necessitated banning not just this French production but also all others similar to it. *Zigomar* had become a problem in other nations as well (it was eventually banned in France, for instance), often because of its supposed elevation of criminality through the figure of an upper-class criminal. While class would become a central problem in later discussions of film censorship in Japan, *Zigomar*'s social portrayals were barely mentioned in the discourse surrounding the film. Many did voice concern that the film was teaching minors the methods of crime, but it is significant that, despite the recommendations of several newspapers,[74] police never pulled any of the *Zigomar*-influenced novels from the bookstore shelves. It was *Zigomar*'s new and unique depiction of crime through the image that was the issue.

The *Asahi* in particular was already citing a driving force behind this evolution in the image: "When people get used to the moving pictures and will no longer be satisfied with most products, it will be necessary to provide something unprecedented and strongly stimulating so as to shock the visual senses."[75] This, the *Asahi shinbun* felt, was what *Zigomar* and its ilk were doing at an accelerating rate: offering a thrilling and singular mode of visual sensation, a new phenomenon that the paper would call "motion-picture-like" (*katsudō shashinteki*).[76] This emerging uniqueness of cinematic narration was itself cited as a problem. Earlier, the newspaper had complained in general about the "unnaturalness" and incomprehensibility of new film techniques such as ellipses and cutting within the scene, arguing that jumping from scene to scene or cutting out (what, in the classical narrative economy, are considered unimportant) actions confused and fatigued spectators, especially younger ones.[77] The transformation of time and space enabled by editing was itself seen as a threat. In *Zigomar*, this was coupled with the villain's ability to appear and disappear, to change costumes in an instant and mysteriously jump from one place to another while eluding his pursuers, but in a way that, the *Asahi* acknowledged, proved absolutely fascinating to new Japanese youth.

This fluidity of space and identity, analogous to the circulatory anonymity of the modern crowd, was, according to Tom Gunning, a central concern of not only early trick films but also nineteenth-century phenomena like photography (which both undermined established forms of identity through mechanical reproduction and instituted new ones by documenting the individual body) and detective fiction (which tried to assert the certainty of an individual's guilt against an ever-changing urban environment).[78] We can speculate that it was this transcendence of space and time and Zigomar's ability to disguise himself and change identities (aided by Jasset's skillful use of trick photography)—elements similar to the "motionless voyage" Noël Burch cites as central to the classical film experience—that both fascinated and disturbed contemporary observers.

That is perhaps why so much of the discourse on these films worried about the audience's ability to recognize and identify who was the villain and who was the hero. If, as Gunning says, *Zigomar* "envisioned a new cinema of narrative integration, moving towards the paradigm of classical filmmaking,"[79] the discourse on film in Japan marked it as the point at which the moving pictures broke with previous paradigms and stepped into the unknown—the simultaneously alluring and threatening modern realm of spatiotemporal dis- and reconnection—and thereby posed the problem of what cinema is. The motion pictures themselves were seen to be like Zigomar. Here we can say that cinema became foreign after it was familiar. The incipient classical mode was being less vernacularized, in Miriam Hansen's sense of "vernacular modernism,"[80] than made alien. The task of film reformers in the 1910s, in what is called the Pure Film Movement (Jun'eigageki Undō), would be to reinvent the familiarity of classical forms, in part by rendering other modes of filmmaking alien to cinema if not also to Japan.[81]

Nagamine Shigetoshi has offered the interesting hypothesis that *Zigomar* and related films were banned only after the Japanese film versions and novels began appearing. Citing the *Asahi* as evidence, he argues that authorities became worried because the stories were becoming domesticated, or Japanized, taking place with Japanese actors in familiar Japanese settings, and thus better able to influence unsuspecting homegrown audiences.[82] That certainly was a fear, and in the following decades censors would come down harder on Japanese films for portraying certain actions such as kissing (which was banned in cinema until after World War II) than on foreign films for portraying the same actions (where an innocent kiss was allowed on occasion). Authorities could sometimes accept images of certain behaviors if these were comfortably framed as "foreign," but not if they crossed the border and entered Japanese everyday life. *Zigomar* was probably one such case, but I emphasize that the majority of discourse on the film focused less on such border crossings in content—and the fear that foreign behavior was becoming familiar—and more on the realization that the cinema, the means by which these actions were shown and which had until then appeared just to be another *misemono*, was itself alien. The parallel anxiety was less that Japanese would become foreign and more that they were already new and different and that cinema both represented and exacerbated this fact.

It was against these anxieties surrounding new media and the idea of identity changing from both within and without, that many discourses on film tried to operate. Just as Gunning emphasizes the important role of regimes of knowledge in processing photographic information so as to refix and reestablish identity within a modern social context, so we can investigate how discourses after the *Zigomar* incident attempted to name and classify this particular visual experience. On the one hand, such discourses, represented by the efforts of educational authorities and newspapers to describe and categorize cinema and its individual texts, laid the foundations for film study in Japan. On the other, in the hands of film reformers like those in the Pure Film Movement in the 1910s, these discussions would work to merge the cinema with the culture of the new Japanese middle class and transform the status of Japanese film and its audiences.

The *Zigomar* incident in this way helped define a central problem with the motion pictures that authorities and social leaders would confront for some time: how to control an alluring but elusive visual (and sometimes physical) mode of signification—one that resisted the regulation of the written or spoken word—and its spectatorship. Recognition of this unique problem was reflected in the reactions of the police to the incident. A few days after banning the film, the Tokyo police issued a set of internal procedural guidelines detailing what to guard against when evaluating applications for film exhibition:

1. Works constructed from a framework that suggests adultery.
2. Works liable to invite or support methods of crime.
3. Works bordering on cruelty.
4. Works constructed from a pattern that covers love relations or that descend into obscenity, especially ones capable of exciting base emotions.
5. Works contrary to morality, that induce mischief by children, or that cause corruption.[83]

The sections covering adultery, cruelty, obscenity, and morality differed little from the theater regulations in force at the time.[84] What had changed in confronting the problem of film was the perception that cinematic works could not only offend established sensibilities or directly harm public morals but also strongly induce objectionable behavior in spectators, especially in certain sectors of the audience. Theater regulations at the time never posited a narrative of behavioral influence, or specified audiences that should be the object of regulative concern. This was a problem thought specific to cinema, which was posited as influencing a newly defined object of correction and control: thought and behavior.[85]

Cinema was a unique problem that demanded particular modes of correction. It was as cinema that *Zigomar* was banned, not as literature. The special attention—or fear—focused on cinema is evident in reports that authorities even tried to prevent producers from making films on the life of General Nogi Maresuke, the military leader who committed *junshi* (ritual suicide on the occasion of one's lord's death) on the night of the Meiji emperor's funeral, only one month before *Zigomar* was banned.[86] Despite the fact that Nogi was already being praised by many as the epitome of *bushidō,* the perfect example of citizenship for Japanese children, cinema and its form of spectatorship were apparently too dangerous to trust them to spread even this important message.

As a Tokyo police official said, there was "a necessity to more strictly watch [the moving pictures] than the theater."[87] The procedure for censoring films started to change. The Tokyo Metropolitan Police attributed their mistake in approving *Zigomar* for exhibition in part to the fact that they had not seen the film beforehand;[88] given the *misemono* regulations that covered cinema at the time, an application required only a written summary of the film or of the *benshi*'s narration.[89] The police did send out officers to investigate the films while they were being screened in the theaters, but this procedure was no different from dispatching foot patrols to the sideshow tents.[90] The *Zigomar* incident made it clear that censoring the content of a film required more than a review of a written summary. The Tokyo police acknowledged that they now needed to base their decisions on preview screenings.[91] The definition of the filmic text itself began to change as censorship procedures started to place importance on the text as a visual object, not just as a written story, as well as on the text as viewed, not just as read. Cinematic meaning came to be conceived as residing in the text before it was exhibited in theaters, produced less in the space of exhibition and more in the space of production. New censorship technologies were deemed necessary (and later proposed in, for instance, the groundbreaking 1917 Tokyo Moving Picture Regulations), ones that molded modern models of subjectivity centered on promoting the internal mental faculties capable of accommodating this visual "stimulation," and ones that regulated the physical side of cinema and created a homology between the structure of the individual subject and the social hierarchy, where the mental (the upper class and the state) would rule over the body (the lower class, the people).

Thus, it is important to stress that reactions against cinema were not simply a manifestation of an existing Japan confronting or domesticating a new or foreign object. Certainly cinema became a mark of the modern, a modern to be feared and regulated, but it was seen as alien only after it was treated as familiar (as a *misemono*). The Japan that encountered it was also assuredly not a traditional entity, given and complete, but one that authorities recognized was already new, different, and changing. And what they proposed against cinema was not the reinforcement of old-time values (although that rhetoric would become more common two decades later, long after these cultural transformations had already begun), but rather a set of new techniques that, as I argue elsewhere, were conducive to constructing a modern subject within a modern nation.[92] Cinema helped prompt these changes, but only insofar as it became subject to a transformative struggle over its form and meaning. What was emerging here was not a battle between old and new but one between different forces or conceptions of modernity. One site of this battle was the rising field of discourse on cinema, which itself was being shaped by the circumstances of film's "discovery" as a problem.

The history of discourse on the moving pictures in Japan as a specific object began only with the realization that discourse was inadequate to define or accommodate its object. Such a realization itself was not sufficient to generate a discourse on the motion pictures: it had to be linked to a description of the medium as a social problem in need of solution. Only with such a perception did the fact that existing discourses, such as those on the *misemono,* failed to treat the cinema as a differentiated sign become an issue. Discourse on cinema developed by first negating existing discourses, establishing the basis of a semiotics of difference within which the cinema would be defined. Such a semiotic negation was doubled in the social realm, because the motion pictures had to be, in a sense, rejected or posited as objectionable in order to gain a positive definition. Again an existing object cinema was not being "discovered"; rather, *cinema* was appearing in discourse as a term considered crucial in identifying central problems of modernity, discourse, visuality, the body, perception, class, and society. Cinema became distinguished in discourse precisely as a medium that exceeded current discourse (if not the word itself), one that utilized a new mode of signification that could not be accommodated in existing forms of speech and writing. It was this contradictory task of delineating in discourse what by definition could not be described—and thus of finding novel forms of discourse to shape and accommodate it—that became the central dynamic of 1910s discourse on cinema in Japan.

Notes

1. Michel Foucault, *The Archaeology of Knowledge and the Discourse on Language,* trans. A. M. Sheridan Smith (New York: Pantheon, 1972), 47–48.

2. Isolde Standish, in using Jean-Louis Comolli to emphasize the determining role of film technologies, argues that "Japanese . . . were constrained by the ideological motivations that led to the development and use of specific technologies and the rejection of others." She tries to temper this technological determinism by arguing for a dialectic between form (technology) and content, but she neither fully complicates that historically fraught binary nor considers such later scholars as John Belton, Rick Altman, or Jim Lastra for examples of technological histories critical of Comolli's model. See her *A New History of Japanese Cinema: A Century of Narrative Film* (London: Continuum, 2005), 20.

3. See, for instance, Sakamoto Kitarō's embellished introduction to the scientific oddities of the known world: *Jitchi ōyō butsuri kikan,* 2nd ed. (Tokyo: Hakubunkan, 1891).

4. "Shin hatsumei kendōki," *Jiji shinpō,* July 13, 1894, reproduced in Tsukada Yoshinobu, *Nihon eigashi no kenkyū* (Tokyo: Gendai Shokan, 1980), 15. Tsukada's book is hereafter abbreviated as *NENK.* All translations from the Japanese are my own unless otherwise indicated.

5. "Shashin, ensetsu o nasu," *Fukuoka nichi nichi shinbun,* April 12, 1891, in *NENK,* 21–22.

6. Newspaper articles did make distinctions between the three inventions, most emphasizing the fact the Cinématographe and the Vitascope, by being projected, were an advancement on the Kinetescope because they presented "all people and things in their natural size" (*Yomiuri shinbun,* February 24, 1897, in *NENK,* 95). Since newspaper articles were also a means of advertising motion picture showings in advance, some would praise Lumière's device over Edison's (or vice versa) if the two were competing in the same market, as they sometimes were. (The two were also differentiated in terms of their Japanese names, a difference stemming from their competing promoters.) For the purposes of my discussion, I have focused only on their points in common.

7. Japanese *utsushi-e* magic lanterns were mostly made of wood and thus more portable than their European counterparts. Performances often featured several projectionists behind a screen moving around with projectors, adding other motion techniques by quickly flipping slides or parts of slides. For more on the *gentō* or utshishie, see Iwamoto Kenji, *Gentō no seiki: Eiga zen'ya no shikaku bunkashi* (Tokyo: Shinwasha, 2002).

8. The *Miyako shinbun* distinguished between the Kinetescope, then showing in Asakusa, from the Vitascope, presented at the Kabukiza, by writing that the latter "took the picture moving machine currently on exhibition at Asakusa Hanayashiki and showed it on a large scale by means of a *gentō*." "Shashin denki katsudō gentō," *Miyako shinbun,* March 4, 1897, in *NENK,* 197.

9. "Katsudo shashin no kyōsō," *Yomiuri shinbun,* March 4, 1897, in *NENK,* 112.

10. See Terada's "Eiga jidai," found in the collection of essays published under his pseudonym, Yoshimura Fuyuhiko: *Zoku Fuyuhiko shū* (Tokyo: Iwanami Shoten, 1932), 284.

11. Dōjin Shiin, *Katsudō shashinjutsu jizai* (Tokyo: Daigakukan, 1903), 101–102.

12. "Suehiroza no shashin gentō chikudōki," *Fusō shinbun,* March 2, 1897, in *NENK,* 172.

13. Komada Kōyō, *Katsudō shashin setsumeisho tsuki Ejison-shi shiden* (Tokyo: Katsudō Shashinkai, 1897), reprinted in *NENK,* 222. Komada lists the article as appearing in the *Mainichi shinbun,* but Tsukada reports that, in scouring through that newspaper, he was unable to find the original version of the piece. Given Komada's skill as a showman, it is not inconceivable that he made up this article that, in the end, speaks quite highly of himself.

14. This was the name used in ads and articles in the *Kyōto hinode shinbun* on March 3 and 4, 1897, in *NENK,* 106–107.

15. *Osaka asahi shinbun,* February 26, 1897, in *NENK,* 102.

16. "Katsudō shashin," *Jiji shinpō,* January 31, 1897, in *NENK,* 53.

17. *Osaka asahi shinbun,* February 26, 1897, in *NENK,* 103.

18. "Shashin katsudōki o miru," *Mainichi shinbun,* January 30, 1897, in *NENK,* 51.

19. As Komatsu Hiroshi argues: "Shinematogurafu to wa nan datta no ka—Ideorogī sōchi to shite no eiga" (What was the Cinematograph?—Film as an ideological apparatus), in *Eiga denrai: Shinematogurafu to "Meiji no Nihon,"* ed. Yoshida Yoshishige, Yamaguchi Masao, and Kinoshita Naoyuki (Tokyo: Iwanami Shoten, 1995), 103–123.

20. So said Saitō Gesshin in his *Bukō nenpyō* when describing Matsumoto's sideshow "Chinzei Hachirō shimameguri," in a fantastic rendition of the fictional hero Chinzei Hachirō's travels in foreign lands that was put on in Edo in 1855. Quoted in Kinoshita Naoyuki, *Bijutsu to iu misemono* (Tokyo: Heibonsha, 1993), 42.

21. Ibid., 57–62.

22. Ibid., 58.

23. Quoted in ibid., 108. Kinoshita reports that one presentation of the Western looking glass, in a kind of precursor to Hale's Tours, was done in a theater shaped like a Western ship, with the looking glasses disguised as portholes.

24. Dōjin, *Katsudō shashinjutsu jizai,* 5, 58.

25. For a short, though somewhat ahistorical, account of the *misemono,* see Katō Hidetoshi, *Misemono kara terebi e* (Tokyo: Iwanami Shoten, 1965), 10–23.

26. One is left with the impression that Dōjin's language resembles that of the sideshow barker introducing a motion picture show or trying to lure customers into his tent. If that is the case, then the writer on film here differs little from the *benshi,* or "lecturer." And if the latter was one of the attractions of the early cinema experience, then so were such florid depictions of the medium. It is possible that many of Dōjin's readers took pleasure less in the "facts" he conveyed than in the wonderful audacity of his claims and the spectacular visions he offered.

27. Ueda Manabu, "Kankyaku no tomadoi: Eiga sōsōki ni okeru shinamatekku no kōgyō o megutte," *Āto risāchi* 7 (2007): 129–139.

28. Examples of such "faked" films produced by the Edison company, *The Battle of Chemulpo Bay* (1904) and *The Battle of the Yalu* (1904), can be viewed on the Library of Congress website: http://lcweb2.loc.gov/intldl/mtfhtml/mfpercep/igpfilms.html. Both were shot in New York.

29. Komatsu Hiroshi, "Transformations in Film as Reality (Part One): Questions Regarding the Genesis of Nonfiction Film," trans. A. A. Gerow, *Documentary Box* (English ed.) 5 (1994), 3–4. Komatsu here clarifies his position on the issue of fiction and nonfiction in early Japanese cinema found in his earlier "Some Characteristics of Japanese Cinema before World War I," in *Reframing Japanese Cinema: Authorship, Genre, History,* ed. Arthur Noletti Jr. and David Desser (Bloomington: Indiana University Press, 1992), 229–258.

30. Komatsu, "Transformations in Film," 3.

31. Abé Mark Nornes, *Japanese Documentary Film: The Meiji Era through Hiroshima* (Minneapolis: University of Minnesota Press, 2003), 10–15.

32. Nagai Kafū, "Asakusa shumi," *Shumi* 4.8 (August 1909), 7.

33. Shimazaki Tōson, "Tōzai no sōi," *Shumi* 4.8 (August 1909), 8.

34. Yoshie Kogan, "Katsudō no omoshiromi," *Shumi* 4.8 (August 1909), 5–6.

35. Kubota Utsubo, "Hajimete katsudō shashin o mini itta hi," *Shumi* 4.8 (August 1909), 10.

36. Yoshiyama Kyokkō, *Nihon eigakai jibutsu kigen* (Tokyo: Shinema to Engeisha, 1933), 121. Yoshiyama's citation is ambiguous, but he implies that this section was included in the original copyright law was when it was issued in 1899, which is not the case. The section regarding film was added in 1910 to bring Japanese law in line with the 1908 revisions of the Berlin international treaty on copyright. Yoshiyama also quotes the law incorrectly, stating that those who reproduce the work of another "will be considered as producers [*seisakusha*]." The law in fact reads: ". . . will be considered as plagiarists [*gisakusha*]." Makino Mamoru, in his history of prewar film censorship, correctly notes the date of the revision but unfortunately reproduces Yoshiyama's misquotation: Makino Mamoru, *Nihon eiga ken'etsushi* (Tokyo: Pandora, 2003), 34. See Yanai Yoshio, *Katsudō shashin no hogo to torishimari* (Tokyo: Yūhikaku, 1929), for a more accurate account of cinema's place in early copyright law.

37. Yanai cites a 1914 court decision, not related to film, which certified the Berne Convention as equivalent to Japanese law, and a 1925 Tokyo court report (which was not binding) claiming the protection of film as intellectual property, as justification for his argument. Yanai, *Katsudō shashin no hogo to torishimari,* 33–92.

38. For one account of this tale, see Yoshida Chieo, *Mō hitotsu no eigashi* (Tokyo: Jiji Tsūshinsha, 1978), 25.

39. Yoshiyama, *Nihon eigakai jibutsu kigen,* 120.

40. See Makino Mamoru, *Nihon eiga ken'etsushi* (Tokyo: Pandora, 2003), 32–76; Makino, "On the Conditions of Film Censorship in Japan before Its Systematization," in *In Praise of Film Studies,* ed. Aaron Gerow and Abé Mark Nornes (Yokohama: Kinema Club, 2001), 46–67; and Okudaira Yasuhiro, "Eiga to ken'etsu," in *Kōza Nihon eiga,* ed. Imamura Shōhei, Satō Tadao, Shindō Kaneto, Tsurumi Shunsuke, and Yamada Yōji (Tokyo: Iwanami Shoten, 1985), 2:303–308.

41. One of the problems of studying early Japanese film history is the unreliability of some facts and figures. The number of Tokyo movie theaters in the last years of Meiji is a case in point. Satō Tadao gives the number 44 (*Nihon eigashi* [Tokyo: Iwanami Shoten, 1995], 1, 113), but Imamura Kanae, in his history of the Japanese film industry, counts over 70 by 1909 (*Eiga sangyō* [Tokyo: Yūhikaku, 1960], 26), and the *Tokyo asahi shinbun* reported 29 theaters in

Asakusa and the rest of the city in early 1912 ("Katsudō shashin to jidō [ichi]: Ichinen happyaku gojū mannin," *Tokyo asahi shinbun,* February 6, 1912, 6). Such discrepancies continue to plague even the most recent research. I have opted for Satō's figure mainly because the Tokyo police reportedly counted 43 theaters in July 1913 ("Katsudō no zōsetsu wa kinshi," *Tokyo nichi nichi shinbun,* July 8, 1913, reprinted in *Taishō nyūsu jiten* [Tokyo: Mainichi Komyunikēshonzu, 1988], 1:87 [hereafter referred to as *TNJ*]).

42. The *Tokyo asahi,* for instance, claimed that there were already 8,500,000 movie tickets sold each year in the Tokyo area alone: "Katsudō shashon to jidō (ichi)." But since this is a piece warning readers of the threat of film's popularity, one must take these figures with a grain of salt.

43. "*Jigoma* (san): Eiga no shushu sentaku," *Tokyo asahi shinbun,* October 7, 1912: 5.

44. See Itō Hideo, *Taishō no tantei shōsetsu* (Tokyo: San'ichi Shobō, 1991). The *Yomiuri shinbun* listed twenty such books: "Katsudōkai no kyōkō," *Yomiuri shinbun,* October 12, 1912, 3.

45. The *Osaka asahi shinbun* said that the film was so popular it was like "if it's not [*Zigomar*], it's not a moving picture." "Eiga *Jigoma* no kinshi to Osaka," *Osaka asahi shinbun,* October 11, 1912, reprinted in *Shinbun shūroku Taishō-shi* (Tokyo: Taishō Shuppan, 1978), 1:73.

46. Nagamine Shigetoshi, *Kaitō Jigoma to katsudō shashin no jidai* (Tokyo: Shinchōsha, 2006).

47. The report not only voiced concern about unsanitary conditions at theaters, the potential deleterious effects customs shown in foreign films had on young Japanese, and the harmful nature of *benshi* explanation and musical accompaniment, it also recommended the production of a greater variety of educational films and the establishment of educational film days. See "Katsudō shashin to jidō (jū): Shōgakusei torishimari no mukō," *Tokyo asahi shinbun,* February 20, 1912, 6. The *Asahi* commented that the recommendations had little effect on film attendance by minors.

48. Masato Hase, "Cinemaphobia in Taisho Japan: Zigomar, Delinquent Boys and Somnambulism," *Iconics* 4 (1998): 87–100.

49. Nagamine (*Kaitō Jigoma to katsudō shashin no jidai,* 165) reports that *Zigomar* did manage to slip into theaters at least once after the Tokyo ban, showing in Asakusa in April 1913 under the title *Tantei kidan* (The strange tale of the detective).

50. "*Jigoma* (ichi): Jigoma to wa nan zoya," *Tokyo asahi shinbun,* October 4, 1912, 5.

51. "Katsudō shashin to jidō (hachi): Kansetsu ni ukuru heigai," *Tokyo asahi shinbun,* February 18, 1912, 6.

52. "*Jigoma* (san)."

53. "*Jigoma* (hachi): Akukanka to akueikyō," *Tokyo asahi shinbun,* October 14, 1912, 5. The police also reiterated this rhetoric: Chief Detective Tsuzura of the Umamichi Police Station (with Asakusa Park in its jurisdiction) told another paper that "it goes without saying that such films cause corruption": "*Jigoma* no kanka," *Miyako shinbun,* October 6, 1912, 5.

54. The *Asahi* had actually said in February that there were no cases of film content causing crime, though it warned of the potential danger: "Katsudō shashin to jidō (shichi): Jidō daraku no jitsurei," *Tokyo asahi shinbun,* February 17, 1912, 6. The researcher Fujio Shigeo declared he could not find any articles providing evidence of *Zigomar* triggering crime ("*Jigoma* genshō to *Jigoma* enzaisetsu," *Gonda Yasunosuke kenkyū* 3 [Fall 1984]), but Nagamine has found one article from June 15, before the ban, claiming a direct connection between watching *Zigomar* and committing crime. However, we must note that the piece appeared in the *Asahi,* the same paper that declared cinema had no benefits and which did not fail to editorialize in this article about how frightening the movies are. As is unfortunately often the case in his well-researched book, Nagamine does not analyze such articles critically, but instead takes this one, likely

biased piece at face value, for instance, as evidence that "the same kind of *Zigomar* incidents had to a certain degree occurred before" the ban (*Kaitō Jigoma to katsudō shashin no jidai,* 138). Nagamine sees the influx of articles after the ban as only the discovery of an existing problem; he thus ignores the role discourse can play in shaping both reality and impressions of it. The fact is that the vast majority of claims about the film causing crime appeared after the ban and were lacking enough details that one can see a cinephobic bias operating therein. For instance, after the *Zigomar* ban was announced, the *Chūgai shōgyō shinbun* reported the existence of a seventeen-year-old criminal from Asakusa named Fujitani Shin'ichi who committed several robberies and called himself "The New Zigomar." The article, however, does not detail how he managed to be corrupted by film ("Jigoma no shin," *Chūgai shōgyō shinbun,* October 15, 1912 [*TNJ,* 1:258]). In the end, most articles only used *Zigomar* as an attention getter; the actual incidents often just involved youths committing crimes less as the result of viewing a film's content than out of a desire to get into the theater.

55. "*Jigoma* (yon): Shigeki no kyōretsuna mono," *Tokyo asahi shinbun,* October 8, 1912, 5. Given the ill effects it believed competition had on the industry, the *Asahi* actually welcomed the formation of the Nikkatsu trust.

56. "*Jigoma* (ni): Katsudō shashin no zaiaku," *Tokyo asahi shinbun,* October 5, 1912, 5.

57. "*Jigoma* (shichi): Akunin sūhai no keikō," *Tokyo asahi shinbun,* October 11, 1912, 5.

58. "*Jigoma* (hachi)."

59. An earlier article offered detailed statistics proving that the air inside Asakusa theaters contained ten times the normal amount of carbon dioxide. Since even a healthy adult would feel dizzy or even faint after spending two hours in such conditions, theater owners, the piece claimed, had made provisions to have doctors on hand during screenings: "Katsudō shashin to jidō (ichi)."

60. For an analysis of early film culture as a heterotopia, see Lynn Kirby, "The Urban Spectator and the Crowd in Early American Train Films," *Iris* 11 (1990): 49–62; and Miriam Hansen, *Babel and Babylon: Spectatorship in American Silent Film* (Cambridge, MA: Harvard University Press, 1991), 107–108.

61. "*Jigoma* (ichi)."

62. "*Jigoma* (ni)."

63. "*Jigoma* (san)." Middle school in the prewar Japanese school system was five years long and included the high school level in the present system. The paper is thus referring to minors of about seven to eighteen years of age.

64. "*Jigoma* (san)."

65. Nagamine reports police claims in 1912 that 30–40 percent of Asakusa spectators were children. The survey by Sandaya Hiraku he cites, however, only found children forming the majority on weekends in some theaters (*Kaitō Jigoma to katsudō shashin no jidai,* 22–24). Kubota Utsubo, however, in his account of going to the movies, registered surprise that his fellow spectators were mostly adult. Given how assertions regarding the number of child spectators were often intimately tied to attempts to impose control on the new medium, we have to view these numbers from a critical distance.

66. The paper then went on to complain of the medium's misuse and posed the combination of the cinema with the phonograph—that is, sound film—as the solution: "Katsudō shashin to chikuonki," *Yomiuri shinbun,* October 20, 1912, 1.

67. The *Asahi* claimed that "this (cruelty) is not the nature of only such children but is an instinct borne by the majority of children in this era" ("Katsudō shashin to jidō (roku): Jidō shinri to eiga," *Tokyo asahi shinbun,* February 16, 1912, 6). The next article emphasized that this character was "inborn" ("Katsudō shashin to jidō (shichi)").

68. "Katsudō shashin to jidō (roku)."

69. The author of a letter to the editor in the *Asahi,* Katatani Seizō, claimed the issue of cinema to be one that demanded attention by education officials. See "Jidō *Jigoma* netsu," *Tokyo asahi shinbun,* October 9, 1912, 5.

70. "*Jigoma* (san)."

71. "*Jigoma* no katsudō shashin kinshi to naru," *Tokyo nichi nichi shinbun,* October 10, 1912, 7.

72. *Jōruri* is a traditional style of sung narration which often accompanied performing arts such as bunraku (puppet theater) and kabuki, but which could also be presented alone. *Naniwa-bushi* is a more recent form of sung narration that was very popular in the Meiji era.

73. "*Jigoma* (san)."

74. Reflecting the fact that many contemporary Japanese newspapers were generally not opposed to greater publications censorship, the *Asahi* ("*Jigoma* mondai kaiketsu") and the *Yomiuri shinbun* ("Katsudōkai no kyōkō") strongly called for banning the publication of this kind of crime and detective novel.

75. "*Jigoma* (yon)."

76. "*Jigoma* (yon): Shigeki no kyōretsuna mono," *Tokyo asahi shinbun,* October 9, 1912, 5. Although this is really the fifth part of the paper's series on *Zigomar,* it is misprinted as number four.

77. "Katsudō shashin to jidō (ni): Jidō no ukuru hirō," *Tokyo asahi shinbun,* February 7, 1912, 6.

78. See Tom Gunning, "Tracing the Individual Body: Photography, Detectives, and Early Cinema," in *Cinema and the Invention of Modern Life,* ed. Leo Charney and Vanessa R. Schwartz (Berkeley: University of California Press, 1995), 15–45.

79. Tom Gunning, "Attractions, Detection, Disguise: *Zigomar,* Jasset, and the History of Film Genres," *Griffithiana* 47 (May 1993): 113.

80. Miram Hansen, "Fallen Women, Rising Stars, New Horizons: Shanghai Silent Film as Vernacular Modernism," *Film Quarterly* 54.1 (Fall 2000): 10–22; Hansen, "The Mass Production of the Senses: Classical Cinema as Vernacular Modernism," in *Reinventing Film Studies,* ed. Linda Williams and Christine Gledhill (London: Edward Arnold, 2000), 332–350.

81. For more on this process, see my *Visions of Japanese Modernity: Articulations of Cinema, Nation, and Spectatorship, 1895–1925* (Berkeley: University of California Press, 2010).

82. Nagamine, *Kaitō Jigoma to katsudō shashin no jidai,* 71–72, 150.

83. Quoted in "*Jigoma* mondai kaiketsu," *Tokyo asahi shinbun,* October 13, 1912, 6.

84. For a copy of the 1900 theater regulations, see Takazawa Hatsutarō, *Gendai engeki sōran,* 2nd ed. (Tokyo: Bunseisha, 1919), 211–229, esp. Article 23, which regulated the content of theater plays.

85. I expand on this in chapter 5 of *Visions of Japanese Modernity.*

86. "Kotogoto," *Miyako shinbun,* October 14, 1912, 2. Such a ban did not last long: films on General Nogi would later become a popular subject in the industry as the government came to recognize cinema's ideological usefulness. Incidentally, Chiba Nobuo has attempted to relate the banning of *Zigomar* to the mood prevailing after the deaths of the emperor and Nogi: as with most entertainments, film theaters were closed during the mourning period, so it is not inconceivable to think that authorities saw the popularity of *Zigomar*-type films as an affront to the emperor. See Chiba Nobuo, "Engeki eiga no jūnen," *Sekai no eiga sakka 31: Nihon eigashi* (Tokyo: Kinema Junpōsha, 1976), 18.

87. "*Jigoma* mondai kaiketsu."

88. One police official was quoted in the *Tokyo nichi nichi shinbun* admitting that they were "too busy" to have seen the film itself: "*Jigoma* no katsudō shashin kinshi to naru."

89. Article 3 of the regulations in effect in Osaka at the time, for instance, merely stipulated: "When the summary of the film or the explanation are under suspicion of violating Section 4 of the previous article, permission will be given after projecting and explaining said work at the said place of exhibition or at another convenient site." Thus screenings were required solely when the written summary was thought dubious, and then only with the necessary accompaniment of the *benshi.* These codes, which were created in 1911 as internal guidelines only, are reproduced in Terakawa Shin, *Eiga oyobi eigageki* (Osaka: Osaka Mainichi Shinbun, 1925), 230–233.

90. The *Tokyo asahi shinbun* explained that the normal procedure for the Asakusa area (since censorship was left to local police stations at the time) was to inspect the film and the *benshi* explanation before it opened; for the rest of the city, the procedure was to check on it after the run had begun: "Katsudō shashin to jidō (kyū): Fujūbunnaru ken'etsu," *Tokyo asahi shinbun,* February 19, 1911, 6. But as we have seen, there were films like *Zigomar* that escaped both procedures for some time.

91. So said the head of the Public Peace Section, while also admitting that at that time, it remained very difficult to view every single film before exhibition. See "*Jigoma* mondai kaiketsu."

92. See chapter 5 of *Visions of Japanese Modernity.*

7 The Crisscrossed Stare

Protest and Propaganda in China's Not-So-Silent Era

Yiman Wang

> [The media] have this power because we empower them with our attention. Someone once startled me with the proposal that if you were to gaze at anybody long enough, you could become enamored with them. *Perhaps the gaze of the camera does the same.*
>
> Loni Ding, "Strangers of an Asian American Filmmaker" (emphasis added)

> When thinking about black female spectators, I remember being punished as a child for *staring*, for those *hard intense direct looks* children would give grown-ups, looks that were seen as confrontational, as gestures of resistance, challenges to authority.
>
> bell hooks, "The Oppositional Gaze: Black Female Spectators" (emphasis added)

Riding the crest of the martial arts film wave in the late 1920s, a southern Chinese businessman, Gao Yongqing, converted a dance hall into the Grand Theatre (*Da guangming daxiyuan*) in 1928. Located on Bubbling Well Road, which stretched across the commercial center and heart of Shanghai's International Settlement, the Grand Theatre was registered as an American theater and soon known as the "No. 1 Movie Theatre in the Far East" (Figure 7.1). As a first-run theater, it exhibited Euro-American films almost exclusively, with the exception (after 1935) of a few Chinese film screenings.[1] As such, it offered a crucial platform for channeling foreign films into China for upper-middle-class Chinese audiences as well as expatriate Western viewers.

The two films I examine here premiered at the Grand Theatre, and each film's reception led to an important incident in the filmic encounter between China and the United States. The first film was Harold Lloyd's *Welcome Danger*

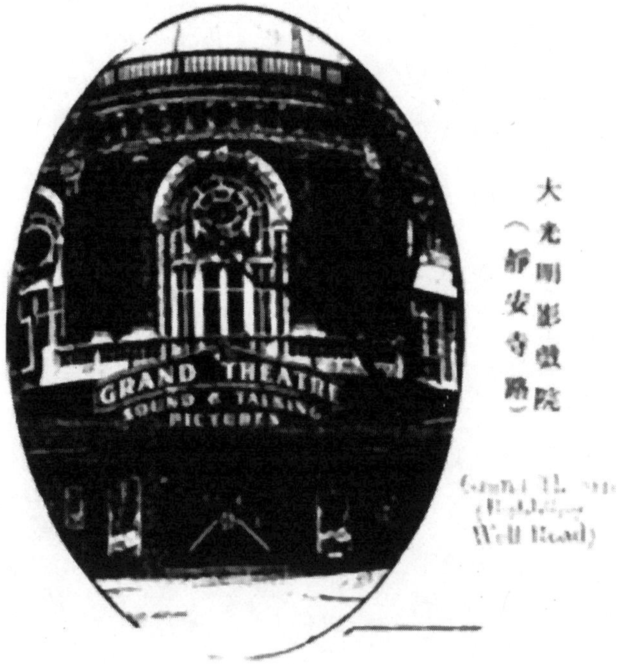

Figure 7.1 Shanghai's Grand Theatre in 1928.

(1929), screened in 1930. With a plot set primarily in San Francisco's Chinatown, a space teeming with long-queued Chinese men involved in opium traffic, this apparently innocuous American comedy precipitated large-scale Chinese protests that led to the temporary closing of the Grand Theatre. The second film was *Tianlun*—better known as *Song of China* (literally "The heavenly bliss," dir. Fei Mu, 1935; see Figure 7.2). This silent Chinese film, accompanied by a specially composed, traditional music track, tells the story of a Chinese family that disintegrates because of urban and commercial corruption, yet ultimately manages to reunite in harmony by recovering Confucian ideals of filial piety and benevolence. By privileging Confucian ideology and traditional Chinese music, *Song of China* offers a model for an indigenous Chinese cinema (distinguished from productions that strove to mimic the Hollywood style). Importantly, when Paramount's Douglas MacLean purchased the film, it was completely re-edited prior to its American screening in 1936.

The crisscrossed reception of *Welcome Danger* and *Song of China* signals two instances of an encounter that brought to the fore the Sino-American mutual misinterpretation and the resulting blocked filmic reception on both sides. In this chapter, I study these two instances of failed communication during the

Figure 7.2 Marquee of the 1935 premiere of *Tianlun* (*Song of China*) at the Grand Theatre, redesigned by L. E. Hudec in 1933.

early twentieth century, when cinema served as a double-sided venue of ideological negotiation and colonial annexation. I argue that the cinematic encounter mobilizes multiple parties to articulate and reconfigure issues of racial, national, and cultural identity in early-1930s China. Importantly, the prolonged silent-to-talkie transition in Chinese cinema leads to an extended discursive focus on cinema's visual register; this focus, in turn, foregrounds a scopic economy born out of the audience's (reviewers, critics, and agitators) engagement with the racial, national, and filmic Other. Such engagement hinges upon scopophilia as well as epistemophilia on the one hand, and constant frustration and readjustment of the desires implied in both scopophilia and epistemophilia on the other.

I argue that this scopic tussle crystallizes in what I call the "crisscrossed stare," which operates not only diegetically, but more importantly, extra-diegetically, in the domain of distribution, exhibition, translation, and reception.[2] These interlocked practices feed back into a larger colonial political economy of the early twentieth century, which determines key facets of the Sino-American power hierarchy. In this context, the crisscrossed stare underpins both the Chinese protest against *Welcome Danger* in 1930 and the American reception of *Song of China* in 1936. If the first instance emblematizes China's opposition to American orientalism, then the export of *Song of China* to the United States signals an infiltration into the American market. Both are anti-colonial strategies that result from and hinge upon a crisscrossed stare that expresses the colonial subject's enhanced self-consciousness through their struggle with what W. E. B. Du Bois calls the "double consciousness."[3] Yet such anti-colonial stances are also problematized by iconoclastic intellectuals such as Lu Xun, a leading voice in modern Chinese literature whose essays demonstrate an incisive critique of the Chinese "national character." Lu Xun's intervention exposes the self-delusion of anti-colonial opposition in order to reorient the stare, turning it inward, producing discourses that reformulate China's racial and national positioning vis-à-vis a dominant Western power.

I deploy the term "stare" in contradistinction to the more commonly used words "look" and "gaze." All three terms are often used interchangeably, with "gaze" accruing the most theoretical capital owing to the sway of Lacanian psychoanalysis in 1970s film studies, especially apparatus studies. If "look" indicates the generic act of exercising the capacity of vision, with no explicit partiality or value judgment, then "gaze," through its connection with psychoanalysis and gaze theory, has been reified as the seat of power, with the gazer being empowered and the gazed being disempowered.[4] Thus, to challenge the existing power inequity and to reconfigure the power structure requires that the marginalized subject acquire the ability to gaze back. This is what bell hooks calls the "oppositional gaze" of black female viewers.[5] In this framework, the dominant Other's gaze objectifies the Self; and the Self must either internalize the gaze or expropriate and repurpose it. In either case, all scopic exchanges are directly translated and locked into a binary power structure that serves either the colonial or anti-colonial agenda. What has been occluded are those scopic moments that defy immediate political interpretation by evoking a range of sentiments such as fascination and wonder as well as disorientation and discomfort.

Such scopic moments are key components of what I am calling the crisscrossed stare. The importance of the "stare" is already implied at the beginning of hooks's essay, where she recalls her childhood experience of being penalized for "staring." However, instead of elaborating on the implications of "stare," especially the childhood sense of wonder, intrigue, bewilderment, and bluntness, hooks quickly slips from "stare" to "gaze," describing "stare" as confrontational and resistant. In this chapter, I refocus the "stare" to develop a paradigm that enables us to analyze filmic exchanges that are produced by a power inequity, yet not immediately translatable into the binary politics of empowerment and disempowerment. Building upon hooks's childhood sense of wonder, I use "stare" to emphasize two dimensions. The first is the *duration* of a sustained, affective attention to the lived experience of an encounter, and the sentiments that result from it. The second is the affective and political ramifications of the "stare," which are situation based and open-ended. The sentiments arising from the extended "stare" during the moment of a benign or violent encounter range from interest, curiosity, and befuddlement to disgust and alienation. What this implies for the disempowered individual or community is that the crisscrossed stare can lead to self-alienation, self-confirmation, or self-reconstruction, or all three at once. This is especially important for our understanding of China's filmic interactions with the West, given China's subordination by the West since the 1840s Opium War, which precipitated China's century-long fight for a modern national and racial identity.

In the following pages, I analyze the crucial role played by China's crisscrossed negotiation with the Western Other, as manifested in the failed reception of *Welcome Danger* in China and *Song of China* in the United States. *Welcome Danger* is a Harold Lloyd comedy set in San Francisco's Chinatown, where Lloyd ultimately outwits the opium-trafficking Chinese. *Song of China,* on the other hand, is introduced to the United States as a quintessential Chinese film that boasts traditional Chinese music, narrative, and aesthetics. The simultaneous exhibition and reception of both films hinges upon a *mise en abyme* of not simply staring at the Other but, more importantly, staring at the Self through the Other's eyes. Such a crisscrossed stare echoes Du Bois's "double consciousness" without duplicating the paralyzing effect suggested by his concept. Instead, the "twoness" in the crisscrossed stare effectively underscores the mutability and mutual implication of Self and Other, which challenge and complicate the binary tension and antinomy between the colonizer (West) and the colonized (China). Thus, the model of an interpenetrative stare offers a new perspective for understanding China's contested racial and national identity that emerges from the affective, multivalent processes of cinematic encounters and interactions.

Welcome Danger Meets an Unwelcoming Audience

Welcome Danger, Harold Lloyd's first talkie—distributed by Paramount in 1929—was initially shot as a silent film, and then reshot with dialogue to take advantage of the rising talkie tide. According to Lloyd, the film had five versions: "a silent film, a talkie, a synchronized version, a version with the conversation recorded on discs, and a version with the conversation on a separate film."[6] The silent version was deemed necessary for international distribution, especially for theaters not yet wired for sound. On February 21, 1930, the film opened to a full house in Shanghai's two first-run theaters, the Grand Theatre and the Capitol Theatre (*Da guangming daxiyuan* and *Guanglu daxiyuan;* both specialized in Paramount pictures).[7] The film narrates the two accomplishments of Harold Lloyd's character, a botany student. First, he experiences a series of dangerous encounters with a menagerie of exotic and shady Chinese characters who stereotypically wear queues and traffic in opium. Yet, thanks to his comic wit (one example being his masquerade in Chinese dress to evade Chinese opium smugglers), Lloyd's character ultimately outmaneuvers the "treacherous" Chinese, convicts the opium traffickers, and saves the one good Chinese individual—a helpless doctor. Meanwhile, he also successfully romances an American girl by enabling her to obtain the doctor's help in treating her sick brother. This seemingly innocuous comedy (laced with romance) gave the film wide appeal in Europe and Japan, as well as the United States.

In China, however, the film's initial success (it got a full house at its premiere) was disrupted the following day by a protest that quickly snowballed into a major campaign against "China-humiliating" (*ruhua*) films. Enraged by the film's stereotypical and demeaning depiction of Chinese characters, Hong Shen, a U.S.-trained Chinese dramatist, screenwriter, and professor, gave an incendiary speech at the Grand Theatre in the middle of a screening on February 22, 1930. Arguing that the film humiliated Chinese people and offended Chinese dignity, he urged the audience to demand a refund, which incited further chaos. Consequently, Hong was arrested by the Western police force in Shanghai's International Settlement and detained for more than three hours. During his detention, a Western police officer tried to convince Hong that the film was no more than a farce and should not be taken seriously. Hong replied, "You Westerners may find it funny. How can we Chinese, in sympathy with the overseas Chinese, possibly enjoy your humor?"[8]

Soon, a protest that had started as a local, intellectual-led event escalated into a concerted political campaign supported not only by social groups of different political persuasions, but also by the ruling Nationalist government, which had successfully united China in 1927, three years prior to the *Welcome Danger* incident. The outcry against *Welcome Danger* provided an ideal opportunity for the government to strengthen its control (via film censorship, for instance) of China's extraterrestrial regions, including Shanghai's International Settlement and French Concession. To support the protest, the Nationalist government's Film Censorship Committee in Shanghai ordered that newspapers stop carrying the two theaters' advertisements, and that the theaters apologize to the public, discontinue and burn the film prints, submit all their future films to the censorship committee before screening, and finally, stop showing any Lloyd films in the future. On February 23, the Censorship Committee published an article in the *Republican Daily* (*Minguo ribao*), urging Chinese audiences to stop watching the film. The Nationalist Party's propaganda department also telegraphed provincial governments, ordering the suspension of all Lloyd films until the U.S. comedian offered an apology.

Shortly after, all the prints of *Welcome Danger* were returned to the film's Chinese distributor, Oriental Pathé, which was located in Shanghai. Ultimately, the drastic box office drop forced both theaters and Lloyd to compromise. The Capitol Theatre apologized to the public on April 5; and newspapers resumed publishing its movie advertisements on April 11. The negotiation with the Grand Theatre dragged on until October 15, when its management finally apologized, agreeing to donate the box office revenue to building schools and to submit its future movies to the film censorship committee. On October 19, newspapers resumed publishing movie advertisements for the Grand Theatre. The interruption in business, however, caused a severe loss, and the theater closed on September 30, 1931. After a two-year period of inactivity, the Grand Theatre was bought by a British Chinese tycoon, Lu Gen, who tore down the old theater and hired Hungarian architect L. E. Hudec to redesign and rebuild it. The new Grand Theatre was opened on June 14, 1933.

Meanwhile, the Nationalist Party's propaganda department contacted the Chinese consul in San Francisco, demanding Harold Lloyd's apology. Lloyd initially refused to comply, arguing that comedy should be dissociated from the politics of representation. "Why, all countries have bad men, but that doesn't mean that a whole race is bad. We've shown bad Americans, too, but think pretty well of our countrymen as a lot. If we start apologizing, who'll we have left to poke fun at?"[9] Lloyd also stressed his film's innocuousness by noting that not a single complaint had originated from Chinese Americans. By August 2, however, the English-language newspaper in Shanghai, the *China Weekly Review*, published Lloyd's formal apology dated May 29, in which he stated his "highest regard" for the dignity of the Chinese nation and expressed his astonishment at the Chinese rage against his film, since it was made with the advice of his China experts. In the end, he did offer his "sincere apologies" and reassured Chinese authorities of his admiration for the Chinese people, civilization, and culture.[10] On September 30, the Censorship Committee lifted the ban on Lloyd's films, which soon returned to Chinese screens.

A comparison of the English- and Chinese-language discourses generated by this incident suggests that *Welcome Danger*'s failed border-crossing reception (from the political perspective at least) has to do with the two sides' contradictory expectations, tastes, and agendas, which led to their crisscrossed stare. American reviewers believed that the film was criticized because the "Chinese don't laugh" even if Lloyd's comedies are "as pure as the driven snow."[11] They argued that the Chinese detractors mistakenly approached a comedy in terms of referential realism.[12] The Chinese critics, however, believed that Hollywood productions (regardless of genre) routinely insulted China by presenting objectionable stereotypes, thereby conveying a negative image to the world. In order to promote a positive Chinese image against Hollywood's negative impact, the newly established filmmaking section of the Shanghai-based Commercial Press decided to make favorable films and distribute them internationally as early as April 1919.[13] In 1921, the mission statement of the inaugural issue of the first Chinese film magazine, *Yingxi zazhi* (Motion Picture Review) criticized Western films for depicting Chinese characters as either troublemakers or slaves (ironically, Lloyd's bespectacled, smiling, full-color face graced the cover of this first issue). To address the problem of misrepresentation, the magazine editor, Gu Kenfu, called for a national cinema that would "restore Chinese dignity in film circles."[14] In this context, *Welcome Danger* was perceived as one more problematic film, following on the heels of Douglas Fairbanks's *Thief of Bagdad* (1924) in which a Japanese actor, Sojin, plays a scheming Mongol prince, which fueled an anti-humiliation protest from some Chinese viewers (Figure 7.3). A similar protest was to be staged again a few years later, targeting Josef von Sternberg's *Shanghai Express* (1932).

All three cases of protest against *ruhua* (China-humiliating) Hollywood productions suggest a growing nationalist reaction against a skewed Western lens in the mid-twenties and early thirties. To an extent, this reaction resembles hooks's notion of an "oppositional gaze." Here the subordinated community/nation does not merely insist on staring back but also wants "to change reality" through the stare.[15] In the Chinese reception of *Welcome Danger,* a reverse stare at Hollywood facilitated change by mobilizing state apparatuses. The Chinese government's overseas representatives, such as Chinese consuls in other countries, joined the protest in pressuring local governments to boycott China-humiliating American films, leading to the withdrawal of *Welcome Danger* in Panama on April 19, 1930. Also, importantly, the Chinese protests strove to debunk the dominant scopic

Figure 7.3 Cartoon lampooning Harold Lloyd: "Do you want to be Douglas Fairbanks No. 2?" *Shanghai sketch,* March 1, 1930.

regime by challenging the racist and/or sexist pleasure inscribed in dominant Western cinema. If bell hooks locates a new form of critical pleasure in an "oppositional gaze" fostered by black female viewers, then the Chinese protesters' reverse stare aimed to deconstruct the hegemonic pleasure generated by an apparently innocuous genre film such as *Welcome Danger.*

As revealed by the Chinese people's reverse stare, the film's pleasure depends upon labeling another race, ethnicity, culture, or nation as less "civilized" (from the Western perspective) and thus available for ridicule and exploitation in comedy. Hong Shen's agitating speech against the Lloyd film's exploitation of the Chinese culture is validated by Lloyd's defensive response—"If we start apologizing, who'll we have left to poke fun at?"—which testifies to the logic of a pecking order.[16] Moreover, as the Chinese protests escalated, an American commentator lamented: "Another source of dramatic villains seems to be drying up. China seemed capable of producing an unlimited supply for plays and pictures until the country began to be infected by civilization and to furnish a market for American productions. So now Chinese villains must go."[17] The next targets down the ladder would be Tibet or Central Africa, although, as the author warned, "we wouldn't guarantee those countries would be available for more than a decade [due to their inevitable self-consciousness through Westernization and civilization]."[18] Ultimately, the question of who could be the safe villain boomerangs, for "the Caucasian himself is the only or nearly the only man who can be presented as the supreme idiot without a protest from those of his own race."[19] By problematizing the pecking order built into comedy's mechanism of representation and pleasure, the Chinese campaign endeavored to control and reorient the scopic regime organized by a broader socio-political power structure.

The stance shared by bell hooks and the Chinese protesters, however, channels resistance toward slightly different goals. If hooks seeks to interrupt white hegemony by exercising her oppositional gaze and fostering a new black women's cinema for the black female audience, then Chinese activists deemed it important to deploy a reverse stare to accost Hollywood in order to transform the Western perception of China, while also disabusing the Chinese mass audience of easy indulgence in Hollywood's brand of visual pleasure. In other words, the Chinese activists sought not to halt but to repurpose the crisscrossed stare arising from the Sino-American filmic encounter. Whereas the attempt to educate the Chinese mass audience hardly had a long-lasting effect (as suggested by Lloyd's regained popularity once the ban was lifted), the state-sponsored protest managed to reconfigure the scopic regime to a considerable extent.

On the Hollywood side, measures were taken to curtail blatant racism in order to secure and expand the international market. In 1927, the MPPDA (Motion Picture Producers and Distributors of America) issued a set of "Don'ts and Be Carefuls" that specifically forbade "willful offense to any nation, race or creed" and recommended "avoiding picturizing [*sic*] in an unfavorable light another country's religion, history, institutions, prominent people, and citizenry." Furthermore, in March 1930, precisely as China was campaigning against Lloyd's films, the Hays Code (the Motion Picture Production Code) was issued to monitor the production of the emerging talkies and to facilitate "a still higher level of wholesome entertainment for all the people." This code contained a section on national feelings, stressing "fair" representation of the "history, institutions, prominent people and citizenry of other nations."[20]

Not surprisingly, China's protest against Lloyd's films further fueled Hollywood self-censorship. A direct result was the rigorous scrutiny of Universal's *East Is West* (dir. Monta Bell, 1930), which was chastised for depicting the Tong wars and the auction of Chinese women. John V. Wilson's letter (on behalf of Jason Joy) to Universal Studios manager Henry Henigson, dated May 23, 1930, points out the script's violation of paragraph X (National Feelings), item 2, of the code (which stipulates fair representation of other nations). It specifically cites China's protest against *Welcome Danger*, a film "mild in comparison to reflections cast on Chinese civilization by the treatment of it in your story [*East Is West*]."

Wilson warned that the script of *East Is West* would "not only be quite injurious [emended from the original word "dangerous"] to your company but a reflection on the industry as a whole."[21] As a remedy, the Hays Office suggested developing a Chinese hero for every Chinese "heavy."[22] Despite these preventive measures, in December 1930 the finished film still incensed the Shanghai Film Censorship Committee upon its informal showing in Shanghai's International Settlement. It was instantly rejected for disagreeable depictions of the Chinese and the potential to trigger racial disturbances.[23] Ultimately, Universal Studios was forced to offer an apology, which appeared in Shanghai newspapers on June 1, 1931.

These trial-and-error cases underscore the interlocking relationship between a Chinese political economy and Hollywood's economic politics, a relationship premised upon their crisscrossed, entangled stare and its correlated mutual decoding and negotiation. Triggered by Hollywood's pejorative perception and portrayal of what was labeled as "China," Chinese filmmakers, intellectuals, and the government stare back (metaphorically speaking) to demand an accurate representation. This reverse stare is in turn registered by the American film industry, which correctly decodes the Chinese demand for positive and respectful depictions in U.S.-produced films as a means of promoting China's international status. Through its censorship mechanisms, the Hollywood "dream factory" exercises its "wish fulfillment" function and offers "wholesome" entertainment. In other words, by responding to China's wish, Hollywood ultimately fulfills its own wish to maintain and expand its market in China (as elsewhere in the world).

To be sure, such interactions, resulting from the crisscrossed stare, do not mean that racist practices are eliminated in Hollywood (yellowface, for instance, continues to be deemed an effective and lucrative casting and acting practice),[24] or that the colonial power inequity becomes irrelevant. However, it does contribute to problematizing, averting, and reorienting Hollywood's scopic lens. To that extent, the crisscrossed stare challenges us to go beyond a dichotomous power framework in order to adequately understand the complex scopic strategies that negotiate power inequities. Such strategies involve a mutual regulation and realignment of Sino-American visual pleasures, which necessitates a retraining of each other's filmic eye that encodes and decodes in a dialogical fashion.

On the American side, the retraining of the gaze into a stare traversed objectification, hostility, and negotiation that led toward engagement and acknowledgment. On the Chinese side, the reverse stare suggests that protesters were, like Sartre and Fanon, fully aware of the importance of the Other's stare in constructing the Self, that is, China's modern, national, and racial identity. Unlike Sartre and Fanon, however, they did not simply resent the Other's stare as an inescapable enslaving force but rather actively sorted out the varied affects and effects of the stare and responded differently. They confronted injurious stereotyping, yet solicited and even demanded a positive fascination with China in order to facilitate nationalistic self-promotion. Additionally, Chinese activists also called for positive films about China that would convey this nationalistic self-perception to the Western audience, thereby re-educating their perception. A case in point is the export of *Tianlun* as *Song of China* to the United States.

Tianlun / Song of China—When an American Audience Meets an Uncanny Chinese Film

Although the intellectual and commercial endeavor to develop a positive national cinema began as early as 1919, overseas distribution of such films remained a challenge, owing in part to colonial power inequities and the perceived backwardness of Chinese cinema. In cases when China-made films (*guopian*) did go overseas, their screening tended to be limited to film festivals and/or diasporic Chinese communities. Consequently, Western audiences were barely introduced to Chinese films. In other words, the images produced by Chinese filmmakers were unable to meet the Western Other's stare on a regular basis—hence the blockage of the loop that would bring the crisscrossed stare full circle.

Tianlun, retitled as *Song of China* for its American release, is one rare example that did find a Western audience and produced what a *New York Times* reviewer described as an "hour-long sober regard" between the film and its American viewers. This late silent film was made in 1935 by the Shanghai-based United China Photoplay and Publishing Service (UPS) (*Lianhua yingye yingshua gongsi*), a studio that actively promoted Chinese national cinema (*guopian*). The film dramatizes a Confucian utopia of heavenly harmony achieved through extending respect to all the elderly and providing care to all children. In doing so, it subscribes to the ideology underpinning the Nationalist Party's New Life Movement, formally launched in 1934, which selectively mobilized and reinterpreted Confucian doctrines with a view to promoting collective hygiene, reinforcing social solidarity, and regimenting everyday life in order to prepare China for military situations. Whereas the film's implicit political message was criticized by some leftist reviewers for conservative evasion of fundamental social problems, *Tianlun* received positive reviews in two major English-language newspapers in Shanghai, namely, the *North China Daily News* (*Zilin xibao*) and *Shanghai Evening Post and Mercury* (*Damei wanbao*). These reviews praised the acting, montage, and use of non-diegetic traditional Chinese music for enhancing the film's universal intelligibility.

As one of the few Chinese films that premiered in Shanghai's first-run Grand Theatre under the banner of "international screening" (*guoji xianying*), the film was soon purchased by Douglas MacLean (a Paramount actor turned producer), who presented it to American audiences. In the process of repackaging the film for the U.S. audience, the original title, *Tianlun,* became *Song of China;* the

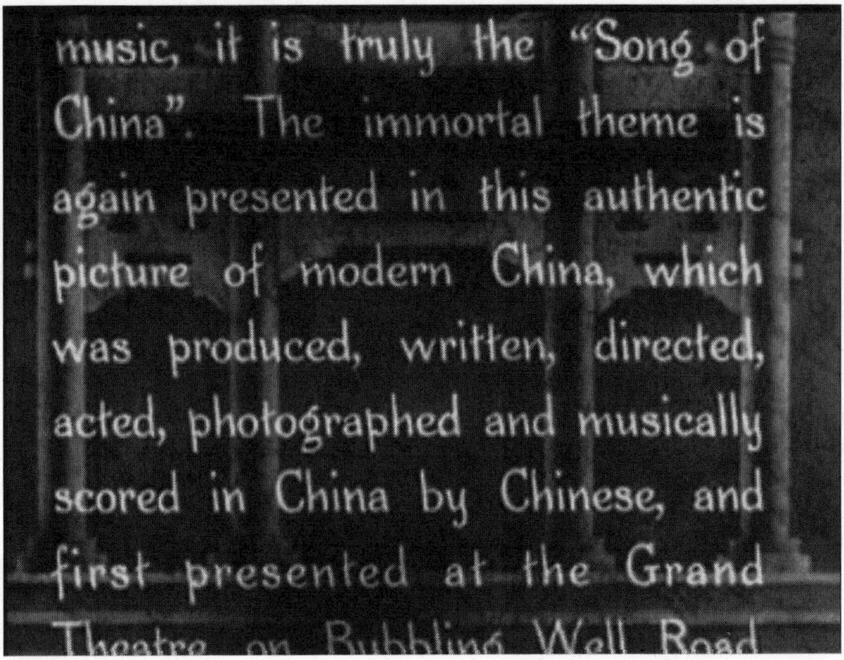
music, it is truly the "Song of
China". The immortal theme is
again presented in this authentic
picture of modern China, which
was produced, written, directed,
acted, photographed and musically
scored in China by Chinese, and
first presented at the Grand

Figure 7.4 Still from the Paramount version of *Song of China*.

original director, Fei Mu, received credit only as co-director; and the original producer, Luo Mingyou (a Christian openly sympathetic with the governing Nationalist Party) was credited as the director. The ending also replaced the death of the patriarchal philanthropist (in the Chinese version) with his recuperation and reunion with his extended family, which gestures toward the Confucian utopia.

None of these modifications, however, were made explicit to the American audience. Instead, the opening title of the U.S.-released version presents the film as an "authentic picture of modern China," produced, photographed, and acted by the Chinese, originally premiered at the Grand Theatre of Shanghai (Figure 7.4). MacLean's packaging of this film as an authentic specimen of Chinese cinema was intended to pique the Western audience's desire to stare, that is, to fetishize "Chineseness," to fantasize about the exotic Other while being reassured as to their superior "Americanness."

This desire to stare (or scopophilia) is complemented and legitimized by epistemophilia, or a desire for knowledge, which assumes that the exotic Other is simply an object to be cognitively grasped, rather than a subject to be engaged in mutual reciprocity. This is demonstrated in the film's publicity strategy. Lin Yutang, one of the earliest Chinese-American bilingual writers, whose book *My Country My People* (1935) played a crucial role in introducing Chinese culture to ordinary Americans,[25] was invited to write an article, "China and Its Film Industry," published in the *New York Times* one day prior to the film's premiere in New York on November 9, 1936. The purpose was to prepare the American audience for a Chinese film—an educational process equivalent to adjusting the audience's lens for the epistemological task of learning how to watch Chinese cinema. The film premiered at the Little Carnegie Playhouse in New York, then toured the United States, coinciding with the screening of *The Good Earth.* Based on Pearl S. Buck's novel, *The Good Earth* is a major MGM production that presents a hardworking and resilient China from a benevolent Western perspective. To ensure its positive portrayal of China, China's Nationalist government sent representatives to MGM to closely monitor its production. The convergence of *Song of China,* a Chinese film repackaged by a Paramount producer, and *The Good Earth,* an American film made with the Chinese government's input, signals a rare moment when stares from both China and the United States engaged with each other for a sustained period of time. Such fascination and engagement, however, do not guarantee rapport.

From the Chinese perspective, *Tianlun,* made under the aegis of the Nationalist Party, showcases a national essence drawn from a Confucian utopia and Chinese music. As such, it constitutes an exemplary response to the nationalist call for an indigenous cinema that would travel overseas to educate foreign audiences about China and its modern national identity. In order to correct China-humiliating films such as *Welcome Danger* that stare at and exploit stereotypical images of China, such as women with bound feet and men with queues, *Tianlun* presents a counterstyle. A tell-tale sign is that, contrary to Lloyd's searching of the entire Pacific Coast for an old Chinese man with an anachronistic queue, *Tianlun* completely *omits* the queue despite the fact that the film opens in the late Qing dynasty, when men were *required by law* to wear their hair in a queue. It also presents a modern China compatible with Western values by fusing the Confucian utopia of heavenly harmony with Christian imagery. In the opening sequence, for instance, a shepherd ushers a stray lamb back into the fold, foreshadowing the benevolent domestic disciplining and reinstatement of Confucian ethics in the main narrative. Thus, the film inscribes an internal position of agency that actively constructs and presents a desired self-image geared for the audiences both within and outside China.

Interestingly, this agency was perceived as a stare from China when the film was shown in New York. The *New York Times* review described the American audience's encounter with the Chinese film in the following terms: "East is East and West is West and the twain met and *regarded each other soberly* for an hour or so yesterday at the Little Carnegie Playhouse."[26] The emphasis on a mutual "sober, hour-long regard"—a sustained attention, or what I am calling the "stare"—implies that despite MacLean's initial packaging of the film as an exotic Other to be easily fetishized and consumed, the American audience was inevitably surprised as it found itself subjected to the Chinese stare inscribed in the film. Thus, the review captures precisely the American viewers' difficult negotiation with an uncanny Other.

On the one hand, the film reinforces American viewers' "settled conviction that the Chinese are not peculiar, just quaint," since the film shows the Chinese as sticking to "sincerity, simplicity, dignity"—qualities that the Americans have been "schooled to distrust." Such "quaint" or antiquated Chineseness, combined with "typical Oriental deliberation" and the "amusingly flowery" English subtitles, endows the film with a "curiosity value" as a retro object; yet it also disqualifies it as "general entertainment" for a contemporary audience. On the other hand, the film also disorients American viewers with its uncannily familiar acting style. According to the reviewer, the acting is thoroughly "Occidental" because cinema is a "modern institution" "served by the moderns of the East," which in turn "disappoints" Western expectations for "the sweeping gestures, the exaggerated pantomime of the traditional Chinese drama."[27]

The reviewer's bifurcated reactions (reassurance and frustration) suggest entangled scopic exchanges and an engagement, or a crisscrossed stare, that both links an orientalist American audience with a self-conscious Chinese film and separates one from the other. The "disappointment" the American reviewer feels with regard to the acting style in *Song of China* pinpoints precisely the incompatibility between an Orientalist expectation for an exotic China and the Chinese film's surprising presentation of an uncanny similarity with Western modernity.

In encountering China's unexpected "coeval-ness" with the West,[28] this sustained Sino-American mutual "sober regard" unleashes the ambivalent effects of the crisscrossed stare. The crisscrossed stare challenges, if not completely debunks, the dichotomous power structure between the colonizer (commonly understood as the gazer) and the colonized subject (who is usually gazed at). To this extent, the Chinese film goes to the West not merely as a hooksian oppositional gaze (that strives to "contest, resist, revision, interrogate, and invent"),[29] but more as a stare that accosts, seduces, and engages with the Western Other's gaze. This exchange disorients and retrains the Western gaze as an open-ended stare that accommodates uncertainty, doubt, and transformation.

Crisscrossed or Introverted?—Lu Xun's Intervention

Both the Chinese protest against *Welcome Danger* and the American "disappointment" with *Song of China* derive from the discrepancy between what the Self expects to see through staring or gazing at the Other and what the stare or gaze actually reveals about the Other and the Self. As different as are the Chinese anger and the American "disappointment," they share two qualities: first, a sustained entanglement of mutual staring that produces sentiments ranging from anger or disaffection to fascination and potential acknowledgment; second, cross-purposes and failed communication between the crisscrossed stares. The continual vacillation between different sentiments characteristic of the crisscrossed stares produces two effects. On the American side, the acquisition of the open-ended stare (in place of the exploitative and preemptive gaze) ambiguates the power structure and potentially undermines the seat of power. On the Chinese side, however, the reverse and crisscrossed stares (especially the tendency of looking toward the West for self-affirmation) risks weakening the anti-colonial project of building an independent Chinese national and cultural identity.

To bring the anti-colonial agenda into sharper focus and to make China a stronger player in the contention over power, Lu Xun, a forerunner of modern Chinese literature and scathing satirist of the flaws in the Chinese national character, redirected the crisscrossed stare toward the introverted stare, urging the Chinese protesters to exercise self-diagnosis and self-improvement. He articulated the self-reflective, introvert stare in his critique of China's protest against China-humiliating films.

Lu Xun argued that the protests stemmed from a major flaw in the Chinese national character, namely, the collective obsession with "face" (or *mianzi*). To maintain "face," the Chinese would try in every way to wriggle out of a corner and feel triumphant (despite an actual failure), which only served to perpetuate their enslavement.[30] On January 16, 1930, shortly after Douglas Fairbanks's visit to China and Japan and just before the eruption of the *Welcome Danger* incident, Lu Xun finished translating an essay by a Japanese leftist critic, Iwasaki Akira. Titled "Senden, sendoo shudan to shite no eiga" (Film as a means of propaganda and agitation) and published in November 1929, this essay was later included in Iwasaki's 1931 book *Eiga to shihon shugi* (Film and capitalism). Lu Xun also attached a long commentary to his translation.[31]

As a leading leftist critic, Iwasaki helped found the Proletarian Film League of Japan (or Prokino) in February 1929 and served on the editorial board for their flagship journal, *Shinko eiga* (The emerging cinema), launched seven months later in September. In his essay, Iwasaki describes cinema as a bourgeois medium and analyzes the ways in which Western (especially Hollywood) cinema maximizes capitalist profits and seduces petty urbanites by occluding class conflicts. Drawing upon Iwasaki's economic analysis, Lu Xun contends that Hollywood exports films to China *not* to humiliate China but rather for profits (just as industrialized countries sell outmoded weaponry to backward countries). He argues that to protest against American stars like Douglas Fairbanks and against Hollywood films like *The Thief of Bagdad* is to miss the fundamental link between cinema and capitalism. Lu Xun rubs against Chinese discourses of self-racialization by stating that the negative portrayal of the Mongolian prince in *The Thief of*

Bagdad should not concern the Chinese, since the Chinese are not Mongolians. Nor should the Chinese criticize Fairbanks for starring in this film, since he was just an actor, not the director, and the film was adapted from the *Arabian Nights*, not an original Hollywood idea.

On the other hand, when the Shanghai Film Association addressed an open letter to Fairbanks, the "great master," asking him to use what he had seen during his China trip to help propagandize China's four-thousand-year civilization to the world, Lu Xun found this plea symptomatic of a simultaneously slavish and arrogant national character stemming from the Chinese empire's past glory and its later degeneration since the mid-nineteenth century. For him, Fairbanks was nothing more than an actor who shamelessly profited from the capitalist and colonial system. As such, he was not qualified to address the problems of *The Thief of Bagdad* or serve as a mouthpiece for China's civilization. Therefore, Lu Xun argues, both the protest and the plea produce a delusion of Chinese agency, one that hinders the critics and the audience from recognizing the true nature of the problem.

Understood in relation to the capitalist nature of cinema, Hollywood productions are problematic and damaging to countries that are in the periphery, but not because of their degrading portrayal of them; rather, the real danger lies in cinema's complicity with Euro-American imperialism and colonialism. Lu Xun sums up the whole package of ongoing exploitation in China as follows: Having thrown China into war and chaos with outmoded weaponry, the United States ships out old Hollywood films to dazzle and befuddle the Chinese audience. When the films become even older, they are shipped inland to further stupefy the broader Chinese population. Thus, China humiliation is no more than a side effect of a larger system of colonial exploitation that extends into economic, political, and cultural domains.[32] Commenting on the origin of films that reputedly humiliate the Chinese, Lu Xun writes in his characteristic satiric style: "Well-fed and warmly-dressed white people need entertainment. Yet they have become tired of the cannibalistic African primitives and beast films. Therefore, they put flat-nosed yellow people on the screen. This leads to the so-called 'China-humiliating films' (*ruhua yingpian*)."[33]

To really solve the problem, Lu Xun argues, the Chinese must learn to face and reflect upon their slavish mentality, born from years of political and economic subjugation. The introverted stare thus serves as a necessary antidote to the crisscrossed stare. According to Lu Xun, protest against China-humiliating films and the export of China-made, China-aggrandizing films are both defense mechanisms that reduce China's capacity for self-reflection and self-improvement. He illustrates this point with an analogy. Those who protest against China-humiliating films are fully aware of China's weaknesses, just as edematous patients are aware of their problem. However, the persistent obsession with maintaining "face" makes them unable to tolerate other people's criticism. They try to foster the illusion that, in terms of the analogy, they are simply fat. When their critics refuse to see things their way, they become humiliated, furious, trying to threaten and scare their critics into taking another close look (or stare) and coming to agree that they are just nicely fat. If their threatening, reverse stare is successful, then they can keep suffering from edema with great peace of mind. Lu Xun concludes that to stop watching "humiliating" films is no different than staying edematous with eyes closed; to watch such films without self-reflection or self-criticism is also harmful. The real task for the Chinese is to diagnose the "edema," to cure it, and to demonstrate with action what defines a respectable new Chinese, rather than demanding or begging for the Western Other's endorsement.

For this purpose, Lu Xun, interestingly, deploys another type of Western stare as a diagnostic mirror for the flawed Chinese Self. The diagnosis comes from an 1894 study of China titled *Chinese Characteristics,* authored by Arthur H. Smith, an American missionary who served in China for fifty-four years.[34] To the extent that Christian missionary work is imbricated with Western colonialist biases, Smith's study inescapably partakes in Orientalist discourses that reduce the Sino-Western encounter to a simplistic binary. Indeed, his observations on Chinese people's treachery and lack of emotion anticipate and justify Hollywood's Orientalist stereotypes. Nevertheless, for Lu Xun, Smith's diagnosis is incisive and compelling because of his lived experience in northern Chinese rural communities for an extended period of time. Instead of fending off Smith's external stare as "China humiliating," Lu Xun emphasizes the importance of acknowledging and internalizing it as an introverted stare, one that instigates a self-re-recognition routed through an outsider's perspective. By critically mobilizing the outsider's position, Lu Xun attempts to provoke Chinese audiences and critics into unflinching self-diagnosis, self-critique, and self-improvement, which can then facilitate the anti-colonial, anti-capitalist agenda.

Interestingly, his dissection of China's problem converges with Homi Bhabha's postcolonial politics in that they both attribute Western colonial stereotyping of the subordinated race to a scopic regime predicated on a politics of vision and visibility. What makes them different, however, is that Bhabha sees the stereotype as a colonizer's "phobia and fetish" that leads to the "colonial fantasy."[35] Inserting "fantasy" as an element of colonial power, Bhabha argues that the stereotype is characterized not by fixation but by ambivalence, which splits the ego of the colonized while engendering the "crucial bind of pleasure and power" for the colonizer.[36] For Bhabha, the splitting and ambivalence of the colonial fantasy render the stereotype an "'impossible' object" where the colonizer's scopic drive necessarily meets the colonized subject's "threaten[ing] return of [his] look," disrupting the attempted closure of the colonial discourse.[37] In Bhabha's conception, "the other question" is not a binary of either absolute dominance or straightforward resistance. Rather, the scopic drive produces an internal fracture in the colonial discourse (including stereotyping), which leads to its self-deconstruction and subversion.

Lu Xun observes a similar split in the subjugated Chinese ego. According to him, Chinese viewers subjected to Hollywood productions that promote "valor and courage" unproblematically feel that the white master is so strong that they themselves can only qualify as slaves.[38] Yet such resignation contradicts their habitual self-conceit as the subjects of an erstwhile Chinese empire. Consequently, their self-positioning is torn between pride in ancestral glory and consciousness of their modern-day subjugation as the racialized and inferior Other. Lu Xun's formulation of the dilemma prefigures what Bhabha understands as the "triply split" ego, one that is scattered among "incongruent knowledges of body, race, ancestors."[39] Yet, contrary to Bhabha, who mobilizes this "split" as a "non-repressive form of knowledge that allows for the possibility of simultaneously embracing two contradictory beliefs" and "a defence towards external reality,"[40] Lu Xun sees it as a national flaw resulting from an awkward combination of blind arrogance and slavishness. And the split Chinese ego can be salvaged only through unflinching self-diagnosis and self-improvement.

If Bhabha emphasizes the ambivalence of colonial discourse, Lu Xun refuses to entertain the idea of ambivalence or its self-deconstructive power. He advocates China's self-strengthening and active resistance against the colonial system. He bases the anti-colonial work on the critical, introverted stare that yields a clear view of both the flawed Self and the Western Other. Challenging the colonial scopic regime, Lu Xun positions himself as an iconoclastic insider-outsider who emphasizes the transformative power of visual agency.

Lu Xun's intervention was undoubtedly necessary for the anti-colonial agenda of the early twentieth century. Yet he failed to take into account the mass audience's fascination with Western cinema, as well his own.[41] By dismissing the audience fascination as guilty pleasure—signaling their co-optation by the colonial, capitalist system, he missed an opportunity to explore the transformative potential of the crisscrossed scopic exchange that arose from China's filmic encounter with the West. By combining Lu Xun's anti-colonial politics with Bhabha's postcolonial emphasis on the "colonial fantasy," we can develop the crisscrossed stare as a new fulcrum for addressing the complexity of (semi-) colonial tensions that simmered between China and the West.

Where Bhabha's "colonial fantasy" mainly refers to the colonizer's fantasy of the colonized, I argue that fantasy also goes in the other direction; the colonized or the semi-colonized subject (as in the case of pre-1949 China) can also fantasize about the colonizer, especially through the mediation of commercial cinema. Thus, the popularity of Hollywood productions in pre-1949 urban China illustrates not only its monopoly overseas but also the degree of fascination on the part of the urban Chinese audience. Such fascination is visually oriented, privileging the audience's scopic investment in moving images projected on the screen, a process that induces disorientation, cognition, agitation, *and* pleasure.

In this light, the protests against China-humiliating films do not contradict the fantasy/pleasure principle but rather reinforce it from the obverse side. For even as the agitators caution the mass audience against indulging in easy visual pleasure, their agitation itself bespeaks the desire for a different fantasy/pleasure principle that requires China's positive representation in order to confirm its self-regard and dignity. In both protesting "China-humiliating" films and sponsoring pro-China films, the potency of image in the border-crossing encounter is fully recognized and actively negotiated with. The concept of the crisscrossed stare underscores precisely the ambivalence of the Sino-American filmic encounter—pleasure and fantasy on the one hand, and frustration and power contention on the other.

Conclusion

I have delineated and analyzed three types of Sino-American scopic encounters from the 1920s and 1930s. These include the Chinese protest against *Welcome Danger,* the sober regard between the American audience and *Tianlun / Song of China,* and Lu Xun's two-pronged project of critiquing Chinese jingoistic campaigns while promoting the self-reflective, introverted stare. Of these, two unfold in the space of the movie theater, which forms an important link in the films' circulation, literally setting the stage for Sino-American and American-Sino filmic encounters. These encounters not only instigate entangled and affective scopic exchanges but also involve viewers in intense physical experiences. Hong Shen was detained by the Western police because of his incendiary speech against *Welcome Danger* in the Grand Theatre; the New York audience was metaphorically held hostage in the Little Carnegie Playhouse by the Chinese film's "hour-long sober regard"; while Lu Xun referenced the pathology of an edematous patient as an analogy with the self-deluding Chinese protesters. Such intense bodily experiences (of suffering and transfixion) are particularly accentuated in the theater space, where moving images impinge upon the audience in a visceral manner.

In this sense, that both *Welcome Danger* and *Tianlun* premiered at the Grand Theatre is not insignificant. As Shanghai's first-run screening venue specializing in Paramount films, its temporary shutdown following the *Welcome Danger* incident underscores the power of Chinese censorship and the ruling Nationalist Party's desire for self-governance, thus vying with Hollywood for dominance of the urban Chinese market. Yet with the theater's relaunching in 1933 under the new ownership of Lu Gen—a British–Hong Kong businessman—the showcasing of Hollywood in urban China resumed. Financially backed by Lu Gen's company registered in the United States, re-designed by the Hungarian architect L. E. Hudec, and boasting state-of-the-art equipment, the Grand Theatre remained a first-run theater dedicated to screening Hollywood productions until 1942 (when the Japanese occupation of Shanghai precipitated the replacement of Hollywood productions with films made by Japan-sponsored Chinese film companies). The pre-1942 screening history of the "No. 1 Theatre in the Far East" was interrupted only on the rare occasions when a China-made film obtained a premiere here. The premiere of *Tianlun* was one such exception, which Douglas MacLean, who happened to be traveling in China, chanced to encounter. He subsequently brought the film to the American audience, resulting in a mutual "hour-long sober regard." Interestingly, the film was then re-imported into Shanghai in its Paramount version and shown again at the Grand Theatre on May 5, 1937, before it was borrowed by Hong Kong's Queen's Theatre to celebrate the British queen's coronation ceremony.

Such continuous circulation and transformation become possible in the contact zone of the movie theater. Within this clamorous space, the Sino-American filmic encounter assumes physical, embodied forms that include Hong Shen's arrest and the American audience's transfixion. As one of the physical enactments of the scopic encounter, such interactions underscore the entanglement, difficulty, inevitability, and *fascination* of not only meeting, even confronting, the colonial Other, but also engaging with the Self *through* the Other. Staged in the theater space, such confrontations challenge the unidirectional, Orientalist, and colonialist nature of scopophilia and epistemophilia, which assume complete disempowerment of the colonized subject. Encompassing a reversed, crisscrossed stare and a self-reflective, introverted stare, the scopic exchanges I study inscribe and respond to a colonial power structure that not only hierarchizes but also interconnects the colonizer and the colonized in a mutually constitutive and ever-shifting network. It is through this simultaneously contentious and fascinating engagement—crystallized in the movie theater—that a multivalent field is opened up, instigating continuous Self-Other realignment.

Thus, even though these scopic exchanges remain overdetermined by the overarching power inequity, they do not presuppose a Self-Other oppositional deadlock. Instead, they point to a *mise en abyme* in which the Self perceives the Other perceiving the Self, producing a new vantage point that may be confusing, offensive, or transformative, but ultimately conduces to potential positional shifts within the power structure. It is precisely through such continuous negotiation, feedback loops, and readjustment that national and racial identity is simultaneously contested and constructed. Border blockages and border crossings, as illustrated in the boisterous reception of *Welcome Danger* and *Song of China,* invite our investment in an embodied, crisscrossed "stare" that challenges and supplements any theory of visual pleasure that presumes a foreclosed system of power.

Notes

I would like to thank the editors for their insightful comments and careful editing of my essay. Any errors that remain are my sole responsibility.

The term in my title, "not-so-silent era," which I proposed at the conference "Border Crossings: Rethinking Silent Cinema" (University of California, Berkeley, 2008), coincides with the title of the published conference proceedings, *Not So Silent: Women in Cinema before Sound,* edited by Sofia Bull and Astrid Söderbergh Widding (Stockholm: Acta Universitatis Stockholmiensis, 2010). This happy coincidence is indicative of an interesting and significant move (initiated by scholars from different linguistic-cultural contexts) toward reconceptualizing and rehistoricizing silent cinema by probing its complex, oftentimes cacophonic social and political as well as cultural and aesthetic configurations.

1. Its first screening of a Chinese film took place on February 3, 1935—the Lunar New Year's Eve. The screening resulted from the vigorous campaign of S. K. Chang (Zhang Shankun), the boss of the newly established Xinhua (New China) Film Studio.

2. By emphasizing the staging of film culture in the public domain, that is, the ways in which a film addresses an audience, and conversely, the ways in which it is contested and resignified by audiences from different backgrounds, I follow Robert Allen's call for a "study of the historical conditions of filmic reception." See Robert C. Allen, "From Exhibition to Reception: Reflections on the Audience in Film History," *Screen* 31.4 (Winter 1990): 355. While Allen restricts his focus to the American market, I scrutinize how audiences across racial, national, and cultural borders engage with each other's cinema by mobilizing industrial, social, *and* state apparatuses.

3. In analyzing the inherent split nature (the "twoness") in Afro-American identity formation, W. E. B. Du Bois famously defines "double consciousness" as a "sense of always looking at one's self through the eyes of others, of measuring one's soul by the tape of a world that looks on in amused contempt and pity." See Du Bois, *The Souls of Black Folk* (1903; New York: Tribeca Books, 2013), 3.

4. The fear of the Other's gaze (or look) as dehumanizing, petrifying, and disempowering is articulated in two widely quoted sources. The first is Jean-Paul Sartre's "bad faith" identity, which derives from the Other's look that simultaneously enslaves and enables the Self. As Sartre puts it, "What anguish to discover that look . . . from which I can't escape! But what a relief as well! I know at last that I am. . . . I need no longer bear the responsibility of my turbid and disintegrating self: he who sees me causes me to be; I am as he sees me." Sartre concludes on a debilitating Self-Other deadlock: "I am as he sees me." See Sartre's 1947 novel *The Reprieve* (trans. Eric Sutton [London: Penguin Books, 1973]). Another traumatic experience of the Other's gaze is depicted in Franz Fanon's encounter with a French girl who exclaims at the sight of him, "Mama, look, a Negro; I'm scared!" (Franz Fanon, *Black Skin, White Masks* (New York: Grove Press, 2008), 91.

5. See bell hooks, "The Oppositional Gaze: Black Female Spectators," in *The Feminism and Visual Culture Reader,* ed. Amelia Jones (New York: Routledge, 2002), 94–104.

6. William Boehnel, "Silent Film Market Necessity, Says Harold Lloyd," October 16, 1929, *Welcome Danger* scrapbook, Margaret Herrick Library, Los Angeles (henceforth MHL).

7. An advertisement of the film's premiere at the Grand Theatre suggests that the sound version was shown. However, in view of the film's transitional status, the predominantly silent film culture in early-1930s China, and the Chinese critics' overwhelming attention to the film's visual representation (compared to a relative lack of interest in its sound dimension), I locate the film's Chinese reception in the broadly defined silent era.

8. See Wang Chaoguang, "'Bu pasi shijian' zhi qianhou jingwei ji qi yiyi" [The reasons, consequences, and ramifications of the *Welcome Danger* incident], http://jds.cass.cn/Article/20070307182135.asp. The translation and others from Chinese sources are mine unless otherwise noted.

9. "Harold vs. Chinese," April 26, 1930, Harold Lloyd scrapbook, MHL.

10. "Harold Lloyd Apologies for *Welcome*," *China Weekly Review*, August 2, 1930.

11. "Chinese don't laugh," March 8, 1930, Harold Lloyd scrapbook, MHL; "[A]s pure as the driven snow," April 27, 1930, Harold Lloyd scrapbook, MHL.

12. One exception that expressed sympathy with the Chinese protest came from a writer self-identified as "Uncle Dudley," who argued that the incident "indicated that the Chinese are human and have feelings like the rest of us." Given the common human nature of "loyalty," "we instantly bristle in defense" when forced to see ourselves "in the light of criticism by an outsider." Since we are all outsiders at times, "it behooves us to treat the failings and eccentricities of others with kindness, lest we find our own feelings unduly ruffled." See Uncle Dudley, "Love My Dog," February 25, 1930, Harold Lloyd scrapbook. While "Uncle Dudley" naturalized the Chinese response as a universal human response, his concluding call for reciprocity, however well intentioned, glossed over the existing and determining structural power inequities. Emphatically, not all "outsiders" occupied the same position; as a semi-colonized territory, China was particularly vulnerable to an external stare.

13. "Shangwu yinshuguan wei zizhi huodong yingpian qing zhun mianshui chengwen" [Appeal for tax exemption for self-made moving pictures by the commercial press], *Shangwu yinshuguan tongxunlu* [Newsletter of the commercial press], May 1919.

14. Gu Kenfu, "Yingxi zazhi: Fakan ci" [Motion Picture Review: Opening words], *Motion Picture Review* 1 (1921).

15. See hooks, "The Oppositional Gaze," 94.

16. "Harold vs. Chinese," April 26, 1930, Harold Lloyd scrapbook, MHL.

17. "No more Chinese villains," February 26, 1930, Harold Lloyd scrapbook, MHL (emphasis added).

18. Ibid. Another example that illustrates Hollywood's indiscriminate exploitation of weak racial/ethnic Others can be found in the report of Douglas Fairbanks as "a quick thinker." When blamed for showing a Chinaman being pulled by his pigtail in *The Thief of Bagdad* (1924), Fairbanks brushes off the trouble by explaining; "That wasn't a Chinese, it was a Korean" ("Chinese Don't Laugh"). The Chinese coverage, however, describes the humiliating scene as a Chinese man shown committing suicide with his queue; there is no mention of Fairbanks's resourcefulness.

19. "A Film Is Banned," February 26, 1930, Harold Lloyd scrapbook, MHL.

20. See http://www.artsreformation.com/a001/hays-code.html.

21. See John V. Wilson's letter (in the absence of Jason Joy) to Universal Studios manager Henry Henigson, May 23, 1930, *East Is West*, MPAA Production Code Administration records (production files), MHL.

22. "Col Joy's Resumé," June 19, 1930, *East Is West*, MPAA Production Code Administration records (production files), MHL.

23. Joy's communication with Mr. Carl Laemmle, Jr., February 25, 1931, *East Is West*, MPAA Production Code Administration records (production files), MHL.

24. Arguably, this practice was tacitly supported by the generally unproblematic acquiescence in, even fascination with, yellowface on the Chinese side. Warner Oland, for instance, was widely adored for his depiction of a "good" Chinese detective, in sharp contrast with the condemnation of Anna May Wong for her humiliating Chinese roles. See Arne Lunde, *Nordic Exposures: Scandinavian Identities in Classical Hollywood Cinema* (Seattle: University of

Washington Press, 2010), chap. 5. For a study of Anna May Wong's "Chinese" acting in relation to yellowface acting, see Yiman Wang, "Anna May Wong: Toward Janus-Faced, Border-Crossing, 'Minor' Stardom," in *Idols of Modernity: Movie Stars of the 1920s*, ed. Patrice Petro (New Brunswick, NJ: Rutgers University Press, 2010), 159–181.

25. According to R. Emmet Kennedy, Lin's *My Country, My People* would convince anyone prejudiced against China of the saying of Confucius, "Within the four seas all men are brothers." See Kennedy, "The East Speaks to the West," *New York Times,* December 8, 1935, sec. 6, 1–2.

26. Frank S. Nugent, "'Song of China,' an All-Chinese Silent Picture, Has a Premiere Here at the Little Carnegie," *New York Times,* November 10, 1936 (emphasis added).

27. Other reviews credited the film for displaying a noble morality and urged Hollywood to shoulder the same task of upholding civilization. For a Chinese translation of some excerpts from the reviews, see Dai Zhongu, "*Tian Lun* de jingcha" [The surprising *Song of China*], *Xinmin wanbao,* December 23, 2007, http://www.news365.com.cn/wxpd/bhygb/shzd/200712/t20071224_1698486.htm.

28. The notion of "coeval-ness" has been advanced by Johannes Fabian, who argues that colonialism operates by relegating the colonized to a backward phase of the teleological history written from the Western perspective, thereby stripping the colonized of coeval-ness. Johannes Fabian, *Time and the Other: How Anthropology Makes Its Object* (New York: Columbia University Press, 1983).

29. hooks, "The Oppositional Gaze," 103.

30. Lu Xun, "Shuo 'Mianzi'" [Observations on Chinese "face"], originally published in *Manhua shenghuo* [Cartoon life] 2 (October 1934).

31. See Lu Xun's commentary to his translation titled "Xiandai dianying yu youchan jieji: yiwen bin fuji" [Modern cinema and the propertied classes: Translation and commentary], originally published in *Mengya Monthly* 1.3 (March 1930). Lu Xun signed his name as "L."

32. Ibid.

33. See Lu Xun, "Lici cunzhao 3" [For future reference #3], originally published in *Zhongliu Semi-Monthly* 1.3 (October 1936).

34. Arthur H. Smith, *Chinese Characteristics* (New York: Fleming H. Revell, 1894).

35. Homi K. Bhabha, "The Other Question: The Stereotype and Colonial Discourse," in *The Sexual Subject: A Screen Reader in Sexuality* (New York: Routledge, 1992), 318.

36. Ibid., 322, 326.

37. Ibid., 327.

38. Lu Xun, "Xiandai dianying yu youchan jieji."

39. Bhabha, "The Other Question," 326.

40. Ibid.

41. Lu Xun's own attraction to Western (including Russian) films is well known. Between 1927 and 1936, he watched 142 films, 121 of which were American. Among his favorites were American documentaries of travels to Antarctica and Africa. According to the recollection of Xu Guangping, his wife, Lu Xun always bought the best and most expensive seat in a movie theater; moviegoing was a significant expense in his life. See Xu Guangping, "Ji Lu Xun xiansheng de yule" [On Mr. Lu Xun's entertainment], in *Lu Xun de xiezuo yu shenghuo: Xu Guangping yi Lu Xun* [The writing and life of Lu Xun: Xu Guangping remembering Lu Xun (selected essays)] (Shanghai: Shanghai wenhua chubanshe, 2006). Lu Xun's visual pleasure derived from capitalist as well as progressive Russian films, which deserves a separate study. Here, suffice it to say that the main target of Lu Xun's critique is the Chinese audience's and pontificators' self-delusion in the face of Hollywood commercial cinema.

8 Around the World in Eighty Minutes

Douglas Fairbanks and the Indian Stunt Film

Anupama Kapse

If a playwright seeks to stick to true history, then he is foregoing his duty to theater. If history is shown on the stage just as it is, it will be unsuccessful as theater.

Kaikhusro Navraji Navrojji, Parsi playwright (1874)

There is no picture like *The Thief of Bagdad*. It is just suitable for Indian audiences.

J. J. Madan, distributor for Madan Films (1928)

One of the most abominable features of Indian films is [the] hopeless acting. It looks like mimicry.

D. D. Sharma, film distributor (1928)

Baghdadmania

When Douglas Fairbanks visited India in 1931, he was almost mobbed. An excited reporter carried the story in the *New York Times:* "Calcuttans . . . mob Douglas Fairbanks."[1] Newspaper reports suggest that his arrival in Calcutta was somewhat compromised by an accident that involved a young teenaged boy who had been knocked down by his car. Even this accident could not deter the eager crowd that had come to see him in person. The experience of being mobbed was not new to the star of *The Mark of Zorro* (1920), *Robin Hood* (1922), and *The Thief of Bagdad* (1924). The Russians had already welcomed Mary Pickford and Douglas Fairbanks—often called Hollywood's first couple—with a display of acute Americanitis when they visited Moscow.[2] But it is not as well known that a Baghdadmania deluged Fairbanks on his otherwise unremarkable trip to India. Within the Hollywood imaginary, India had often figured as a land of bejeweled rajahs and wild tigers.[3] The size of the massive, somewhat affluent and urbane crowd gave

Fairbanks his first inkling of new audiences in an unexpected venue where his silent films continued to hold sway, although his popularity was fading in Hollywood. As eager fans waited to catch a glimpse of the celebrated "thief of Bagdad," Fairbanks arrived with the intention of shooting his sassy new film, *Around the World in Eighty Minutes with Douglas Fairbanks* (1931).[4] The idea was to make *Thief*'s oriental world come alive—to enact a "real" hunt in the actual "orient." But Fairbanks would soon discover that it would be impossible to supplant the fantastic world of *Thief* with this actual footage of urban India in *Around the World.*

Making no reference to the injury reported in the *New York Times,* Fairbanks opens *Around the World* with the following statement, literally "stepping off" from his star image (which presides over a map of the world) by undercutting the perceived experience of his visit: "I have just made a trip around the world—not in the interests of science or international goodwill, or anything like that. My sole idea was to have a good time . . . the world is essentially funny. It's a great place for laughs. It's also the dwelling place of magic. Absolutely anything can happen, especially in the orient, where we spent most of our time." As it turns out, *Around the World*'s "magic map" erases any topographic traces of India, roving over a cinematic vision of what India *ought* to be. For Indians, too, Fairbanks was no less an exotic presence: he incarnated a spectacular screen charisma that was at once magical and accessible—with an essential presence that had been evacuated of all signs of corporeality. In a sequence that focuses on his trip to India, an immaculate Fairbanks, dressed in a formal black suit and tie, is seen alighting from a ship in Calcutta. He waves to a party of wealthy gentlemen (in Parsi headgear) as his voiceover congratulates them on establishing a successful film industry in India.[5] Paradoxically, this little segment from an otherwise dreamlike *Around the World* (which also includes trips to Thailand and Malaysia) provides visual, documentary evidence of a long-lost connection between Fairbanks and Indian cinema. Dramatizing a tense relationship between imagination and fact, Fairbanks is, on the one hand, at great pains to live up to his extraordinarily "orientalized" star image, but on the other hand, confronted by the material immediacy of India. Eventually, however, the witty fiction of going around the world in a matter of minutes prevails and he gives up any pretense of offering factual evidence of his trip to India.

By the mid-twenties, Fairbanks was the center of attention in India's nascent film industry. Released in India during the summer of 1925 (a year after it was released in New York in March 1924), *Thief* was described as a "super production" by Indian directors and distributors.[6] Super—not only as a spectacular, lavish costume drama but as the biggest crowd puller of 1925. *Thief* played to packed houses wherever it was shown, be it the big city or small town. Freight trains rushed prints to the remotest cantonments in India and across to Burma and neighboring countries.[7] Owners of cinema halls noted that *Thief* held a unique appeal for both ruler and ruled, bringing them into the same viewing space. Its fabled world was potent enough to unify vastly different viewing constituencies on the Indian side: British and Indian, Hindu and Muslim, rich and poor. The phenomenon continued unabated even during repeat showings, something no other film, whether British, Indian, or American, had accomplished so effortlessly until that point. *Thief* represented a catch-all genre that could draw people of whatever age, race, or persuasion into the cinema hall, with Fairbanks emerging as *star extraordinaire*.

Erik Barnouw and S. Krishnaswamy contend that "by the 1920s . . . the stunt film, inspired by the popular serials and by the features of Douglas Fairbanks, became an obsession with Indian film-makers . . . [so much so that] film production broke out like a rash [after that]."[8] The word "rash" encapsulates a seminal view of *Thief*'s infectious ability to take root in a foreign culture. Unlike popular reports extolling Fairbanks, critical opinion has been undivided in suggesting that the popular star had caused an allergy of sorts, forcing the body politic to break out in a hysterical cinematic inflammation. For the industry, however, *Thief* emerged as the urtext of an Indian dream factory that was waiting for recognition.

As its name suggests, the film is set in the famed city of Baghdad and tells the coming-of-age story of a thief, Ahmed, who must learn that "happiness must be earned" (and not stolen). Adapted from a spectacular ballet called *Scheherazade*, the movie was based on a well-known tale from the *Arabian Nights*. Indian spectators would have noted that Ahmed's journey strings together a fantastic set of adventures as he falls in love with a princess and saves her from a Mongol prince, flying to her rescue on a magic carpet. Stories from the *Arabian Nights* were dramatized repeatedly on the nineteenth-century stage in India and had popularized a distinctly Indian Islamicate aesthetic.[9]

Unlike most other films set in the orient, including those starring Rudolph Valentino—in which the woman is usually white and the man of Eastern origin—*Thief*'s two leads both play Arabs, creating a diegetically "pure" Arabian landscape on celluloid. As most viewers may recall, an extraordinary set piece on the magic carpet closes *The Thief of Bagdad:* a depiction of the prince and the princess flying over the vast expanse of a world above which they seal their love, with a kiss. Fairbanks strove to re-create the same "flight of fantasy" in *Around the World.* Watching an Indian boy as he performs the rope trick (which recalls an important gag in *Thief*), he asks in a surprised tone, "Where did you learn that?" "Why, from *The Thief of Bagdad*!" quips the boy. This episode stages the central conceit of *Around the World:* a borderless world where source and origin, fact and fiction, East and West are conjoined inseparably on the world map. Only in a paradigmatically cinematic sense could the so-called "Doug" have "crossed" the world in eighty minutes. Borrowed from the fairy tale structure of the *Arabian Nights,* this fantastic premise struck a deep chord with Indian audiences, although, as Yiman Wang explains in the preceding essay in this section, the Mongol prince would signal Hollywood's manifest racial stereotyping during much of the late silent era. But Indian audiences, well schooled in tales from the *Arabian Nights,* had eyes only for Douglas Fairbanks.

The crowd's adulation was not simply a sign of the recognition and broad appeal of American cinema but also an expression of India's long-standing love for an enchanting Baghdad whose new mascot was Douglas Fairbanks. Consider the following titles, the likes of which continued to appear well beyond the silent era: *Siren of Baghdad* (1931), *Bulbul* (nightingale) *of Baghdad* (1934), *Thief of Delhi* (1934), *Fighting Chevalier* (1931), *Lion-Hearted* (1931), and *Gallant Hearts* (1931): such titles could not speak more loudly of the Baghdadmania that was sweeping India. As an advertisement for *Siren of Baghdad* put it, "Do you know the fascination of Arabian atmosphere? Baghdad, where moonbeams light the blue sky, where pure love is the religion, where nature dances in nude form."[10] Here Baghdad epitomizes a luminous, exotic world characterized by spectacular sets, physical gags, magical transformations, and epic characters pitched at Indian eyes. Such films launched the popular stunt genre, which recast the Hollywood version by adding elements from British historical fiction while drawing liberally from Indian heroic tales and stories from the *Arabian Nights* (Figure 8.1).

Not surprisingly, the stunt film's meteoric rise caused considerable anxiety to the colonial government, which took *Thief* as its key exemplar. As Priya Jaikumar points out in another essay in this volume, the coming of cinema and photography brought about a massive shift in perceptions of the space and geography of India. While Jaikumar examines the increasing spatialization of colonial govermentality, my essay focuses on the British government's anxious reaction to the triumph of a new visual culture epitomized by the stunt film. It was in this spirit that the British government set up the Indian Cinematograph Committee (ICC) to amass data for assessing the extent of "native" film production.[11] Expressing concern about cinema's effect on Indian tastes and viewing habits, the ICC attempted to address British anxiety about moving pictures, predominantly the idea that images of white women would fuel uncontrollable lust in Indian men.[12] But beyond the fear of rape was the dread that moving images might create novel and unprecedented forms of intimacy between a white ruling class and its colonial subjects, an ideologically fraught scenario that was made dangerously desirable by the new medium of the cinema. After conducting hundreds of interviews that could not stop extolling the success of *Thief,* the committee ruled that *Sacrifice* (1926; based on a story by the poet laureate Rabindranath Tagore) was the best and most representative silent film from India, followed by *Light of Asia* (1926). Not a single Indian producer cited *Sacrifice* as a model (a government-approved, experimental film with no notable star, few stunts, and spare production values), while others agreed that "realistic" films such as *Light of Asia* were

Figure 8.1 Cover of publicity booklet for *Bulbule Baghdad* (1941). An early sound film in the stunt genre, now lost. Courtesy of the National Film Archive of India.

too new-fangled for Indian tastes. Interestingly, *Light of Asia* (a film about the Buddha's enlightenment) was a lavish Indo-German co-production. Shot in India's scenic tourist spots and opulent palaces, its producer, Himansu Rai, wanted to depict India "as it was." While both *Thief* and *Light of Asia* are films set in the so-called orient, it is telling that, by and large, spokesmen from the Indian film industry chose *Thief* as their key text.

On the other side, the British administration described *Sacrifice* and *Light of Asia* as films that followed the norm of empire films, which would be produced in Britain or in India with the permission of the colonial government so that profits could be shared.[13] For the empire, *Thief* was an alarming sign of its dwindling monopoly: it represented the coming of an autonomous Indian industry with the capacity to overrule the didactical imperatives of a *Sacrifice* or *Light of Asia.* As such, *Thief*'s steady popularity inaugurated a fertile but contested arena that mobilized stardom, stunts, and costume dramas as the organizing elements of a rapidly commercializing film industry.

A look at *Thief*'s production process reveals the complex nature of its economic intervention on the international film circuit. While *Thief* was being filmed in California, a rival unit transported its entire crew to Algeria to film an ethnographic spectacle, *A Son of the Sahara* (1924). Edwin Carewe, its director, cited racial realism—"the difference between good coffee and tinted water"—as the main reason for filming in Africa. Another motivation was saving money: "It cost DeMille $25 a day for each camel in *The Ten Commandments*. . . . I don't think there are more than 100 camels in the United States. . . . We used 587, at 50 cents a day."[14] In contrast, consider a *New York Times* review which notes that *Thief* was a film with no explorers, no expeditions, and no ethnographic views. Readers were expressly informed that "Bagdad" was a total fiction, a "flight" of pure fantasy, *entirely imaginary,* so much so that *Thief* was described as "a satire on the orient."[15] Produced at a stupendous cost of $1,135,654.65, the film was shot on a massive set spread out over six and a half acres.[16] Filming took more than sixty-five weeks, an unusually long period for its time, but nothing compared to how long it might have taken if the crew had traveled abroad. More than five hundred extras were used, the largest number in a Hollywood film at the time. Indeed, the repainting and remodeling of space remained central to *Thief*'s production ethic. At first glance, these tactics appear to support Edward Said's famous characterization of the orient as a "total absence," an empty space for imagining absolute power.[17] Said argues that, paradoxically, the abstraction of knowledge went hand in hand with an intimate cartography of the orient, schematized by extensive railroad networks, roads, and maps. Considering the West's heightened attention to the authenticity of detail, it is remarkable that from the outset Fairbanks pokes fun at the very principle of cartography and its realist project—repeatedly—in both *Thief* and *Around the World.* The latter explicitly overwrites the map of the world, while the cinematic Baghdad insists on its fictionality, obscuring all accurate details about its precise time, location, place, and history. A souvenir booklet of *Thief*'s initial screenings sold at the time underlines the power of make-believe:

> Fantasy is elusive . . . [but] when a thing is photographed, it is given substance and reality. This was *overcome* by building acres of glazed floor, which reflected the buildings, destroying the reality of solid foundations. . . . [It] imparted the illusion of floating, so that the magnificent structures . . . seemed to have the fantastic quality of hanging from the clouds rather than being set firmly on the earth.[18]

The souvenir booklet makes every attempt to situate the viewer in a world that is "out of proportion to human fact," telling us that *Thief*'s landscape is all magic—unabashedly capricious in its spatial inventiveness, like its fabled source. Architecturally, Baghdad was set up to reflect only its virtual image, appearing as a hall of mirrors where space was a placeless place—something that mimed the free, unbounded flight of its protagonist. In effect, the booklet positions the cinematic apparatus as a space determined by the authenticity of its fictional location. Here all material "substance" needed to be *overcome* to make room for the experience of a world *not* witnessed during actual travel. As we will see, in their own way and for their own reasons, both the Indian side and Fairbanks himself would remain deeply committed to the ideal of a fantastic time and place that was far removed from the actual world.

Although Fairbanks's early work is known primarily for his boyish, athletic—if nutty—charm, two films reveal his intense preoccupation with dreams and fantasies: *The Mystery of the Leaping Fish* (1915) and *When the Clouds Roll By* (1919). The first, a satire on the Sherlock Holmes mysteries and their quest for objective truth, features surreal stunts, executed by Fairbanks in a cocaine-induced haze. The second engages explicitly with Freud's theory of the unconscious, treating dreams as spatial landscapes that can be filled with scenarios of unrepressed, free, and radical forms of movement. Both films unfold in an experimental register that is imbued with a sharp comic edge. They would constitute Fairbanks's early and successful experiments with transforming film space into a nebulous domain that maximized opportunities for displaying his exceptional gymnastic skill, grace, and fluidity—which would be rivaled only by his smiling face, which became an abiding feature of his stardom.

The Physiognomy of a Brown Hero

Up until the beginning of the twentieth century, empirical data about the shape, structure, and contours of the face were repeatedly used to determine deviant behavior, particularly while studying Eastern races or ethnic types.[19] However, the institution of the cinema would make a different investment in and room for the exotic. The iridescent face of the film star was especially useful in reframing scientific imagery that was used to validate discourses of aberration. I need hardly say that a mug shot of a so-called thief from Baghdad would bear little resemblance to Fairbanks's grinning visage. Indeed, the star's face reveals more about cinema's treatment of space than we have been willing to admit, particularly in the context of colonial domination. Béla Balázs describes the face as itself a kind of map: "The human face is not yet completely discovered—there are still many white patches on its map. One of the tasks of film is to show us, by means of its 'microphysiognymics,' . . . the soulful, beautiful physiognomy hiding behind the typically course and ugly features of an uncultured race."[20] The word "typical" encapsulates Balázs's subtle jibe at cinema's ability to at once create and debunk racial stereotypes. In fact, physiognomy played a key role in Fairbanks's celebration on the other side of the globe as the Indian film industry redrew the face of the brown man for both Indians and Americans by picturing an audaciously robust personality cut loose from racial stereotypes.[21]

I am particularly concerned with the stunt film here, which made expedient use not only of Fairbanks's agility but also his face in order to abstract the time and place of the British Raj in its numerous renditions of *Thief*-style films. Unlike empire photography, the stunt film turned the Indian terra firma into a dreamlike site of spatial mobility and kinetic exploration, choosing Fairbanks as its figurehead. Balázs notes that the face could loosen all reference to location: "Facing an isolated face takes us out of space[;] our consciousness of space is cut out so that we are in another dimension[,] that of physiognomy."[22] By virtue of the magnitude of his stardom, Fairbanks was able to condense his intense physical routine into the single geography of his face. An image of his dark face dominates advertisements for his films in Indian newspapers and journals even though Fairbanks was known less for being handsome and more for his acrobatics; references to his acrobatics accompanied illustrations of his smiling face (drawn from such films as *The Mark of Zorro, Robin Hood,* and *Thief*). The wide grin represented cinema's subversive play with iconographies of masculinity and empire: a mere close-up could destabilize the visual centrality of the old landscape of domination (see Figure 8.2).

The ICC includes repeated discussions about the industry's intense quest for the right cinema faces. Asked if Indians had the right face for acting in cinema, one writer replied that they did not.[23] While this might seem like an embarrassing confession of racial lack (especially since it was coming from an Indian scenarist), it is significant that most filmmakers agreed that the Hollywood star possessed the correct physiognomy for embodying masculine vigor in Indian cinema. J. J. Madan eulogizes Fairbanks's face when he describes it as perfectly "*suit[ed]* to the Indian market."[24] In British India, such a face could instantly telescope the vision of a robustly empowered brown man. Fairbanks was so dark that his mother would hide him from her neighbors, afraid that they would accuse him of being a "half-breed."[25] But Fairbanks would turn these very slurs—including that of being "mentally retarded"—into the constituent elements of his machismo and free-spiritedness in his career as a movie star. The star recalls being stigmatized because of his skin color during his childhood: "I was the blackest baby you ever saw. . . . I was so dark [that] even my mother was ashamed of me," he confessed in an interview.[26] Indeed, his dark color, virile physique, and spectacular costumes held a potent appeal that could easily be appropriated by Indian actors. Directors like Madan capitalized on the opportunity to recast the "servile" brown man as a vigorously athletic, healthy, and attractive Indian type. Local look-alikes of Fairbanks prompted the elite accusation that "Indian acting looks like mimicry," but such views often co-existed with a low-brow, unbridled admiration for cinema's new faces.

To describe the search for an idealized American physiognomy as simple mimicry, however, would be to follow the British perspective. The idea of the appropriate film face became influential precisely because it promised to unhinge the racial lineaments that had come to signify the effeminate but sexually

Figure 8.2 Advertisement for *Robinhood* (1922), featuring a large close-up of Douglas Fairbanks's face, from *The Statesman,* March 17, 1923.

lascivious Indian man: small, servile, and dark skinned. Whether it was the foppish brown sahib or the dark, secretly threatening native, the old stereotype signified an ineffectual and powerless subject whose physical constitution was weak. The Fairbanks-inspired, robust new image, by contrast, signified energy, exuberance, and a newly rejuvenated brown body.

If his face conveyed intense joie de vivre, his physical stunts developed an expressive repertoire that could convey the underdog's freedom to range over his homeland. Once again, Bąlázs is useful for understanding Fairbanks's distinct charm. In *Theory of Film,* Balázs writes that walking, or human movement, is "the most expressive and specific cinematic gesture . . . because actors on the stage rarely [had] an opportunity to use the walk as a characteristic gesture."[27]

Balázs alludes to walking as a specifically cinematic invention that could generate an infinite play of space—a vessel for a distinct gestural idiom. As a star who often galloped rather than walked, Fairbanks exploited this expressive potential to its fullest effect. "To walk [or move] is to lack a place," writes Michel de Certeau. Certeau compares walking to transpositions of meaning in figures of speech (such as the synecdoche), which enact a profound metamorphosis in space.[28] As a matter of fact, the thief's gestural repertoire could be readily appropriated precisely because it represented a moment of intense spatial metamorphosis, one that could easily be translocated to Indian soil. Walking, leaping, jumping—all restructure and transform the limits of colonial geography, landscape, and place into a profusion of cinematic space.

Indeed, Gandhi, the architect of India's freedom, would also rely on the simple act of walking to express his right to belong to an unconquerable homeland. His characteristic brisk walk would quickly be schematized into a deeply charged national physiognomy—embodied in his saintly, toothless, dark, and smiling face, his skinny body pictured with an energetic walking stick. Gandhi walked repeatedly during his campaign, transforming this everyday practice into an idiom of protest, using it to great rhetorical effect in the famous Salt March of 1931. In spite of these ideological, expressive, and institutional resonances, scholarship on silent film has been reluctant to recognize the stunt film's significance in heralding a self-sufficient film industry that had successfully reinvented Hollywood's production style and aesthetics to suit its own progress. In the absence of reliable pecuniary sources, acting schools, exhibition venues, and well-equipped studios, *Thief* functioned as a virtual how-to book, offering information on the advantages of having a star system, ideas about acting, costumes, set design, and techniques of publicity: new film companies channeled these lessons into their work, which had begun to transform a startup industry into an organized cinematic institution.[29] Earlier work by Parag Amladi and Ashish Rajadhyakhsa, for example, privileges an aesthetic of realism, implying that the stunt film strove toward but usually fell short of the imperatives of nationalism because of its oblique treatment of history.[30] Amladi argues that "all the early films are, in a sense, variations on oppositions to history. . . . In the indigenous versions of the feudal romances, the emphasis is less on the truth than on the fantasies of aristocratic power and privilege." Rajadhyaksha, on the other hand, positions *Gallant Hearts* (G. P. Pawar, Agarwal Film Company, 1931)—one of two silent stunt films to have survived in near-complete form—as an "oriental spectacular," describing it as the first film "to spearhead the introduction of plot in the silent cinema." He is particularly struck by its "apparent realism of object-picturization and causality."[31] Amladi and Rajadhyaksha are right to point out that history appears in an altered, quasi-realistic form in the stunt film; but this need not be taken as a problem. Many of these films are set in a nominal past that

Figure 8.3 Cover of publicity booklet for *Siren of Baghdad* (1931). Courtesy of the National Film Archive of India.

papers over the exact setting and place to imagine a time when neither the British nor the Mughals before them had arrived in India. Rather than understanding such obfuscation as a sign of failed realism, we need to attend to the stunt film's peculiar fascination with abstraction as a sign of its play with and destabilization of entrenched notions of history, identity, time, and space (see Figure 8.3).

The genre depended on a frenetic relay of swashbuckling gags, key attractions that would be advertized loudly on billboards. As an advertisement for a typical stunt film, *Lion-Hearted* (1931) declares: "The very stones of the earth shake. HE-MEN fight, the battlefield thunder[s]. If you want to experience such thrills, then you must see *Lion-Hearted.* Featuring Miss Mumtaz, Mr. Madhav

Kale, and Prabhashanker. He comes like the whirlwind. He dashes against danger like [a] dare-devil."[32] Zunzarrao Pawar, who acted in and directed many of these early stunt films, recalls that his stunts involved "dashing up trees, galloping, wrestling [with] ten opponents . . . diving from dizzy heights into the sea, and frenzied battle scenes with real weapons."[33]

Typically, no attempt was made to periodize or locate the film in an actual historical milieu. Advertisements mentioned only the high point of stunts and thrills. Many of the films would be released with two titles—the novel *The Prisoner of Zenda* was adapted as a Rajput romance and released as *Raseeli Rani,* or *Triumph of Love* (1929). Its hero, one of the leading practitioners of the Fairbanks "school," recalls that the films of Douglas Fairbanks were his main "inspiration. . . . Nobody [had] done stunts like that and I learn[ed] by watching him . . . whether it was falling off a horse or jumping off a building."[34] The intertitles reflect the pressing physicality of the hero's performance, which would underscore a whole array of kinetic gestures in an "acoustic" typographical register:

> Down! Down!
> You dirty dog! Be a man!
> . . . cast this rogue in the dungeon!
> Not so fast, my little girl! You C-A-N-N-O-T go! (*Gallant Hearts*)
>
> Enough of this age-long tyranny! Ye! Freedom-loving sons of the soil! Gird up your loins and fight for your birthright!!! (*Marthanda Varma,* 1931)[35]

Even the style and pace of production was breathless, yet prolific. It subordinated narrative to spectacle, although each film could run for over two hours. As Jairaj, an actor-director known for his work in stunt films, recalls: "Films were made expediently and cheaply. . . . A film took eleven to twenty days . . . most of them twelve reelers, and cost as little as five to seven thousand rupees."[36] In contrast, even before *Thief* was completed, interviews with Fairbanks provided detailed information on the epic cost and grand scale of production. The bazaars of Baghdad alone, created outside the palatial Fairbanks-Pickford residence, Pickfair, cost twenty thousand pounds; the buildings "towered above Robin Hood's castle, dwarfing it to quite ordinary proportions."[37] In a significant departure, Fairbanks began a new collaboration with Morris Gest, a well-known theater personality and entrepreneur of "artistic" films, to market *Thief* at New York's Liberty Theater, which could house 15,000 viewers at one time. Fairbanks, speaking in an interview, praised Gest for having no equal in "presenting artistic entertainment to the public," while Gest remarked that he had undertaken the project because he wanted to "present to Europe this great triumph of American art . . . even Russia."[38]

No one anticipated the near stampede that took place when *Thief* was finally released in New York on March 17, 1924. Pickford and Fairbanks were "nearly crushed" by the crowd, which delayed the premiere for several hours as the police rushed to the spot to manage the situation. The campaign was so successful precisely because of its ambition toward artistry—Fairbanks claimed that he wanted outdo his German rival Fritz Lang, particularly the latter's *Destiny* (1921). Following the stampede, advertisements in the *New York Times* labeled it the "artistic revelation of the century."[39] Fairbanks's collaboration with Gest (son-in-law of the grand dramaturge David Belasco) resulted in a marketing coup that telescoped Hollywood into new markets, ensuring that *Thief* had an even greater success outside the United States, particularly in Russia and the Far East.

On the other side of the world, in the absence of a fully functional star system, *Thief*'s Indian counterparts had little financial backing and were completed, if and when money became available, for a few thousand rupees. Production was immediate, rapid, and continuous, lasting as little as eleven days. Films were shot on actual location in open studios with reflectors that brightened natural light. Here the re-enactment of Hollywood scenarios served as an appropriate (rather than appropriated) filmic citation, while famous literary texts functioned as strategies for aggrandizing the stunt film, where location pictured an orient made *in, about,* and *for* an orient that could, ironically, never be precisely identified. The makeshift nature of the location and extreme simplicity of characterization transgress the dominant Hollywood aesthetic of illusionism while borrowing visibly from *Thief*'s exemplary outlandishness.

It is not surprising that Pawar glosses over the small scale of production. Instead, he highlights the literary source, which became the major creative inspiration for stunt films, an impulse that was never recognized by the ICC, just as it also ignored references to Fairbanks and *Thief,* which were essentially demands for recognition of artistic merit. Pawar recollects that his "part in *Hawk* was based on the *Hunchback of Notre Dame*. . . . [It] was very popular. I also played a double role in an Indian version of *Dr. Jekyll and Mr. Hyde*."[40] As in silent cinemas elsewhere, literary material was particularly useful for attracting "socially minded," cultivated patrons, a fact that once again belies the notion that the stunt film had a limited audience, just as it draws attention to its practiced narrative sophistication, which went unnoticed owing to the raw physicality of its action. The genre continued to borrow eclectically from a variety of literary sources: *Fight unto Death* was based on a popular Rajput historical romance; *My Mother Land* was based on a novel by Baroness Orczy and set against a Rajput background; *Queen of Fairies* was based on an *Arabian Nights* story of a princess and her poor people.[41]

Actor-director Jairaj recalls popular novels, claiming that they were necessary "to make a *good* film . . . [one] read Raphael Sabatini for sea adventures, Alexander Dumas for action, and Charles Dickens for character."[42] Narrative coherence came from recognizing literary allusions which signified the overriding theme of freedom from oppression; the kinetic mise-en-scène enacted this central problem as a series of extravagant fight sequences that unfolded in the open space of exterior locations. Jairaj's account underlines the stunt film's emotional appeal, which combines "the adventurousness of a Sabatini or a Dumas with the melodramatic pathos of Dickens."[43] Finally, the frenetic pace of production imitated Hollywood's expansionist model, prompting the ICC's soubriquet that such movies were nothing but "infectious [t]rash."[44]

Unmasking Amboo: The Fairbanks of *Gallant Hearts* (1931)

I am hardly suggesting that the Indian film industry could not have launched itself without Douglas Fairbanks. I am suggesting, however, that Fairbanks's appeal is too staggering to be ignored and that, at its peak, his popularity was imbricated not only in genre formation but also in thinking and speaking about an industry of epic proportions. An added consequence is the unintentional role Fairbanks played in setting up a new female iconography that is specific to Indian silent cinema and particularly noteworthy in the context of the expansion of its film industry.[45] In what follows, I examine *Thief*'s trajectory in relation to *Gallant Hearts* (*Diler Jigar*; G. P. Pawar, Agarwal Film Company, 1931), the only extant example of Fairbanks's considerable impact on Indian silent cinema.[46] Widespread during the late 1920s, the stunt film would be relegated to the B circuit by the early 1930s. With the coming of sound, the rhetoric of fantasy and action gave way to a preoccupation with cinematic realism, one that depended on the purity of the female actress's voice, costume, and dramatically Indianized appearance.[47] Yet such ideals could not have been realized without the intervention of the patriotic, often cross-dressed stunt film heroine. As we will see, cross-dressing afforded the woman unprecedented freedom of movement, enabling her to embody a new norm of femininity made possible by the rapid institutionalization of the stunt genre.

Released in 1931, *Gallant Hearts* features Lalita Pawar as its heroine and is advertised as a film that speaks "not with [the] tongue but with actions."[48] The reference to sound is explicit and pointed—sound is *not* the main focus of the film.[49] Pawar is credited as Amboo, possibly a natal name that was later changed to Lalita Pawar after her marriage to the stunt film maker G. P. Pawar (also the director of *Gallant Hearts*), the name by which she came to be known, ever since she played the tyrannical matriarch in Guru Dutt's *Mr. and Mrs. 55* (1955). In *Gallant Hearts*, the heroine Saranga (Amboo) grows up on the street and earns a living by performing with a troupe of acrobats that includes her friend Hameer (played by a gymnast or "bodybuilder," also named Hameer), with whom she has grown up.[50] The absence of parental or indeed any controlling authority is striking. Saranga has no home to speak of except the street. Uncannily, the story echoes Amboo's own journey into the film industry. Growing up with no immediate family, she began by performing bit roles in early mythologicals, the most popular genre before the rise of the stunt film, when she was barely ten. In a telling anecdote, she recalls climbing over a wall to spy on a production unit and reiterates her quest for adventure, though she also notes that she fell on her face and bled profusely after one such attempt. First aid was administered, and she was cast in her first film because of her fearless taste for risk-taking. The incident marks the beginning of her cinematic career as an actor. Pawar (formerly Amboo) maintains that that's where she grew up: on the film set, which took the place of both playground and home.

Both *Gallant Hearts* and Amboo's subsequent interviews emphasize the landscape of the film set, street, and fairground, treating them not only as metaphors of home but also as emancipated spaces, available for exploring new social, psychic, and artistic possibilities. Soon after Pawar established herself as an actress, still going by the name Amboo, a slap from a co-star permanently scarred her face. This traumatic moment coincided with the coming of sound, ironically reprising the iconographic shift that would transform silent cinema's relatively unknown Amboo into sound cinema's fearful Lalita Pawar. As such, it signifies a critical transformation which required Amboo to give up stunts for other, less physical and more overtly emotional modes of acting and performance. With her face partially paralyzed, Amboo never played the daredevil again, returning to the screen as the demonic, sharp-tongued Pawar—the very antithesis of the courageous silent film heroine.[51] I refer to her as Amboo in the rest of my essay in order to emphasize this previous identity, which was closely tied to a type of female performativity that depended on a feel-good stunt persona that would be significantly obscured by Pawar's later screen life as an evil mother-in-law.[52]

Amboo has been largely forgotten: Pawar herself recounts in interviews that she excelled in the role of the mother-in-law, singling out details that show how she used her handicap to strategic advantage.[53] To that end, Amboo's role in *Gallant Hearts* offers a rare testimony of her work as a stuntwoman. While it is hard to ascertain exactly how and when *Gallant Hearts* was completed, it is quite clear that its release coincided with Douglas Fairbanks's visit to India at the time when he was filming *Around the World*. Just as Fairbanks himself would reprise the antics of *Zorro, Robin Hood,* and *Thief* in that film, *Gallant Hearts* conjoins all three in its expressive repertoire. Not surprisingly, it avoids any reference to the more contemporaneous *Around the World*. Nor does it ever *directly* reveal or refer to Fairbanks's work, relying instead on the greater power of suggestion and insinuation. *Gallant Hearts* opens with a point-of-view shot that reveals a king gazing at his people, showering them with silver coins. At the very outset, we are introduced to a vertical space that represents the king's grandeur and is pitched against the horizontal level of the street. But the camera destroys the king's primacy in the next shot: breaching the stability of his sovereignty, it repeatedly violates the 180 degree rule, a pattern that immediately alerts us to a transformation of the Hollywood norm. Whether or not this is deliberately intended—there is no evidence to suggest that such "jerky" movements were intended to be self-reflexive—they evoke the experimental address characteristic of an emerging film industry that was enthusiastically embracing new cinematic techniques. Here the overall effect is one of intense social upheaval and sudden unrest. The mise-en-scène reveals an unsettling décor that refuses to provide a stable point of identification—the interior of the castle comes across as a cavernous, flickering space with corners that jut out expressionistically as heavy drapes cast dark, sinister shadows on looming walls, augmented by innovative lighting effects. The palace is rife with a blood feud: the king's own brother, Kalsen (Daniel),[54] poisons him and usurps the throne. In contrast to the grand and expansive view that opens the film, the palace now appears as a cramped, labyrinthine space full of intrigue. A loyal minister saves the king's infant son, whisking him off to the woods to protect the successor. It is this prince who grows up to become the bodybuilder Hameer—a lowly position that literally requires him to perform at a street level while earning his living as a fairground acrobat. Thus the bound, confined place of the castle is pitted against the unbound space of the street.

Once they grow up, Saranga and Hameer, both street performers, fall in love. And as Kalsen, Daniel plays a hypnotic, moustache-twirling, Daliesque villain who is lasciviously attracted to Saranga as she dances sensuously during one of her performances, twisting and thrusting her hips seductively (see Figure 8.4). He invites Saranga to his castle—a lure to bring her into his harem. Hameer follows in hot pursuit. A trap door lands Saranga in Kalsen's clutches. Kalsen entices her with his jewels. Knowing that she is trapped, Saranga makes a plan to escape. She tries on each jewel, displaying her attraction to both Kalsen and the jewels but hoping to escape with her treasure. Hameer arrives unannounced upon the scene and believes that Saranga has sold herself to Kalsen's harem. Outraged, he saves Saranga, but only to reject her as a woman kept by Kalsen. In a stunning sequence, the camera follows Saranga in a rhythmic forward tracking motion (enhanced by the makeshift nature of the technology, which sensuously mimics her thrusting movements) as she throws each jewel into the river, as if she were discarding the fragments of an empowered self. Kalsen now captures Hameer, but this time it is Saranga who rescues Hameer. Disguised as a masked crusader à la Douglas Fairbanks, she breaks into the castle with a gag that depends on the difference between the homely space of the street and the ominous alienation of the castle.

References to Fairbanks's mask, cape, and trademark smile are unmistakable. Strikingly, Amboo's "Doug," instead of being bare-chested, wears an excess

Figure 8.4 As Saranga in *Gallant Hearts* (1931): Amboo dances seductively. Author's screen shot.

of accoutrements that noticeably quote Fairbanks's signature leaps, grin, and aggressive posture. Of these, Doug's mask is the most prominent feature of the Zorro-like female Indian incarnation. *Gallant Hearts* clearly reprises Fairbanks's machismo in Amboo's costume, while distributing his leaps, sword fights, whip cracking, rope tricks, and sprints evenly across the performances of its two lead actors—blending these "spice[s]" into a perfectly coupled amalgam.[55] In other words, Amboo is endowed with Fairbanks-like attributes in order to structure a coup d'état that not only spices up the scene but also arranges a climactic finale that ultimately leads to a recognition of her extraordinary bravura.

Indeed, the acrobatic Fairbanks, with his dark tan, stunning physique, and mannequin- like facility for "dressing up," supplied unexpectedly rich fodder for staging female dramas of liberation. By the late teens, the agile Fairbanks had a string of successes to his credit, particularly *Double Trouble* (1915) and *Wild and Woolly* (1917). As these titles suggest, Fairbanks's stardom grew on the basis of a double persona—that of a mollycoddle, a "nut" with a "feminine" side, together with that of a macho, swashbuckling pirate or caped crusader; he often combined both into a double persona in key roles in films such as *The Mark of Zorro* (1920). Far from being effeminate, the figure of the mollycoddle became necessary in order to manage the surplus generated by his hypermasculinity. Take the aristocratic fop who carries an umbrella instead of a sword, with a silk handkerchief to boot in *The Mark of Zorro.* As Don Diego Vega (Zorro's alter ego), Fairbanks sports a curly bang and sniffles delicately at his snuff box. Upon seeing the aristocratic fop, Lolita—the heroine of *The Mark of Zorro*—recoils instantly, exclaiming that Don Diego Vega is "not a man, [but] . . . a fish!" Lolita's description of the aristocratic fop as a fish out of water lampoons his lopsided nobility—only to accentuate a modernized, classless Zorro who emerges resplendent in a cape, mask, and sword. Zorro's spectacular introduction is followed by a swashbuckling display of his penetrating swordsmanship, where he literally brands his opponents with the letter *Z.*

In turn, Fairbanks's ultramasculine persona would often be tempered by exotic, scanty costumes that revealed as much as possible of a body offered for feminized display, to a point that tested all acceptable limits of decency. Daniel Cornell points out that no Hollywood star enjoyed dressing up as much as Fairbanks—he literally "stole" many of the key attributes of the costume drama, which was traditionally a woman's genre.[56] The combination of elaborate costumes with terrific acts of valor orchestrated an alluring form of masculinity that was, in all senses of the word, pleasurable to look at instead of being intimidating. In Indian incarnations, Fairbanks's appeal is further enhanced with the help of costumes and gestures that conjure a persona drawn from Indian heroic tales and Islamicate fables. While his effeminate persona was essential for managing his hypermasculine feats on the American screen, Indian appropriations called for an enhanced masculinity that was constructed with the help of indigenous costumes which function as historical referents in an exotic spectacle of India's mythical past. The drama of what such performative approximations should signify extends to an erotic contest between the couple, as both man and woman "fight" over who should act and dress like Fairbanks, and to what end. While as actors both Hameer and Amboo dress and act like the thief, surprisingly it is Amboo who more closely appropriates the outlandish Fairbanks, maximizing her transgression, while Hameer is in turn more imperiled than hypermasculine (retaining some traces of Fairbanks's double-edged American persona).

Indeed, Amboo's makeup authorizes a repertoire of actions that showcase the daredevilry of the new woman and are given an unusual amount of screen time. Citations of Fairbanks are for the most part overtly masculinized in *Gallant Hearts:* the Indian stunt film had little use for his effeminate persona. Whether we see them as stolen gags or adulation, such references help to imagine a woman at the center of the nationalist struggle, even as Fairbanks's heroism is split and distributed across the two principal roles. In turn, Amboo's masculine attire resonates with early cinema's theatrical history in India, where men would often appear in the role of women—a practice that arose from an increased demand for

Figure 8.5 Hameer unmasks Saranga in *Gallant Hearts*. Note how Saranga resembles the Fairbanks of *The Mark of Zorro* (1920), while Hameer resembles the Fairbanks of *The Thief of Baghdad* (1924). Author's screen shot.

strong female roles in a culture that prohibited women from appearing in public. But if male cross-dressing required the illusion of perfect femininity, female cross-dressing in cinema flirted with theatrical protocols to orchestrate gags that depended on the appropriation of male privileges; indeed, the woman, as woman, did not need to be perfect.[57] Scenes of unmasking—such as the one that closes *Gallant Hearts*—orchestrate and underline a prohibited, sensational view of the female face. They also recall the exclusive male privilege of lifting the bride's veil on the wedding night, this time in full view of the filmgoing public, thus enhancing the erotic appeal of seeing the woman's face while adding to the drama of revelation (Figures 8.5 and 8.6).

As such, Fairbanks's sexualized masculinity also served a new, transformed femininity that could disable the older, submissive variety: one which complemented, reflected upon, and amplified the new ideal of a robust Indian masculinity. In turn, the ultimate function of this public and therefore masculinized femininity would be to underscore and support unseen, sensational forms of female action, including the erotically charged act of being unveiled in public. If early Indian cinema deployed the trope of the angel in the house repeatedly to

Figure 8.6 Cover of publicity booklet for the stunt film *Dilawar* (Braveheart, 1936). Images of female bravura dominate, featuring both the cross-dressed heroine (inset, with moustache and hat), and a scene of unmasking, where her hair cascades in an erotic revelation of her femininity. Courtesy of the National Film Archive of India.

picture the white man as an invader and potential rapist—a fear that confined the woman to the space of the home—then Amboo's dual identity is vital for domesticating the street, usually a metaphor for homeless, "loose" women. In *Gallant Hearts,* the open area of the street becomes a metaphor for the institution of the cinema, which, through the facility of its expanded landscape, liberates the woman from the limited spatiality of the home, picturing Amboo as a brave heroine rather than a woman who has "fallen" by appearing in the movies. Amboo's "Douglasization" exposes the female actress's struggle to be seen and understood as heroic. Also mimicking the brown man's struggle to be recognized in spite of his emasculation, Amboo's cross-dressing in turn foregrounds complex layers of race-gender appropriations made possible by cinema's new trafficking of identities. Thus the camera lingers over Amboo in a medium close-up as Hameer removes her mask, while Amboo grins playfully through a gesture that recalls Fairbanks's trademark smile. A governing tension between the feminized, homely Amboo and the free-ranging, masked stranger telescopes a range of binaries critical to the popular imagination of India's emancipation from colonial rule: inside/outside, woman/man, interior/exterior, homemaker/warrior, wife/prostitute, caregiver/performer, weak/powerful, and home/street—all of which highlight the strain placed on a body politic envisaged as powerfully feminine. *Gallant Hearts* is exemplary in its unique privileging of the female subject, since the performative arena of the hypermobile, fairground-like street is triumphantly identified as Amboo's first home. In refusing to cast a slur on its heroine for her bold display of "acting," *Gallant Hearts* reprises cinema's own, slurred association with prostitution to symbolically set the medium free.

After sound arrived, the Indian stunt film reinvented itself with the help of a Caucasian star, Nadia.[58] In almost every film, Nadia straddled the roles of an alluring and simultaneously "fearless" femininity with ease and panache. Traces of Fairbanks's persona remain embedded in the whip she cracks, the mask on her face, her breeches and flowing cape, and the swashbuckling stunts she executes astride a horse. Ironically, because Nadia was of Caucasian origin, her films "whiten" Fairbanks's dark persona into an Anglo-American presence that is significantly at odds with the new norms of Indianized femininity. Generically, Nadia's star presence evacuates performative references to older, lesser-known female stunt actors such as Amboo, just as it moves the stunt genre out of the A circuit, reserved for educated Indian actresses who came from respectable families and spoke with an appropriate diction. The most telling example here is Nadia's inability to say the line usually spoken by the proverbial, virtuous damsel in distress, "Mujhe chod do" (Let go of me), which came out instead as "Mujhe chod do" (Have sex with me).[59] Even as her films remain patriotic in their use of themes and plots, the line effectively clinches Nadia's vexed relationship with the typical ideal of an "Indian" femininity in a split that was radically exacerbated by the coming of sound.

Some of the best-known female stars of the silent era came from mixed racial backgrounds and went on to have successful careers precisely because they were not required to talk—a practice that allowed actresses to re-create the safe, glamorous illusion of an unthreatening Indian femininity. Also, quite simply, Anglo-Indian women replaced earlier cross-dressed male performers. In contrast, Amboo was one of the few actresses who risked incarnating *herself* and took on an unapologetically "public" identity that was set against light-skinned female stars such as Sulochana, Patience Cooper, and Ermeline, who dominated the screen in the late silent era.[60] Which is to say that Amboo's earthy stunts were predicated on a free-spiritedness that challenged not only the prevailing ideals of glamor and beauty but also female propriety. Such notions were later accentuated by the constitution of a new, pronounced difference between the serious, well-spoken actress and Nadia's flamboyantly Caucasian appearance and accent, which fashioned an Anglicized, glamorous stunt queen whose Hindi emphasized rather than hid her extraordinary whiteness.[61] As someone who "spoke not with [the] tongue but with actions," Amboo's short-lived career as a stuntwoman went largely unnoticed—but it begs to be revalued both as an impression of Fairbanks and as an exemplar of the unwritten history of women in Indian silent film.

As it happened, the ugly scar eventually led to Amboo's screen demise, but not before the daredevil side of her persona paved the way for Nadia's louder play with outré femininity. Amboo's heroic public persona was soon appropriated by dulcet, respectable female successors who indeed spoke with the tongue rather than with actions. Needless to say, the ICC's recommendations were eventually realized in the long term, but not before Amboo and her male cohorts had put up a good fight. Stunt films soon gave way to studio films with high production values in a cinema that foregrounded themes identified as specifically Indian. The rash was gone. If the Fairbanks of *Around the World* had circled India in less than eighty minutes, the Fairbanks of Indian silent film would persist through Amboo into Nadia's less-than-mainstream performance and into the work of educated female figures who sublimated physical action into other modes of sensational performance, particularly song renditions. Impressions of Fairbanks can be seen well into the 1950s in swashbuckling films from Bombay and other regions, which preserved the legacy of *Gallant Hearts* in the form of historical nostalgia. To that end, it is in the cross-dressed figure of the intrepid, dark-skinned Amboo that Fairbanks may have performed his most valiant stunt.

Notes

I thank the staff of the National Film Archive of India, Pune, particularly Mr. Deewar, for making *Gallant Hearts* available, and Arti Karkhanis and Lakshmi Iyer for their invaluable help in scanning booklet covers. Thanks are also due to Linda Williams, Christine Gledhill, Rosie Thomas, Jennifer Bean, Laura Horak, Ira Bhaskar, Nitin Govil, and Anuj Vaidya for their help in polishing earlier versions of this essay.

1. *New York Times*, March 17, 1931 (henceforth *NYT*); see also *Times of India*, March 16, 1931 (henceforth *TOI*).

2. Denise Youngblood puts it succinctly: "The Soviet response to American and European movies was clear: they loved them." "'Americanitis': The Amerikanshchina in Soviet Cinema,"*Journal of Popular Film & Television* 19.4 (January 1, 1992): 148, http://www.proquest.com.queens.ezproxy.cuny.edu:2048/.

3. For a nuanced account of this view, see Daisuke Miyao, "Sessue Hayakawa: The Mirror, the Racialized Body, and *Photogenie*," in *Flickers of Desire: Movie Stars of the 1910s*, ed. Jennifer M. Bean (New Brunswick, NJ: Rutgers University Press, 2010), 112. Miyao tracks the career of the Japanese star Sessue Hayakawa, who played the role of an Indian in such films as *Hidden Pearls* (1918) and *The Man Beneath* (1919). He shows how Hayakawa's exotic appeal was simultaneously mobilized and repressed through a process of Americanization in films produced by the Lasky company. Paradoxically, the more Americanized he became, the more his Japanese fans admired him for successfully breaking into the Hollywood industry.

4. *Around the World in Eighty Minutes*, dir. Victor Fleming and Douglas Fairbanks (United Artists, 1931; Phoenix, AZ: Grapevine Video, n.d.), DVD.

5. The Parsis represented a wealthy, Anglicized sector of Indian society. Among them, Madan Theatres was owned by the Parsi entrepreneur J. J. Madan, whose company was one of the first to successfully import British and American films. According to Ashish Rajadhyaksha and Paul Willemen, by 1927 Madan controlled roughly "half of India's permanent cinemas."

See the *Encyclopaedia of Indian Cinema*, ed. Ashish Rajadhyaksha and Paul Willemen, rev. ed. (London: British Film Institute; New Delhi: Oxford University Press, 1999), 139.

6. *Report of the Indian Cinematograph Committee: Report and Evidence*, 5 vols. (Calcutta: Government of India, Central Publication Branch, 1927–1928), 1:505, 3:584 (henceforth *ICC*).

7. *ICC*, Report: 135.

8. Erik Barnouw and S. Krishnaswamy, *The Indian Film* (New York: Oxford University Press, 1980), 21–22.

9. For an introduction to Islamicate genres and idioms in Indian cinema, see Ira Bhaskar and Richard Allen, *Islamicate Cultures of Bombay Cinema* (New Delhi: Tulika, 2009), 4–5. See also Rosie Thomas, "Distant Voices, Magic Knives: *Lal-e-Yaman* and the Transition to Sound in Bombay Cinema," in *Beyond the Boundaries of Bombay Cinema: The Many Forms of Hindi Cinema*, ed. Rachel Dwyer and Jerry Pinto (New Delhi: Oxford University Press, 2011), 53–76; and Thomas, "Still Magic: An Aladdin's Cave of 1950s B-Movie Fantasy," *Tasveer Gar*, http://tasveerghar.net/cmsdesk/essay/103/.

10. *Statesman*, November 21, 1929.

11. *ICC*, Report: 1–3.

12. Priya Jaikumar, "More than Morality: The Indian Cinematograph Committee Interviews (1927)," *Moving Image* 3.1 (Spring 2003): 82–109.

13. See Priya Jaikumar, *Cinema at the End of Empire: A Politics of Transition in Britain and India* (Durham, NC: Duke University Press, 2006), 44–49.

14. *NYT*, March 16, 1924.

15. Ibid.

16. Jeffrey Vance, *Douglas Fairbanks* (Berkeley: University of California Press, 2008), 153.

17. Edward Said, *Orientalism* (New York: Vintage, 1979), 27, 208.

18. *The Thief of Bagdad*, dir. Raoul Walsh (United Artists, 1924; New York: Kino, 2004), DVD (my emphasis).

19. Cesare Lombroso, *Criminal Man*, trans. Mary Gibson and Nicole Hahn Rafter (Durham, NC: Duke University Press, 2006).

20. Béla Balázs, *Theory of the Film: Character and Growth of a New Art*, trans. Edith Bone (New York: Dover, 1970), 83.

21. Gaylyn Studlar's "Building Mr. Pep: Boy Culture and the Construction of Douglas Fairbanks" (in *This Mad Masquerade: Stardom and Masculinity in the Jazz Age* [New York: Columbia University Press, 1996]) includes a detailed discussion of Fairbanks's boyish charm (10–89). For an account of the conditions of Fairbanks's rapid rise to stardom in the United States, see Scott Curtis, "Douglas Fairbanks: Icon of Americanism," in Bean, *Flickers of Desire*, 118.

22. Balázs, *Theory of the Film*, 61.

23. *ICC*, 2:682.

24. Ibid. (my emphasis).

25. Vance, *Douglas Fairbanks*, 14.

26. Quoted in ibid.

27. Balázs, *Theory of the Film*, 135.

28. Michel de Certeau, *The Practice of Everyday Life*, trans. Steven Rendall (Berkeley: University of California Press, 1984), 103.

29. Following *Thief*'s success, Warner, Universal, and Paramount studios showed a keen interest in negotiating exhibition contracts with Indian film distributors. *ICC*, 2:154, 843, 1068. The report of the U.S. Bureau of Commerce also picked up news of *Thief*'s success from the ICC. Its *Trade Information Bulletin No. 601* (Washington, DC: U.S. Department of Commerce, Bureau of Foreign and Domestic Commerce, 1929) indicates that U.S. producers were torn

between echoing the sentiments of the empire and celebrating Hollywood's initial success in India. "The production of feature films in India exceeds, both in number and footage, that of the United Kingdom, a fact which is *generally not recognized.* In 1925 the production of feature films in the United Kingdom was 34 . . . by Indian concerns (including Burma) . . . in 1925–26 [that number equaled] 111. . . . Indian films are *very popular* with native audiences. . . . The majority of films shown in India, however, are imported, mostly American" (1) (my emphasis).

30. Parag Amladi, *New Apprehensions: The Ambivalence of Modernity in Early Indian Cinema* (PhD dissertation, New York University, 1997), 212.

31. Ashish Rajadhyaksha, "India's Silent Cinema: A 'Viewer's View,'" in *Light of Asia: Indian Silent Cinema, 1912–1934,* ed. Suresh Chabria (New Delhi: Wiley Eastern, 1994), 33–35.

32. *Bombay Chronicle,* March 22, 1931.

33. Shashikant Kinikar, "The Rise and Fall of a Stunt King," *Cinema Vision* 1.1 (1980): 48.

34. Interview with Jairaj, *Asian News Age,* January 2, 1997.

35. P. K. Nair, "Titling Techniques," *Cinema Vision* 1.1 (1980): 115.

36. Uma da Cunha, "Jairaj," *Cinema Vision* 1.1 (1980): 83.

37. *NYT,* July 29, 1923.

38. *NYT,* March 1, 1924.

39. *NYT,* March 19, 1924.

40. Shashikant Kinikar, "Zunzarrao Pawar: Best Fighter," *Cinema Vision* 1.1 (1980): 48.

41. Not dated.

42. Da Cunha, "Jairaj," 84.

43. Ibid.

44. Dumas's popularity is evident from an advertisement in the Sunday edition of the *Statesman* (November 21, 1929), which describes Douglas Fairbanks's *The Three Musketeers* as "the greatest action picture ever made . . . the biggest production ever staged. Ransack all the libraries of the world, search the literatures of all the nations of the earth, and nowhere will you find the equal of Dumas's undying story of thrilling romance and stirring adventure." The advertisement appears in English in the Calcutta edition, suggesting that the stunt film's target audience consisted of English viewers and educated Indians who appreciated *The Three Musketeers* as a "classic" that was "better than the literature of all the [other] nations" of the world.

45. The index to *The Encyclopedia of Indian Cinema* (p. 580) lists nearly a dozen films with the name *Thief of Baghdad: Baghdad Gajadonga* (1968), *Baghdad Nu Baharvatiyo* (1929), *Baghdad Nu Bulbul* (1931), *Baghdad Ka Badmash,* (1932), *Baghdad Ka Chor* (1934), *Baghdad Ka Chor* (1946), *Baghdad Ka Chor* (1955), *Baghdad Ka Jadu* (1956), *Baghdad ki Ratein,* and *Baghdad Perazhagi* (1973). The genre was revived by the regional film industries after the coming of sound, notably in the South, where it was particularly influential in establishing N. T. Rama Rao (*Pathala Bhairavi / The Magician of the Netherworld,* 1951) and M. G. Ramachandran (*Baghdad Thirudan / Thief of Baghdad,* 1960) as popular stars.

46. 35mm print held at the National Film Archive, Pune, India. Of *Gallant Hearts'* original length of 9,632 feet, 8,672 feet survive. The original Gujarati title is *Diler Jigar. Pitru Prem* (*A Father's Love,* 1929) is another surviving example; this film, however, is better characterized as a social melodrama and shows little influence of Fairbanks. See Suresh Chabria, "Notes on the Indian Silent Cinema Retrospective, Pordenone, 1994," 46, 55.

47. By 1931, a number of "ladies from [the] educated classes" had begun to act in the movies. After the arrival of female stars, the disguise motif lost much of its rhetorical power as a device for interrogating the norms of femininity. Instead, the new female star drew her rhetorical power from appearing and singing on screen as a woman and often mobilized her education

and voice as the sites of female emancipation. See Durga Khote's autobiography, *I, Durga Khote* (New Delhi: Oxford University Press, 2006).

48. Advertisement, *Bombay Chronicle*, July 12, 1931.

49. The reference is to *Alam Ara* (dir. Ardeshir Irani, 1931), the first sound film, which included a significant number of songs.

50. The only other surviving silent stunt film, *The Fall of Slavery / Ghulami Nu Patan* (1931) features a woman who grows up under the care of her father (hence her tomboyishness)—unlike Amboo, who grows up without a family. Since the heroine of *The Fall of Slavery* is brought up by her father, she is also required to perform the nurturing tasks of a wife or daughter for much of the film. This film is less representative of the genre—as Ashish Rajadhyaksha points out ("India's Silent Cinema," 34), *The Fall of Slavery* lacks the stylish camerawork of *Gallant Hearts*.

51. Lalita Pawar, "It Has All Been Worth It" [interview], in *70 Years of Indian Cinema 1913–1983*, ed. T. M. Ramachandran (Bombay: Cinema International, 1985), 78.

52. Pawar was active well into the 1980s, though she went on to play a variety of roles. Well-known examples of her role as an "evil" mother-in-law include *Neel Kamal* (The blue lotus; Ram Maheshwari, 1968) and *Shriman Shrimati* (Mr. and Mrs.; Vijay Reddy, 1982), as well as numerous other films—a list so long that it cannot be cited here.

53. Pawar, "It Has All Been Worth It," 78.

54. The actor's last name is not credited; it is common to refer to Indian actors by their first name or a mononym.

55. *ICC*, 2:495.

56. Daniel Cornell, "Stealing the Spectacle: Gay Audiences and the Queering of Douglas Fairbanks's Body," *Velvet Light Trap* 42 (Fall 1998): 76–90.

57. See Kathryn Hansen, "Making Women Visible: Gender and Race Cross-Dressing in the Parsi Theatre," *Theatre Journal* 51.2 (May 1999): 127–147, http://www.jstor.org/stable/25068647.

58. See Rosie Thomas, "Not Quite (Pearl) White: Nadia, Queen of the Stunts," in *Bollyworld: Popular Indian Cinema through a Transnational Lens*, ed. Raminder Kaur and Ajay J. Sinha (New Delhi: Sage, 2005), 54.

59. The joke hinges on her accent: *chod* (pronounced "ch-hoad") means "let go of me"; Nadia's accent rendered the word more softly, pronouncing it "cho-athe," which means "have sex with me."

60. See Neepa Majumdar, *Wanted Cultured Ladies Only!: Female Stardom and Cinema in India, 1930s–1950s* (Urbana: University of Illinois Press, 2009), 93–94, 108–109.

61. "Fearless: the *Hunterwali* Story" [interview with Nadia], dir. Riyadh Wadia, ca. 1987 courtesy National Film Archive of India), VHS. Girish Karnad recounts the story in "This One Is for Nadia," in *70 Years of Indian Cinema (1913–1983)*, ed. T. M. Ramachandran (Bombay: Cinema India–International, 1985), 266. For further discussion on Nadia, see Rosie Thomas, "*Miss Frontier Mail*: The Film That Mistook Its Star for a Train," in *Sarai Reader 7: Frontiers*, ed. Monica Narula, Shuddhabrata Sengupta, Jeebesh Bagchi, and Ravi Sundaram (New Delhi: Center for the Study of Developing Societies, 2007), 294–308; for an account of the stunt film's transformation of the individual, see Kaushik Bhaumik, "Heroes in the Metropolis: Imagining the Romantic Individual in Early Bombay Cinema," in *Beyond the Boundaries of Bollywood: The Many Forms of Hindi Cinema*, ed. Rachel Dwyer and Jerry Pinto (New Delhi: Oxford University Press, 2010), 47–52. Both argue that Nadia inhabited a far more privileged world filled with machines and Westernized items of luxury.

Part IV
Cosmopolitan Sexualities and Female Stars

Introduction

Jennifer M. Bean

In asking how female screen stars play highly symbolic roles during this period of imperial and industrial modernization, contributors to this section share the conviction that the conjunction of the terms "cinema" and "woman" assume governing status in debates surrounding the transformation of traditional cultures around the world. Each chapter also asks if the "problem of cinema," to borrow Aaron Gerow's phrase from part 3 of this volume, is separable from what Joanne Hershfield elsewhere terms the "'problem' of women." In an insightful analysis of early sound film in Mexico, Hershfield observes that "modernity in Mexico was marked by debate and anxiety concerning the rapidly changing role of women in the home and in social and economic spaces, and it is not surprising that the 'problem' of women, especially their sexuality, was of major concern to Mexican (male) public intellectuals."[1] While Hershfield's analysis lingers over the modern Mexican woman as signifier of change and transformation in *Santa* (Antonio Moreno, 1931), starring Lupita Tovar, it is of particular interest here to note that Mexico's first film star, Emma Padilla, not only bore an uncanny resemblance to the seductive, sometimes anguished, and often arrogant Italian diva Pina Menichelli but also "copied her mannerisms and gestures."[2] The imitation was hardly coincidental. Padilla's star status emerged following her performance in *La luz* (The light; Ezequiel Carrasco, 1917), the second feature-length fiction film produced in Mexico and one that overtly "plagiariz[ed] the popular Italian film *Il fuoco* (The light; Piero Fosco, 1915), starring Menichelli."[3]

Whether the Italian diva's replication on Mexican soil generated anxiety for male public intellectuals remains a matter of speculation, contingent on further research. But the concern aroused by a Turkish penchant for plagiarizing the diva's mannerisms in 1920s Istanbul is relatively clear. In a fascinating essay, Canan Balan reveals that young women's enthusiasm for filmgoing generated grave concerns for Turkish authors, social commentators, and government officials in the years after World War I, when the fall of the Ottoman Empire and the establishment of the new Republic of Turkey inaugurated a virulent nationalizing project. During the 1920s, Istanbul supported a booming film culture, but a Turkish film industry had not yet evolved and exhibitors depended on an international system of distribution. Although French, German, and U.S. prints also penetrated the market, among the most popular imports may have been Italian melodramas starring Pina Menichelli, whose "imitators amongst young Turkish women" simultaneously distressed and fascinated author Sermet Muhtar Alus. "Without hesitating to hide his own temptation," writes Balan, "he recalls women trying to impress men by copying Menichelli's gestures, her décolleté, her flirtatious glance and her half-open lips."[4] The at-once moralistic and lascivious tone adopted by Alus reflects what Balan describes as a pervasive discourse at the time concerning cinema's impact on women's more liberated lifestyles and public visibility, a phenomenon perceived by male intellectuals and commentators as a distinct threat to traditional family structures and patriarchal norms.

Although the three chapters included in this section discuss neither the Italian diva nor her impact on early Turkish and Mexican film cultures, I begin with these examples because they frame the intellectual concerns most germane to this section, in three ways. First, they flaunt the degree to which large-scale processes of global/industrial modernization and the liveliness of cinema's "transnational popular circuit" in the early twentieth century impacted men and women differently, not only transforming gender relations but also altering constructions of masculinity and femininity. Second, my ability to sketch these examples as an introductory gambit draws attention to the flood of very good work from an array of international scholars now assessing the absolute centrality of women to early cinema in every aspect of the medium, not only as stars but also as directors, writers, producers, editors, journalists, distributors, and fans.[5] Insofar as these historical investigations become "a discovery process with open-ended results and multiple points of entry" necessary to "inform our theory," as Vicki Callahan cannily observes, then the third point evoked by these examples concerns the concepts mutually at stake in histories of female stardom and feminist theories of subjectivity.[6]

This point warrants further elaboration. In an era when Judith Butler's understanding of gender as an "effect" of performance has become axiomatic for feminist theories of subjectivity, critical assessments of female stardom in a cross-cultural context offers a vibrant site for examining how sexual/gender identity is neither an essential quality nor even an intentional "performance," but rather the product of multiple, overlapping, reiterated discursive practices. Indeed, the challenge Butler assumes in *Gender Trouble*—to rethink gender categories outside the "metaphysics of substance" granted by a pre-given body or a thinking subject; to consider instead how identity is "performatively constituted"—finds an exemplary correlative in the methodologies necessary for discussing stardom, in part because a "star" is never reducible to a person, self, or bodily presence.[7] A star's identity, rather, exists *only* as a palimpsest of texts: images in films, photographs, portraits, caricatures, etchings, imprinted objects, and sketches; a flurry of stories, rumors, allusions, imitations, advertisements, press books, interviews, and eye-witness testimonies; a series of jokes, limericks, songs, dances, and so on.

That the diverse media formats constituting any "star text," to employ Richard Dyer's well-known phrase, also render star identities prone to dynamic transformation and appropriation in diverse cultural contexts can be gleaned by glancing back to Anupama Kapse's chapter in part 3 of this book.[8] Taking the popular reception in India of American superstar and swashbuckling hero Douglas Fairbanks as her point of departure, Kapse argues that Fairbanks's "dark color, virile physique, and spectacular costumes held a potent appeal that could easily be appropriated by Indian actors." She skillfully reveals how the literally dozens of Indian-produced stunt films in the 1920s "unhinge the racial lineaments that had come to signify the effeminate but sexually lascivious Indian man in the British imaginary: small, servile, and dark-skinned." One of the formidable strengths of her chapter lies in its capacity to steer the argument away from too-facile political critiques of "Americanitis" as cultural imperialism and toward a more nuanced reading of cultural history whereby popular images and identities imported from the United States galvanized Indian filmmakers to retool the images and identities discursively reiterated by the British Empire. Read as a precursor to this section's focus on female stars, it is worth repeating her convincing argument that Indian filmmakers not only "Douglasized" male actors; they also transferred this playful bravura to a female actress, Amboo (later Lalita Pawar), whose cross-dressed performance in *Gallant Hearts* (1931) and capacity to stunt freely across an emancipated space form, in Kapse's analysis, a highly symbolic emblem of national pride.[9]

In 1920s Sweden, the struggle to recuperate a national "soul" through the production of domestic films, and particularly via homegrown female stars, pervaded public discourse. As Jan Olsson clarifies in the chapter that opens this section, the term "soul" obtains acute signifying status in Swedish discourse at the time, functioning as a signpost for the "spiritual" health and tradition of the nation. It also forms a binary with terms such as "skin"—meaning the slick sheen of surfaces and crass commercialism—associated with the influx of film imports from the United States and, particularly, with American female stars. In a tour-de-force argument that juxtaposes perspectives from writers in multiple European countries, stretching to include even the correspondence of those based in locations such as Egypt, he traces "the intertwined issues of national screen identity and of feminine beauty as a casting concern." Taking the caustic question posed by French actor Pierre Daltour in 1923—why are Swedish actresses "so ugly"?—as his point of departure, Olsson charts the effects of what he terms "the pulchritude thesis," that is, an investment in women's appearances as the sign either of national health or of its other—a glittery, glamorous cosmopolitanism emptied of "soul." The "cosmopolitanism" of which Olsson speaks became the dominant trend for Svenska Filmindustri in the course of the decade, even as the box-office success of films such as Dimitri Buchowetzki's *Karusellen* (*The Whirl of Passion* / The carousel; 1923), featuring the Norwegian actress turned German film star, Aud Egede-Nissen, emblematized for some an end to the sanctity of Swedish art and culture and inevitable cultural suffocation. In this sense, *Karusellen*'s international success and its impact on industrial production policies in 1920s Sweden offers a prescient variation of what Ackbar Abbas calls a "new capitalism, global capital, [which] is freshly able to act, constantly outpacing the interventions of the nation-state and making it look heavy-footed."[10]

Is a comparatively fleet-of-foot industrial capitalism the progenitor of cosmopolitanism in its early-twentieth-century forms? Does this phenomenon replicate the ideological snare of an Enlightenment universalism that allegedly embraces a worldwide brotherhood of men (I use these gendered terms advisedly) while simultaneously inscribing the particularities of that universalism as European or, as in Olsson's study, "American"? Alternately, is it possible to understand the resistance of Swedish commentators to their film industry's lucrative cosmopolitan groove as a sort of narrow parochialism masquerading as tradition? What role did women play in articulating a relationship to national identity and to a cinematic aesthetics predicated on "'feminine beauty as a casting concern"? Insofar as Olsson's chapter implicitly raises such questions, the finesse lies in accepting the impossibility of a singular or definitive answer.

As a case in point, countervailing perspectives from European intellectuals regarding cinema's impact on national or local consciousness in the 1920s warrant at least momentary attention. Czech author Bedřich Václavek, for instance, cheered what he termed cinema's "cosmic consciousness" in his 1924 essay "On the Sociology of Film." In what may remain to date the most vocal celebration of popular cinema's capacity to induce a habit of mind that would enable loyalty to humanity as a whole, Václavek declares that the "cinema educates":

> [It] pulls a person at a remote end of the world out of isolation and connects him [de facto] to the whole world. It is "everyone's general instruction." It informs. It teaches a new sociability. In the cinema, country villagers see the hustle and bustle of the metropolis, its flood of lights, cars, hotel facades, and train stations. City dwellers see wooded mountain ranges, the melancholic lines of telegraph cables along isolated paths, and the serenity of the countryside. Central Europeans see deserts, seas, China, India, and life there. The Japanese participate in American and European life. *A new consciousness of world unity* emerges.[11]

This conception of popular cinema as a sort of educational program emphasizing the commonalities and responsibilities of global citizenship similarly informed the thinking of British author Dorothy Richardson, whose writings regularly focused on film viewing as a means of broadening the horizon of women's lives and experiences. In her 1928 essay "The Cinema in Arcady," however, Richardson considers the impact of filmgoing on the generation coming of age in small towns and rural areas. At the cinema, she writes, "these youths and maidens in becoming world citizens, in getting into communication with the unknown, become also recruits available . . . for the world-wide conversations now increasingly upon us in which the cinema may play, amongst its numerous other roles, so powerful a part."[12]

In contemporary academic parlance, positive connotations of the term "cosmopolitanism" share an oblique but discernible consonance with Václavek's giddy "cosmic consciousness," as well as with the imaginative process of "becoming world citizens," as Richardson would have it.[13] The lure posed by the term shimmers at its hyphenated root: the *cosmos* (meaning the ordering of the universe or world) conjoins with the *polis* (meaning the body of the state, or the body politic). To be cosmopolitan means that one belongs to, or at least struggles to imagine and inhabit, the world qua world. It involves transcending the tyranny of the nation-state, leaving behind the trappings of nationalism's cry for unification and the mantra of patriotism in favor of what Ulf Hannerz has recently described as "a willingness to engage with the Other . . . an intellectual and aesthetic stance of openness toward divergent cultural experiences."[14] Anthropologist James Clifford adds that "it [cosmopolitanism] recognizes something important: worldly, productive sites of crossing; complex, unfinished paths between local and global attachments."[15]

Often understood as a condition of subjectivity, and as a conceptual rubric capable of unsettling assumptions that attachments to the nation are either natural or fixed, "cosmopolitan theories" in recent years might be perceived as sharing a sort of distant kinship with Judith Butler's investment in unsettling assumptions of a pre-given gender identity. Yet as Patrice Petro stresses in her chapter that closes this section, most critical conversations on cosmopolitanism today have little to say about gender or sexual identity. And they overlook entirely the connotations that the term shares specifically with women (including the magazine *Cosmopolitan*, launched in the United States in 1886 as a "family" magazine and marketed specifically to women after 1960).

Petro goes a long way toward filling that critical lacuna by considering how iconic female stars in the silent era enabled viewers in different parts of the world to imagine "divergent cultural experiences," including freedom from traditional (local and national) mores. I am tempted to recall the diva-esque behavior of young women in 1920s Istanbul in this context. But other supra-modern female icons in that same decade—Anna May Wong, Marlene Dietrich, and Leni Riefenstahl—form the focus of Petro's analysis. Significantly, that analysis restricts its focus almost exclusively to several photos of these three women shot by the young Alfred Eisenstaedt in a Berlin nightclub in 1928, reprinted in a 1938 issue of *Look* magazine and published more recently in a 2004 Berlin Film Museum newsletter. In the context of late-1920s Germany, Petro argues, the photograph "documents the circulation of artists and actresses and film personnel, which connected Hollywood, New York, London, Paris, and Berlin" while also documenting a moment that "valu[ed] the risks of social deviance." Reading the women's dress and position relative one to another—the iconic cigarette clenched in Dietrich's hand; Riefenstahl's arm wrapped around Wong, whose central position in the photo recalls her prominent international status at the time—Petro argues that appearing or performing as lesbian or bisexual or gay in twenties Berlin was "not only proof that 'one was modern' but was also indicative of an emergent form of cosmopolitanism, especially for women, newly enfranchised and eager to think, dress, and perform beyond national borders and traditional identities."

As a border-crossing figure par excellence, Greta Garbo would seem to present us with a feminine identity emblematic of what it means above all else to be modern and cosmopolitan, worldly and emancipated. Her arrival in the United States in 1926 coincided with the economic boom of 1920s Jazz Age culture and the heyday of those energetic, self-sufficient, and sexually liberated female stars such as Clara Bow, Colleen Moore, and (by 1928, following the release of Harry Beaumont's *Our Dancing Daughters*) Joan Crawford.[16] Admittedly, fast-paced (and short-skirted) performances of the Charleston or the Turkey Trot were never part of executives' plans for the exilic Swedish actress, Greta Garbo. But her initial vehicles in the United States—*The Torrent, The Temptress,* and *Flesh and the Devil* (all 1926)—collectively promote an onscreen identity for the star as the most worldly of women, a female as dangerously avant-garde as the stylistic domain she inhabits. It is particularly illuminating, then, to consider the difficulties that press agents faced in assimilating their newly imported talent from Sweden into Hollywood-style cosmopolitan glamour of the late 1920s, as Laura Horak argues in her chapter here.

Combing an archive comprised of popular magazines, trade-oriented publications, and even interoffice memos, Horak details an American public's puzzled perception that Garbo did not participate in Jazz Age fun. She rarely visited speakeasies and shunned many acclaimed dinner parties of the Hollywood elite. She kept to herself, an aloofness that partially coincided with her onscreen persona of the dangerously seductive woman. But her penchant for mannish dress and sundry sorts of odd behaviors off-screen conflicted sharply with major components of her "star text," a contradiction that threatened to fray and split asunder the projection of a complete and coherent identity. More to the point, Horak observes, the fan press hinted that Garbo's secretive domestic lifestyle, her resistance to speaking with the press, and her altogether unglamorous appearance in daily life were not simply different but more precisely *deviant,* a "female invert" of the sort that sociologist Havelock Ellis defined in the early twentieth century when diagnosing women who were attracted to other women. Sexuality may very well prove the exemplary site of private, personal interiority—the very stuff on which the U.S. star system fed—but this sort of sexual secret required a cover story.[17] Horak's research thus teases out a fascinating displacement—from selfhood to nationhood—that distinguishes Garbo's star text in the United States. The numerous journalistic genres that depended on a hermeneutic model of surface and depth, on the reporter's ability to peer behind closed doors, to scratch through the transparent surface of the public face or mask, revealed (and reveled in) Garbo's Swedishness. A flurry of adjectives re-scripted the meaning of such images: Horak uncovers numerous accounts in which her mannish dress appears "peasant-like" while her secretive demeanor signifies the "shy timidity" of a newly arrived immigrant, one not yet accustomed to speaking English properly.

As the sole chapter in *Silent Cinema and the Politics of Space* that focuses exclusively on tensions internal to the United States, Horak's study of Garbo's stardom offers a particularly resonant addition to this volume's broader project. Rather than tout once again the hegemonic power and vertically integrated efficiency of Hollywood as a well-oiled machine, Horak reveals the female star's capacity to influence the machinery itself, a power attained through Garbo's undeniable box-office appeal. As Horak puts it, by the time she starred in *Queen Christina* (1933), her most enduring and iconic vehicle, Garbo had acquired "veto power over the director, screenwriter, and actors." A particularly significant result of Garbo's professional clout surfaces in the artful integration of her presumably "odd" off-screen identity with her glamorous onscreen persona in the 1933 film. Horak puts it succinctly: "The queen is Swedish, craves solitude, wears men's clothes, has a forthright demeanor, and—importantly—displays open affection for a female friend—Ebba Sparre, the queen's lady-in-waiting (Elizabeth Young)," whom she kisses in a justly famous scene.

It should be clear by now that star identities flout cultural ideals, anxieties, and often conflicted desires—perhaps especially so when female sexuality is at stake. As the chapters that follow collectively insist, the discursive construction of star identities also make clear the degree to which gender identities—performed and conceived as normative or deviant, feminine or androgynous, traditional or modern, national or cosmopolitan—are prone to dynamic transformation. Even the meaning of a singular and presumably isolable text—say a photograph taken in 1928 Berlin—shifts, cracks apart, and re-performs the past as it resurfaces in another present. In the paragraphs that close this section, and likewise this volume, Patrice Petro cannily reveals how the Eisenstaedt photograph from 1928 Berlin resurfaced in 1930s Germany, where the meticulous inscription of captions and other written text revitalized the dead letter of female androgyny and cosmopolitanism, specifically the image of Leni Riefenstahl, to signify a non-decadent, athletic, and authoritatively masculine German nationalism. More recently, heated debates over the meaning (and even the date) of this photograph, which was reprinted in a 2004 newsletter, remind us in no uncertain terms that the identity of "history" (as with gender; as with the body; as with the nation) is never stable or static. Whatever meanings the past now signifies can be found or located only by examining a culture's discursive constructions and geopolitical imagination at any given moment—and in any given space.

Notes

1. Joanne Hershfield, "Visualizing the Modern Mexican Woman: *Santa* and Cinematic Nation-Building," in Vicki Callahan, ed., *Reclaiming the Archive: Feminism and Film History* (Detroit: Wayne State University Press, 2010), 333.

2. The quoted phrases come from Ana M. López, who offers a passing observation about Padilla's mimicry of Menichelli in her magisterial essay "Early Cinema and Modernity in Latin America," *Cinema Journal* 40.1 (2000), 68–69.

3. Ibid.

4. See Canan Balan, "Wondrous Pictures in Istanbul: From Cosmopolitanism to Nationalism," in Abel, Bertellini, and King, *Early Cinema and the "National,"* 181. For a detailed history of Menichelli's career and the aesthetic/cultural implications of her film vehicles, as well as those of other iconic Italian divas such as Francesca Bertini and Lyda Borelli, see Angela Dalle Vacche, *Diva: Defiance and Passion in Early Italian Cinema* (Austin: University of Texas Press, 2008).

5. It would be an impossible task to delineate this body of work in any detail. Over a decade ago, Diane Negra and I sought to collect and organize a representative selection of scholarship emerging at that time in our edited collection *A Feminist Reader in Early Cinema* (Durham, NC: Duke University Press, 2002). Since then, feminist historical work on silent era cinema has escalated dramatically, not least given the coalitions scholars have formed through the Women and Film History International Association and the now bi-annual Women and the Silent Screen (W&SS) conferences. (Even as this volume goes to press in early fall 2013, the seventh W&SS conference is taking place in Australia, hosted by the University of Melbourne). For an overview of the methodological and theoretical implications of the Women Film Pioneer Project, as well as an excellent conceptualization of how feminist histories of cinema refract "transnational perspectives," see Monica Dall'Asta, "On Frieda Klug, Pearl White, and Other Traveling Women Film Pioneers," *Framework: The Journal of Cinema and Media* 51.2 (Fall 2010): 310–323. Valuable resources for ongoing work in this area include Antonia Lant's edited collection *Red Velvet Seat: Women's Writing on the First Fifty Years of Cinema* (New York: Verso, 2006) as well as the freely accessible Women Film Pioneer Project database: https://wfpp.cdrs.columbia.edu/.

6. See Vicki Callahan, introduction to *Reclaiming the Archive: Feminism and Film History* (Detroit: Wayne State University Press, 2010), 4.

7. Judith Butler, *Gender Trouble: Feminism and the Subversion of Identity* (New York: Routledge, 1990), 25.

8. The idea that a film star's identity depends on an assembly of media texts (and is thus more properly known as a "star text") has been foundational to theories of stardom, introduced in Anglophone studies by Richard Dyer's *Stars* (London: British Film Institute, 1979).

9. Indian filmmakers' appropriation of an individual "star text" from the United States may very well anticipate what Neepa Majundar describes, in a groundbreaking study, as the Indian film industry's appropriation of the U.S. "star system" more generally, which was noticeably modified to exclude information pertaining to the player's *personal* life. Rather than probe the "inner essence of the person," or indulge in salacious gossip and innuendo regarding a performer's off-screen life, the incipient star system in India traded in what Majumdar calls a "discourse of surfaces" (8). Such a discourse rendered the cinema and its stars at once well known—widely circulated through images, promotional hype, media texts, and so on—and yet also respectable or cultured. Maintaining discretion in regard to female stars in particular proved imperative to the realignment of star virtue with normative Hindu womanhood, Majumdar argues, and thus to a version of femininity that enabled the cinema and its mass appeal to participate in a nationalist discourse imperative to the struggle for independence. See Neepa Majumdar, *Wanted Cultured Ladies Only!: Female Stardom and Cinema in India, 1930s–1950s* (Urbana: University of Illinois Press) 2009.

10. Ackbar Abbas, "Cosmopolitan De-Scriptions: Shanghai and Hong Kong," *Public Culture* 12.3 (2000): 781.

11. Bedřich Václavek "On the Sociology of Film," in *Cinema All The Time: An Anthology of Czech Film Theory and Criticism, 1908–1939,* eds. Jaroslav Anděl and Petr Szczepanik, trans. Kevin B. Johnson (Prague: National Film Archive, 2008), 157–158; emphasis in original.

12. Dorothy Richardson, "The Cinema in Arcady," in *Close Up 1927–1933: Cinema and Modernism,* ed. James Donald, Anne Friedberg, and Laura Marcus (Princeton, NJ: Princeton University Press, 1998), 186.

13. A detailed study regarding the historical use of the term "cosmopolitanism" relative to silent era cinema remains the task of another, most welcome, volume altogether. For a historically informed set of discussions that employ "cosmopolitanism" as a rubric for rethinking art-historical modernist canons, see Kobena Mercer's edited collection *Cosmopolitan Modernisms* (Cambridge, MA: MIT Press, 2005).

14. Ulf Hannerz, "Cosmopolitans and Locals in World Culture," in *Global Culture: Nationalism, Globalization and Modernity,* ed. Mike Featherstone (London: Sage, 1990), 239.

15. James Clifford, "Mixed Feelings," in *Cosmopolitics: Thinking and Feeling beyond the Nation,* ed. Pheng Cheah and Bruce Robbins (Minneapolis: University of Minnesota Press, 1998), 362.

16. These 1920s female stars present a figuration of the "New Woman" that, as Olsson observes, differs markedly from the serial stunt queen and physically proactive female heroines that America exported widely in the 1910s, emblematized by stars such as Pearl White and Ruth Roland. On the promotion of Roland's courageous physicality and serial vehicles in 1920s Tehran, see Kaveh Askari's chapter in part 2 of this volume.

17. This conception of U.S. stardom dates back to Richard deCordova's 1986 study *Picture Personalities,* which focuses on the decade prior to an industrially organized star system in the United States. He argues that the "film star" proper emerges in 1914 and attains definition by virtue of a specific type of knowledge production—namely, knowledge regarding the player's "private" life. This emphasis on *personal* identity distinguishes the "film star" from earlier "picture personalities" whose names and *professional* identities—talents, acting experience,

and so on—circulated in the press (albeit released somewhat reluctantly by studios and producers at the time) beginning around 1909–1910. See his *Picture Personalities: The Emergence of the Star System in America* (Urbana: University of Illinois Press, 1990). As noted above, this investment in a star's private life is precisely what Neepa Majumdar pinpoints as antithetical to India's incipient star system in later decades.

9 National Soul / Cosmopolitan Skin

Swedish Cinema at a Crossroads

Jan Olsson

A provocative stance—formulated in French—hovered over Swedish film culture in the fall of 1923: Swedish film actresses—why are they so ugly? People in Stockholm were quite offended by this insult from visiting actor Pierre Daltour. Flustered directors retorted, journalists published lists of name to counter the preposterous contention, and upscale magazines assembled photographs as comely evidence *pace* Daltour's temerity.

The magazine *Veckojournalen* (see Figure 9.1) even mustered two new faces from the not-yet-released *Gösta Berlings saga* (*The Atonement of Gosta Berling*; 1924) for additional punch—Greta Garbo, still Gustafsson in the caption, being one of them. Finally, the leading local company, Svensk Filmindustri (SF), compiled a filmic rebuttal (now lost, alas), as part of the program when the still fabulous Skandia Theater opened in September 1923, a week after Daltour's musings. Presumably, SF's film compilation celebrated more or less the same actresses as the article in *Veckojournalen*. According to Daltour, Swedish actresses were quite accomplished, but not beautiful. "They are cut out to be mothers or old ladies, but, heroines?! . . . We Frenchmen believe that all young beautiful women have emigrated to the U.S."[1]

Shortly before Daltour's arrival, the Swiss newspaper *Neue Zürcher Zeitung* had voiced fears from a different perspective concerning the future of Swedish cinema. Once, the anonymous Swiss writer contended, Swedish cinema was a haven of otherness compared to indistinguishable products from Hollywood, Paris, and Berlin. Currently, however, the Swedes were on the verge of substituting their national distinctiveness for a form of bland cosmopolitanism and thus risked losing their celluloid soul. "Soul" emerged as a key concept in the debate setting a Swedish cinema of spiritual values apart from Hollywood's implied crass commercialism. The Swiss article was translated in one of Stockholm's morning papers and spawned scores of comments in the trade press.[2] During 1922, SF was apparently intensely courted from afar by prospective contributors and collaborators such as Romain Rolland and Elinor Glyn, and in December the company actually hired Dimitri Buchowetzki, a Russian émigré actor/director who had

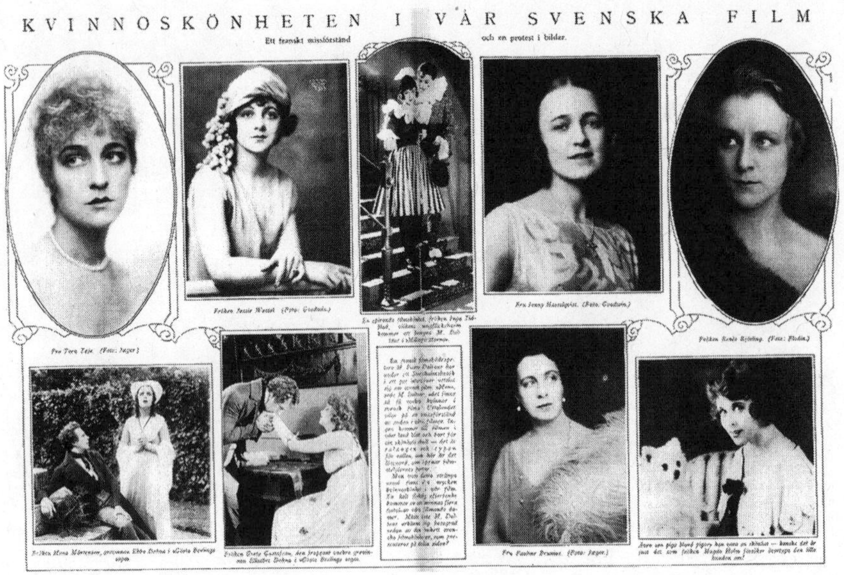

Figure 9.1 *Veckojournalen* offered this mash-up of Swedish screen beauties in order to disentangle a "French misunderstanding" by way of a "visual protest," No. 38 (September 23, 1923), 910–911.

been working in Germany, as director for a film we will return to as our centerpiece for tracing the company's change of strategy from the national in a wide sense to a cosmopolitan mode of production.[3]

The Pulchritude Thesis

In the debate instigated by Pierre Daltour's casual comments, screen heroines from France, Sweden, and Hollywood were discursively lined up and pitted against each other as emblematic of their respective film cultures. The sensitive issue around homely versus comely actresses, framed by Daltour as matrons versus heroines, came to bear on film culture more generally in interesting ways, and especially on how a small national cinema at a crossroads could position its production in relation to the fickle vagaries of both domestic and international market conditions. Pointedly, the Swiss analysis mentioned the suppression of the star system as a particularly praiseworthy feature of Swedish cinema, which is an alternative framing of Daltour's observation—or, rather, its obverse. A full-fledged star system might have engendered the type of female heroines Daltour sorely missed on Swedish screens and that he suspected had emigrated to the greener pastures in the United States.

Figure 9.2 A postcard featuring actor Pierre Daltour. From the author's collection.

Good-looking himself, as Figure 9.2 evidences, Pierre Daltour had been enlisted by Pierre-Auguste Renoir to model as a shepherd for the first draft of *Jugement de Paris,* but other bodies were eventually substituted for the young actor as the painting evolved from sketches to canvas. Pierre Daltour's career on the big screen also ran its course rather quickly. The short roster of film roles for this actor from Theatre Odéon begins in 1920 and ends in 1926.[4] Daltour did not throw the first French stone at the Swedes, however; Louis Gaumont, one of pioneer

Léon's three sons, had waxed eloquent along similar lines a few months earlier. Explaining the difficulties in marketing Swedish cinema for the general French audience, Gaumont explained to interviewer Inga Gaate that Swedish films are "too heavy, too serious" for the French mass market. Furthermore, he reflected, "Why don't you have any beautiful, captivating women? Especially since your actors are so wonderful. *Vraiment, un type adorable!*" he exclaimed, although he omitted mentioning specific names for corroboration.[5]

The Gallic misgivings peaked in 1925 as both director Jean Epstein and Russian émigré actor Ivan Mosjoukine, while ignoring Swedish actresses, declared themselves in interviews unimpressed by the celebrated Swedish repertoire in general. This criticism generated a lengthy debate concerning cultural differences in relation to casting, audience preferences, and popular cinema versus avant-garde experiments that eventually harked back to Daltour's stance.[6] He at least was very enthusiastic about Swedish cinema and praised it as the best in the world, citing in particular Mauritz Stiller's then recent *Gunnar Hedes saga* (*The Blizzard;* 1923), which he deemed more fluent and less gloomy than previous Swedish titles. Jean Epstein showed no mercy when dismissing the entire Swedish repertoire except for a single scene as non-cinematic. The exception: the finale on the ice in *Herr Arnes pengar* (*Sir Arne's Treasure;* 1919). For him this was the only Swedish moment of genuine cinema in a wasteland of filmed theater.

This pointed criticism twice over from outsiders bruised local pride and vanity. The ensuing debates interface with several strands of Swedish film culture at a time of unprecedented uncertainty as to production practices and general business strategies. The first half of the 1920s was indeed a troublesome time for Swedish cinema, and not only for the big-name directors, Victor Sjöström and Mauritz Stiller, caught in the clutches of hard-nosed bookkeepers according to the portal premise for Swedish authorship studies: true artists fighting losing battles against the custodians of commerce.[7]

As Pierre Daltour arrived late in the summer of 1923, Sjöström had already emigrated to Goldwyn for Hollywood's opportunities and resources. SF still regarded him as their commodity and even hoped to secure the rights for Goldwyn's production as part of the deal. Stiller, meanwhile, struggled with *Gösta Berlings saga* and a production fraught with obstacles from mid-August 1923 to early February 1924, when shooting was wrapped up. A voting contest for the most popular film screened in 1924 offered some indications as to a shift in audience preferences. Here Stiller's Lagerlöf epic came in only second after Rex Ingram's historical epic *Scaramouche.*[8] By then Stiller was contracted by a German producer, Trianon, with SF's blessing. This agreement came to naught at Christmas after a detour for shooting in Istanbul. Soon Stiller and his entourage, including Garbo, who had most recently worked with G. W. Pabst, arrived in Hollywood. The transfer did not diminish her screen beauty in years to come.[9]

Spelled out in commercial terms, Daltour's thrust can be reformulated as a market paradox: why were Swedish actresses not cast in the mold of Hollywood's screen heroines, given that Hollywood movies dominated Swedish film exhibition? Hence, Daltour's offhand observation highlighted casting as critical for how a locally grounded mode of production negotiated Hollywood's screen modernity and feminine ideals in its casting practices. From such a perspective, Daltour's reflection can be expanded into a set of binaries concerning the overlapping realms of preferred source material, roster of genres, and casting choices at SF midstream between the national and cosmopolitan.

In the debate, popular genres were pegged as an amalgamation of Hollywood/superficial/cosmopolitan, and comedic rather than dramatic, while the contested glory of Swedish high-class cinema was spelled out as national (or grounded in Nordic literature of repute), spiritual, and with cultural depth to boot—summed up with "soul" as a discursive focal point. Casting choices bearing on this genre polarity differentiated Hollywood films from Swedish productions and were fleshed out as young versus old, skin versus soul, advertising models versus trained actresses. A discursive case in point, albeit with French cinema vicariously standing in as the non-Swedish other after Daltour's analysis was published, may be provided by director John Brunius's comment in a follow-up piece: "French cinema for sure has quite a few beautiful women, but in general they are soulless. . . . Swedish directors have never strived toward some form of beauty contest."[10] For Brunius, soul and soulful beauty are the pivotal terms that contrast with the merely skin-deep dazzle sought after elsewhere. Much of the debate hinged on this polarity and its multiple derivations.

Hollywood's screen heroines in the early 1920s, to recast Brunius's argument in relation to the most conspicuous and ubiquitous non-Swedish cinema, were not cut from the cloth of progressiveness and middle-class values indicative of the first generation of American "new women"—those hailing from the decades before cinema.[11] Instead, the very newest generations of American women, on and off the screen, embodied wider ranges of womanhood and femininity concerning class, lifestyles, ideals, and fields of action. In the mid-1910s, the serial queens—for example, Pearl White as the eponymous heroine in *The Perils of Pauline* (1914) or Grace Darling in *Beatrix Fairfax* (1916)—initially needed a man to help out, even though these stars were advertised as "fearless." Pearl White was, however, in more independent command in her later serials, not least in *Plunder*, produced during the year in focus here, 1923.[12]

Arguably, this wider paradigm of feminine wherewithal and its onscreen cultural options were intimately correlated with modernity and the emerging consumerist culture in Sweden, for which Hollywood functioned as a prime advertising window, one primarily geared toward women. This paradigm was in turn further disseminated via local fan magazines touting ideals and templates for lifestyles open for vernacular emulations and negotiations across borders.[13] This intense flow of U.S. products and Hollywood films ran parallel to Daltour's jesting reflections concerning the type of femininity local film producers elected to showcase.

The Spirit of the Market: Export and Emigration

In regard to source material, and to a certain extent casting as well, local film production in the late 1910s operated with a Nordic rather than Swedish cultural home base, in a model cast by the film adaptation of Henrik Ibsen's *Terje Vigen* (*A Man There Was;* 1917). In the early 1920s, this carefully cultivated and celebrated brand of film culture faced a rapidly changing market as the conditions that had favored Swedish production gradually waned. Such perceptions motivated the trustlike formation of SF, a combine of the old Svenska Biografteatern (Swedish Biograph) and its rival, Skandia, in late 1919, a preemptive initiative obviously orchestrated in order to meet the looming challenges. The Skandia group had emerged only the year before by consolidating Hasselblad, Swedish Pathé, and Victoria. Following the formation of SF, the exhibition market in Sweden went through a series of transformations as Hollywood's dominance escalated in tandem with the gradual resurgence of film imports from war-ravaged countries such as France, England, and Germany.

In sheer numbers, the U.S. films imported to Swedish screens at this time represented a veritable deluge. Given this ubiquitous presence, what impact did Hollywood's overwhelming dominance exert concerning local production and audience preferences, and as a cultural interface in relation to modernity as well as the more intangible issues of modern femininity? Daltour's unwelcome casting observations impinged on these intertwined issues for an entrenched film culture that for a time had prided itself on being an alternative to cosmopolitan cinema, mainly Hollywood, precisely owing to its local grounding and deep cultural roots. As Daltour from an oblique, idiosyncratic, and decidedly French point of view elected to zoom in on Swedish cinema according to his detractors, SF was hedging their bets by testing the international waters prior to adopting a full-scale model of co-production together with several European companies during the second half of the 1920s.

Since the mid-1910s, big business had an escalating stake in Swedish Biograph in the form of a corporate empire headed by the match king Ivar Kreuger. His control was transferred over to the new company and was further solidified as SF was forced to sell off some of its real-estate holdings to Kreuger's construction company to generate capital as revenue dropped.

Already, 1920 had come with worries concerning the exhibition side of the industry in Sweden as the boom from the war years had gradually trickled into the red, especially for small houses in the provinces and for exhibitors without ties to distributors and domestic producers. One morning paper attributed the previous attendance records to a temporary shift in leisure patterns and described the sharp drop at the box office as the end of "the golden age" of movie theaters. A key factor for this newspaper, *Svenska Morgonbladet,* affiliated with the Mission Union Church, was that the strict rationing of liquor had diverted monies during the war in other directions, to the benefit of cinema. Now, the writer maintained, "people are back to boozing and abandon the theaters."[14]

The bankruptcy filed in late 1922 by one of the vertical competitors to SF, Skandinavisk Filmcentral, clearly evidences this downward exhibition trend. Waiting in the background were novel ways of factoring in the international market, at all levels of the film business, and of balancing the national—or the Nordic peasant line based on hallmarked literature, if you will—with a more cosmopolitan type of filmmaking aligned with current audience preferences for Hollywood movies. A critical aspect for ushering in novel strategies in Sweden was the gradual reopening of both the British and American markets for film import after years of exorbitant import tariffs. Historiographically, it is well known that SF in the mid-1920s embarked on a cosmopolitan mode of co-productions as joint ventures with film companies in the UK, Germany, and France, but the process leading up to this production model is still in the main under-researched.[15] From its very outset in 1919, after the big merger of Swedish Biograph and Skandia into SF, the new company set a keen eye toward England after successful trade screenings in 1919 of Stiller's *Sången om den eldröda blomman* (*The Flame of Life* / The song of the scarlet flower). The chief rationale for the merger, which launched a virtual monopoly for a time, was to facilitate inroads into the international film market after the war. In this spirit, SF's precursor, Swedish Biograph, published a booklet titled *Swedish Film Abroad* and subtitled *The Export Prospects for Our Film Industry.*[16] It came with a long section of celebratory clippings from trade screenings in London concerning *The Song of the Scarlet Flower.* Arguably, this film, based on a Finnish novel, is the magnum opus in the peasant genre and was even awarded a full symphonic score commissioned by Swedish Biograph and composed by Armas Järnefelt, then musical director at the Stockholm Opera.

The strategic rethinking of production practices within SF involved story content, casting choices, and export prospects as the box office drop became noticeable. As a form of market feelers, stories set outside the Nordic countries seemingly presented themselves as potentially viable options for turning around the domestic box-office drought as well as for selling more film copies abroad. In this spirit Stiller directed *De landsflyktige* (*Guarded Lips* / The exiled; 1921) and John Brunius directed *Kärlekens ögon* (*A Scarlet Angel* / Eyes of love; 1922), both set in Russia. Brunius's film featured luxurious cosmopolitan nightclub settings and an intrigue brimming with crimes and passions leading up to redemption of

Figure 9.3 Production still from *Det omringade huset*. Victor Sjöström is seated between Meggie Albanesi and Uno Henning. Courtesy of the Swedish Film Institute.

sorts. Simultaneously, Stiller, Sjöström, and CEO Charles Magnusson registered a short-lived production company within SF for which Sjöström, as the story goes, was forced to direct *Det omringade huset* (*Honour* / A house surrounded; 1922). This is the only lost Swedish film directed by Sjöström from the 1920s. Here the cosmopolitan turned exotic, again with an eye toward courting markets in Britain. Based on a French play, the film featured a British battalion on a military mission in North Africa. During the preparation for shooting, the idea of co-producing this film with German interests was entertained, as well as the possibility of even shooting part of the film in Berlin. This did not happen; instead the desert scenes were shot on an island in the unexotic Swedish archipelago.[17] Presumably as a segue to the British market, Meggie Albanesi (born of an English mother and an Italian father) was brought over from successes on the London stages and some minor film roles during 1921 to play the only female lead in this otherwise military affair (see Figure 9.3). Albanesi's film career, however, was tragically nipped in the bud when she died a year later at the age of twenty-four.

The production of *A House Surrounded* was rushed and sandwiched into the shooting of Sjöström's big vehicle that summer, *Eld ombord* (*Jealousy* / Fire on board; 1923), a film based on Hjalmar Bergman's original manuscript, and again with an English name in the cast, this time the renowned Shakespearean

Figure 9.4 Anna Q. Nilsson, the first Swedish movie star in the United States. Publicity photo from the author's collection.

actor Matheson Lang (who was born in Canada). Meanwhile, small-time regional producers with director Gustaf Edgren picked up some of the slack left over from SF's so-called peasant-film era. Edgren directed two famous folk plays at this juncture by returning to material from the very earliest phase at Swedish Biograph and shying away from highbrow literature. The most notable aspect of these productions was the choice of casting Anna Q. Nilsson in one of the films, *Värmlänningarna* (*Harvest of Hate* / The Varmlanders; 1921). Nilsson (see Figure 9.4) was a Swedish model turned actress early on in the United States and this was her only role in Sweden. Her American career, which began at the Kalem Company, lasted from 1911 to 1954. In 1923 she was famous enough for a cameo appearance in two metafilms, James Cruze's *Hollywood* (Famous Players–Lasky, 1923) and Rupert Hughes's *Souls for Sale* (Goldwyn Pictures, 1923). In 1950 she appeared together with Hollywood veterans Buster Keaton and H. B. Warner in *Sunset Blvd.* (Paramount, 1950) as stars of the past. In a sense, her career was a veritable template for Daltour's analysis. Combined, Nilsson's two 1923 titles succinctly sum up the spiritual corruption threatening Swedish cinema if it succumbed to the spell of American film culture.

But Anna Q. Nilsson was not the only young Swedish woman seeking a better life in the United States. Between 1892 and 1923, a sizeable portion of the Swedish population passed through Ellis Island, leaving behind the Old World's bleak prospects for the attractions and dreamscapes of the New World and its hoped-for opportunities for young men and women. Around a million émigrés left Sweden for the United States in these years, although the bulk of departures occurred prior to 1917 as immigration became increasingly circumscribed when the United States entered the Great War. Even so, the Swedish population in the United States soared from six million in 1897 to seven million in 1923.[18]

The transformations wrought by the twinned effects of emigration and population expansion in these years must be understood as part of a broader shift in domestic culture from a rural or agrarian to an urban or modern lifestyle. As the Swedish countryside was depleted by emigration, Stockholm's population expanded from 300,000 in 1900 to 450,000 in 1925. Modernity, reaching a Sweden relatively unscathed by World War I, gradually changed outlooks and future prospects as the agrarian economy and culture became intertwined with its industrial and urban counterpart. Simultaneously, Swedish cinema mixed up its peasant predilection with cosmopolitan forays. In the process, cinema's wide distribution net and its imaginary windows to other worlds came to touch virtually everyone. As living conditions improved and the odds for making a decent living in Sweden seemingly changed for the better after the war, a young generation of Swedes could get in tune with ideals and modern lifestyles, predominantly American and often "advertised" and showcased by way of the movies, without necessarily having to leave Sweden. To what extent cinema fueled new mind-sets and an everyday life with an urban or even cosmopolitan slant is of course impossible to conclusively gauge. Film reformers, however, did not hesitate in pronouncing cinema to be seductive by default and an engine for almost infectious emulation in a multitude of ways, while hoping for celluloid education to get the upper hand on mere entertainment.[19]

Enter Buchowetzki—A Full-Scale Test

The most elaborate and daring cosmopolitan endeavor at SF, however, was the production of *Karusellen* (*The Whirl of Passion* / The carousel; 1923). This production took the earlier experiments with actors recruited from the English-speaking world to a new level by completely discounting Swedish performers in favor of an international cast—and this production was finished prior to

Daltour's trash talk. The film was primarily shot in Berlin and directed by Dimitri Buchowetzki, a Russian émigré actor/director who had worked previously in Germany and would work subsequently in Hollywood. The deal apparently came about as he visited Stockholm for the opening of his film *Peter the Great* at SF's recently acquired theater, the Palladium, on December 25, 1922. In the process a deal was negotiated for at least one film. Seemingly, Buchowetzki already had Alfred Feteke's script more or less finished when courting SF. In an interview, the director announced that his next project was a modern film, in contrast to his previous historical cycle.[20] This was obviously *The Carousel,* for which SF signed him up a few days later. The film's only Swedish links turned out to be the financing of the production and the camera crew headed by Julius Jaenzon. At the time, the film market in Weimar Germany was plagued with uncertainty in a country with inflation running rampant and disastrous social conditions, which might explain Buchowetzki's Swedish detour.

The storyline for *The Carousel* is quite simple and set against the backdrops of reckless stock speculation and hectic, metropolitan nightlife, but opens and closes as an almost pastoral family idyll in a country villa, true to the circular movement implied by the title. In the opening of the film, a woman is rescued from her runaway horse by a man in an automobile. Afterwards, he is invited to the country house where she lives with her husband and son. Falling in love with her rescuer, she abandons her family. As it turns out, her new beau is a speculator. He loses everything and in the process steals jewels from her. Meanwhile, her husband takes up his former profession as a crack shot at a circus. When the woman learns that their son is part of the attraction in a Wilhelm Tell routine, her affair has already fallen apart. In the nick of time she shows up at the circus, stops the routine, and the family is reunited and moves back to the country house.

The female lead was played by the Norwegian actress Aud Egede-Nissen, a firmly established star in Germany who had been working for the most reputable directors—Fritz Lang, Ernst Lubitsch, and F. W. Murnau, among others. She was not Buchowetzki's first choice for the role. After having being showcased on the front page of SF's house organ / fan magazine *Filmnyheter* as the female lead in *The Carousel,* the Prague actress Suzanne Marwille (see Figure 9.5) was for some reason dropped and replaced by Egede-Nissen. In the featured article, SF claimed that Marwille's "interesting face" was "beautiful, but furthermore it also has soul [critical, of course], and it shows both temperament and nerves."[21] According to the director, she was destined to become another Pola Negri, the latter an early protégé of Buchowetzki and again his star when he left for Hollywood after his single contribution to Swedish cinema. During the production, both Swedish and German reporters were invited to watch him direct some of the more spectacular scenes in a former zeppelin hangar outside Berlin.[22]

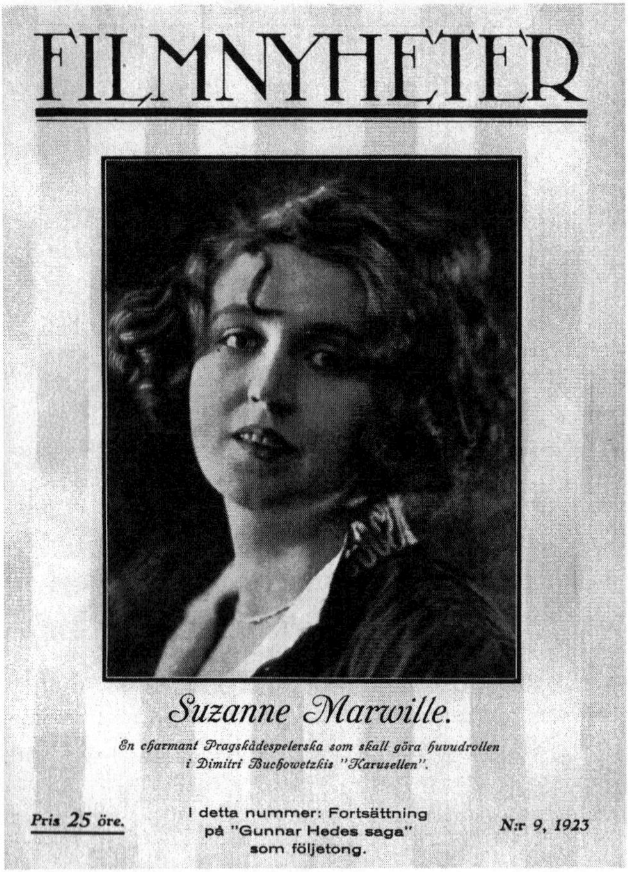
FILMNYHETER
Suzanne Marwille.
En charmant Pragskådespelerska som skall göra huvudrollen
i Dimitri Buchowetzkis "Karusellen".
Pris 25 öre.
I detta nummer: Fortsättning
på "Gunnar Hedes saga"
som följetong.
N:r 9, 1923

Figure 9.5 Suzanne Marwille featured on the cover of *Filmnyheter* 4.9 (February 26, 1923).

The Carousel opened at Skandia during the debate incurred by Daltour's disparaging of Swedish actresses, and some of the film's critics picked up on the debate. One reviewer pronounced Aud Egede-Nissen "an elegant film phenomenon, but perhaps not beautiful to the degree foreign experts on feminine beauty wish for"[23] (see Figure 9.6). The most detailed tie-in comment concerning the beauty thesis came from the anonymous critic in *Svenska Dagbladet:* "Aud Egede-Nissen does not ruin her part, in fact, she has pretty good and strong moments, but she is surely not pleasant to watch. Bearing in mind the recent French complaint concerning the absence of feminine comeliness in Swedish films, one wonders what the party in question would express concerning this heroine. Swedish cinema could most certainly have furnished an actress at least equally competent and a bit more beautiful to boot."[24] As to the film's standing vis-à-vis contemporary

Figure 9.6 Aud Egede Nissen featured on the cover of *Filmnyheter* 4.16 (September 17, 1923).

Swedish cinema, one critic opined that overall expectations had been lowered by recent productions. Consequently, most critics considered the film somewhat superficial but still reluctantly admired Buchowetzki's superb direction, the luxurious settings, and the whirling pace, while deliberating on its questionable Swedish status. A fan magazine comment is most indicative of this negotiation between Swedishness and the cosmopolitan. According to the anonymous writer, "*Swedish* film and *The Carousel* cannot be mentioned at the same time. The film has two Swedish features: the financing and the photographer. But as the entire film is miles apart from everything that characterizes our national film art, it would be almost an insult to award it with such a hallmark. With all due respect concerning the ingenious execution, *The Carousel* is an over-strung product of what Buchowetzki himself once described as cocaine-infested Berlin. . . . It's good, but meaningless—an un-Swedish quality film from a Swedish producer."[25] This criticism picks up the drift concerning Swedish cinema's lost soul from the analysis in *Neue Zürcher Zeitung*.

The film's restless pace and atmosphere were read in intertextual terms by at least one critic, who perceptively noted Buchowetzki's accomplished use of parallel editing as a principal compositional feature that was also working on a microlevel within blocks of scenes. Before the film eventually comes full circle, in line with the carousel metaphor, sensational and riveting scenes in the circus ring reestablish the family circle while simultaneously preparing for closure and a return to the setting of the film's opening. This critic attributes the compositional method to American cinema, which by way of a "rapid switch of scenes offers an exhaustive depiction of a course of events"[26] (see Figure 9.7). Heaping accolades on the film, the most enthusiastic and renowned Swedish film critic, Bengt Idestam-Almquist, analyzed the film in terms of expressionism, but as a version "cloaked in naturalism." He meticulously describes Buchowetzki's method of casting, mise-en-scène, and editing. His analysis is worth quoting at length, as he takes off from the nervous mode of postwar Western Europe. According to Idestam-Almquist:

> [Buchowetzki] does not want to tell a story, but rather to convey a frame of mind. . . . All conceivable means are mobilized to impart this restless, hectic atmosphere, resulting from sick and overtaxed nerves. Buchowetzki wants only this—and diligently eliminates everything that could detract from this overall impression. By choice, his cast consists of pretty commonplace actors, and he muffles their acting, turns it impersonal. He turns them into marionettes. To put across the nervousness, he pulls the strings gently, sometimes violently. He dresses them up flamboyantly, even tastelessly—on purpose. He makes the interiors nervous—on purpose. And the pace. From the outset it is furious. After relaxing the spectators for a while by way of a stupid, grotesque joke, he again cranks up the pace. It becomes a feverish dream. . . . The storytelling surpasses everything I've seen.[27]

Summing up, Idestam-Almquist pronounced *The Carousel* an unrivaled production. In the process, he writes, Buchowetzki turns Stiller's *Erotikon* (1920) and Erich von Stroheim's *Foolish Wives* (1922) "smallish and anemic by comparison."[28]

In Transit: National Screen Identity and Beauty

This carousel movement brings us back to our point of departure: the intertwined issues of national screen identity and of feminine beauty as a casting concern. Pulchritude was made irrelevant by Idestam-Almquist for *The Carousel* by an

Figure 9.7 Frame enlargements from *The Carousel* (SF, 1923).

alleged conscious casting choice seeking out a female type toned down in this respect. As we've noted, writers taking exception to Daltour's thrust directed at Swedish actresses by way of reflex got back at French actresses. Vera von Kraemer, after starting out in this manner and singling out French actresses Gina Palerme (short career 1921–1925) and Pierette Madd (even shorter career 1921–1923) and a roster of alleged Swedish film beauties, landed in Hollywood, a putative haven for unsurpassed beauty. "An American screen beauty is flawless," von Kraemer writes; "she is slim yet has firm, round arms, perfect teeth, big eyes, beautiful mouth, and well-groomed and beautiful hair. . . . She can market any type of cosmetic product. . . . If Swedish producers are going to do luxurious comedies and bathing-suit films, then Swedish actresses have to endure pain to get beautiful skin, because they are not that beautiful. But for quality films, in which the star is not going to advertise day or night cream, the female type we have will suffice."[29] Thus, we infer, Swedish actresses project soul and depth rather than showing off toned bodily features. Von Kraemer's argument is connected to genres when she contrasts the somewhat vague designation "quality film" to the less weighty "luxurious comedies and bathing-suit films." The premise here is that Hollywood casts models rather than actresses proper.

In a condensed analysis from the year before, an anonymous writer in the same SF house organ, presumably also von Kraemer, put the current ideals of beauty as defined by Hollywood in a historical perspective. The beauty benchmark from the past, the writer maintains, was Lillian Russell (see Figure 9.8) and her full-bodied type of female opulence, in contrast to the frailty of the current Griffith heroines, Mary Pickford and the Gish sisters.

Discounting fearless serial queens, other types, the writer claims, are relegated to being mothers, like Mary Alden, or unnamed vamps. From a Swedish perspective, English actress Meggie Albanesi imported for Sjöström's *A House Surrounded* arguably should be placed in the Griffith camp. By way of further example concerning the current Hollywood ideal, described as the short, girlish type of woman inaugurated by Pickford and the Gish sisters (see Figure 9.9), a spin-off list is presented, containing such names as Mae Murray, Marie Prevost, Viola Dana, Colleen Moore, and Alla Nazimova. A beautiful woman who never would become a star by virtue of being too big and not graceful enough, we learn, is Katherine MacDonald.[30]

What was the outcome for Swedish cinema of the twists and turns of the pulchritude debate, which ran parallel to a series of cosmopolitan test films? If nothing else, SF elected to turn fully cosmopolitan in the wake of its test endeavors, not least of them *The Carousel*, with a series of co-productions featuring international names such as Lil Dagover, as well as the Swedish actress Margit Manstad (see Figure 9.10). This new star emerged as emblematic of a novel brand of modern Swedish femininity in films such as *Women of Paris* (1928), after playing the

Figure 9.8 Lillian Russell. Publicity photograph. Courtesy of the Academy of Motion Picture Arts and Sciences.

Figure 9.9 Upper left: Lillian Gish in *The Scarlet Letter,* directed by Victor Sjöström for MGM in 1926. Courtesy of the Swedish Film Institute. Upper right: Dorothy Gish in *Romola,* directed by Henry King for Inspiration Pictures in 1924. Courtesy of the Swedish Film Institute. Lower left: Mary Pickford. Publicity photograph. Courtesy of the Swedish Film Institute. Lower right: Katherine MacDonald in *White Shoulders,* directed by Tom Forman for B. P. Schulberg Productions in 1922. Courtesy of the Academy of Motion Picture Arts and Sciences.

Figure 9.10 Margit Manstad at the Joinville studio lot during the shooting of *Hjärtats röst* (Les Studios Paramount, 1930), a Swedish version of Paramount's *Sarah and Son*, directed by Dorothy Arzner. Courtesy of the Swedish Film Institute.

small but quite illustrative role as Karin in *En piga bland pigor* (A peasant maid among peasant maids; 1924).

A society comedy–cum-burlesque, *En piga bland pigor* both introduced and reformed a full-fledged Swedish flapper girl. The jazzy upper-class girl Alice, played by Magda Holm, is temporarily ditched by her fiancé, Sven, a painter. Sven is annoyed that his girlfriend sleeps until lunch, and the film shows in great detail that she is as spoiled as her lapdog, while her sister Karin (Margit Manstad) makes herself useful in the background. Apart from being a fashion fiend, Alice adopts a rigorous workout regime, thereby emulating the superficial genre types deemed inappropriate for Swedish actresses in the debate. Moreover, Alice smokes, never a good sign for women in Swedish films, and she flirts, albeit quite innocently, when entertaining herself at afternoon tea dances. To prove her mettle after a fight with Sven, she embarks on a spirited masquerade by advertising her services as a maid seeking employment in order to relocate to a country farm. In the process, the film shifts from a society comedy set in a moneyed Stockholm context to a burlesque folk comedy with rural bumpkins aplenty as a backdrop for the project of Alice's reform. After scores of predictable cultural clashes and considerable havoc caused by the displaced Alice among the caricatured country folks, Alice makes good and blends in among the locals; she even proves herself resourceful when a snake bites one of the girls. Eventually, of course, she is reunited with Sven. After having learned her lesson according to the film's logic, Alice will presumably be a "better girl" in the future in the manner of her industrious sister.

The film toys with and merges two types of caricatured genres and strikes a balance between them as Alice subjects herself to a process of de-flappering incurred by Sven's disapproval. Even the name Sven, devoid of all foreign connotations, hints at a sober grounding in good old Swedish values. Passing images featuring Alice's sister offer the ideal feminine template—affluent, metropolitan, even beautiful, yet unaffected and industrious. Alice will seemingly reinvent herself in the manner of this wholesome well-to-do girl and discard her former spoiled and flapper-like persona.[31]

Traveling Swedishness

Finally: the problematic Swedishness. As noted, the degree of Swedishness concerning *The Carousel* was already in question before the opening of the film. Abroad, it was at times perceived as cosmopolitan beyond belief. The Swedish ambassador to Egypt thus wrote home to the State Department suspecting a fraud in the making when the film, under the title *La cible vivant,* was marketed as Swedish in Cairo. The ambassador presumed that some international distributor was trying to capitalize on Swedish cinema's stellar international reputation. Confirming that this indeed was a Swedish-produced film, the head of the Swedish censorship bureau informed the State Department that "the film has no real value even if it received favorable reviews here as do most films."[32] Still, the fate of *The Carousel* convinced SF to favor the cosmopolitan trend, which turned into the guiding production model during the mid-1920s, as noted, bemoaned, and feared by the *Neue Zürcher Zeitung.*

These processes became conspicuous in 1925 when Stiller and his entourage joined Sjöström in Hollywood and SF simultaneously imported the Viennese screenwriter/director Paul Merzbach to spearhead the co-production ventures. According to author Erik Lindorm's witty analysis, "the folk-costume stage is only a short, sentimental episode in the history of cinema. . . ." Film, he opines, "is the most international phenomenon conceivable, it shatters national borders and language barriers. . . . In its nature rests a fertile seed of national abandonment, a need to raid the bottomless depository of international motifs, an obliteration of national borders. . . . No, I do not believe in Swedish cinema, but

American. The entire globe will soon be Americanized; even the little Swedish patch is now retreating toward the Arctic Circle."[33] Swedishness for Lindorm equals provincialism, as well as the idyllic, and is thus out of touch with an era of progress and new values. In prescient verbal imagery, Lindorm claims that future Sjöström films will "no longer come with the wild-strawberry fragrance of Sweden, but instead an international smell of petrol from all over the globe." The peasant culture onscreen, the wild-strawberry cinema, if you will, therefore must yield to the promises/threats of consumerism represented by the young and vigorous American culture unshackled by stifling traditions and national pride. In line with Daltour's claim, Hollywood heroines—and heroes—best embody this new, modern film- and lifestyle, decoupled from the performers' national origin.

Already in 1923, at our critical juncture, Lindorm reflected on movie stars in light of consumerism and especially fast-paced culture's quick turnaround of goods and screen gods and goddesses. Hollywood's luminaries, from his vantage point, are shooting stars in the screen firmament and they come and go, a reflection inspired by his wife's current infatuation with a certain Rudolph Valentino. After sizing Valentino up by looking at publicity images outside a theater, the author is convinced that his wife will have forgotten Valentino in a few weeks. The writer's reflections on Valentino's presumedly fleeting fame lead him to remember what he claims to be the sorry fate of the once-brightest movie star of them all—Asta Nielsen. She is still active in Berlin but, according to the scribe, now sadly forgotten. "A whole galaxy of American stars have drowned her in their light and she will never regain her former luster. Her films are rolled up and stored on history's shelf, i.e., the shelf of oblivion."[34]

For Lindorm, the blinding light from Hollywood drowns not only film stars but also local film cultures. Hence, in his terms, there is no future in hoping for a small national cinema—and no past glory to bask in for Swedish filmmaking, if one accepts Epstein's dismissive analysis. Hard pressed by the market conditions that exacerbated such analyses, SF turned to co-productions seeking out screen beauty, pep, and "It" by way of Hollywood-inspired emulations with a European touch. Alongside homegrown cosmopolitanism, of course, Swedish screens could still supply vernacular raw material for transatlantic transformation, as the case of Garbo (see Figure 9.11) clearly evidences.

Notwithstanding the bleak trajectory we have charted, with French voices as detractors of Swedish cinema's past, present, and future glory, there was at least one dissenting, optimistic forecast formulated in French. Folke Holmberg, a Swede in Paris and for decades SF's film ambassador to France, valiantly came to the rescue in an article published in the prestigious Parisian journal *Cahiers du mois*. Not a clairvoyant, he initially declined to talk about the future of Swedish cinema, which depended, he claimed, mainly on the Americans and to a certain extent on the Swedes themselves. After praising the productions of Sjöström and

Figure 9.11 Greta Garbo (at the time still Greta Gustafsson; shown in the foreground) in *Luffar-Petter* (Peter the tramp, Petschler-Film, 1922). MGM turned her into a very different type of commodity. Courtesy of the Swedish Film Institute.

Stiller, and obviously convincing himself in the process, Holmberg promised there would still be glorious days ahead for Swedish cinema: "Alors, il y aura encore de beaux jours pour le cinema suédoïs!"[35] Penned by a representative of SF, Holmberg's French stance more than anything resides in the realm of wishful thinking.

Notes

1. Robin Hood [Bengt Idestam-Almquist], "Äro de svenska filmdivorna fula?" [Are the Swedish film divas ugly?], *Stockholms-Tidningen,* September 8, 1923, 8; see also "Finns det inga vackra kvinnor i svensk film?" [Are there no beautiful women in Swedish cinema?], *Stockholms Dagblad,* September 8, 1923, 5. *Dagens Nyheter* published comments on September 8 (p.7), September 10 (p. 7), September 11 (p. 7), and September 13 (pp. 8–9). Directors Sigurd Wallén and John Brunius were interviwed in *Aftonbladet* on September 9 (p. 5). Daltour commented on the debate, especially director Wallén's temperamental reaction, but otherwise mainly reiterated his overall appreciation of Swedish cinema. Pierre Daltour, "De svenska filmaktrisernas skönhet" [Swedish film actresses' beauty], *Stockholms Dagblad,* September 12, 1923, 7. Coincidentally, perhaps, Daltour's comment foreshadows G. W. Pabst's reported difficulties in finding a truly beautiful girl in Europe for the part of Lulu in *Pandora's Box* (1929)—this according

to Louise Brooks, the film's American star, in Richard Leacock and Susan Woll's film *Lulu in Berlin* (1984).

2. "Kinematographisches," *Neue Zürcher Zeitung,* March 29, 1923 (Drittes Mittagsblatt, No. 430), 1; translated in *Svenska Dagbladet,* "Svensk film i fara att mista särtypen och förflackas" [Swedish cinema risks losing its distinctiveness and becoming shallow], April 19, 1923, 3. For comments, see, for example, "Den svenska filmens standard" [The standard of Swedish cinema], *Filmnyheter* 4.17 (April 23, 1923), 1, 5; "Är den svenska filmen i fara?" [Is the Swedish cinema in peril?], *Filmbladet* 9.9 (May 1, 1923), 293; and "Börjar vår film förflackas?" [Is our cinema getting shallow?], *Biograf-Revyn* 2.8 (May 7, 1923), 3. The Swiss article was in turn inspired by an essay in the Swedish trade journal *Biografbladet* under the byline Romulus [Knut Jeurlin], "'What Does Swedish Film Signify?'" 4.5 (March 1, 1923), 240–241.

3. "Den svenska filmen lockar" [The lure of Swedish cinema], *Filmnyheter* 3.41 (December 4, 1922), 1, 10.

4. That year he had the misfortune of being arrested and imprisoned as allegedly insane after altercations with his landlady; he was subsequently released from the psychopathic ward. "Our Paris Letter," *Evening Post* (Wellington), July 17, 1926, 13.

5. Inga Gaate, "Ingen kvinnoskönhet i svensk film?" [No feminine beauty in Swedish cinema?], *Filmjournalen* 5.25 (August 5, 1923), 410.

6. Ture Dahlin, "Svensk film—fotograferad teater" [Swedish cinema—photographed theater], *Filmjournalen* 7.3 (January 25, 1925), 48, 57. The magazine's editor, Ragnar Cederstrand (writing as Mr. Gynt), vigorously championed the honor of Swedish cinema against Jean Epstein's "gibberish" in multiple installments and again when Ture Dahlin upped the ante in an interview featuring Ivan Mosjoukine. The Russian émigré actor admired Victor Sjöström's acting but confessed to being "utterly unmoved by *The Phantom Chariot* and the mysticism it seemingly hopes to express." Ture Dahlin, "'Alla kvinnors avgud' intime" ["Every woman's idol" *intime*], *Filmjournalen* 7.6 (February 15, 1925), 107, 120; quotation from p. 107. The most appreciative evaluation of the Swedish films and filmmakers dismissed by Epstein can be found in a short chapter in Léon Moussinac's book *Naissance du cinéma* (Paris: J. Povolozky, 1925), 103–107. For a discussion of Moussinac's analysis and a critical discussion of Swedish cinema in France, see Bo Florin, *Den nationella stilen: Studier i den svenska filmens guldålder* (Stockholm: Aura, 1997), 51–58.

7. Concerning Sjöström, see Bengt Forslund, *Victor Sjöström: His Life and His Work* (New York: New York Zoetrope, 1988); concerning Stiller, see Gösta Werner, *Mauritz Stiller: Ett livsöde* (Stockholm: Prisma, 1991).

8. Dr. Lagerlöf herself was less than pleased with Stiller's adaptation and only after having her arm twisted consented to endorse the production with an onscreen credit statement. Privately, in a letter to Stiller, she declared that she wouldn't accept free adaptations in the future.

9. For an account of Stiller's involvement with the German production firm Trianon, see Patrick Vonderau, *Bilder vom Norden: Schwedisch-deutsche Filmbeziehungen, 1914–1939* (Marburg, Germany: Schüren-Verlag, 2007), 250–308.

10. "Svenska filmen och de vackra kvinnorna" [Swedish cinema and the beautiful women], *Aftonbladet,* September 9, 1923, 5.

11. For a comprehensive discussion, see Kathy Peiss, *Cheap Amusements: Working Women and Leisure in Turn-of-the-Century New York* (Philadelphia: Temple University Press, 1986).

12. For excellent discussions of female agency in American serial films, see Jennifer Bean, "Technologies of Early Stardom and the Extraordinary Body," *Camera Obscura* 16.3 (2001): 9–57, and Marina Dahlquist, ed., *Exporting Perilous Pauline: Pearl White and the Serial Film Craze* (Urbana: University of Illinois Press, 2013).

13. For the correlation between the lure of American consumer culture and media, see Victoria de Grazia, *Irresistible Empire: America's Advance through 20th-Century Europe* (Cambridge, MA: Belknap Press of Harvard University Press, 2005), and Roland Marchand, *Advertising the American Dream: Making Way for Modernity, 1920–1940* (Berkeley: University of California Press, 1985). As for the concept "vernacular cinema," see Miriam Hansen, "The Mass Production of the Senses: Classical Cinema as Vernacular Modernism," *Modernism/Modernity* 6.2 (1999): 59–77.

14. "Är biografernas guldålder förbi? Publikfrekvensen minskad med 25 proc" [Has the golden age of movie theaters passed? Attendance figures down 25 percent], *Svenska Morgonbladet*, October 16, 1920, 2.

15. The most detailed discussions of the co-productions against the backdrop of Hollywood's market dominance are Mats Björkin, *Amerikanism, Bolsjevism och korta kjolar* (Stockholm: Aura, 1998), and Anna-Sofia Rossholm, *Reproducing Languages, Translating Bodies: Approaches to Speech, Translation and Cultural Identity in Early European Sound Film* (Stockholm: Acta Universitatis Stockholmiensis, 2006). For additional perspectives on Swedish cinema in the 1920s, see Florin, *Den nationella stilen;* Vonderau, *Bilder vom Norden;* Tommy Gustafsson, *En fiende till civilisationen: Manlighet, genusrelationer, sexualitet och rasstereotyper i svensk filmkultur under 1920-talet* (Lund, Sweden: Sekel, 2007); and Christopher Natzén, *The Coming of Sound Film in Sweden 1928–1932: New and Old Technologies* (Stockholm: Acta Universitatis Stockholmiensis, 2010).

16. *Svensk film i utlandet: Några ord om exportmöjligheterna för vår filmindustri och om en svensk filmsuccés i London* (Stockholm: Svenska Biografteatern, 1919). This unpublished booklet, "Swedish Film Abroad: Remarks about the Export Prospects for Our Film Industry and about a Swedish Film Success in London," was authored from within Svenska Biografteatern.

17. The distinction between the malleable studio space, standing in for "other spaces," in Michel Foucault's sense of heterotopias, and location shooting, the latter alluding to camera presence outside the studio at the named or inferred place, is truly a blurred one. For a discussion of the parameters for camera presence on location, see Mark Sandberg's essay in this collection, "Location, 'Location': On the Plausibility of Place Substitution." For a comprehensive discussion of place strategies in early Swedish cinema, see Pelle Snickars, *Svensk film och masskultur 1900* (Stockholm: Aura, 2001).

18. Statistiska Centralbyrån, *Historisk statistik för Sverige. Del 1: Befolkning, 1720–1967* [National Central Bureau of Statistics, Historical Statistics of Sweden, Part 1: Population, 1720–1967] (Stockholm: Allmänna Förlaget, 1969).

19. For such debates and their relation to film censorship and reform initiatives, see my essay "Svart på vitt: Film, makt och censur" [Black on white: Cinema, power, and censorship], *Aura. Filmvetenskaplig tidskrift* 1.1 (1995): 14–46. The Swedish censorship bureau classified films in three color-coded categories—white: banned from screening; red: approved for all audiences; yellow: approved for patrons at least fifteen years old.

20. Mr. Gynt [Ragnar Cederstrand], "Stockholm ett paradis—kontinenten kokainförgiftad" [Stockholm a paradise—the continent cocaine poisoned], *Filmjournalen* 4.24 (December 17, 1922), 654. As an aside to the reception of *The Carousel,* it is interesting to note that Buchowetzki in the interview singled out Stiller's *Erotikon* for praise when asked about his impression of Swedish cinema: "It's a masterpiece in terms of directing and featuring a more lavish mise-en-scène than any continental or American luxury film could accomplish."

21. *Filmnyheter* 4.9 (February 26, 1923), 2.

22. Filmör, "Bland sköna damer och ståtliga kavaljerer i Dimitri Buchowetzkis ateljé [Among beautiful ladies and fine-looking cavaliers in Dimitri Buchowetzki's studio],

Filmnyheter 4.21 (May 22, 1923), 10–11; and Hake [Harald Hansen], "Ett imponerande regissörsarbete: Svenska filmare i den största innescen som gjorts i Tyskland" [Impressive directing: Swedish cinematographers in the biggest studio scenes shot in Germany], *Svenska Dagbladet,* May 27, 1923, Sunday Supplement, 4. From a German perspective the shooting was reported in an unsigned trade article: "Aus dem Glashaus" [From the studio], *Der Kinematograph* 17.846 (May 6, 1923), 12.

23. "Karusellen" [The carousel], *Stockholms Dagblad,* October 2, 1923, 8.

24. "Karusellen" [The carousel], *Svenska Dagbladet,* October 2, 1923, 12.

25. "Ett Mästerverk på gott och ont" [A masterpiece—pros and cons], *Filmjournalen* 5.33 (October 14, 1923), 563.

26. Ragnar Allberg, "Karusellen" [The carousel], *Saisonen* 8.20 (October 10, 1923), 667.

27. Robin Hood [Bengt Idestam-Almquist], "Karusellen" [The carousel], *Stockholms-Tidningen,* October 2, 1923, 9.

28. Ibid.

29. Maudlin [Vera von Kraemer], "Äro de svenska filmskådespelerskorna icke vackra?" [Aren't Swedish actresses beautiful?], *Filmnyheter* 4.30 (September 17, 1923), 1–2.

30. "Skönhetstypen i världen förändrad" [Our world's beauty ideal has changed], *Filmnyheter* 3.24 (July 31, 1922), 12–13.

31. For a perceptive analysis of *En piga bland pigor,* see Björkin, *Amerikanism, Bolsjevism och korta kjolar,* 150–168.

32. The correspondence can be found in the Swedish censorship bureau's archive at the Swedish National Archives: Fritz Henriksson (forwarding a query from Egyptian envoy Harald Bildt), letter to Gunnar A. Bjurman, April 21, 1925; Gunnar A. Bjurman, letter to Fritz Henriksson, April 23, 1925; both letters in EI:8, Korrespondens i chefsärenden, Statens Biografbyrå, Riksarkivet, Arninge, Sweden.

33. Erik Lindorm, "Farväl svenska film!" [Adieu Swedish film!], *Svenska Dagbladet,* April 26, 1925, A:11; a digest of the article was published in *Biografbladet* 6.10 (May 15, 1925), 473.

34. Johansson med hjärnan [Johansson with the brain] [Erik Lindorm], "Det stora filmstjärnfallet" [Grandiose shooting stars], *Social-Demokraten,* January 26, 1923, 7. The thesis seems somewhat contradictory given that the author found it worthwhile to reprint the article two years later: *Bonniers Veckotidning* 2.21 (May 23, 1925), 27.

35. Folke Holmberg, "Un exemple: L'avenir du film suédois," *Cahiers du mois* 2.16/17 (September/October 1925): 208–211.

10 Queer Crossings

Greta Garbo, National Identity, and Gender Deviance

Laura Horak

Greta Garbo's star persona has proved remarkably flexible. Her famous blankness—derived from both her restrained acting style and her infamous obsession with privacy—has left the image of Garbo open for any number of projects, ranging, for example, from Roland Barthes's contemplation of Garbo's face as Platonic mask to Diana McClellan's gossipy exposé of early Hollywood lesbian networks.[1] However, the various ways in which Garbo has been used in the decades since her films were produced has obscured the nature of her star persona during her first years in the United States and how her now-celebrated transgressions were first described. In particular, Garbo's Swedishness is less visible and has different meanings today than it did during her career because Swedish-Americans have been assimilated into American whiteness. In this essay, I argue that Swedishness was an essential element of Garbo's early star persona in the United States and that, furthermore, it was key to making her gender and sexual deviance palatable. Garbo offers a useful case study of the complex ways in which the burgeoning star system exploited shifting lines of national, ethnic, gender, and sexual identity as international film personnel were relocated to Hollywood. Although the effects of her national border crossings have become less visible as her sexual and gender crossings have become more so, I will argue that Garbo's multiple modes of crossing required each other in order for her to be successful.

No account of Garbo's arrival in the United States failed to mention her Swedishness. Typical is the first mention of Garbo in the *New York Times*, a photograph with the caption: "Scandinavia Sends Another Star to America: Greta Garbo, the New Swedish Screen Actress with Metro Goldwyn."[2] Amidst the influx of European actors, directors, and technicians to Hollywood in the 1920s, these imports were often differentiated by their nationality.[3] Although this was, on the one hand, a pragmatic way of sorting the newcomers, it also helped reify U.S. stereotypes of national characteristics describing the incoming waves of immigrants and encouraged the creation of star personae based on these stereotypes. In *Nordic Exposures: Scandinavian Identities in Classical Hollywood Cinema,* Arne Lunde insightfully analyzes the ways in which the American press described the successful waves of Scandinavian film personnel emigrating to Los Angeles in the 1920s and 1930s and how these emigrés negotiated American whiteness.

Garbo's performance in *Queen Christina* has been important to histories of gay and lesbian representation in Hollywood film (particularly Christina's transvestism and full-mouth kiss of Ebba Sparre).[4] A limitation of many star biographies and histories of gay and lesbian cinema, however, is that they rely so heavily on retrospection. The result is that scholars and fans read stars through decades of accumulated star discourse and it is difficult to determine just what audiences might have thought of a star in earlier times. To comprehend how Garbo was understood when she first came to the United States, I have consulted newspapers, general-interest magazines, fan magazines, and trade journals between 1925 and 1934, from Garbo's arrival on American shores to the release of her most iconic film, *Queen Christina* (Rouben Mamoulian, 1933/1934). Departing from previous scholarship, I argue that the U.S. press began constructing Garbo as a lesbian even before *Queen Christina,* that stereotypes of Swedishness allowed the press to flirt with insinuations of lesbianism without provoking a backlash, and that the film *Queen Christina* succeeded in creating a coherent persona for Garbo that was both Swedish and lesbian, where earlier written discourse had positioned her national and sexual identities as competing explanations.

I am not interested in determining the "truth" of Garbo's sexual life, but rather in when and how rumors of her lesbianism began to circulate publicly and why they never provoked much of a backlash. While biographers often dismiss rumors about a star's sexual life (and particularly rumors of homosexuality) as unfounded gossip, feminist and queer scholars like Irit Rogoff and Gavin Butt have pointed out that gossip is often the only way that sex lives (particularly deviant sex lives) enter into discourse and that gossip insistently puts sexuality into discursive play, regardless of whether it is true or false.[5] While gossip polices cultural norms, it also generates fantasies of transgressing those norms and circulates concepts for making sense of such transgressions. Thus, the history I want to trace here is not who had sex with whom, but how concepts of sexual and gender identity circulated in the public sphere and under what terms.

"The Two Greta Garbos"

Garbo, more than perhaps any other star, was described as a "mystery" to be solved. Journalists obsessively articulated a contradiction between Garbo's on-screen persona as a confident, feminine woman of the world and her off-screen, allegedly "true" self—a timid, somewhat mannish Swedish immigrant. A 1930

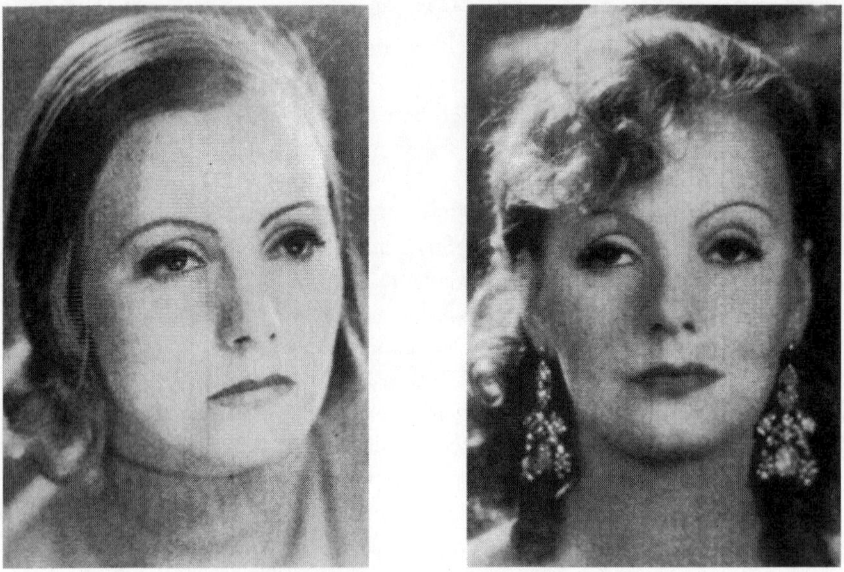

Figure 10.1 The "two Greta Garbos," from "What Greta Garbo Thinks of Hollywood," *Photoplay* (August 1930), 65. Courtesy of the Media History Digital Library.

profile of Garbo in *Photoplay* offers a typical account, in a caption below two photographs of the star (Figure 10.1):

> The two Greta Garbos that make up one of the most romantic and glittering figures in all screen history. At the left is a plain girl, with simple tastes, who lives her own life and minds her own business. She likes children, and funny stories, and is timid in a crowd. At the right is the other Garbo—glittering, mysterious, exotic. The Greta of the screen whose allure is so powerful a magnet that she is talked about by millions of fans.[6]

The journalist later compares the "vague exotic mystery woman" of the screen with "the Swedish girl called Greta who likes her native food and loves anchovies, is always cold, suffers from insomnia, wears bedroom slippers between scenes, . . . is terrified of meeting strange people and is actually timid and embarrassed in a crowd."[7] Virtually every profile of Garbo during this period repeats this contrast—between the glamorous, exotic femme fatale of Garbo's film roles and the strange young woman who shuns fashionable clothing, marriage, and the Hollywood social scene. Richard deCordova argues that the star discourse that developed in the late 1910s and 1920s was founded on a "play of surface and depth," in which "the private lives of the players were constituted as a site of knowledge and truth."[8] Garbo epitomizes this particular dynamic.

Following Michel Foucault, deCordova posits the sexual as "the most private, and thus the most truthful, locus of identity" and describes the explicit coverage of actors' (hetero)sexual scandals during the 1920s.[9] In the case of Garbo, however, the supposed "secret" that journalists continually reveal is her timidity, her plain taste in clothing and food, and her bulky, asexual clothing. This is a complex kind of revelation. The traits fit stereotypes of Swedish immigrant women. Thus, journalists posit Garbo's *nationality* as the "secret" behind her placeless screen persona. Even after years in the United States, journalists insist that Garbo retains her essential Swedishness.[10] She may *play* Russian or French, but she *is* Swedish. Not until five years into her U.S. career (around 1930) does the press begin to suggest that these traits could alternatively be read as evidence of a deviant sexual/gender identity, as I will discuss shortly.

Swedishness in the United States

If Garbo's off-screen persona was constructed as intractably Swedish, what did "Swedishness" mean in the United States at this point? As Olsson states in the previous chapter of this volume, around one million Swedes emigrated from Sweden to the United States between 1892 and 1923. Many became farmers in the Midwest and laborers in big cities such as New York and Chicago. (In fact, by 1910, Chicago was second only to Stockholm in terms of Swedish population.) Swedes were an identifiable ethnic group, like the Italians or Irish. In a variety of popular entertainments, Swedes were portrayed as large, none-too-bright, country folk, and the "dumb Swede" was a staple of American vaudeville. Two stereotypical versions of Swedish womanhood were the mannish working woman and the vulnerable immigrant girl. The mannish working woman was a comic type epitomized by "Sweedie, the Swedish maid," a popular character in a series of Essanay film comedies (1914–1916), played by the American actor Wallace Beery in drag (see Figure 10.2). This female type was large, working class, awkward, and overtly masculinized. The vulnerable immigrant girl, on the other hand, was imagined to be a naïve country girl alone in the big city. This type was popular in sensationalistic tales of white slavery, such as the record-breaking film *A Traffic in Souls* (George Loane Tucker, 1913). In this film, two Swedish girls in peasant garb are led to a brothel labeled "Swedish Employment Agency," where they are kidnapped and forced to become sex workers. Swedish girls were popular victims of these tales, which played into melodramatic narratives of racial threat to white womanhood, as the slavers were often swarthy immigrant men.[11] Though stereotypes of vulnerable immigrant girls and mannish working women were clearly not confined to Swedes, they were key configurations for representing Swedish femininity.

In Garbo's case, Swedishness had a certain recuperative power that Pola Negri's Polishness or Rudolph Valentino's Italianness, for example, did not have.[12]

Figure 10.2 Wallace Beery as "Sweedie, the Swedish Maid," 1915. From the author's collection.

Diane Negra has argued that Negri's "resistant ethnicity" caused the backlash that ended her career. Likewise, Gaylyn Studlar and Miriam Hansen have argued that Valentino's ethnicity compounded his social transgressions.[13] Swedes had a complicated relationship to American whiteness during this period. As Lunde demonstrates, Swedes and other Scandinavians who migrated to the United States were sometimes excluded from the category "white folks," even while conceptions of a Nordic race figured into European and American theories of white supremacy.[14] Like other immigrant groups, Lunde shows, Swedes became "white" by assimilating to U.S. norms and differentiating themselves from other, ostensibly "non-white" groups. Nonetheless, even if Swedish-Americans were not fully included in American whiteness by this time, they were certainly considered "more" white than Southern or Eastern European immigrants or African-Americans.

Garbo's Deviations

When Garbo arrived in Hollywood in July 1925, MGM remade her physical appearance through dieting, orthodontic work, a new hairstyle, and possibly plastic surgery (as Michaela Krützen contends).[15] Nonetheless, it was not long before journalists noticed that Garbo deviated noticeably from American and Hollywood norms of sociality, gender, and sexuality. She spent little time with her peers in Hollywood, granted few interviews, and dodged personal questions in the few interviews she gave. When not filming, she wore loose-fitting, androgynous clothing. By 1930 and 1931, she had established a trademark look, consisting of an ulster (a man's loose overcoat), a shapeless sweater, low-heeled shoes, and a slouch hat. After a highly publicized romance with co-star John Gilbert between 1926 and 1929, she did not allow the studio or the press to romantically pair her with any other men. When repeatedly asked what she thought of "American men," she dodged the question.[16] Around 1931, she developed close friendships with women such as screenwriter Salka Viertel and the flamboyant bisexual playwright Mercedes de Acosta. These deviations, in fact, played an essential role in her stardom.

As early as October 1926, Katherine Lipke of the *New York Times* noted that Garbo did not like fine clothes, did not want to get married, and kept away from her Hollywood peers. Lipke writes that "clothes bore the blonde Miss Garbo slightly" and quotes Garbo as saying, "Ne-ever until two months ago do I go out in the evening. I do not like to go[;] I would rather stay at home." Nor is she interested in (heterosexual) romance or marriage. Regarding the rumor of romance between Garbo and Gilbert, Lipke writes: "An interview with her on the subject leaves her non-committal and the interviewer with curiosity unsatisfied. 'I do not want to get married!' This much she does say, over and over like a well-learned lesson."[17]

Lipke tries to explain Garbo's peculiarities by fitting them within the narrative of a vulnerable immigrant girl. Lipke establishes Garbo as uncertain and uncomfortable with the English language—and, by extension, with her place in the United States. She writes that "the Swedish Greta" speaks "with all the slow earnestness caused by a new and laborious language." As was a common strategy in interviews with foreign stars, Lipke rendered Garbo's speech with incorrect word order, dropped prepositions, and a phonetically described "Swedish" accent. (The accent may reflect vaudeville conventions of Swedish-American speech more than Garbo's actual speech. Several years later, the director of her first talkie complained that she had to be taught how to say "yust" and "yob" instead of "just" and "job" in order to sound "authentic.")[18] Lipke suggested that Garbo avoided people because she was so shy and because English was such a strain for her. Lipke attempted to soften Garbo's statement against marriage by prefacing the quote with a preemptive explanation: "As for Greta herself—well, Greta does not speak the English language easily. It is so easy for her to misunderstand a direct question—so hard for her to reply." By saying that Garbo repeated her refusal of marriage "like a well-learned lesson," Lipke implied that Garbo had memorized these words as a stock response to questions she didn't understand. This is rather an odd way to interpret what seems like a fairly straightforward statement on Garbo's part.

Garbo resisted this strategy of attributing her oddities to Swedishness when she asserted that "Swedish women, though, like clothes joost as mooch as Americans do. Women are the same the world over, I think. They all want the same things." Here Garbo contradicted Lipke's strategy of casting Garbo's eccentricities within the explanatory framework of the Swedish immigrant girl. Journalists continued to use this strategy, however, throughout Garbo's career—the Swedish story growing stronger, in fact, as Garbo grew more distant from Sweden and other explanations for her behavior increasingly suggested themselves.

"Her favorites are pansies and violets": Insinuations of Lesbianism

As it turned out, Garbo's deviance could not be entirely explained by nationalizing her idiosyncrasies. Such traits were not dismissed as accidental oddities, though. Journalists tossed out a number of theories—that she was suffering from childhood trauma; that she was mourning the death of her one true love, the director Mauritz Stiller (who was in fact gay); that her silence was a publicity stunt; or even that she was suffering from anemia. However, beginning around 1930, a number of journalists also began to insinuate that Garbo was a lesbian. The timing coincided with Hollywood's broader exploitation of public fascination with illicit sexuality and criminal behavior in the so-called pre-Code films. It also occurred on the heels of New York's so-called pansy craze and the national controversy around the lesbian plays and novels of the late 1920s (particularly Édouard Bourdet's *The Captive* and Radclyffe Hall's *Well of Loneliness*), which I discuss in my dissertation.[19] Film scholar Ronald Gregg has described how MGM exploited insinuations of "wisecracking" star William Haines's homosexuality in the late 1920s and early 1930s to capitalize on the "pansy craze."[20] This shift also coincides with Garbo's alleged relationships with Lilyan Tashman and, in 1931, with de Acosta—two women at the center of international, lesbian, artistic circles. I would surmise that MGM was aware of and tacitly endorsed these insinuations, as reporters (particularly from the fan magazines) would not have wanted to jeopardize their relationship with the studio and MGM was using a similar strategy to promote William Haines at that time.

If we must ask ourselves what Swedishness meant in the 1920s, it is equally important to ask what lesbianism meant at this time. Sex between women had long been acknowledged and named (e.g., the terms "tribade," "Sapphist," and "lesbian" date back to antiquity), but in the late nineteenth century, European and American activists, scientists, and writers began trying to describe variant sexual desires in earnest, coining new terms such as *Urning* (Karl Ulrichs, 1864), *homosexualität* (Károly Mária Benkert, aka Kertbeny, 1869), and *conträre Sexualempfindung* (Carl von Westphal, 1870; this became *sexual inversion* when translated into English in 1897). At this same time, sexual deviance became increasingly visible to the public through a succession of French novels and plays, growing communities of deviants in cities such as Paris, Berlin, and Harlem, and several highly publicized trials (e.g., the 1892 Alice Mitchell trial in the United States, the 1895 Oscar Wilde trials in England, and the 1907–1909 Harden-Eulenburg affair in Germany). In 1928, the English novelist Radclyffe Hall published *The Well of Loneliness*, which achieved international fame as the result of censorship trials in England and the United States. The novel called for increased tolerance of the female "invert," embodied in the semi-autobiographical protagonist Stephen Gordon. In the novel, Stephen is strong and athletic, noble and self-sacrificing, with a slight masculine cast to her face and body. She dresses in the clothes of a British country gentleman. Film scholar Patricia White has argued that Garbo's star persona in *Queen Christina* intersected with this newly circulating type, though she has not attended specifically to how this happened.[21] By 1930, the term "invert" was becoming less common and the word "lesbian" was making its way from high-cultural circles into the U.S. popular press. The notion of a broader gender inversion, however, still accompanied the idea of lesbianism (as, in fact, it continues to do). Thus, of the range of terms that circulated at the time, I will use the word "lesbian" here, as it was in the process of becoming the dominant term, but I want to retain the connotation of gender inversion more explicit in the term "invert."

Garbo's lesbianism was communicated in a number of different ways. A small set of journalists made fairly straightforward insinuations, describing Garbo's relationships with certain women and using established code words. Journalists began commenting on Garbo's close friendships with actresses Lilyan Tashman and Fifi D'Orsay in 1930. Tashman was a Broadway actress who had married gay actor Edmund Lowe in 1925. Her lesbianism was an open secret in Hollywood and she was known for her Natalie Barney–like *salons*. D'Orsay was a French-Canadian vaudeville performer and Hollywood hopeful who had invented a Parisian past for herself. In February 1930, one magazine reported:

> Greta Garbo and Fifi Dorsay have become inseparable friends. Everywhere that Greta goes, Fifi is sure to tag along and vice versa. Greta stays in her shell and is so reserved that Hollywood has been greatly amused and interested in this dalliance. Fifi is Greta's first pal since Lilyan Tashman and Greta parted company. . . . Just how long it will last no one knows, but the two "gals" are certainly a colorful pair—so different and both so foreign.[22]

Garbo and D'Orsay's relationship, though explicitly labeled a "friendship," is nonetheless described in terms often used for romantic relationships—a "dalliance," Tashman and Garbo "parted company" like a couple breaking up, people wonder "how long" the next one "will last." Several suggestive words are used to describe Garbo and D'Orsay: "colorful," "different," and "foreign." Eight months later, the *New York Times* published an interview with d'Orsay:

> "One night Geegee [her pet name for Miss Garbo] called me up," Miss d'Orsay exclaimed, "and she said to me: 'Baby, I mus' come over and see you for dinnaire tonight.' But I tell her I have people come to my house for dinnaire. So she say, 'T'row them out.' So I throw them out and Geegee come over."[23]

Both articles allude to a particular intimacy between Garbo and her friend d'Orsay.[24]

Describing sex between women as a practice of "foreign" peoples has been a persistent strategy (even back to Greek and Roman texts), and this was no less the case in the United States. Here we can see how Garbo is described as "foreign" in a general sense, along with the seemingly French D'Orsay. "Foreign" here means both ambiguously European and, simply, "other." Indeed, Garbo's peculiarities were sometimes attributed to her being "foreign," broadly speaking. This is particularly the case in late-1930s profiles that align her with competitor Marlene Dietrich. Describing these women as "foreign" also aligns them with the international cosmopolitan scene that Patrice Petro describes in the last essay in this volume. Though this strategy was used at times, it is nonetheless surprising how often journalists made the effort to differentiate Garbo as specifically Swedish, not merely foreign/European.

In 1931 and 1932, journalists began to note Garbo's close friendships with screenwriter Salka Viertel and de Acosta. The gossipy "Rambling Reporter" of the *Hollywood Reporter* noted coyly on August 21, 1931, that "Greta Garbo has a new love," and another source wrote, in December of that year: "Maybe Mercedes de Acosta is giving Greta good advice. The two girls are inseparable companions."[25] In January 1932, the "Rambling Reporter" announced, "Despite the 'law' against nance entertainers, the hottest speakeasy spot in N.Y. is on Sixth Avenue, with fifty lavender boys serving the likker—Greta Garbo, Fifi Dorsay and Joe Schenck amongst its patrons."[26] Later that month, they joked about a rivalry between Garbo's two companions, de Acosta and Viertel:

> This is supposed to have happened when Mrs. Berthold Viertel went to the Pasadena station to meet Greta Garbo who was arriving from New York a few weeks ago. Mrs. V. came into the station in a very tailored attire, flat-heeled shoes, etc., and was immediately swamped with reporters. . . . When it was all over the reporters said, "Thank you very much, Miss D'Acosta." (!)[27]

Garbo was repeatedly linked with de Acosta throughout 1932: "Mercedes De Acosta, fond friend of Greta Garbo," "[Garbo was] accompanied by her close friend, Mrs. Mercedes De Acosta Poole," "Mercedes de Acosta became the great Garbo's chum."[28]

The journalist Rilla Page Palmborg was responsible for many of the most direct hints that Garbo was a lesbian or invert. Palmborg had married a Swedish man, which, she insinuated, gave her an advantage in getting close to Garbo, though she had no Swedish background or language skills herself.[29] Palmborg published two articles on "The Private Life of Greta Garbo" in *Photoplay* in September and October 1930 and an unauthorized biography by the same name in 1931.[30] Though she introduced the first article by noting that Garbo had been seen around town with a "tall, blond, handsome young Swede," she concludes that this young man "is infatuated with Garbo, but he knows that there is not a chance for him."[31] Indeed, Palmborg says, "In the summer of 1929, Garbo did not seem to be devoted to any particular man."[32] She notes elsewhere that "Lilyan Tashman was reported to be Garbo's pal. Then Fifi Dorsay was supposed to be her chum. Others declared that Nils Asther was the only person she invited to her house. Garbo succeeded in keeping the public ignorant of her innermost private life."[33] Just in case a reader might mistake Asther for a love interest, Palmborg added: "Hollywood never has taken the friendship between Nils Asther and Greta Garbo the way Hollywood usually takes friendship."[34]

Palmborg went even further, using established code words for lesbianism. At one point, she revealed, "Garbo has always been fond of flowers. Her favorites are pansies and violets. . . . A bunch of violets was almost always to be found at the head of her bed."[35] In the 1920s, women gave violets to their female lovers, inspired by one of Sappho's poems in which the poet and her female lover wear garlands of violets. The practice was publicized in the United States via the New York production of Édouard Bourdet's *The Captive* in 1926, as the protagonist (played by Helen Menken) receives violets from her female lover. For years after the play, newspapers remarked on the negative impact this association had had on violet sales. One popular syndicated columnist remarked: "Florists believe the continued slump in the sale of violets is due solely to Helen Menken's play with a Lesbian theme, The Captive. Violets symbolized perversion throughout the drama."[36] Additionally, "pansy" was an established slang term for an effeminate gay man by the turn of the century.[37]

Palmborg furthermore mentioned that "word got out in Hollywood that Garbo's next picture was to be *Sappho.*"[38] Though she is likely referring to Alphonse Daudet's novel *Sapho,* which describes an entirely heterosexual affair between a young man and an older woman, the name "Sappho" assuredly evoked same-sex female desire for those in the know. Like the publicity that associated William Haines with pansies and interior decorating, Palmborg and others described Garbo using codes that would be recognizable to quite a few readers.[39]

Lesbian or Swedish?

However, far more common than accounts of Garbo's female friendships or affinity for violets were descriptions of her masculinity and obsessive privacy. These two traits, which could serve as evidence of sexual inversion, were explained away as characteristics of either the mannish Swedish working woman or the vulnerable Swedish immigrant girl. Much attention was paid to Garbo's masculine-style clothing, and the word "mannish" consistently cropped up. Journalists described her as "a tall, lanky, mannishly attired woman" or reported that "she wears a mannish walking-suit of brown, with leather jacket. . . . She swings a stick with masculine effort."[40] Palmborg's description of Garbo's clothing, quoted here, even resembles the narrator's description of Stephen Gordon's clothing in *The Well of Loneliness:*

> [Garbo] always wore heavy, low-heeled slippers. Oftenest these were the smallest size obtainable in men's low shoes. . . . She wore men's tailored shirts. She owned dozens of men's silk ties, in all colors. At night she wore men's pajamas, in soft shades of silk and in stripes. Her hats were of soft felt in mannish style. When her manservant brought her shoes, she would laugh and say, "Just the kind for us bachelors, eh?"[41]

Reporters also described Garbo's furnishings as being distinctively masculine. They wrote that she "likes solid substantial furniture and hates feminine geegaws" and that "her home contains no feminine appointments. The furnishings are solid and mannish."[42] Palmborg described Garbo's bedroom: "This room was furnished in heavy walnut, as though it were intended for the master of the house."[43] Even her style of walking was described as masculine. Palmborg quotes two of Garbo's male friends: "'Garbo strides along like a man and fairly races across the ground.' 'She plays tennis like a man, too.'"[44]

Garbo's off-screen masculinity was one of the key "mysteries" that journalists hoped to solve. Clearly sexual inversion was an explanation that could not be stated in print. Journalists sometimes struggled visibly to find a language that could make sense of these gender violations. For example, in 1929, Adela Rogers St. Johns wrote: "It is misleading to call Garbo mannish. Or masculine. But it is difficult to find exactly the right word to describe a certain something about her which calls those words to mind."[45] Certain readers would not have had too hard of a time finding the right word . . . But St. Johns cut off this line of thinking, suggesting, "Perhaps bigness will do. She is a big person, mentally and physically, and she likes bigness." This struggle to find the right language to describe Garbo resembles journalists' attempts to describe the butch director Dorothy Arzner during this same period, as Judith Mayne has shown.[46] Mayne writes that "writers employ various turns of phrase to suggest that Dorothy's appearance is not easily readable, and that her character is not easily decipherable."[47] The same strategy was applied to Garbo.

Most often, journalists attributed Garbo's masculine clothing, furnishings, and physical comportment to her identity as a Swedish peasant. For example, Palmborg reports that one of her informants told her that "Greta Garbo is a peasant at heart."[48] This refrain is repeated throughout the writings about Garbo. Palmborg emphasizes Garbo's intrinsic Swedishness by detailing the star's food preferences. Garbo's "favorite lunch," she says is "some cold meat, a salad, and a bottle of near beer."[49] She is fond of "Swedish hardtack" and asks her chef to make her "Bruna Bönor, Swedish hardtack, cake, and coffee."[50] Palmborg even explains to readers that "Bruna Bönor is a rich, heavy dish made of Swedish brown beans cooked with cubes of salt pork and sweetened with brown sugar." Garbo's large, androgynous body, Palmborg and others imply, is the body of a Swedish peasant, not a sexual invert.

At other times, journalists describe Garbo's penchant for masculine clothing as a disguise to avoid publicity (publicity which she shuns because of her timidity). For example, the author of one *Los Angeles Times* article wrote: "Her boon companions are the caddy boys at a golf course in her neighborhood; she shoots craps with them. Once, in a boy's coat and boy's shoes, she attended an afternoon tea at a house on the hills above Beverly. They saw her come in; then they missed her. Again she had escaped."[51] Likewise, St. Johns described her as "an awkward, lonely girl wrapped from curious eyes in a heavy, boy's coat and from curious minds in an armor of protective silence." In contrast to the Swedish peasant, this explanation mobilized the vulnerable immigrant girl type, and St. Johns even describes Garbo's arrival in Hollywood as that of a "girl in her ten-dollar checked suit, bewildered, frightened, unhappy."[52]

Many journalists asked what Garbo may be hiding behind her obsessive secrecy. Typical headlines read "The Hollywood Hermit," "The Reason Why Greta Garbo Will Not Talk," "Why Garbo Plays Dumb," and "Garbo Heads World's Strangest Secret Society." The 1931 *Los Angeles Times* article, "The Reason Why Greta Garbo Will Not Talk," is a good example of this line of questioning.[53] The author first describes Garbo's pathological silence ("A Trappist monk—under the vows of eternal silence—is a garrulous little chatterbox compared to the mysterious Swede"), then asks, "What is the reason for her silence?" Several possible answers are put forward: "Is it a haughty nature? A business policy? Orders from the publicity department?" The author then triumphantly discloses the truth: "The truth is that the delectable Greta is afraid." This fear is the timidity of a young Swedish immigrant girl. After the death of her mentor, Mauritz Stiller: "A cautious, cold Swede, she solved the bewilderment of the situation by going into her shell. She resolutely refused to talk to reporters because she did not know what to say." When Mary Pickford encouraged her to attend a party, "the Swedish girl, with a frightened light in her eyes, whispered, 'I can't go. I'm afraid.'" Swedishness is particularly prominent in these descriptions of her timidity; her pathological shyness is explicable because she is a "Swedish girl" and a "cautious, cold Swede."

Of course, the possibility that her secrecy was used to hide romantic relationships with women could not be said explicitly, but this interpretation often hovered below the surface. This was particularly true of articles from 1933 and after, such as "Garbo Heads World's Strangest Secret Society" and "Why Garbo's Friends Dare Not Talk." In these increasingly mean-spirited accounts, the Swedish immigrant tale is *not* used and Garbo's secrecy remains pathological. In "Secret Society," for instance, the journalist reports that Garbo's friends remain silent because "they dread incurring the glamorous vestal queen's displeasure."[54] In "Why Garbo's Friends Dare Not Talk," the reporter shares: "Another current Garbo legend has to do with the luckless big player who quoted the star to a newspaper reporter—and *was never seen or heard of in Hollywood, thereafter*."[55] This account completely contradicts the notion of Garbo as a shy, overwhelmed Swedish immigrant.

With Garbo's masculinity, then, and her obsessive secrecy, the stereotypes of the mannish Swedish woman and the timid immigrant offered journalists a safer way to explain Garbo's deviations. Because Swedishness was comparatively neutral, it could recuperate these gender, sexual, and social deviations without incurring a backlash.[56]

"Garbo is entirely Queen Christina"

Whereas the press repeatedly offered evidence that could be interpreted as lesbianism but described it as Swedish instead, the film *Queen Christina* offered an explanation of how Garbo could be both lesbian *and* Swedish. This film did more than any other to shape Garbo's public persona. Images of the star in wax museums today and in recently issued U.S. and Swedish postage stamps invariably use Garbo's look from this film. In the BFI Companion to this film, Marcia Landy and Amy Villarejo concur: "*Queen Christina* is a [*sic*] film with which the image of Greta Garbo is most intimately fused."[57] More than any other film, *Queen Christina* took on the task of explaining Garbo herself, and, unlike the writings that were also trying to do this, it consolidated a coherent star persona that reconciled the contradictory national, gender, and sexual narratives that had been applied to the actress.

Garbo had a great deal of control over the film. Salka Viertel says that Garbo chose the topic and asked Viertel to write a treatment, which Garbo then presented to Thalberg. Garbo had veto power over the director, screenwriter, and actors, "what in effect amounted to her own production company" at MGM, write Landy and Villarejo.[58] As Garbo's fame grew, her onscreen roles began to align more closely with her off-screen persona. In *Anna Christie,* she played a working-class Swedish woman (which legitimized her accented voice in her talkie debut, argues Lunde). In *Grand Hotel* (Edmund Goulding, 1932), she played a moody Russian ballerina, who famously tells her assistants, "I want to be alone." Even more than *Grand Hotel,* though, *Queen Christina* built a protagonist for Garbo that explicitly played on her off-screen persona. The queen is Swedish, craves solitude, wears men's clothes, has a forthright demeanor, and—importantly—displays open affection for a female friend—Ebba Sparre, the queen's lady-in-waiting (Elizabeth Young). It also included Garbo's previously off-screen references to herself as a "bachelor." The film is Garbo's first and only to include explicit references to lesbianism.

Essentially, *Queen Christina* collapses and incorporates both of the "two Garbos" into itself. By writing the "off-screen" Garbo onto the screen, the film collapses the dichotomy that had been operating in her fan discourse and, in doing so, turns the film into an explanation of the "real" Garbo. Garbo's insistence that her former lover John Gilbert be cast as her on-screen lover only contributed to this effect. The film's first half articulates the "off-screen" Garbo: Christina wears men's clothing, seeks privacy, kisses her female friends, and displays jealousy of her friend's relationship with a man. The second half articulates the "on-screen" Garbo: Christina falls in love with the character played by John Gilbert (Don Antonio, a Spanish ambassador), wears glamorous dresses, inadvertently causes the death of the man she loves, and leaves Sweden for an unrepresentable European continent. The elaboration of Christina's character functions as an elaboration of Garbo's two characters.

Writings about the film obsessively paralleled Garbo and Christina. Finally journalists could explain Garbo, because this seemingly illegible being had precedent. Press coverage often described the historical figure of Christina as an astonishing double of Garbo. Typical was the *New York Herald*'s claim that "Queen Christina is entirely Garbo, and Garbo is entirely Queen Christina."[59] In an article in *Photoplay,* "Two Queens Were Born in Sweden," Helen Dale alternated between descriptions of Christina and Garbo, using the same language to describe each ("moody," "headstrong," "distinctly masculine taste in clothes," "refuses to marry," etc.).[60] After describing Christina, Dale asks the reader, "Could not those very well be Garbo's sentiments?" and suggests, "You could substitute the name of Garbo anywhere in this paragraph." Dale wrote: "Christina's hands were beautiful and white, but strong and virile; her eyes might have belonged to either sex, and they were extremely intelligent; her voice was clear, deep and emotional. It would be difficult to find a more exact description of Garbo." Landy and Villarejo remind us that the apparent "coincidence" of Garbo's resembling Christina is "not a coincidence at all," as this conjunction was "selected and painstakingly constructed."[61]

Dale draws an almost supernatural connection between Garbo and Christina. She describes Garbo as Christina's "reincarnation": "For Greta Garbo might easily be the reincarnation of Christina, so closely are the two related, emotionally, intellectually and spiritually." In this reading, Garbo and Christina are one person who happens to exist in two different times, the historical past and the present day. This idea of Garbo's being outside of time aligns her with Virginia Woolf's ageless androgyne, Orlando. (The novel *Orlando* was published in 1928, only five years before *Queen Christina* was released.)

However, Dale also renders the parallel as an intimacy between two women separated by time:

> Across the centuries, the two queens clasp hands, their eyes meeting in perfect understanding. . . . Garbo certainly feels a close kinship with Christina. . . . She must acknowledge, deep within herself, that emotional accord linking the two most famous Swedes in history—that harmony of mood that stretches back through the years like a golden cord and makes them both say, one to the other, "I understand."[62]

Here the relationship between the two women begins to seem romantic: they clasp hands, meet eyes, are bound by a golden cord. Lesbianism (in the form of the dead Christina) becomes a specter haunting this account. This was a popular strategy, according to Terry Castle in *The Apparitional Lesbian*, and the uncanny relationship between Garbo and Christina echoes the structure that Patricia White detects in later lesbian gothic films such as *Rebecca* (1940) and *The Uninvited* (1944).[63] White writes: "Narrativity in a film like *Rebecca* . . . works to position the heroine . . . in relationship to a desirable female object. Yet the genre enacts prohibition against their representation *together*, since one of the women is dead."[64] The description of Garbo and Christina likewise draws on ghostly doubling and the imagined desire between two women.

Like previous written discourse about Garbo, the film suggests that Christina may be lesbian by depicting her intimate female friendship and her masculinity. Famously, Christina kisses her friend and lady-in-waiting, Ebba Sparre, and then gets angry when she overhears Ebba planning to marry a guardsman (see Figure 10.3). It is clear that both the studio and the Production Code Administration

Figure 10.3 Christina (Greta Garbo) kisses Ebba (Elizabeth Young) in *Queen Christina*.

(PCA) were aware of the lesbian possibilities of Christina's relationship with Ebba. A reader's report from one of the first versions of the script praises the fact that "even in the inference of Christina's passion for a woman, the scenes are delicately handled so that only the 'wise' can get the idea.'"[65] Salka Viertel says in her memoir that producer Irving Thalberg asked her if she had seen *Mädchen in Uniform* (1932), a German film about a schoolgirl's crush on her teacher (marketed in the United States as "an unusual love story").[66] Viertel said that she had, and he asked her, "Does not Christina's affection for her lady-in-waiting indicate something like that?" He apparently urged her "to keep it in mind" because "if handled with taste it would give us very interesting scenes."[67] However, James Wingate of the PCA asked MGM to change the scene in which Christina gets upset over Ebba's marriage in order to correct "the tinge of lesbianism in the relationship between Christina and Ebba."[68] Wingate furthermore warned: "Even with these changes, we assume that you will be careful to avoid anything in the portrayal of the scene which may be construed as lesbianism."

The same year that the film was released, Margaret Goldsmith published what she termed a psychological biography of Christina that took up the question of Christina's "sexual abnormality" and baldly stated that "many contemporary documents, and Christina's own letters, make it quite clear that she was attracted by her own sex."[69] Goldsmith cited a recent German biography, too, which claimed that Christina, "whose study of the classics had made her familiar with Lesbos, played with the idea of experimenting in Lesbian love." The biography likely encouraged some viewers to label Garbo's somewhat ambiguous representation of Christina's feelings toward Ebba as definitely "Lesbian."

As in written descriptions of Garbo, the film highlights Christina's masculinity. In the first shots of the adult queen, the spectator is invited to confuse her for a man (see Figures 10.4a and b). In a series of extreme long shots, we see two small figures on horseback racing through the woods, with a hunting dog following close behind. Each wears a riding jacket, hat, and trousers. As the figures ride up to the castle, the camera gets a little closer, and the figure on the lead horse dismounts and runs up the castle steps. However, the figure keeps its back to the camera and rushes up steps and through doorways in a series of shots, always running away from the camera. When the figure finally stops in front of two advisors and is addressed as "Your Majesty," the camera cuts in for a medium close-up, but the face is still obscured by the wide, black brim of a hat. Finally, after an agonizing moment, the figure turns toward the camera slightly and slowly removes the hat, dramatically revealing the snowy white face of Garbo. This sight gag contrasts the seeming maleness of the body (when seen from behind) with the dramatic femaleness of the face. Christina is also mistaken for a man by spectators in the diegesis (twice by Antonio and also by the patrons of the rural inn). Like descriptions of Garbo's own house, Christina's furniture is solid and "mannish."

However, as with reporters' descriptions of Garbo's off-screen masculinity, the film offers multiple lenses through which to interpret Christina's masculinity.[70] For one, the young Christina was crowned "King" of Sweden, and her masculine habiliments and comportment are, in a sense, the uniform for the job. Certainly sovereign power was often imagined to masculinize its female bearers (think of Queen Victoria or Catherine the Great). Additionally, the costume could connote an emancipated modern woman. Christina is educated, independent, and assertive, yet brings a "womanly" love of peace to her war-mongering male court. She could be read as an argument for women's increased participation in the political sphere. Finally, though, her psychological masculinity, particularly when paired with her affection for Sparre, fits her into the paradigm of the sexual invert described by sexologists like Havelock Ellis and writers like Radclyffe Hall. One of the film's taglines was particularly suggestive: "She was crowned King of Sweden . . . lived and ruled as a man . . . But surrendered to love."[71] Though the tagline may explicitly mean that Christina surrendered to her love for Antonio, the statement is actually somewhat ambiguous. If she "lived and ruled as a man," is it possible that she also loved "as a man"?

(a)

(b)

Figure 10.4 The first shots of the adult Christina.

The film allowed Christina/Garbo to be visibly lesbian, but contained this meaning in two key ways—through the romance with Antonio and, in a more complicated way, by cordoning off the same-sex desire to early modern Swedish history. Within the film, Christina's affection for Sparre is only a brief interlude between her casual fling with Magnus de la Gardie (Ian Keith) and her love for Antonio. Christina even has a reputation for promiscuity, as the inn patrons argue whether their queen has had six or nine lovers in the past year. Christina, in disguise, corrects them: "The truth is that the queen has had *twelve* lovers this past year. A round dozen!" Audiences may assume that these lovers were men, but this is never explicitly stated by the inn patrons or Christina herself.

This recuperation of Christina's attraction to Ebba is not entirely successful, though, for a number of reasons. For one, heterosexual endings never truly foreclose the spectacle of sexual deviance that occurs earlier on.[72] Furthermore, Garbo's off-screen persona and biography work against the recuperation that occurs narratively. Writings about Garbo had already established a sense that the masculine, solitary Garbo was the "real" Garbo and that the feminine woman who fell in love with men was the "performing" Garbo.

Furthermore, although the film depicts Christina progressing from masculinity and love for a female friend to femininity and love for John Gilbert (in the familiar logic of "all she needed was a good man"), spectators may have recognized that this trajectory in fact inverted Garbo's own biography. Garbo started her career in the United States with a more feminine style and a romance with Gilbert and then progressed to a more masculine style and rumors of romance with female companions. The fan press framed Garbo's casting of Gilbert as a gracious favor to an old friend down on his luck, not as a re-igniting of their romance. One *Photoplay* article, titled "'Now I Help You,' says Garbo to Gilbert," noted that "Garbo and her friend, Mrs. Berthold Viertel, had worked on the story—had, in fact, a well-organized scenario to present—before Jack was even mentioned for the part."[73] In this description, Garbo and Viertel are the inseparable pair and Gilbert is the odd man out.

Swedishness did not function the same way in *Queen Christina* as it did in the print discourse. Rather than being an alternative explanation, Swedishness permitted Christina/Garbo to be recognizably lesbian. However, it simultaneously relegated her to another time and place—early modern Sweden. Rather than operating as competing stories—is she lesbian or just Swedish?—Swedishness allowed Garbo to be whatever it was that Christina was. The movie's claims to historical authenticity through its publicity, sets, and costumes gave it permission to depict Christina's apparent sexual inversion, including one of the most explicit kisses between women in classical Hollywood. The more realistically the film could render its designated time and place, the more effectively it cordoned off Christina/Garbo from the time and place of the spectators. Publicity for the film boasted that "historical archives serve as guides for authentic sets in Queen Christina."[74] Indeed, the castle's vast interiors have a feeling of solidity and realness, as do the exterior shots of the forest that were clearly filmed in an outdoor location. The film was only concerned with the *impression* of realness, though, as the "historical advisor" hired by MGM was largely ignored.[75] Though the film altered the events of Christina's life to fit a conventional romance narrative, the film used publicity, sets, and costumes to convince spectators that it accurately re-created early modern Sweden. This claim to authenticity legitimized the inclusion of Christina's affection for Ebba while exiling it from the here and now.[76]

This sequestering to the past is complicated by some of the taglines used to advertise the film: "A Queen whose romance was as modern as tomorrow's tabloids" and "A seventeenth century maid who loved with a twentieth century madness."[77] Rather than sending Garbo into the past, these lines would seem to drag Christina into the present or even the future. Although the "modern" romance and "twentieth century madness" may explicitly refer to Christina's all-consuming love for Antonio, it could also describe her affection for Ebba. Indeed, same-sex love was often described as a troubling "modern" development. For example, Havelock Ellis and John Addington Symonds wrote in 1897 that "it has been stated by many observers who are able to speak with some authority—in America, in France, in Germany, in England—that homosexuality in increasing among women."[78] A 1914 vice investigation revealed that "members of the [male] homosexual community in southern California . . . referred to oral sex as the 'Twentieth Century Way.'"[79] However, even as lesbianism was described as hypermodern, it was simultaneously located in the distant past, most often in the times of Sappho, the decadent Roman empire, or the court of Marie Antoinette. There is thus a tension between the publicity around the film's historical authenticity, which projects Christina's same-sex desire into the distant past, and the film's taglines, which could suggest to some readers that this desire might exist in the present. Overall, however, the film and its publicity recuperated Christina's same-sex desire through the heterosexual teleology of the narrative and the claims to historical authenticity made by the mise-en-scène and publicity.

Through her star persona, Garbo created and popularized a new Swedish female type in America—the brooding, introverted woman. Though certain exposés of Garbo and even some recent biographies still trot out the timid immigrant and mannish peasant narratives, Garbo was more often explained through a newly legible kind of Swedish woman. Rather than working-class and dense, this type is regal and assertive—a step up the class ladder. It is a female version of an emergent Scandinavian male type—the brooding natural philosopher, embodied, in the film industry, by Lars Hanson and Victor Sjöström.

Swedishness provided an important cover for the press's insinuations of Garbo's lesbianism. *Queen Christina* provided a way to integrate Swedishness and lesbianism, creating a coherent persona for Garbo and a newly recognized Swedish type. Through this case study we can see how a star discourse can insist that a national and ethnic truth lies beneath the apparent placelessness or ethnic ambiguity of a Hollywood star. Furthermore, it is likely that Garbo's gender and sexual transgressions could not have been successfully exploited without the recuperative work of the Swedish stereotypes that were applied to her. In other words, Garbo's national border crossings seem to have facilitated and made palatable her significant gender and sexual crossings.

Notes

Ett stort tack to Arne Lunde and Christopher Oscarson, who shared their research materials and their enthusiasm with me, as well as to Mark B. Sandberg, Dean Krouk, and Amanda Doxtater. Thanks also to the Swedish Film Institute, the Margaret Herrick Library, the New York Library for Performing Arts, the Pacific Film Center, and the Scandinavian Studies Library at the University of California, Berkeley. Earlier versions of this essay were presented at Border Crossings: Rethinking Silent Cinema (Berkeley, CA, February 2008) and the Society for the Advancement of Scandinavian Studies (Seattle, WA, March 2010).

1. Roland Barthes, "The Face of Garbo (1957)," in *Mythologies*, translated by Annette Lavers (New York: Hill and Wang, 2001), 56–57; Diana McLellan, *The Girls: Sappho Goes to Hollywood* (New York: LA Weekly Books, 2000).

Other key works on Garbo include: Peter Matthews, "Garbo and Phallic Motherhood: A 'Homosexual' Visual Economy," *Screen* 29.3 (1988): 14–42; Jane M. Gaines, "The Queen Christina Tie-Ups: Convergence of Show Window and Screen," *Quarterly Review of Film & Video* 11.1 (1989): 35–60; Michaela Krützen, *The Most Beautiful Woman on the Screen: The Fabrication of the Star Greta Garbo* (Frankfurt: P. Lang, 1992); Brian Gallagher, "Greta Garbo Is Sad: Some Historical Reflections on the Paradoxes of Stardom in the American Film Industry, 1910–1960," *Images: A Journal of Film and Popular Culture* 3.7 (1997), http://www.imagesjournal.com/issue03/infocus.htm; Lucy Fischer, "Greta Garbo and Silent Cinema: The Actress as Art Deco Icon," *Camera Obscura* 16.3 (2001): 82–111; Arne Lunde, "'Garbo Talks!': Scandinavians in Hollywood, the Talkie Revolution, and the Crisis of Foreign Voice," in *Screen Culture: History and Textuality*, ed. John Fullerton (Bloomington: Indiana University Press, 2004), 21–40; and Melinda Szaloky, "'As You Desire Me': Reading 'The Divine Garbo' through Movement, Silence and the Sublime," *Film History: An International Journal* 18.2 (2006): 196–208.

On Garbo and lesbianism, see: Andrea Weiss, *Vampires and Violets: Lesbians in Film* (New York: Penguin Books, 1993), chap. 1; Terry Castle, *The Apparitional Lesbian: Female Homosexuality and Modern Culture* (New York: Columbia University Press, 1993), chap. 1; Axel Madsen, *The Sewing Circle: Hollywood's Greatest Secret: Female Stars Who Loved Other Women* (Secaucus, NJ: Carol Publishing Group, 1995); Patricia White, *Uninvited: Classical Hollywood Cinema and Lesbian Representability* (Bloomington: Indiana University Press, 1999), chap. 1; McLellan, *The Girls;* and Patricia White, "Black and White: Mercedes de Acosta's Glorious Enthusiasms," *Camera Obscura* 15.3 (2000): 227–264.

2. "Scandinavia Sends Another Star to America: Greta Garbo," *New York Times,* September 13, 1925, 5. Other examples include Mordaunt Hall, "A New Swedish Actress," *New York Times,* February 22, 1926, 14; and Barbara Miller, "Swedish Screen Star Gains International Experience," *Los Angeles Times,* August 22, 1926, C25.

3. Articles addressing this "foreign invasion" include "Americans Hold Own in Pictures," *Los Angeles Times,* December 6, 1925, C41; Ivan St. Johns, "The Foreign Legion in Hollywood," *Photoplay,* July 1926, 28; "Citizenry in Film Capital Topsy-Turvy," *Los Angeles Times,* January 2, 1927, C30; "Many Nationalities Represented," *Los Angeles Times,* July 27, 1927, B1; and "Victorious Invaders!," *Los Angeles Times,* May 6, 1928, J1.

4. See, for example, Vito Russo, *The Celluloid Closet: Homosexuality in the Movies* (New York: Harper and Row, 1987); Richard Barrios, *Screened Out: Playing Gay in Hollywood from Edison to Stonewall* (New York: Routledge, 2003); Weiss, *Vampires and Violets;* and White, *Uninvited.*

5. Irit Rogoff, "Gossip as Testimony: A Postmodern Signature," in *The Feminism and Visual Culture Reader,* ed. Amelia Jones (London: Routledge, 2003), 268–276; Gavin Butt, *Between You and Me: Queer Disclosures in the New York Art World, 1948–1963* (Durham, NC: Duke University Press, 2005).

6. Katherine Albert, "What Garbo Thinks of Hollywood," *Photoplay,* August 1930, 64–66, 120; 65. Another good example occurs in Adela Rogers St. Johns, "Garbo, the Mystery of Hollywood," *Liberty,* July 27, 1929, 15–22.

7. Albert, "What Garbo Thinks of Hollywood," 65.

8. Richard deCordova, *Picture Personalities: The Emergence of the Star System in America* (Urbana: University of Illinois Press, 1990), 98.

9. Ibid., 140.

10. A 1928 profile in the *Los Angeles Times,* for instance, writes that "Greta is probably a very lonely individual, still frightened, after two and one-half years in this country, where has poured down upon her, as an avalanche of snow in Sweden, the adulation of hundreds of thousands of fans." Muriel Babcock, "Greta Lacks Temperament," *Los Angeles Times,* January 8, 1928, C19.

11. On white slave films in the United States, see Shelley Stamp, *Movie-Struck Girls: Women and Motion Picture Culture after the Nickelodeon* (Princeton, NJ: Princeton University Press, 2000), chap. 2. On U.S. racial melodramas, see Linda Williams, *Playing the Race Card: Melodramas of Black and White from Uncle Tom to O. J. Simpson* (Princeton, NJ: Princeton University Press, 2001).

12. On Pola Negri, see Diane Negra, *Off-White Hollywood: American Culture and Ethnic Female Stardom* (London: Routledge, 2001), chap. 3. On Rudolph Valentino, see Miriam Hansen, *Babel and Babylon: Spectatorship in American Silent Film* (Cambridge, MA: Harvard University Press, 1991), chaps. 11 and 12; and Gaylyn Studlar, *This Mad Masquerade: Stardom and Masculinity in the Jazz Age* (New York: Columbia University Press, 1996), chap. 3.

13. I don't think Negri's "resistant ethnicity" is the sole reason her career in Hollywood ended. In the early 1930s, the studios laid off many actors as they tightened their belts and converted to sound. Negri's acting style was passing out of fashion and the typical career of female stars was not much longer than her eleven years in Hollywood. Like Garbo, Marlene Dietrich's German whiteness may have been able to recuperate her sexual transgressions, especially when she was placed in "exotic" foreign locales, as in *Morocco.* However, there are important differences between Dietrich's Germanness (associated with the free-wheeling cabaret life of Berlin) and Garbo's Swedishness (associated with drab peasant life). It would also be worthwhile to consider how the African-American Josephine Baker's cross-dressing performances were understood, though this gender deviance seems to have been considered part of her performance repertoire rather than a sign of lesbian identity.

14. Lunde mentions several examples on pages 42 and 43 of *Nordic Exposures.*

15. Krützen, *The Most Beautiful Woman on the Screen,* 66–71.

16. See, for example, St. Johns, "Garbo, the Mystery of Hollywood," 22; and Rilla Palmborg, *The Private Life of Greta Garbo* (Garden City, NY: Doubleday/Doran, 1931), 71.

17. Katherine Lipke, "Greta Garbo Most Alluring," *New York Times,* October 17, 1926, C19.

18. "[Director Clarence] Brown's chief difficulty in directing the star, he added, was in persuading her to do justice to a Swedish accent! . . . 'Just' and 'job,' in especial, were, likely as not, to emerge in the playbacks as either 'yust' and 'job,' or 'just' and 'yob.'" Philip K. Scheuer, "A Star Falls to Earth," *Los Angeles Times,* January 26, 1930, B15.

19. On the so-called pansy craze, see George Chauncey, *Gay New York: Gender, Urban Culture, and the Making of the Gay Male World, 1890–1940* (New York: Basic Books, 1995), chap. 11. On the national controversy over lesbian protagonists in the late 1920s and the incorporation of lesbianism in U.S. cinema culture, see my dissertation: Laura Horak, "Girls Will Be Boys: Cross-Dressed Women and the Legitimation of American Silent Cinema" (PhD dissertation, University of California, Berkeley, 2011), chap. 5.

20. Ronald Gregg, "Gay Culture, Studio Publicity, and the Management of Star Discourse: The Homosexualization of William Haines in Pre-Code Hollywood," *Quarterly Review of Film and Video* 20.2 (January 1, 2003): 81–97.

21. White, *Uninvited,* 13–14.

22. "Greta Garbo and Fifi Dorsay have become . . . ," [unknown newspaper], February 16, 1930, Greta Garbo clipping file, Margaret Herrick Library, Los Angeles (henceforth MHL).

23. "Young Star's Rapid Rise," *New York Times,* October 5, 1930, X3.

24. It is not entirely clear what became of this relationship. A July 1935 profile of Garbo claimed that Garbo broke off her relationship with D'Orsay after the girl mentioned their friendship to the press. Dorothy Calhoun, "Why Garbo's Friends Dare Not Talk," *Motion Picture,* July 1935, 28–29, 74. Diana McLellan and E. J. Fleming make the same claim in *The Girls* (2000) and *The Fixers* (2005), respectively, although they disagree on who leaked the information—McLellan says Salka Viertel, Fleming says MGM fixer Eddie Mannix. Indeed, four months after the "inseparable friends" article, D'Orsay denied the rumor to the *Los Angeles Record,* stating, "I have seen Greta Garbo maybe four times in my whole life. I like her. I theenk she is zee greatest of all actresses. You can tell everybody, Fifi say that. But I am not her . . . insepairable friend, even eef I would like to be" (quoted in McLellan, *The Girls,* 98). However, Garbo evidently did not cut off contact with D'Orsay after the February 1930 article, because the *New York Times* report about their friendship came out in October of that year and the *Hollywood Reporter*'s gossip columnist saw the women together at a speakeasy in 1932 (see n. 29 below).

25. [Unknown newspaper], December 22, 1931, Greta Garbo clipping file, MHL.

26. "Rambling Reporter," *Hollywood Reporter,* January 7, 1932, 2.

27. "The Lowdown," *Hollywood Reporter,* January 27, 1931, 2.

28. Alma Whitaker, "Celebrities Overflow Cinemaland's Rosters," *Los Angeles Times,* May 1, 1932, B19; "Garbo, Going Home, Leads Wild Chase in New York," *Los Angeles Times,* July 26, 1932, 1; Nancy Randolf, "Debut Party on Eve of Race at Belmont Park," *Chicago Daily Tribune,* August 21, 1932, G3.

29. Rilla Page Palmborg, "The Private Life of Greta Garbo," *Photoplay,* September 1930, 38–40, 90, 92; 38. Many of the most in-depth reports about Garbo were written by Swedish or Swedish-American people. These reporters suggested that only fellow Swedes could understand her and also that she only allowed Swedes to get close to her.

30. Ibid., 38–40, 90, 92; Palmborg, "Chapter Two of *The Private Life of Greta Garbo,*" *Photoplay,* October 1930, 36–39, 142–143; Palmborg, *The Private Life of Greta Garbo* (Garden City,

NY: Doubleday/Doran, 1931). Excerpts from the book were also published in newspapers, such as the *Milwaukee Journal* (October and November 1931).

31. Palmborg, "Private Life of Greta Garbo," 92.
32. Palmborg, "Chapter Two," 143.
33. Palmborg, "Private Life of Greta Garbo," 39.
34. Palmborg, "Chapter Two," 102.
35. Ibid., 142.
36. O. O. McIntyre, "New York Day by Day," *The Day,* New London, CT, November 4, 1931, 6. Other references to *The Captive*'s influence on violet sales include Edwin Schallert, "Bourdet Play at the Egan," *Los Angeles Times,* February 1, 1928, A11; and "Style Chats," *San Jose Evening News* (San Jose, CA), April 25, 1932, 11.
37. Chauncey, *Gay New York,* 125.
38. Palmborg, *Private Life of Greta Garbo,* 275.
39. I argue in my dissertation that mass-circulation newspapers and magazines spread these codes to increasingly large numbers of readers during the 1920s and 1930s. Thus, they would not have been confined to gay and lesbian readers. See Horak, "Girls Will Be Boys," chap. 5.
40. "Greta, Incognito, Plays Tag with Reporters," [unknown newspaper], December 28, 1931, and Harry D. Wilson, "Why Garbo Plays Dumb," *Motion Picture,* August 1931, 27, 93; both in Greta Garbo clipping file, MHL.
41. Palmborg, "Chapter Two," 142.
42. Albert, "What Garbo Thinks of Hollywood," 65; "Call Quiet Swedish Star 'Portrait of a Recluse,'" *Detroit Free Press,* May 4, 1930, Greta Garbo clipping file, MHL.
43. Palmborg, *Private Life of Greta Garbo,* 113.
44. Palmborg, "Private Life of Greta Garbo," 40.
45. St. Johns, "Garbo, the Mystery of Hollywood," 22.
46. Judith Mayne, *Directed by Dorothy Arzner* (Bloomington: Indiana University Press, 1994), 151–174.
47. Ibid., 156.
48. Palmborg, "Private Life of Greta Garbo," 39.
49. Ibid., 40.
50. Palmborg, *Private Life of Greta Garbo,* 180.
51. "The Reason Why Greta Garbo Will Not Talk," *Los Angeles Times,* August 9, 1931, B9.
52. Palmborg, "Private Life of Greta Garbo," 40.
53. "The Reason Why Greta Garbo Will Not Talk," B9.
54. Edwin Schallert, "Garbo Heads World's Strangest Secret Society," *Los Angeles Times,* August 27, 1933, A1.
55. Dorothy Calhoun, "Why Garbo's Friends Dare Not Talk," *Motion Picture,* July 1935, 28–29, 74; 29.
56. Or, in fact, only a very minor backlash, from writers such as Edwin Schallert and the hyperbolic Leonard Hall. See, for example, Schallert, "Garbo Heads World's Strangest Secret Society," and Hall, "Garbo-Maniacs," *Photoplay,* January 1930, 60–61, 106.
57. Marcia Landy and Amy Villarejo, *Queen Christina,* BFI Film Classics (London: British Film Institute, 1995), 68.
58. Ibid., 9.
59. As quoted in Landy and Villarejo, *Queen Christina,* 21.
60. Helen Dale, "Two Queens Were Born in Sweden," *Photoplay,* October 1933, 28–29, 113; 28.
61. Landy and Villarejo, *Queen Christina,* 73.

62. Dale, "Two Queens Were Born in Sweden," 28.

63. Castle, *Apparitional Lesbian,* chaps. 1 and 3; White, *Uninvited,* chap. 3.

64. White, *Uninvited,* xxi.

65. Jessie Burns, "Readers Report," Academy of Motion Picture Arts and Sciences file on *Queen Christina,* 1932, as quoted in Landy and Villarejo, *Queen Christina,* 16.

66. Salka Viertel, *The Kindness of Strangers* (New York: Holt, Rinehart and Winston, 1969), 175; "An Unusual Love Story," program for *Maedchen in Uniform, Maedchen in Uniform* clipping file, Billy Rose Theatre Collection, New York Public Library for Performing Arts, New York.

67. Viertel, *Kindness of Strangers,* 175.

68. James Wingate to E. J. Mannix, "Queen Christina," August 7, 1933, *Queen Christina* file, MPAA/PCA Collection, MHL.

69. Margaret Goldsmith, *Christina of Sweden: A Psychological Biography* (London: Arthur Barker, 1933), 68. For a perceptive analysis of the differing biographies of Christina Vasa, see Sarah Waters, "'A Girton Girl on a Throne': Queen Christina and Versions of Lesbianism, 1906–1933," *Feminist Review* 46.1 (1994): 41–60.

70. Jane Gaines argues that Adrian's costume design in this film synthesizes Garbo's masculine and feminine traits into a new configuration and deconstructs the nature of power and femininity as a "costume." Gaines, "The Queen Christina Tie-Ups," 40–54.

71. As quoted in Landy and Villarejo, *Queen Christina,* 19.

72. See Chris Straayer, *Deviant Eyes, Deviant Bodies: Sexual Re-Orientations in Film and Video* (New York: Columbia University Press, 1996), 42.

73. Martin Stevers, "'Now I Help You,' says Garbo to Gilbert," *Photoplay,* October 1933, 74.

74. *Queen Christina* pressbook, quoted in Landy and Villarejo, *Queen Christina,* 19.

75. Alexander Walker, *Garbo: A Portrait* (New York: Macmillan, 1980), 142.

76. Within the diegesis, the deviant Christina is exiled from the national space of Sweden to an unrepresented other space (the "Spain" of her imagination). Yet in the larger discourse around the film, Garbo is symbolically relocated from Hollywood/America to Sweden.

77. As quoted in Landy and Villarejo, *Queen Christina,* 19.

78. Havelock Ellis and John Addington Symonds, *Sexual Inversion* (London: Wilson and Macmillan, 1897), 99.

79. Sharon Ullman, "'The Twentieth Century Way': Female Impersonation and Sexual Practice in Turn-of-the-Century America," *Journal of the History of Sexuality* 5.4 (1995): 595–596.

11 Cosmopolitan Women

Marlene Dietrich, Anna May Wong, and Leni Riefenstahl

Patrice Petro

RECENT YEARS HAVE witnessed new scholarly interest in concepts and practices of cosmopolitanism across a range of disciplines, even as the term itself remains contested and elusive. As Steven Vertovec and Robin Cohen argue,

> For some contemporary writers on the topic, cosmopolitanism refers to a vision of global democracy and world citizenship; for others it points to the possibilities for shaping new transnational frameworks for making links between social movements. Yet others invoke cosmopolitanism to advocate a non-communitarian, post-identity politics of overlapping interests and heterogeneous or hybrid publics in order to challenge conventional notions of belonging, identity, and citizenship. And still others use cosmopolitanism descriptively to address certain socio-cultural processes or individual behaviors, values or dispositions manifesting a capacity to engage cultural multiplicity.[1]

Humanists as well as social scientists have explored the multiple meanings of the term "cosmopolitan," as evidenced by the variety of scholarly books published in the past decade and more that explore cosmopolitanism in relationship to nationalism, transnationalism, and globalization. Particularly noteworthy in this regard are Pheng Cheah and Bruce Robbins's collection of essays *Cosmopolitics: Thinking and Feeling beyond the Nation* (1998) and Kwame Anthony Appiah's monograph *Cosmopolitanism: Ethics in a World of Strangers* (2006).[2]

In everyday parlance, however, "cosmopolitanism" evokes neither philosophical nor social-scientific notions, but rather images and ideas derived from popular culture, especially as addressed to women. The "cosmopolitan," for example, is a popular cocktail consisting of vodka, Cointreau, cranberry, and lime (made famous on the television series *Sex and the City*). It also is the name of a glossy women's magazine, which was launched in 1886 as a "family magazine," only to become a specifically "women's magazine" in the 1960s, known for its advice to "cosmo girls" about sex, beauty, and fashion. If the relationship among women, popular culture, and cosmopolitanism is thus obvious, having entered the vernacular in our own time through an explicit address to women, why haven't more scholars explored it? Or, to ask a different but related question, is the popular association between women and cosmopolitanism rooted in the post-1960s era or can we trace the gendering of the term to an earlier time in the twentieth century, specifically to the histories and cultural practices of the 1920s and 1930s?

Rebecca Walkowitz's work on literary modernism provides some preliminary answers. Her 2006 book, *Cosmopolitan Style: Modernism beyond the Nation,* maintains that modernist literary style was crucial to new and gendered ways of thinking and acting, precisely because it engaged debates about politics large and small, from fascism, world war, colonialism, and displacement, to issues of privacy, intimacy, sexuality, and education—all in an effort to test and refine what counted as international politics and engagement.[3] Like Vertovec and Cohen, Walkowitz argues that there is not one meaning of cosmopolitanism, but several. She explains that "late twentieth century theories of cosmopolitanism rely on three, somewhat different traditions of thought." First, she says, there is "a philosophical tradition that promotes allegiance to a transnational or global community, emphasizing detachment from local cultures and the interests of the nation." Second, she points to "a more recent anthropological tradition that emphasizes multiple or flexible attachments to more than one nation or community, resisting conceptions of allegiance that presuppose consistency and uncritical enthusiasm." Finally, she mentions "a vernacular or popular tradition that values the risks of social deviance and the resources of consumer culture and urban mobility."[4]

While Walkowitz complicates any simple understanding of cosmopolitanism and attends to the gendered aspects of the term, her focus on literary modernism and the work of such writers as Oscar Wilde, Virginia Woolf, James Joyce, and Joseph Conrad precludes attention to the vernacular or popular traditions she mentions—those that value the risks of social deviance and rely on the resources of consumer culture and urban mobility. Another recent collection of essays, however, addresses this gap in our thinking by exploring the global circulation of the "Modern Girl" in films, advertisements, and illustrated magazines during the 1920s and 1930s, in cities from Beijing to Bombay, Tokyo to Berlin, and Johannesburg to New York. Edited by an interdisciplinary group of scholars at the University of Washington, including Alys Eve Weinbaum, Lynn M. Thomas, Priti Ramamurthy, Uta G. Poiger, Madeleine Yue Dong, and Tani E. Barlow, *The Modern Girl around the World* (2008) demonstrates how popular culture in the interwar years provides the material for "a study of globalization before the invention of the term" because it promoted a variety of cosmopolitan experiences for women—some emphasizing detachment from local cultures and the interests of the nation, others encouraging both, and still others promoting multiple or flexible attachments to more than one nation or community.[5] These experiences, moreover, incorporated dissenting as well as conforming individualisms, hyphenated identities as well as more collective and transnational forms of allegiance, across boundaries of gender, sexual orientation, class, race, ethnicity, and nation. As I will also argue, these cosmopolitan experiences are crucial to our understanding of border crossings across cinemas in the 1920s and beyond.

Indeed, *The Modern Girl around the World* project allows us to see how cosmopolitan and international styles were promoted via a gendered aesthetic rooted in the interwar years that was fundamentally visual in nature. As the editors explain, "lithography, photography, and cinema together enabled the easy reproduction of visual representations. These durable and cheap technologies were the sine qua non of the Modern Girl's near simultaneity since everywhere she became visible in and through these common media. Multinational corporations, film industries, international reporting and artistic circuits, and the distribution of illustrated magazines from metropoles to colonies, and from urban centers to remote locations, facilitated the circulation of a Modern Girl iconography."[6] This iconography, moreover, typified by "visual representations of women with bobbed hair, cloche hats, elongated bodies, and open easy smiles," could be found on all five continents in a range of visual media.[7] As historian Uta Poiger points out in her own contribution to the *Modern Girl* collection, this "cosmopolitan aesthetic" combined a range of racial markers, including blond hair, brown skin, and stylized eyes and embraced a variety of political projects including socialism and nationalism.[8] Her analysis of German popular magazines in the 1920s and 1930s reveals a marked transition from a cosmopolitan and internationalist identification with racial and ethnic "others" in the 1920s to the promotion of "nationalized female figures" in the 1930s. Her findings with respect to German popular culture resonate with my own research on the U.S. reception of cosmopolitan female film stars during the interwar years, which similarly troubled but also shored up conventions of race, sexuality, and gendered hierarchies—and, indeed, continue to provoke our thinking about women and cosmopolitanism today.[9]

To ground these ideas, I turn to a remarkable photographic image (see Figure 11.1). Taken in Berlin by the young Alfred Eisenstaedt, who was at the time an amateur photographer, it features three icons of twentieth-century cinema: Marlene Dietrich, Anna May Wong, and Leni Riefenstahl. Eisenstaedt's photograph depicts twenties-Berlin nightlife at its pinnacle. Here is a young, pre-Hollywood, sexually assertive Dietrich, looking directly into the camera, cigarette holder clenched in her teeth, hands on her hips, displaying an attitude at once defiant and playful. Here, too, is Anna May Wong, signature bangs framing her face, wearing a long string of pearls, a simple sheath dress, and a flower in her hair. Finally, there is Leni Riefenstahl, her arm around Wong's waist, more matronly

Figure 11.1 Marlene Dietrich, Anna May Wong, and Leni Riefenstahl in 1928 Berlin. Photograph by Alfred Eisenstaedt. Courtesy of the Getty Institute.

or at least fuller figured than the other women—soft hair, strained smile, in a shimmering, sequined gown. The photograph conjures up worlds of flappers and glamour and lost sophistication. It also documents the circulation of artists and actresses and film personnel, which connected Hollywood, New York, London, Paris, and Berlin.

But when and where in Berlin was the photograph taken, exactly? Historians and commentators list various dates for the photograph, ranging from 1928 to 1930.[10] Establishing the exact year, however, is crucial to understanding its circulation and consumption, especially within the quotidian contexts (the movie theater and the home-delivered photo magazine) that constructed a cosmopolitan imaginary in popular culture in the United States and abroad.

For instance, knowing that the photograph was taken early in 1928 (and not in 1930, as some commentators have claimed) allows us to understand something about the impulse behind its creation. This photograph was taken before Dietrich's performance in *The Blue Angel* (1930) crystallized her persona forever as a worldly woman with a cool and sardonic exterior. It was taken before Leni Riefenstahl became known as "Hitler's filmmaker," the much-celebrated and later vilified documentarist of *Triumph des Willens* (*Triumph of the Will;* 1935) and *Olympia* (1938). Riefenstahl was a rising German star in 1928, having gained a reputation on Berlin's dance circuit before she quickly moved into making a series of *Bergfilme,* or "mountain films," for Arnold Fanck. Indeed, at the time this photograph was taken, Wong was the only international film star among the three women pictured—which is why she occupies the center position in the image. As Yiman Wang has argued, Wong had made several films in Hollywood in the 1920s that garnered an international audience, appearing in stunning if still supporting roles (her breakthrough film was Douglas Fairbanks's *The Thief of Bagdad* in 1924, in which she played a Mongol slave). Frustrated with typecasting and the dearth of opportunities in Hollywood, Wong left for Europe in 1928. Like many female performers before and after her (notably, Josephine Baker and Louise Brooks), she was drawn to Berlin, which explains how she ended up in a photograph taken at a Berlin ball in 1928 with two up-and-coming but still national film stars.[11]

But if the 1928 date helps to explain why the three women appeared together in this photograph, it does not fully exhaust speculation about what it is they were doing there. A Berlin Film Museum newsletter, published in 2004, remarks on the revived interest in the Eisenstaedt photograph, especially on the occasion of what would have been Wong's one hundredth birthday. The newsletter reports on several new books about Wong but focuses on one in particular, Graham Russell Gao Hodges's *Anna May Wong: From Laundryman's Daughter to Hollywood Legend* (2004). The newsletter states: "This one we got hold of. It looks serious, it reads seriously but it has its unserious moments. The famous Eisenstaedt photograph showing Anna May, Marlene and Leni Riefenstahl at a ball in Berlin makes the author speculate: Did Anna May have a love affair with Marlene in Berlin; did Marlene have a love affair with Leni; couldn't it possible [*sic*] be that there was a 'ménage a trios' [*sic*]? All this leads to the question which we have to ask the author: What kind of sex life do you have to ask questions like this? Certainly not one that satisfies your needs" (February 5, 2004).[12]

If the caustic (verging on puritanically coy) tone of the newsletter suggests that "serious" historical matters hardly extend to sexual promiscuity, much less to affairs between women, then a question worth asking of the museum becomes, why highlight Hodges's study in the first place? To answer this question, I turned to Hodges's book to see exactly what he had written. There, he references the Eisenstaedt photograph as well as others taken at the time that featured Wong and Dietrich and claims that they "reveal an intimacy and warmth beyond a publicity friendship." "Were they lovers?" he asks, only to answer:

> Biographers of Dietrich have assumed so and stated that Dietrich seduced Wong because she was an exotic personality. . . . No doubts are ever expressed; rather, Anna May was simply another conquest for Dietrich, who used sex to express casual friendship rather than deeper affection. Wong's reputation suffered greatly from rumors of the liaison. It was one principal reason for the shame her family felt toward her career. There is no definite proof that Dietrich and Wong, or for that matter, Wong and Riefenstahl, were ever lovers. At the same time, Dietrich probably would not accept less of a public companion. Gay women were everywhere in Berlin, and arriving at a party with someone of the same sex simply proved one was modern.[13]

Although defensive on Wong's account and reluctant to explore the issue further, Hodges is on to something crucial. Being a lesbian or bisexual or gay in twenties Berlin (and outwardly appearing and performing as such) was not only proof that "one was modern" but also indicative of an emergent form of cosmopolitanism, especially for women, newly enfranchised and eager to think, dress, and perform beyond national borders and traditional identities. Speculations about Dietrich's or Wong's or Riefenstahl's sexuality are thus not merely or simply voyeuristic and prurient (or evidence of a deficient sex life). They also testify to the circulation of images that bind features of a cosmopolitan imaginary to popular culture and everyday life.

In this regard, it is important to note that while the Eisenstaedt photograph seems to document a singular moment in history, frozen in time, it is actually one of several photographs taken of the three women at a 1928 Berlin ball, all of which circulated well into the 1930s and beyond. As I have already described it, one photograph depicts a cigarette-smoking, hands-on-hips Dietrich, with a defiant, almost swaggering look at the camera. She is joined by Wong and Riefenstahl, and it is Riefenstahl who has her arm around Wong, which perhaps explains the speculation that they, too, were lovers. But there is another photograph of the threesome which seems nearly identical, although it is notable for its softening of Dietrich's image (see Figure 11.2). Here, Dietrich's cigarette and holder are gone; her arms are at her side and her shoulders are bare. She is smiling, and glances beyond the photographer taking the picture, as if addressing someone outside of the frame. Wong's arms are now fully in view, hands clasped in front, while Riefenstahl's eyes seem somewhat vacant, her smile hesitant, even forced.

What are we to make of this second, nearly identical photograph? As Dietrich biographers have pointed out, long before her big break with *The Blue Angel*,

Figure 11.2 A second photograph by Alfred Eisenstaedt of the three stars in 1928 Berlin. From the author's collection.

Dietrich often approached photographers with this request: "Take some pictures of me that will make me a star."[14] Clearly, as we now know, Eisenstaedt took multiple shots of the three women, who have obviously posed for the carefully constructed photograph. Dietrich's outfit in all of the photographs taken at the 1928 ball remains of special interest. A curator of the Dietrich collection at the Berlin Film Museum writes: "These were the years of costume balls. Everyone tried to outdo one another. Marlene arrived in her own creation of sexy pirate—assembled from odd pieces of her soon-to-be famous *Blue Angel* costume."[15] That her "sexy pirate" costume would serve to shape the image of the mature Lola Lola in the final sequence of *The Blue Angel* testifies to the distinctive self-fashioning Dietrich brought to the movies, derived from her everyday life in twenties Berlin.[16]

Needless to say, other actresses of the period also incorporated their own styles into their screen personas. For instance, Lea Jacobs points out that fashion was critically important to the success of Norma and Constance Talmadge's star images; "the fact that Schenck's studio was in New York," she explains, "meant that the Talmadges had access to the best fashion designers, such as Lucile and Mme. Francis, and this gave them an edge on the actresses restricted to shopping in the more provincial Los Angeles."[17] As Charlotte Herzog and Jane Gaines have argued, elite fashion magazines like *Vogue* and *Harper's Bazaar* insisted in the 1920s on Paris over Hollywood as a site for women's fashion—although this changed in the 1930s, as Hollywood forged new relationships between the motion picture industry and women's clothing industries (such as Macy's department store) and eclipsed Paris as the oracle of international style.[18] Lucy Fischer's work on Garbo and art deco aesthetics similarly shows how fashion played a central role in shaping and defining cosmopolitan culture—both for female stars and for their fans and audiences.[19] In the case of Garbo, an identification with art deco fashions (and her constitution as one of its pivotal emblems) helped to shape the international style of the new woman (a sophisticate who operated with sexual and social autonomy). As such, it offered a route to influence, emulation, and a form of democratization for women, perhaps especially for women of color, as they experimented with and performed conventionalized roles and identities.[20] Indeed, Wong also used her own personal Chinese wardrobe in her performances. As Yiman Wang has shown, while this was "meant to reinforce her affinity and natural fit with her racialized roles . . . one may argue that by clothing her characters in her own Oriental costumes, Wong did not simply naturalize her transitive bond with the roles but also highlighted the constructedness of the Orientalist fantasy. In these terms, she achieved two things at the same time: collaborating in the production of the Orientalist fantasy and, more important, highlighting her self-conscious fabrication and reification of the fantasy."[21]

But just as fashion changes with the times, so do the contexts in which it is experienced and viewed. In this respect, the second photograph from 1928 is of special interest because its depiction of a more demure Dietrich was reproduced in the 1930s, notably in the pages of *Look*, a general interest magazine known more for its photographs than its articles. *Look* was considered by some to be a second-rate version of *Life* magazine. Prior to World War II, *Look* also specifically addressed itself to "women in the news" and news for women and regularly covered issues of politics, ethnicity, and race.

Shirley Jennifer Lim is the first scholar to analyze the Eisenstaedt photograph as it appeared in a 1938 issue of *Look* magazine. In her recent book on Asian American women's public culture, *A Feeling of Belonging: Asian American Women's Public Culture, 1930–1960* (2006), she points out that extended coverage of Wong in this issue of *Look* established the star's hyphenated Chinese-American identity, while the inclusion of the Eisenstaedt image underscored her cosmopolitan woman-of-the-world status for American audiences—precisely because it showed her in the company of world-famous (and in the case of Riefenstahl, politically infamous) German stars. Here, the tension between nationalism and cosmopolitanism in thirties culture comes into view: Wong is both American and Chinese-American—a nationally hybrid star and woman of the world.

The March 1938 issue of the magazine featured Wong on the cover and included a two-page pictorial inside, under the title "The World's Most Beautiful Chinese Girl." As Lim explains:

> The pages devoted to Anna May Wong heightened her glamour, clothing and, not surprisingly, given the moniker the "world's most beautiful Chinese girl," her physical attributes. . . . Underneath a still of Wong from the British movie *Chu Chin Chow,* the pictorial explained that Wong had only recently visited China and that, despite her appearance, she was American-born. In case the point was not understood, the next picture clarified Wong's nationality as a sophisticated American citizen: "Anna May Wong, seen here with one of her brothers, Roger Wong, wears clothes unusually well. In 1934 the Mayfair Mannequin society designed her as the world's best-dressed woman. . . . An American citizen, she has given up plans to return to China."[22]

Lim traces Wong's career in Hollywood throughout the 1930s and shows how she ultimately moved beyond earlier exotic typecast characters to attain professional Chinese-American film roles. She argues that various historical shifts in the United States and in its relationship to China laid the groundwork for this transformation by changing the way that "Orientals" were portrayed on the screen. Lim points out, for example, that the Sino-Japanese War, triggered in 1931 by Japan's invasion of Manchuria, resulted in greater sympathy for China and Chinese-Americans. Wong took advantage of the improved image of China in the United States to pay a visit there, but Chinese audiences, or rather Chinese critics, did not embrace her, since Wong's modern cosmopolitanism was at odds with Chinese nationalism.

While changes in international relations had an impact on the representation of ethnic identities, so did the Production Code, which was established in 1930. Although the code did not prohibit ethnic stereotyping, there was a general stipulation, under the heading of "national feelings" (itself an interesting formulation), that the history, institutions, prominent people, and citizenry of all nations be treated fairly, a provision that clearly reflected the MPPDA's (Motion Picture Producers and Distributors of America) concern about the potential loss of foreign revenue from various national markets. According to Ruth Vasey, the Chinese government was keenly interested in Hollywood's depiction of Chinese characters at least as early as 1930.[23] After 1934, the Hays Office was sensitive to changing political relations between the United States and China, and Production Code Administration practices reflected this. The more interesting point, however, is that the new distinction that emerged between Japanese and Chinese "Oriental" characters was drawn on national lines. That is to say, "ethnic" specificity was defined in terms of "national" differences, which speaks to the broader issue of the emerging power of national distinctions in the 1930s.

Lim's analysis led me to the pages of *Look*, where I discovered that the infamous Eisenstaedt photograph had also appeared a year earlier in the inaugural, February 1937, issue of the magazine, this time featuring Nazi commander Hermann Goering on its cover. The caption accompanying the image of Goering, shown giving a bottle to a docile full-grown lion perched in his lap, reads: "Goering—Germany's Strange Bridegroom." Strange and perverse, indeed. Although not another word is written about Goering in this issue of the magazine, it nonetheless comments on the perversity of gender politics in Hitler's Germany. Recall that the 1938 issue of *Look* reprints the Eisenstaedt photograph to underscore Wong's international star status (because she appears with the now world-famous Dietrich and Riefenstahl, who, ironically, were relatively unknown and certainly not of Wong's stature when the photograph was taken). In 1937, by contrast, the Eisenstaedt photograph is enlisted not to call attention to Wong or Dietrich, but to an imminent danger in international politics—the threat of Hitler's Germany to world order as evidenced by its impact on these women's apparent friendships (see Figure 11.3).

The title above the image reads: "Parted by a Nation's Hatred . . . and Hitler . . . Hitler Won't Like This Picture—It Can Never Be Taken Again." In three columns that line up under each woman in the photograph, we learn the following (the text is brief and worth quoting in full):

> Marlene Dietrich. When Marlene Dietrich, Anna May Wong, and Leni Riefenstahl posed together for this remarkable photo a decade ago, Adolf Hitler had not yet come to power to tear apart their friendship. Today he hates two of them, bestows his favors on the third. In 1933, the Nazi government ordered German film artists abroad to return home to assist "in the great cultural upbuilding of Germany," by working for German film producers. Marlene declined to return, although Hitler warned German artists they would be regarded not only as unpatriotic but as actual traitors if they ignored the edict. Since then Marlene has never returned to Germany, because she says, "They don't like me." She insists she is Aryan. Her picture, "Song of Songs," was banned by Germany in 1934. Although Marlene was born and reared in Germany, she has sent her daughter to school in England.
>
> Anna May Wong. Anna May, recently received most hospitably in the Orient, would not be allowed on a Berlin stage because she is not "Nordic." Hitler regards "non-Aryan" blood as a menace to Germany, but this does not worry Anna May. She once turned down a plastic surgeon who offered to operate on her nose to make her look "more Nordic." She ran into the same prejudice which Hitler holds, however, when she was making pictures in England. In spite of her good acting, British censors ruled that the lips of an English actor touching the mouth of a Chinese woman would offend the British public. All scenes of Anna May kissing were cut out.[24]

While Dietrich receives three paragraphs and Wong two, Riefenstahl garners the greatest attention, with five paragraphs devoted to her story. (Under her

Women in the News Page 3

Parted by a Nation's Hatred . . . *and Hitler*

. . . Hitler Won't Like This Picture—It Can Never Be Taken Again

Marlene Dietrich

When Marlene Dietrich, Anna May Wong and Leni Riefenstahl posed together for this remarkable photo a decade ago, Adolf Hitler had not yet come to power to tear apart their friendship. Today he hates two of them, bestows his favors on the third.

Miss Dietrich and Miss Wong, almost unknown when this picture was taken, are now Hollywood stars, while Leni has become Hitler's favorite.

√

In 1933 the Nazi government ordered German film artists abroad to return home to assist "in the great cultural upbuilding of Germany," by working for German film producers. Marlene declined to return, although Hitler warned German artists they would be regarded not only as unpatriotic but as actual traitors if they ignored the edict.

√

Since then Marlene has never returned to Germany, because she says, "They don't like me." She insists she is Aryan. Her picture, "Song of Songs" was banned by Germany in 1934. Although Marlene was born and reared in Germany, she has sent her daughter to school in England.

Anna May Wong

Anna May, recently received most hospitably in the Orient, would not be allowed on a Berlin stage because she is not "Nordic." Hitler regards "non-Aryan" blood as a menace to Germany, but this does not worry Anna May. She once turned down a plastic surgeon who offered to operate on her nose to make her look "more Nordic."

√

She ran into the same prejudice which Hitler holds, however, when she was making pictures in England. In spite of her good acting, British censors ruled that the lips of an English actor touching the mouth of a Chinese woman would offend the British public. All scenes of Anna May kissing were cut out.

√

Leni Riefenstahl is Hitler's ideal of pure German womanhood: energetic, good at sports and mannishly attractive. She had his permission to make exclusive cinema recordings of the 1936 Olympic games and with this power made herself unpopular with foreign cameramen. They would be all set to take certain pictures, then receive orders that it was forbidden by Fraulein Riefenstahl.

Leni Riefenstahl

(Pronounced "Lane-i Ree-fen-shtahl")

She is 28, the daughter of a Berlin plumber. She began her career as a ballet dancer in Munich in 1923, progressed to the movies where she refused to have a double for dangerous film sequences. Fond of mountain climbing, she is nicknamed, not too prettily, "the Oily Goat."

√

Hitler liked her screen work, engaged her to advise him when he posed for photographs. On Leni, Hitler has showered countless special privileges enjoyed by no other woman.

√

Berlin gossips talked about her when she lived six months on Mount Blanc unchaperoned with eight men in a movie cast. She taught the men how to ski.

√

Of her relationship with Hitler, even the most skeptical quote an article on "Hitler's Love," which a Paris newspaper published, to the great annoyance of the German dictator. The article quoted Miss Riefenstahl as saying, "The Realmleader could not love except platonically." The paper was banned immediately from the newsstands.

Figure 11.3 Inaugural issue of *Look* magazine, February 1937. From the author's collection.

name in boldface type, the proper English pronunciation of her German name is provided, further reinforcing her foreign, German origins and suggesting, too, that hers was not a household name in the United States.) The text reads:

> Leni Riefenstahl is Hitler's idea of pure German womanhood: energetic, good at sports and mannishly attractive. She had his permission to make exclusive cinema recordings of the 1936 Olympic games and with this power made herself unpopular with foreign cameramen. They would be all set to take certain pictures, then receive orders that it was forbidden by Fraulein Riefenstahl. She is 28, the daughter of a Berlin plumber. She began her career as a ballet dancer in Munich in 1923, progressed to the movies where she refused to have a double for dangerous film sequences. Fond of mountain climbing, she is nicknamed, not too prettily, "the Oily Goat." Hitler liked her screen work, engaged her to advise him when he posed for photographs. On Leni, Hitler has showered countless special privileges enjoyed by no other woman. Berlin gossips talked about her when she lived six months on Mount Blanc unchaperoned with eight men in a movie cast. She taught the men

> how to ski. Of her relationship with Hitler, even the most skeptical quote an article on "Hitler's Love," which a Paris newspaper published, to the great annoyance of the German dictator. The article quoted Miss Riefenstahl as saying, "The Realmleader could not love except platonically." The paper was banned immediately from the newsstands.[25]

What is stunning about these captions is the way in which they document how popular culture in the United States became increasingly nationalized in the 1930s, accompanied by a shift from outward signs of bisexuality and gender play to heavily laden gender, racial, and national stereotypes. Marlene "insists she is Aryan," even though Nazi Germany considers her a traitor for refusing to return to the Reich. Anna May isn't allowed on German stages because "she is not Nordic" and refuses plastic surgery to make her appear so, but allegedly faces similar discrimination in Britain, where the censors prohibit ethnic mixing. Ironically, as scholars have pointed out, this sort of censorship of Wong's films did not occur in Britain but prevailed in the United States.

But in what is perhaps the most striking formulation in the text, Riefenstahl is described as "mannishly attractive." This is remarkable, because in twenties Berlin and in at least one of the Eisenstaedt photographs, it is Dietrich, and not Riefenstahl, who would seem to be the most mannishly attractive of all. She is the brazen, bisexual, troubling figure, donning a "sexy pirate" costume, cigarette holder in her teeth, defiantly addressing the camera. To be sure, Dietrich's image would be recast during World War II as the uniformed booster of the Allied cause, complete with WAC-like wide-shoulder military blouse, jacket, and tie. Clearly, cosmopolitan androgyny was recast and modified under the pressure of wartime politics. But this is 1937, before the outbreak of war, and here the Eisenstaedt photograph is enlisted to soften Dietrich's persona and feminize her image. The written text then does the work of masculinizing Riefenstahl, who stands as a larger symbol for a censoring, aggressive German nationalism. This nationalism is strikingly anti-feminine and asexual (not only in the person of Hitler, who loves platonically, but also in the example of Riefenstahl, who receives favors unlike any other woman and who lives unchaperoned with eight men on a film shoot but engages in nothing other than teaching them how to ski). It is evidence of a non-decadent modernity—and an allegiance to masculine values of authority, discipline, athleticism, and sport.

While by no means uncomplicated, the nationalizing trend in the world film industries throughout the 1930s is unmistakable. For instance, although Dietrich refused to return to Nazi Germany, her popularity there nonetheless continued unabated until the latter part of the 1930s, when she applied for U.S. citizenship and publicly renounced Nazi racial policies. Historian Erica Carter observes that "Third Reich stars were modeled in part as replicas of Hollywood's counterparts,

'Germanicised American' prototypes of a hybrid star aesthetic."[26] National differences, in other words, while understated, were nonetheless deeply understood by actors and audiences alike. As Carter explains: "Hollywood stars [in Germany] were admired for their spectacular quality, but denigrated also for their status as inauthentic, serially produced doubles or replicas, the manufactured products of a film industry oriented around profit, not art." Thirties German stars fashioned in Hollywood's image—actresses such as the Hungarian Marika Rökk or the Swedish-born operetta and revue diva Zarah Leander—therefore "always risked embodying a profane commercialism that the Third Reich film commentary abhorred. But German stars were uncanny doubles in a second, psycho-symbolic sense, representing as they did an imagined return to German screens of figures 'repressed' through mass purges and censorship."[27]

Dietrich's films were ultimately banned in Hitler's Germany. Wong's films were also banned in China for what was perceived to be their anti-Chinese sentiments. Even Leni Riefenstahl's 1935 film *Triumph of the Will,* which was a rousing success in Europe (receiving an award for the best foreign documentary at the Venice Biennale in 1935 and the gold medal and the Grand Prix from France in 1937) was widely banned in the United States. A purging and censorship of images occurred worldwide in the 1930s, as did a revision of the meaning and significance of images produced in earlier times. Perhaps most infamous in this regard was the Nazi exhibition *Entartete Kunst* (Degenerate art) in 1937, which exhibited over 650 confiscated paintings, sculptures, prints, and books from the collections of thirty-two German museums in an effort to incite revulsion against modernism and the "perverse Jewish spirit" penetrating German culture.

However much we prefer to distance ourselves from the more flagrant abuses of the past, history is never "just" history. Indeed, the meaning and significance of images produced in earlier times remains under revision, a process through which these stars and their symbolic status as emblems of national fictions continue to matter. Thus, I return for a final time to the 1928 Eisenstaedt photographs and to yet another recent Berlin Film Museum newsletter, which weighs in on the purported significance of the relationships between the two German stars. The newsletter reports:

> Yes, there are two photographs by Alfred Eisenstaedt taken at a Berlin journalists ball. . . . Marlene is chatting with Anna May Wong and Leni Riefenstahl. So what? Remember, the year is 1930 [this is incorrect, of course; the photograph was taken in 1928, and yet the newsletter further reports, with accuracy, that] *The Blue Angel* hasn't yet been shown in public and it took another three years till Hitler came to power. Leni Riefenstahl in her memoirs remembers that she suggested Marlene to Sternberg for the part of Lola Lola. The story was first published in the German yellow press journal "Bunte" in May 1987. Marlene cabled "Bunte" on June 3rd 1987: "The Riefenstahl story is

> so ridiculous that Sternberg and Remarque would have laughed themselves to death if they wouldn't be dead already." "Bunte" in reply offered Marlene as many pages as she would like to tell her version of the story. Awaiting the scoop of his lifetime "Bunte" editor told the biggest German daily "Bild" about the "Last showdown of the old ladies." But this did not happen as Marlene wisely did not react. In June 1991 Marlene was asked in a letter to meet Leni Riefenstahl. "She would like to clear up a few things which to the great regret of Leni Riefenstahl might be standing between her and you." Marlene just noted on that letter "Nazi." They never met again. The main difference between Marlene and Leni? Leni Riefenstahl fell for the Nazis, Marlene fought against the Nazis. And that sums up the whole story of their relationship. (August 16, 2002)

While presuming to be the final word on the matter, the newsletter's view of Dietrich and Riefenstahl has been further complicated by Elisabeth Bronfen, who briefly references the 1928 Eisenstaedt photograph in an essay on stardom and German nationalism.[28] For Bronfen, Wong remains a largely forgotten Chinese-American film star who merely anchors "the two women from Berlin" in the photograph; in a kind of uncanny foreshadowing, Bronfen points out that it is telling that Dietrich and Riefenstahl studiously avoid touching one another. Bronfen further argues that Dietrich and Riefenstahl "would go quite different ways within two years after this photograph was taken" but would nevertheless share much in common in the postwar German imaginary. Their movie star status, she argues, is now "invariably seen in light of the attitude they assumed towards National Socialism: Marlene Dietrich—an icon of seduction—was one of the few Hollywood stars to speak out against the Nazis. Leni Riefenstahl—an icon of the seduced—was, according to Goebbels, the only one who understood the National Socialist politico-cultural project so perfectly that she could be entrusted, without misgivings, with the job of documenting the Reich Party convention in Nuremberg in 1934 . . . as well as the Olympic Games in 1936."[29] Bronfen is less interested in the Eisenstaedt photograph itself than in Dietrich's and (mostly) Riefenstahl's careers after 1945. Her essay nonetheless underscores the ways in which images, especially star images, have been enlisted in symbolic fictions about women and nationalism as well as cosmopolitanism and political engagement.

In thinking about border crossings in silent and early sound cinema, this much is clear: the late 1930s ushered in an era of intensely nationalist rhetoric, despite the cross-cultural fluency of actors, directors, and audiences alike, who had long mastered a more complicated understanding of cinematic symbolism and meanings. The interwar years were nonetheless an auspicious time for thinking both within and beyond nationalism and for sustaining multiple and flexible attachments to more than one community. Women like Dietrich, Wong, and Riefenstahl were part of a deeply cosmopolitan cultural imaginary, forged in the interwar years and disseminated across various popular, everyday, and quotidian forms, such as the movies and illustrated magazines. They helped to shape our ideas about gender, nationalism, and popular culture, together with the sights and sounds of cultural mimicry and hybridity that remain with us today.

Notes

1. Steven Vertovec and Robin Cohen, eds., *Conceiving Cosmopolitanism: Theory, Context, and Practice* (New York: Oxford University Press, 2002), 1.

2. Pheng Cheah and Bruce Robbins, eds., *Cosmopolitics: Thinking and Feeling beyond the Nation* (Minneapolis: University of Minnesota Press, 1998); Anthony Appiah, *Cosmopolitanism: Ethics in a World of Strangers* (New York: W. W. Norton, 2006).

3. Rebecca L. Walkowitz, *Cosmopolitan Style: Modernism beyond the Nation* (New York: Columbia University Press, 2006).

4. Ibid., 9.

5. Alys Eve Weinbaum, Lynn M. Thomas, Priti Ramamurthy, Uta G. Poiger, Madeleine Yue Dong, and Tani E. Barlow, *The Modern Girl around the World: Consumption, Modernity, and Globalization* (Durham, NC: Duke University Press, 2008).

6. Ibid., 12.

7. Ibid., 13.

8. Uta G. Poiger, "Fantasies of Universality? *Neue Frauen,* Race, and Nation in Weimar and Nazi Germany," in *The Modern Girl around the World,* ed. Weinbaum et al., 317–345.

9. Significantly, Poiger stresses that while Nazi political propaganda narrowed the range of what was politically and ideologically acceptable vis-à-vis representations of the modern woman in the 1930s, even National Socialism could not completely contain the cosmopolitan aesthetic that emerged in the 1920s. As she explains:

> Representations of Modern Girls in cosmetics ads reveal how race and international relations manifested themselves in the everyday workings of capitalism. In the late 1920s at a time when modernization was not yet a widespread concept, universalistic fantasies and a business logic associated with a cosmopolitan aesthetic imagined growing numbers of people in increasing areas of the world in pursuit of the same commodities, including modern fashion and cosmetics, striving toward a standardized way of living. The Modern Girl was perhaps the central icon of such fantasies. National Socialism was one of many possible reactions against such visions. However, in spite of repeated denunciations of "Girlkultur," the Third Reich did not simply leave the Modern Girl behind. (340–342)

10. For instance, Hodges dates this image to the fall of 1928, whereas the 2002 Berlin Film Museum newsletter lists the date as early 1930. Graham Russell Gao Hodges, *Anna May Wong: From Laundryman's Daughter to Hollywood Legend* (New York: Palgrave Macmillan, 2004). Other sources identify the photograph as having been taken in January 1928 at the annual press ball at the Hotel Adlon, while still others identify the date as February 1928 at the Berlin Reimann ball. For a contemporary account of the Reimann ball, see Horst Wagner, "Harfenjule, Penner und Patentluden beim Zilleball," *Berliner Tageblatt,* February 4, 1928, 72–74, http://www.luise-berlin.de/bms/bmstxt99/9902novd.htm. Wagner writes, for instance: "An unusually large number of balls took place this first February weekend of 1928 in Berlin," but "the brightness of the ball scene increased on Saturday, February 4, 1928 at the costume festival, the so-called Reimann Ball." He continues:

> The *Vossische Zeitung,* which is normally reserved in matters of pleasure, even sent its famous feature writer "Sling," otherwise known as Paul Schlesinger, because the

> festival offered "the first opportunity to see the new Kroll'schen Festival Halls in action." The architecture there, according to Sling, is "seemingly modern, but not so much that it makes a person crazy." Actually, one could not really discern anything exactly, because the light kept changing—now blue, now pink, now yellow—great atmosphere." About the female ball goers, Sling reported, "One can say, each wore in average half of a costume. . . . One had only something made of black lace, just so that those she met would not catch cold." (translation mine)

For additional photographs of the three women at this event, see http://www.marlenedietrich.org.uk/id18.html. These additional photographs show the trio preparing for the formal portrait; one features Wong playfully adjusting Dietrich's cigarette holder, another shows Dietrich and Riefenstahl with their arms around an unidentified man, and still another depicts Dietrich posing alone in her "sexy pirate" costume.

11. Werner Sudendorf remarks on Dietrich's status at this time: "Professionally, 1928 and 1929 were successful years for Marlene. She had played central figures in five films, besides performing in plays and revues. And although her films were only received moderately well and her performances on stages outside of Berlin went almost unnoticed, she was no longer unknown. Nevertheless, she could not compete with the fame of an Olga Tschechowa, the beauty of a Brigette Helm or the class of a Louise Brooks. She was first choice for second-rate films." Werner Sudendorf, "Marlene Dietrich: Von Kopf bis Fuss / Marlene Dietrich: From Head to Toe," in *Filmmuseum Berlin*, ed. Wolfgang Jacobsen, Hans Helmut Prinzler, and Werner Sudendorf (Berlin: Deutsche Kinemathek and Nicolaische Verlagsbuchhandlung, 2000), 138.

12. FilmMuseum Berlin, *Newsletter*, no. 60 (February 5, 2004), www.marlenedietrich.org/pdf/News62.pdf. Various English-usage and spelling errors occur in the text, which appears to be an English translation from the original German text.

13. Hodges, *Anna May Wong*, 87.

14. Donald Spoto, *Blue Angel* (New York: Cooper Square Press, 2000), 37.

15. Jean-Jacques Naudet, Maria Riva, and Werner Sudendorf, comps., *Marlene Dietrich: Photographs and Memories* (New York: Random House, 2001), 6.

16. This was not the first or last time her style would find its way into pictures. Cast as an amoral flapper in a 1926 film, Dietrich arrived at the first rehearsal and was told by director Leopold Jessner that she looked just right in her own outfit—"silk trousers, a dark jacket and a startling monocle—and that she should wear all these in the performances" (Spoto, *Blue Angel*, 37).

17. Lea Jacobs makes this argument in her essay "The Talmadge Sisters: A Forgotten Filmmaking Dynasty," in *Idols of Modernity: Movie Stars of the 1920s*, ed. Patrice Petro (New Brunswick, NJ: Rutgers University Press, 2010), 71.

18. Charlotte Cornelia Herzog and Jane Marie Gaines, "'Puffed Sleeves before Tea-Time': Joan Crawford, Adrian and Women Audiences," in *Stardom: Industry of Desire*, ed. Christine Gledhill (New York: Routledge, 1991), 75–78.

19. Lucy Fischer, *Designing Women: Cinema, Art Deco, and the Female Form* (New York: Columbia University Press, 2003), chap. 4.

20. On this point, see Shirley Jennifer Lim, *A Feeling of Belonging: Asian American Women's Public Culture, 1930–1960* (New York: NYU Press, 2006), and Yiman Wang, "The Art of Screen Passing: Anna May Wong's Yellow Yellowface Performance in the Art Deco Era," *Camera Obscura* 20.3 (2005): 159–191. On Wong's career in Europe, with particular attention to the differences in the ways her films were received in Germany and Britain, see Tim Bergfelder, "Negotiating Exoticism: Hollywood, Film Europe and the Cultural Reception of Anna

May Wong," in *"Film Europe" and "Film America": Cinema, Commerce and Cultural Exchange 1920–1939,* ed. Andrew Higson and Richard Maltby (Exeter, UK: University of Exeter Press, 1999), 274–345.

21. Wang, "The Art of Screen Passing," 175.

22. Lim, *A Feeling of Belonging,* 77.

23. Ruth Vasey, *The World According to Hollywood, 1918–1939* (Madison: University of Wisconsin Press, 1997, 153. See also Yiman Wang's discussion of the Chinese government's ban of Harold Lloyd's *Welcome Danger* (1929) in this volume.

24. FilmMuseum Berlin, *Newsletter,* no. 42 (August 16, 2002), www.marlenedietrich.org/pdf/News42.pef.

25. Ibid.

26. Erica Carter, *Dietrich's Ghosts: The Sublime and the Beautiful in Third Reich Film* (London: British Film Institute, 2004), 16.

27. Ibid.

28. Elisabeth Bronfen, "Leni Riefenstahl und Marlene Dietrich: Zwei deutsche Stars / Leni Riefenstahl and Marlene Dietrich: Two German Stars," in Jacobsen, Prinzler, and Sudendorf, *Filmmuseum Berlin,* 169–190.

29. Ibid., 170.

Bibliography

Abbas, Ackbar. "Cosmopolitan De-scriptions: Shanghai and Hong Kong." *Public Culture* 12.3 (2000): 769–786.

Abel, Richard, Giorgio Bertellini, and Rob King, eds. *Early Cinema and the "National."* New Barnet, UK: John Libbey, 2008.

Adorno, Theodor. *Minima Moralia: Reflections from Damaged Life.* Translated by E. F. N. Jephcott. New York: Verso, 1978.

Allen, Robert C. "From Exhibition to Reception: Reflections on the Audience in Film History." *Screen* 31.4 (Winter 1990): 347–356.

Altman, Rick. "General Introduction: Cinema as Event." In *Sound Theory, Sound Practice,* 1–14. New York: Routledge, 1992.

Ames, Eric. *Carl Hagenbeck's Empire of Entertainments.* Seattle: University of Washington Press, 2008.

Amladi, Parag. *New Apprehensions: The Ambivalence of Modernity in Early Indian Cinema.* PhD dissertation, New York University, 1997.

Amy de la Bretèque, François, Michel Cade, Angel Quintana Morraja, and Jordi Pons I Busquet, eds. *Les cinémas périphériques dans la périod des premiers temps / Peripheral Early Cinemas.* Perpignan, France: University of Perpigan Press, 2010.

Anderson, Benedict. *Imagined Communities: Reflections on the Origin and Spread of Nationalism.* New York: Verso, 1991.

Andrew, Dudley. "Time Zones and Jet Lag: The Flows and Phases of World Cinema." In *World Cinemas, Transnational Perspectives,* edited by Nataša Ďurovičová and Kathleen Newman, 59–90. New York: Routledge, 2010.

Appadurai, Arjun. "Disjuncture and Difference in the Global Cultural Economy." *Public Culture* 2.2 (1990): 1–24.

———. *Modernity at Large: Cultural Dimensions of Globalization.* Minneapolis: University of Minnesota Press, 1996.

Appiah, Anthony. *Cosmopolitanism: Ethics in a World of Strangers.* New York: W. W. Norton, 2006.

Arondekar, Anjali. *For the Record: On Sexuality and the Colonial Archive in India.* Durham, NC: Duke University Press, 2009.

Atabaki, Touraj, and Zürcher, Erik. *Men of Order: Authoritarian Modernization under Atatürk and Reza Shah.* London: I. B. Tauris, 2004.

Balan, Canan. "Wondrous Pictures in Istanbul: From Cosmopolitanism to Nationalism." In *Early Cinema and the "National,"* edited by Richard Abel, Giorgio Bertellini, and Rob King, 172–184. New Barnet, UK: John Libbey, 2008.

Balázs, Béla. *Theory of the Film: Character and Growth of a New Art.* Translated by Edith Bone. New York: Dover, 1970.

Balio, Tino, ed. *The American Film Industry.* Madison: University of Wisconsin Press, 1985.

Bao, Weihong. "From Pearl White to White Rose Woo: Tracing the Vernacular Body of *Nüxia* in Chinese Silent Cinema, 1927–1931." *Camera Obscura* 20.3 (2005): 193–231.

Barnouw, Erik, and S. Krishnaswamy. *The Indian Film*. New York: Oxford University Press, 1980.

Barrios, Richard. *Screened Out: Playing Gay in Hollywood from Edison to Stonewall*. London: Routledge, 2003.

Barthes, Roland. "The Face of Garbo (1957)." In *Mythologies*, translated by Annette Lavers, 56–57. New York: Hill and Wang, 2001.

Bean, Jennifer M. "Charles Chaplin: The Object Life of Mass Culture." In *Flickers of Desire*, 242–263.

———, ed. *Flickers of Desire: Movie Stars of the 1910s*. New Brunswick, NJ: Rutgers University Press, 2011.

———. "Technologies of Early Stardom and the Extraordinary Body." *Camera Obscura* 16.3 (2001): 9–57.

Bergfelder, Tim. "Negotiating Exoticism: Hollywood, Film Europe and the Cultural Reception of Anna May Wong." In Higson and Maltby, *"Film Europe" and "Film America,"* 274–345.

Bertellini, Giorgio. "Introduction." In "Early Italian Cinema." Special issue, *Film History* 12.3 (2000): 235–239.

———. "Italian Imageries, Historical Feature Films, and the Fabrication of Italy's Spectators in Early 1900s New York." In Maltby and Stokes, *American Movie Audiences*, 29–45.

———. *Italy in Early American Cinema: Race, Landscape, and the Picturesque*. Bloomington: Indiana University Press, 2010.

———, ed. *Silent Italian Cinema: A Reader*. Bloomington: Indiana University Press, 2013.

Bhabha, Homi K. "The Other Question: The Stereotype and Colonial Discourse." In *The Sexual Subject: A Screen Reader in Sexuality*, 312–331. New York: Routledge, 1992.

———. *The Location of Culture*. London: Routledge, 2004.

Bhaskar, Ira, and Richard Allen. *Islamicate Cultures of Bombay Cinema*. New Delhi: Tulika, 2009.

Bhaumik, Kaushik. "Heroes in the Metropolis: Imagining the Romantic Individual in Early Bombay Cinema." In *Beyond the Boundaries of Bollywood: The Many Forms of Hindi Cinema*, edited by Rachel Dwyer and Jerry Pinto, 30–52. New Delhi: Oxford University Press, 2010.

Biswas, Moinak. "Mourning and Blood Ties: Macbeth in Mumbai." *Journal of the Moving Image*, no. 5 (December 2006): 78–85.

Björkin, Mats. *Amerikanism, bolsjevism och korta kjolar*. Stockholm: Aura, 1998.

Bloch, Ernst. "Nonsynchronism and the Obligation to Its Dialectics." *New German Critique*, no. 11 (1977): 22–38.

Bloom, Peter. *French Colonial Documentary: Mythologies of Humanitarianism*. Minneapolis: University of Minnesota Press, 2008.

Bois, Yve-Alain. "Introduction. Sergei Eisenstein: Montage and Architecture." Translated by Michael Glenny. *Assemblage*, no. 10 (December 1989): 110–131.

Bottomore, Stephen. "'She's Just Like My Granny, Where's Her Crown?': Monarchs and Movies, 1896–1916." In *Celebrating 1895: The Centenary of Cinema*, edited by John Fullerton, 172–181. Sydney: John Libbey, 1998.

———. "The Sultan and the Cinematograph." *Early Popular Visual Culture* 6.2 (2008): 121–144.

Bowser, Elaine. *The Transformation of Cinema, 1907–1915*. Berkeley: University of California Press, 1990.
Bratia Vasilievy. Sobranie sochinenii v trekh tomakh [The Vasiliev brothers. Collected works in three volumes]. Moscow: Iskusstvo, 1981.
Bronfen, Elisabeth. "Leni Riefenstahl und Marlene Dietrich: Zwei deutsche Stars / Leni Riefenstahl and Marlene Dietrich: Two German Stars." In Jacobsen, Prinzler, and Sudendorf, *Filmmuseum Berlin*, 169–190.
Brummet, Palmira. *Image and Imperialism in the Ottoman Revolutionary Press, 1908–1911*. Albany: SUNY Press, 2000.
Bruno, Giuliana. *Atlas of Emotion: Journeys in Art, Architecture and Film*. London: Verso, 2007.
———. *Streetwalking on a Ruined Map: Cultural Theory and the City Films of Elvira Notari*. Princeton, NJ: Princeton University Press, 1993.
Bull, Sofia, and Astrid Söderbergh Widding, eds. *Not So Silent: Women in Cinema before Sound*. Stockholm: Acta Universitatis Stockholmiensis, 2010.
Butler, Judith. *Gender Trouble: Feminism and the Subversion of Identity*. New York: Routledge, 1990.
Butt, Gavin. *Between You and Me: Queer Disclosures in the New York Art World, 1948–1963*. Durham, NC: Duke University Press, 2005.
Callahan, Vicki, ed. *Reclaiming the Archive: Feminism and Film History*. Detroit: Wayne State University Press, 2010.
Carter, Erica. *Dietrich's Ghosts: The Sublime and the Beautiful in Third Reich Film*. London: British Film Institute, 2004.
Castle, Terry. *The Apparitional Lesbian: Female Homosexuality and Modern Culture*. New York: Columbia University Press, 1993.
Ceram, C. W. *Archaeology of the Cinema*. New York: Harcourt Brace, 1965.
Chakrabarty, Dipesh. *Provincializing Europe: Postcolonial Thought and Historical Difference*. Princeton, NJ: Princeton University Press, 2000.
Chakravarty, Gautam. *The Indian Mutiny and the British Imagination*. Cambridge, UK: Cambridge University Press, 2005.
Chaudhary, Zahid. "Phantasmagoric Aesthetics: Colonial Violence and the Management of Perception." *Cultural Critique* 59 (Winter 2005): 63–119.
Chauncey, George. *Gay New York: Gender, Urban Culture, and the Making of the Gay Male World, 1890–1940*. New York: Basic Books, 1995.
Cheah, Pheng, and Bruce Robbins, eds. *Cosmopolitics: Thinking and Feeling beyond the Nation*. Minneapolis: University of Minnesota Press, 1998.
Chiba Nobuo. "Engeki eiga no jūnen." In *Sekai no eiga sakka 31: Nihon eigashi*. Tokyo: Kinema Junpōsha, 1976.
Chisolm, Brad. "Reading Intertitles." *Journal of Popular Film and Television* 15.3 (1987): 137–142.
Christensen, Thomas G. "Nordisk Films Kompagni and the First World War." In *Nordic Explorations: Film before 1930*, edited by John Fullerton and Jan Olsson, 12–18. Sydney: John Libbey, 1999.
Conley, Tom. *Cartographic Cinema*. Minneapolis: University of Minnesota Press, 2007.
Cook, David. *A History of Narrative Film*. New York: W. W. Norton, 2008.

Cornell, Daniel: "Stealing the Spectacle: Gay Audiences and the Queering of Douglas Fairbanks's Body." *Velvet Light Trap* 42 (Fall 1998): 76–90.

Crafton, Donald. *The Talkies: American Cinema's Transition to Sound, 1926–1931.* Berkeley: University of California Press, 1999.

Croy, Homer. "Shadows of Asia." *Photoplay* 11 (1917): 61–63.

Curtis, Scott. "Douglas Fairbanks: Icon of Americanism." In Bean, *Flickers of Desire,* 218–241.

da Cunha, Uma. "Jairaj." *Cinema Vision* 1.1 (1980): 81–85.

Dabashi, Hamid. *Close-Up: Iranian Cinema, Past, Present and Future.* New York: Verso, 2001.

Dahlquist, Marina, ed. *Exporting Perilous Pauline: Pearl White and the Serial Film Craze.* Urbana: University of Illinois Press, 2013.

Dall'Asta, Monica. "On Frieda Klug, Pearl White, and Other Traveling Women Film Pioneers." *Framework: The Journal of Cinema and Media* 51.2 (Fall 2010): 310–323.

Dalle Vacche, Angela. *Diva: Defiance and Passion in Early Italian Cinema.* Austin: University of Texas Press, 2008.

de Certeau, Michel. *The Practice of Everyday Life.* Translated by Steven Rendall. Berkeley: University of California Press, 1984.

de Grazia, Victoria. *Irresistible Empire: America's Advance through 20th-Century Europe.* Cambridge, MA: Belknap Press of Harvard University Press, 2005.

de la O Castellanos, Ana Maria. "Las vivencias cinematográficas en la memoria de los pueblos de Zapopan y Unión de Tula." In *Microhistorias del cine en México,* edited by Eduardo de la Vega Alfaro, 153–169. Guadalajara: Universidad de Guadalajara; Mexico City: UNAM / IMCINE / Cineteca Nacional / Instituto Mora, 2000.

de Téramond, Guy. *Le tigre sacré.* Paris: Les Romans Cinéma, 1920.

deCordova, Richard. *Picture Personalities: The Emergence of the Star System in America.* Urbana: University of Illinois Press, 1990.

Di Bello, Patrizia. *Women's Albums and Photography in Victorian England: Ladies, Mothers and Flirts.* Aldershot, UK: Ashgate, 2007.

Ding, Loni. "Strangers of an Asian American Filmmaker." In *Moving the Image: Independent Asian Pacific American Media Arts,* edited by Russell Leung, 46–59. Los Angeles: UCLA Asian American Studies Center, 1991.

Dōjin Shiin. *Katsudō shashinjutsu jizai.* Tokyo: Daigakukan, 1903.

Du Bois, W. E. B. *The Souls of Black Folk.* 1903. New York: Tribeca Books, 2013.

Dulac, Nicholas. "Distribution sérielle et synchronization du spectateur aux premiers temps du cinéma." In *Networks of Entertainment: Early Film Distribution 1895–1915,* edited by Frank Kessler and Nanna Verhoeff, 167–179. Eastleigh, UK: John Libbey, 2007.

Ďurovičová, Nataša. "*Los Toquis,* or Urban Babel." *Rouge* 6 (2005). http://www.rouge.com.au/7/urban_babel.html.

———. "Vector, Flow, Zone: Towards a History of Cinematic *Translatio.*" In *World Cinemas, Transnational Perspectives,* edited by Nataša Ďurovičová and Kathleen Newman, 90–120. New York: Routledge, 2010.

Dyer, Richard. *Stars.* London: British Film Institute, 1979.

Eisenstein, Sergei. "Dickens, Griffith and Ourselves." In *S. M. Eisenstein: Selected Works,* Vol. 3, *Writings 1934–47,* translated and edited by Richard Taylor, 193–239. London: British Film Institute; Bloomington: Indiana University Press, 1996.

———. *Film Form*. Edited and translated by Jay Leyda. New York: Harcourt, Brace and World, 1949.
Ellis, Havelock, and John Addington Symonds. *Sexual Inversion*. London: Wilson and Macmillan, 1897.
Elsaesser, Thomas. "The New Film History as Media Archaeology." *Cinemas* 14.2–3 (Spring 2004): 75–117.
———. "The "Return" of 3-D: On Some of the Logics and Genealogies of the Image in the Twenty-First Century." *Critical Inquiry*, no. 39 (Winter 2013): 217–246.
Engberg, Marguerite. *Dansk Stumfilm: De Store År*. 2 vols. Copenhagen: Rhodos, 1977.
———. "Plagiarism and the Birth of the Danish Multi-Reel Film." In *100 Years of Nordisk Film*, edited by Lisbeth Richter Larsen and Dan Nissen, 73–79. Copenhagen: Danish Film Institute, 2006.
———. *Registrant over Danske Film 1896–1914*. Vol. 1. Copenhagen: Institut for Filmvidenskab, 1977.
Fabian, Johannes. *Time and the Other: How Anthropology Makes Its Object*. New York: Columbia University Press, 1983.
Fanon, Franz. *Black Skin, White Masks*. New York: Grove Press, 2008.
Fischer, Lucy. *Designing Women: Cinema, Art Deco, and the Female Form*. New York: Columbia University Press, 2003.
———. "Greta Garbo and Silent Cinema: The Actress as Art Deco Icon." *Camera Obscura* 16.3 (2001): 82–111.
Floor, Willem. *The History of Theater in Iran*. Washington, DC: Mage, 2005.
Florin, Bo. *Den nationella stilen: Studier i den svenska filmens guldålder*. Stockholm: Aura, 1997.
Forslund, Bengt. *Victor Sjöström: His Life and His Work*. New York: New York Zoetrope, 1988.
Foucault, Michel. *The Archaeology of Knowledge and the Discourse on Language*. Translated by A. M. Sheridan Smith. New York: Pantheon, 1972.
———. "Of Other Spaces." Translated by Jay Miskowiec. *Diacritics* 16 (1986): 22–27. http://www.jstor.org/stable/464648.
Friedberg, Anne. *The Virtual Window: From Alberti to Microsoft*. Cambridge, MA: MIT Press, 2006.
———. *Window Shopping: Cinema and the Postmodern*. Berkeley: University of California Press, 1993.
Gad, Urban. *Filmen: Dens Midler og Maal*. Copenhagen: Gyldendal, 1918.
Gaines, Jane M. *Fire and Desire: Mixed-Race Movies in the Silent Era*. Chicago: University of Chicago Press, 2001.
———. "Micheaux's *Within Our Gates:* Now Available in Videotape." *Oscar Micheaux Society Newsletter* 3 (Summer 1994).
———. "The Queen Christina Tie-Ups: Convergence of Show Window and Screen." *Quarterly Review of Film & Video* 11.1 (1989): 35–60.
Gallagher, Brian. "Greta Garbo Is Sad: Some Historical Reflections on the Paradoxes of Stardom in the American Film Industry, 1910–1960." *Images: A Journal of Film and Popular Culture* 3.7 (1997). http://www.imagesjournal.com/issue03/infocus.htm.
Gerow, Aaron. *Visions of Japanese Modernity: Articulations of Cinema, Nation, and Spectatorship, 1895–1925*. Berkeley: University of California Press, 2010.

Ghaffary, Farrokh. "Cinema I: History of Cinema in Persia." In *Encyclopedia Iranica Online,* 2005. http://www.iranicaonline.org/articles/cinema-i.

———. *Le cinéma en Iran.* Tehran: Conseil de la Culture et des Arts, Centre d'Étude et de la Coordination Culturelle, 1973.

Goldsmith, Margaret. *Christina of Sweden: A Psychological Biography.* London: Arthur Barker, 1933.

Gordon, Sophie. "A City of Mourning: The Representation of Lucknow, India in Nineteenth-Century Photography." *History of Photography* 30.1 (Spring 2006): 80–91.

Gregg, Ronald. "Gay Culture, Studio Publicity, and the Management of Star Discourse: The Homosexualization of William Haines in Pre-Code Hollywood." *Quarterly Review of Film and Video* 20.2 (January 1, 2003): 81–97.

Gregson, Nicky, and Louise Crewe. *Second-Hand Cultures.* Oxford, UK: Berg, 2003.

Grieveson, Lee, and Peter Krämer. *The Silent Cinema Reader.* London: Routledge, 2004.

Grieveson, Lee, and Haidee Wasson, eds. *Inventing Film Studies.* Durham, NC: Duke University Press, 2008.

Guha, Ranajit. "The Prose of Counter-Insurgency." In *Selected Subaltern Studies,* edited by Ranajit Guha and Gayatri Spivak, 45–86. New York: Oxford University Press, 1988.

Gunning, Tom. "An Aesthetic of Astonishment: Early Film and the (In)credulous Spectator." In *Viewing Positions: Ways of Seeing Film,* edited by Linda Williams, 124–133. New Brunswick, NJ: Rutgers University Press, 1994.

———. "Attractions, Detection, Disguise: *Zigomar,* Jasset, and the History of Film Genres." *Griffithiana* 47 (May 1993): 137–156.

———. "The Cinema of Attraction: Early Film, Its Spectator and the Avant-Garde." *Wide Angle* 8.3–4 (1986): 63–70.

———. "Modernity and Cinema: A Culture of Shocks and Flows." In *Cinema and Modernity,* edited by Murray Pomerance, 297–315. New Brunswick, NJ: Rutgers University Press, 2006.

———. "Tracing the Individual Body: Photography, Detectives, and Early Cinema." In *Cinema and the Invention of Modern Life,* edited by Leo Charney and Vanessa R. Schwartz, 15–45. Berkeley: University of California Press, 1995.

———. "The Whole World within Reach: Travel Images without Borders." In Ruoff, *Virtual Voyages,* 25–41.

Gustafson, Anita Olson. "Swedes." In *Encyclopedia of Chicago.* Chicago: Chicago History Museum and the Newberry Library, 2005. http://encyclopedia.chicagohistory.org/pages/1222.html.

Gustafsson, Tommy. *En fiende till civilisationen: Manlighet, genusrelationer, sexualitet och rasstereotyper i svensk filmkultur under 1920-talet.* Lund, Sweden: Sekel, 2007.

Hagener, Malte. "Programming Attractions: Avant-Garde Exhibition Practices in the 1920s and 1930s." In *The Cinema of Attractions Reloaded,* edited by Wanda Strauven, 265–279. Amsterdam: Amsterdam University Press, 2006.

Hannerz, Ulf. "Cosmopolitans and Locals in World Culture." In *Global Culture: Nationalism, Globalization and Modernity,* edited by Mike Featherstone, 237–252. London: Sage, 1990.

Hansen, Kathryn. "Making Women Visible: Gender and Race Cross-Dressing in the Parsi Theatre." *Theatre Journal* 51.2 (May 1999): 127–147.

Hansen, Miriam. *Babel and Babylon: Spectatorship in American Silent Film.* Cambridge, MA: Harvard University Press, 1991.

———. "Fallen Women, Rising Stars, New Horizons: Shanghai Silent Film as Vernacular Modernism." *Film Quarterly* 54.1 (Fall 2000): 10–22.

———. "The Mass Production of the Senses: Classical Cinema as Vernacular Modernism." *Modernism/Modernity* 6.2 (1999): 59–77.

———. "The Mass Production of the Senses: Classical Cinema as Vernacular Modernism." In *Reinventing Film Studies*, edited by Christine Gledhill and Linda Williams, 332–350. London: Arnold; New York: Oxford University Press, 2000.

———. "Universal Language and Democratic Culture: Myths of Origin in Early American Cinema." In *Myth and Enlightenment in American Literature,* edited by Dieter Miendl and Friedrich W. Horlacher, 321–351. Erlangen: Erlanger Forschungen, 1985.

———. "Vernacular Modernism: Tracking Cinema on a Global Scale." In *World Cinemas, Transnational Perspectives,* edited by Nataša Ďurovičová and Kathleen Newman, 287–314. New York: Routledge, 2009.

Hase, Masato. "Cinemaphobia in Taisho Japan: Zigomar, Delinquent Boys and Somnambulism." *Iconics* 4 (1998): 87–100.

Heinink, Juan B., and Robert G. Dickson. *Cita en Hollywood: Antología de las películas norteamericanas habladas en español.* Bilbao, Spain: Ediciones Mensajero, 1990.

Hershfield, Joanne. "Visualizing the Modern Mexican Woman: *Santa* and Cinematic Nation-Building." In *Reclaiming the Archive: Feminism and Film History,* edited by Vicki Callahan, 329–344. Detroit: Wayne State University Press, 2010.

Herzog, Charlotte Cornelia, and Jane Marie Gaines. "'Puffed Sleeves before Tea-Time': Joan Crawford, Adrian and Women Audiences." In *Stardom: Industry of Desire,* edited by Christine Gledhill, 74–91. New York: Routledge, 1991.

Higson, Andrew, and Richard Maltby, eds. *"Film Europe" and "Film America": Cinema, Commerce and Cultural Exchange, 1920–1939.* Exeter, UK: University of Exeter Press, 1999.

Hjort, Mette, and Scott MacKenzie, eds. *Purity and Provocation: Dogma 95.* London: British Film Institute, 2003.

Hjort, Mette, and Duncan Petrie, eds. *The Cinema of Small Nations.* Bloomington: Indiana University Press, 2007.

Hodges, Graham Russell Gao. *Anna May Wong: From Laundryman's Daughter to Hollywood Legend.* New York: Palgrave Macmillan, 2004.

Holmberg, Folke. "Un exemple: L'avenir du film suédois." *Cahiers du mois* 2 (September/October 1925): 208–211.

hooks, bell. "The Oppositional Gaze: Black Female Spectators." In Jones, *Feminism and Visual Culture Reader,* 94–104.

Hoover, Herbert. "American Relations." *Hispania* 10.3 (May 1927): 129–138.

Horak, Laura. "Girls Will Be Boys: Cross-Dressed Women and the Legitimation of American Silent Cinema." PhD dissertation, University of California, Berkeley, 2011.

Imamura Kanae. *Eiga sangyō.* Tokyo: Yūhikaku, 1960.

Iwasaki Akira. "Senden, sendō shūdan to shite no eiga" [Film as a means of propaganda and agitation]. In *Eiga to shihon shugi* [Film and capitalism]. Tokyo: Sekaisha, 1931.

Indian Cinematograph Committee. *Report.* 1928.
Issari, Mohammad Ali. *Cinema in Iran, 1900–1979.* London: Scarecrow Press, 1989.
Itō Hideo. *Taishō no tantei shōsetsu.* Tokyo: San'ichi Shobō, 1991.
Iwamoto Kenji. *Gentō no seiki: Eiga zen'ya no shikaku bunkashi.* Tokyo: Shinwasha, 2002.
Jacobs, Lea. "The Talmadge Sisters: A Forgotten Filmmaking Dynasty." In *Idols of Modernity: Screen Stars of the 1920s,* edited by Patrice Petro, 65–86. New Brunswick, NJ: Rutgers University Press, 2010.
Jacobsen, Wolfgang, Hans Helmut Prinzler, and Werner Sudendorf, eds. *Filmmuseum Berlin.* Berlin: Filmmuseum Berlin, Deutsche Kinemathek, and Nicolaische Verlagsbuchhandlung, 2000.
Jaikumar, Priya. *Cinema at the End of Empire: A Politics of Transition in Britain and India.* Durham, NC: Duke University Press, 2006.
———. "More than Morality: The Indian Cinematograph Committee Interviews (1927)." *Moving Image* 3.1 (Spring 2003): 82–109.
Jani, Pranav. "Karl Marx, Eurocentrism, and the 1857 Revolt in British India." In *Marxism, Modernity and Postcolonial Studies,* edited by Crystal Bartolovich and Neil Lazarus, 81–97. Cambridge, UK: Cambridge University Press, 2002.
Jarvie, Ian. *Hollywood's Overseas Campaign: The North Atlantic Movie Trade, 1920–1950.* Cambridge, UK: Cambridge University Press, 1992.
Jones, Amelia, ed. *The Feminism and Visual Culture Reader.* New York: Routledge, 2003.
Karnad, Girish. "This One Is for Nadia." In *70 Years of Indian Cinema 1913–1983,* edited by T. M. Ramachandran, 258–268. Bombay: Cinema India–International, 1985.
Katō Hidetoshi. *Misemono kara terebi e.* Tokyo: Iwanami Shoten, 1965.
Keddie, Nikki. *Modern Iran: Roots and Results of Revolution.* Updated edition. New Haven, CT: Yale University Press, 2006.
Kejlbo, Ib Rønne, ed. *Kongelig Hoffotograf Peter Elfelt: En billedkavalkade.* Copenhagen: Det Kongelige Bibliotek, 1989.
Kennedy, Joseph, ed. *The Story of the Films.* Chicago: A. W. Shaw, 1927.
Khote, Durga. *I, Durga Khote.* New Delhi: Oxford University Press, 2006.
King, Rob. "Uproarious Inventions: The Keystone Film Company, Modernity, and the Art of the Motor." In *Slapstick Comedy,* edited by Tom Paulus and Rob King, 114–136. New York: Routledge, 2010.
Kinikar, Shashikant. "The Rise and Fall of a Stunt King." *Cinema Vision* 1.1 (1980): 45–48.
———. "Zunzarrao Pawar: Best Fighter." *Cinema Vision* 1.1 (1980): 44–45.
Kinoshita Naoyuki. *Bijutsu to iu misemono.* Tokyo: Heibonsha, 1993.
Kirby, Lynne. *Parallel Tracks: The Railroad and Silent Cinema.* Durham, NC: Duke University Press, 1997.
———. "The Urban Spectator and the Crowd in Early American Train Films." *Iris* 11 (1990): 49–62.
Klaver, Claudia. "Domesticity under Siege: British Women and Imperial Crisis at the Siege of Lucknow, 1857." *Women's Writing: The Elizabethan to Victorian Period* 8.1 (2001): 21–58.
Komada Kōyō. *Katsudō shashin setsumeisho tsuki Ejison-shi shiden.* Tokyo: Katsudō Shashinkai, 1897.

Komatsu Hiroshi. "Shinematogurafu to wa nan datta no ka—Ideorogī sōchi to shite no eiga." In *Eiga denrai: Shinematogurafu to "Meiji no Nihon,"* edited by Yoshida Yoshishige, Yamaguchi Masao, and Kinoshita Naoyuki, 103–123. Tokyo: Iwanami Shoten, 1995.

———. "Some Characteristics of Japanese Cinema before World War I." In *Reframing Japanese Cinema: Authorship, Genre, History,* edited by Arthur Noletti Jr. and David Desser, 229–258. Bloomington: Indiana University Press, 1992.

———. "Transformations in Film as Reality (Part One): Questions Regarding the Genesis of Nonfiction Film." Translated by A. A. Gerow. *Documentary Box* (English ed.) 5 (1994): 3–4.

Koolhaas, Rem. "Junkspace." *October* 100 (2002): 175–190.

Krützen, Michaela. *The Most Beautiful Woman on the Screen: The Fabrication of the Star Greta Garbo.* Frankfurt: P. Lang, 1992.

LaMarre, Thomas. *Shadows on the Screen: Tanizaki Jun'ichirō on Cinema and "Oriental" Aesthetics.* Michigan Monograph Series in Japanese Studies 53. Ann Arbor: Center for Japanese Studies, University of Michigan, 2005.

Landy, Marcia, and Amy Villarejo. *Queen Christina.* BFI Film Classics. London: British Film Institute, 1995.

Lant, Antonia, ed. *Red Velvet Seat: Women's Writing on the First Fifty Years of Cinema.* London: Verso, 2006.

Laporte, Dominique. *History of Shit.* Boston: MIT Press, 2000.

Lefebvre, Henri. *The Production of Space.* Translated by Donald Nicholson-Smith. Malden, MA: Blackwell, 1991.

Liepa, Torey. "Figures of Silent Speech: Silent Film Dialogue and the American Vernacular, 1909–1916. PhD dissertation, New York University, 2008.

Lifson, Ben. "Beato in Lucknow." *Artforum* (May 1988): 99–103.

Lim, Shirley Jennifer. *A Feeling of Belonging: Asian American Women's Public Culture, 1930–1960.* New York: NYU Press, 2006.

Llewellyn-Jones, Rosie. *A Fatal Friendship: The Nawabs, the British and the City of Lucknow.* In *The Lucknow Omnibus,* edited by Abdul Halim Sharar, Rosie Llewellyn-Jones, and Veena Talwar Oldenberg. New Delhi: Oxford University Press, 2001.

Lombroso, Cesare. *Criminal Man.* Translated by Mary Gibson and Nicole Hahn Rafter. Durham, NC: Duke University Press, 2006.

López, Ana M. "Early Cinema and Modernity in Latin America." *Cinema Journal* 40.1 (2000): 48–78.

Lu Xun. "Lici cunzhao 3" [For future reference #3]. Originally published in *Zhongliu Semi-Monthly* 1.3 (October 1936).

———. "Shuo 'Mianzi'" [Observations on Chinese "face"]. Originally published in *Manhua shenghuo* [Cartoon life] 2 (October 1934).

———. "Xiandai dianying yu youchan jieji: yiwen bin fuji" [Modern cinema and the propertied classes: Translation and commentary]. Originally published in *Mengya Monthly* 1.3 (March 1930).

The Lucknow Album. Calcutta: Baptist Mission Press, 1874.

Lunde, Arne. "'Garbo Talks!': Scandinavians in Hollywood, the Talkie Revolution, and the Crisis of Foreign Voice." In *Screen Culture: History and Textuality,* edited by John Fullerton, 21–40. Bloomington: Indiana University Press, 2004.

———. *Nordic Exposures: Scandinavian Identities in Classical Hollywood Cinema*. Seattle: University of Washington Press, 2010.

Madsen, Axel. *The Sewing Circle: Hollywood's Greatest Secret: Female Stars Who Loved Other Women*. Secaucus, NJ: Carol Publishing Group, 1995.

Mahadevan, Sudhir. "Traveling Showmen, Makeshift Cinemas: The *Bioscopewallah* and Early Cinema History in India." *Bioscope: South Asian Screen Studies* 1.1 (January 2010): 27–48.

Majumdar, Neepa. *Wanted Cultured Ladies Only!: Female Stardom and Cinema in India, 1930s–1950s*. Urbana: University of Illinois Press, 2009.

Makino Mamoru. *Nihon eiga ken'etsushi*. Tokyo: Pandora, 2003.

———. "On the Conditions of Film Censorship in Japan before Its Systematization." In *In Praise of Film Studies*, edited by Aaron Gerow and Abé Mark Nornes, 46–67. Yokohama: Kinema Club, 2001.

Malmkjær, Poul. *Gøgler og Generaldirektør: Ole Olsen, grundleggeren af Nordisk Film*. Copenhagen: Gyldendals Bogklubber, 1997.

Malraux, André. *Esquisse d'une psychologie du cinéma*. Paris: Gallimard, 1946.

Maltby, Richard, and Melvyn Stokes, eds. *American Movie Audiences: From the Turn of the Century to the Early Sound Era*. London: British Film Institute, 1999.

———. *Hollywood Abroad: Audiences and Cultural Exchange*. London: British Film Institute, 2004.

Maltby, Richard, and Ruth Vasey. "The International Language Problem: European Reactions to Hollywood's Conversion to Sound." In *Hollywood in Europe: Experiences of a Cultural Hegemony*, edited by David. W. Ellwood and R. Kroes, European Contributions to American Studies 28, 68–93. Amsterdam: VU University Press, 1994.

Mannoni, Laurent. *Le grand art de la lumière et de l'ombre: Archéologie du cinema*. Paris: Nathan, 1995.

Marchand, Roland. *Advertising the American Dream: Making Way for Modernity, 1920–1940*. Berkeley: University of California Press, 1985.

Martineau, Harriet. "Suggestions towards the Future Government of India." *Calcutta Review* 30 (January–June 1858): 358.

Marx, Karl. *Capital: A Critique of Political Economy*. Vol. 1. Translated by Ben Fowkes. Harmondsworth, UK: Pelican Books, 1990.

Massey, Doreen. *for space*. London: Sage, 2010.

Mathur, Saloni. *India by Design: Colonial History and Cultural Display*. Berkeley: University of California Press, 2009.

Matthews, Peter. "Garbo and Phallic Motherhood: A 'Homosexual' Visual Economy." *Screen* 29.3 (1988): 14–42.

Mayne, Judith. *Directed by Dorothy Arzner*. Bloomington: Indiana University Press, 1994.

McLellan, Diana. *The Girls: Sappho Goes to Hollywood*. New York: LA Weekly Books, 2000.

Miyao, Daisuke. "Sessue Hayakawa: The Mirror, The Racialized Body, and *Photogénie*." In Bean, *Flickers of Desire*, 91–112.

Moore, Paul. *Now Playing: Early Moviegoing and the Regulation of Fun*. Albany: SUNY Press, 2008.

Mottahedeh, Negar. "Collection and Recollection: On Studying the Early History of Motion Pictures in Iran." *Early Popular Visual Culture* 6.2 (2008): 103–120.
———. *Representing the Unrepresentable: Images of Reform from the Qajars to the Islamic Republic of Iran.* Syracuse, NY: Syracuse University Press, 2008.
Moussinac, Léon. *Naissance du cinéma.* Paris: J. Povolozky, 1925.
Musser, Charles. *Thomas A. Edison and His Kinetographic Motion Pictures.* New Brunswick, NJ: Rutgers University Press, 1995.
———. "The Travel Genre in 1903–1904: Moving towards Fictional Narrative." In *Early Cinema: Space, Frame and Narrative,* edited by Thomas Elsaesser, 123–132. London: British Film Institute, 1990.
Naficy, Hamid. "For a Theory of Regional Cinemas: Middle Eastern, North African, and Central Asian Cinemas." *Early Popular Visual Culture* 6.2 (2008): 97–102.
———. "Self-Othering: A Postcolonial Discourse on Cinematic First Contacts." In *The Pre-Occupation of Postcolonial Studies,* edited by Fawzia Afzal-Khan and Kalpana Seshadri-Crooks. Durham, NC: Duke University Press, 2000.
———. *A Social History of Iranian Cinema,* vol. 1, *The Artisanal Era, 1897–1941.* Durham, NC: Duke University Press, 2011.
———. "Theorizing 'Third-World' Spectatorship." *Wide Angle* 18.4 (1996): 3–26.
Nagamine Shigetoshi. *Kaitō Jigoma to katsudō shashin no jidai.* Tokyo: Shinchōsha, 2006.
Nagib, Lúcia. "Towards a Positive Definition of World Cinema." In *Remapping World Cinema,* edited by Stephanie Dennison and Song Hwee Lim, 30–37. London: Wallflower Press, 2006.
Nair, P. K. "Titling Techniques." *Cinema Vision* 1.1 (1980): 114-116.
"Nationalfilmografien." Danish Film Institute. http://www.dfi.dk/FaktaOmFilm/Nationalfilmografien.aspx.
Natzén, Christopher. *The Coming of Sound Film in Sweden 1928–1932: New and Old Technologies.* Stockholm: Acta Universitatis Stockholmiensis, 2010.
Naudet, Jean-Jacques, Maria Riva, and Werner Sudendorf, eds. *Marlene Dietrich: Photographs and Memories.* New York: Random House, 2001.
Negra, Diane. *Off-White Hollywood: American Culture and Ethnic Female Stardom.* London: Routledge, 2001.
Nichols, Bill. *Introduction to Documentary.* Bloomington: Indiana University Press, 2001.
Nornes, Abé Mark. *Cinema Babel: Translating Global Cinema.* Minneapolis: University of Minnesota Press, 2007.
———. *Japanese Documentary Film: The Meiji Era through Hiroshima.* Minneapolis: University of Minnesota Press, 2003.
Oakes, T. S. "Ethnic Tourism and Place Identity in China." *Environment and Planning D: Society and Space* 11 (1993): 47–66.
Okudaira Yasuhiro, "Eiga to ken'etsu." In *Kōza Nihon eiga,* edited by Imamura Shōhei, Satō Tadao, Shindō Kaneto, Tsurumi Shunsuke, and Yamada Yōji, 2:303–308. Tokyo: Iwanami Shoten, 1985.
Oldenberg, Veena Talwar. *The Making of Colonial Lucknow: 1856–1877.* In *The Lucknow Omnibus,* edited by Abdul Halim Sharar, Rosie Llewellyn-Jones, and Veena Talwar Oldenberg. New Delhi: Oxford University Press, 2001.

Olsen, Ole. *Filmens Eventyr og Mit Eget.* Copenhagen: Jespersen og Pios Forlag, 1940.

Olsson, Jan. "Svart på vitt: Film, makt och censur" [Black on white: Cinema, power, and censorship]. *Aura. Filmvetenskaplig tidskrift* 1.1 (1995): 14–46.

Palmborg, Rilla. *The Private Life of Greta Garbo.* Garden City, NY: Doubleday/Doran, 1931.

Paranaguá, Paulo Antonio. *Tradición y modernidad en el cine de América Latina.* Madrid: Fondo de Cultura Económica de España, 2003.

Pawar, Lalita. "It Has All Been Worth It." In *70 Years of Indian Cinema 1913–1983,* edited by T. M. Ramachandran, 276–280. Bombay: Cinema International, 1985.

Peiss, Kathy. *Cheap Amusements: Working Women and Leisure in Turn-of-the-Century New York.* Philadelphia: Temple University Press, 1986.

Perry, John. "Language Reform in Turkey and Iran." *International Journal of Middle East Studies* 17 (1985): 295–311.

Peterson, Jennifer Lynn. "Travelogues." In *Encyclopedia of Early Cinema,* edited by Richard Abel, 640–643. New York: Routledge, 2005.

———. "World Pictures: Travelogue Films and the Lure of the Exotic, 1890–1920." PhD dissertation, University of Chicago, 1999.

Petro, Patrice. *Joyless Streets: Women and Melodramatic Representation in Weimar Germany.* Princeton, NJ: Princeton University Press, 1989.

Pinney, Christopher. *The Coming of Photography in India.* London: British Library, 2008.

Poiger, Uta G. "Fantasies of Universality? *Neue Frauen,* Race, and Nation in Weimar and Nazi Germany." In Weinbaum et al., *Modern Girl around the World,* 317–344.

Rajadhyaksha, Ashish. *Encyclopedia of Indian Cinema.* London: Oxford University Press, 1994.

———. "India's Silent Cinema: A 'Viewer's View.'" In *Light of Asia: Indian Silent Cinema, 1912–1934,* edited by Suresh Chabria, 25–40. New Delhi: Wiley Eastern, 1994.

Rajadhyaksha, Ashish, and Paul Willemen. *Encyclopaedia of Indian Cinema.* Rev. ed. London: British Film Institute; New Delhi: Oxford University Press, 1999.

Report of the Indian Cinematograph Committee: Evidence. 4 vols. (Calcutta: Government of India, Central Publication Branch, 1927–1928).

Rhodes, John David, and Elena Gorfinkel, eds. *Taking Place: Location and the Moving Image.* Minneapolis: University of Minnesota Press, 2011.

Richardson, Dorothy. "The Cinema in Arcady." In *Close Up 1927–1933: Cinema and Modernism,* edited by James Donald, Anne Friedberg, and Laura Marcus, 184–186. Princeton, NJ: Princeton University Press, 1998.

Rocha, Gregorio. "*La venganza de Pancho Villa* (*The Vengeance of Pancho Villa*): A Lost and Found Border Film." *Journal of Film Preservation* 65 (December 2003): 24–31.

Rogoff, Irit. "Gossip as Testimony: A Postmodern Signature." In *The Feminism and Visual Culture Reader,* edited by Amelia Jones, 268–276. London: Routledge, 2003.

Rosenberg, Emily. *Spreading the American Dream: American Economic and Cultural Expansion, 1890–1945.* New York: Hill and Wang, 1982.

Rossholm, Anna-Sofia. *Reproducing Languages, Translating Bodies: Approaches to Speech, Translation and Cultural Identity in Early European Sound Film.* Stockholm: Acta Universitatis Stockholmiensis, 2006.

Ruoff, Jeffrey, ed. *Virtual Voyages: Cinema and Travel.* Durham, NC: Duke University Press, 2006.

Russell, Catherine, ed. "New Women of the Silent Screen: China, Japan, Hollywood." Special issue, *Camera Obscura* 20.3 (2005).
Russo, Vito. *The Celluloid Closet: Homosexuality in the Movies.* New York: Harper and Row, 1987.
Sadr, Hamid Reza. *Iranian Cinema: A Political History.* London: I. B. Tauris, 2006.
Said, Edward. *Culture and Imperialism.* London: Vintage, 1994.
———. *Orientalism.* New York: Vintage, 1979.
Sakamoto Kitarō. *Jitchi ōyō butsuri kikan.* 2nd ed. Tokyo: Hakubunkan, 1891.
Sandberg, Mark B. "Mastering the House: Performative Inhabitation in Carl Th. Dreyer's *The Parson's Widow.*" In *Northern Constellations: New Readings in Nordic Cinema,* edited by C. Claire Thompson, 23–42. Norwich, UK: Norvik Press, 2006.
———. "Multiple-Reel Feature Films: Europe." In *Encyclopedia of Early Cinema,* edited by Richard Abel, 452–456. New York: Routledge, 2005.
———. "Pocket Movies: Souvenir Cinema Programs and the Danish Silent Cinema." *Film History* 13.1 (Fall 2001): 6–22.
Sartre, Jean-Paul. *The Reprieve.* Translated by Eric Sutton. London: Penguin Books, 1973.
Satō Tadao. *Nihon eigashi.* Tokyo: Iwanami Shoten, 1995.
Schivelbusch, Wolfgang. *The Railway Journey: The Industrialization of Time and Space in the 19th Century.* Berkeley: University of California Press, 1986.
Schnaidt, Claude. *Hannes Meyer: Bauten, Projekte und Schriften / Buildings, Projects and Writing.* London: Tiranti, 1965.
Scurr, Ruth. *Fatal Purity: Robespierre and the French Revolution.* New York: Henry Holt, 2006.
Serna, Laura Isabel. "'As a Mexican I Feel It Is My Duty': Citizenship, Censorship, and the Campaign against Derogatory Films in Mexico, 1922–1930." *The Americas: A Quarterly Review of Inter-American Cultural History* 63.2 (October 2006): 225–244.
Shanks, Michael, David Platt, and William Rathje. "The Perfume of Garbage: Modernity and the Archaeological." *Modernism/Modernity* 11.1 (2004): 61–83.
Shinbun shūroku Taishō-shi. Tokyo: Taishō Shuppan, 1978.
Shklovsky, Viktor. "The Work of the Re-Editor." In *The Film Factory: Russian and Soviet Cinema in Documents 1896–1939,* edited by Richard Taylor and Ian Christie, 168–169. London: Routledge and Kegan Paul, 1988.
Shohat, Ella, and Robert Stam. *Unthinking Eurocentrism: Multiculturalism and the Media.* London: Routledge, 1994.
Singer, Ben. *Melodrama and Modernity: Early Sensational Cinema and Its Contexts.* New York: Columbia University Press, 2001.
Sinha, Babli. "Lowering Our Prestige: American Cinema, Mass Consumerism, and Racial Anxiety in Colonial India." *Comparative Studies of South Asia, Africa and the Middle East* 29.2 (2009): 291–305.
Smith, Arthur H. *Chinese Characteristics.* New York: Fleming H. Revell, 1894.
Smith, Michael. "Cinema for the Soviet East: National Fact and Revolutionary Fiction in Early Azerbaijani Film." *Slavic Review* 56.4 (1997): 645–678.
Snickars, Pelle. *Svensk film och masskultur 1900.* Stockholm: Aura, 2001.
Soja, Edward. *Postmodern Geographies: The Reassertion of Space in Critical Social Theory.* New York: Verso, 1989.
———. *Seeking Spatial Justice.* Minneapolis: University of Minnesota Press, 2010.

Sollors, Werner. Introduction to *The Multilingual Anthology of American Literature: A Reader of Original Texts with English Translations*. Edited by Marc Shell and Werner Sollors. New York: NYU Press, 2000.

Spoto, Donald. *Blue Angel*. New York: Cooper Square Press, 2000.

Stamp, Shelley. *Movie-Struck Girls: Women and Motion Picture Culture after the Nickelodeon*. Princeton, NJ: Princeton University Press, 2000.

Standish, Isolde. *A New History of Japanese Cinema: A Century of Narrative Film*. London: Continuum, 2005.

Statistiska Centralbyrån. *Historisk statistik för Sverige. Del 1: Befolkning, 1720–1967* [National Central Bureau of Statistics. Historical Statistics of Sweden, Part 1: Population, 1720–1967]. Stockholm: Allmänna Förlaget, 1969.

Steer, Valentia. *The Romance of the Cinema: A Short Record of the Development of the Most Popular Form of Amusement of the Day*. London: C. Arthur Pearson, 1913.

Steimatsky, Noa. *Italian Locations: Reinhabiting the Past in Postwar Cinema*. Minneapolis: University of Minnesota Press, 2008.

Stein, Gertrude. *Narration: Four Lectures*. Introduction by Thornton Wilder. Chicago: University of Chicago Press, 1993.

Stewart, Jacqueline Najuma. *Migrating to the Movies: Cinema and Black Urban Modernity*. Berkeley: University of California Press, 2005.

Stites, Richard. *Revolutionary Dreams: Utopian Vision in the Russian Revolution*. New York: Oxford University Press, 1989.

Straayer, Chris. *Deviant Eyes, Deviant Bodies: Sexual Re-Orientations in Film and Video*. New York: Columbia University Press, 1996.

Strasser, Susan. *Waste and Want: A Social History of Trash*. New York: Metropolitan Books, 1999.

Strauss, William Victor. "Foreign Distribution of American Motion Pictures." *Harvard Business Review* 8.3 (April 1930): 307–315.

Streible, Dan. "The Role of Orphan Films in the 21st Century Archive." *Cinema Journal* 46.3 (2007): 124–128.

Studlar, Gaylyn. *This Mad Masquerade: Stardom and Masculinity in the Jazz Age*. New York: Columbia University Press, 1996.

Sturken, Marita. *Tourists of History: Memory, Kitsch, and Consumerism from Oklahoma City to Ground Zero*. Durham, NC: Duke University Press, 2007.

Sudendorf, Werner. "Marlene Dietrich: Von Kopf bis Fuss / Marlene Dietrich: From Head to Toe." In Jacobsen, Prinzler, and Sudendorf, *Filmmuseum Berlin*, 131–168.

Szaloky, Melinda. "'As You Desire Me': Reading 'The Divine Garbo' through Movement, Silence and the Sublime." *Film History* 18.2 (2006): 196–208.

Taishō nyūsu jiten. Tokyo: Mainichi Komyunikēshonzu, 1988.

Takazawa Hatsutarō. *Gendai engeki sōran*. 2nd ed. Tokyo: Bunseisha, 1919.

Taylor, Paul S. *Mexican Labor in the United States: Chicago and the Calumet Region*. Berkeley: University of California Press, 1932.

Terakawa Shin. *Eiga oyobi eigageki*. Osaka: Osaka Mainichi Shinbun, 1925.

Thissen, Judith. "Jewish Immigrant Audiences in New York City, 1905–1914." In Maltby and Stokes, *American Movie Audiences*, 15–28.

Thomas, Rosie, "Distant Voices, Magic Knives: *Lal-e-Yaman* and the Transition to Sound in Bombay Cinema." In *Beyond the Boundaries of Bombay Cinema: The*

Many Forms of Hindi Cinema, edited by Rachel Dwyer and Jerry Pinto, 53–76. New Delhi: Oxford University Press, 2011.

———. "*Miss Frontier Mail:* The Film That Mistook Its Star for a Train." In *Sarai Reader 7: Frontiers,* edited by Monica Narula, Shuddhabrata Sengupta, Jeebesh Bagchi, and Ravi Sundaram, 294–308. New Delhi: Center for the Study of Developing Societies, 2007.

———. "Not Quite (Pearl) White: Fearless Nadia, Queen of the Stunts." In *Bollyworld: Popular Indian Cinema through a Transnational Lens,* edited by Raminder Kaur and Ajay Sinha, 35–69. New Delhi: Sage, 2005.

———. "Still Magic: An Aladdin's Cave of 1950s B-Movie Fantasy," *Tasveer Gar,* http://tasveerghar.net/cmsdesk/essay/103/.

Thompson, Kristin. *Exporting Entertainment: America in the World Film Market, 1907–1934.* London: British Film Institute, 1985.

Thorsen, Isak. "The Rise and Fall of the Polar Bear." In *100 Years of Nordisk Film,* edited by Lisbeth Richter Larsen and Dan Nissen, 53–71. Copenhagen: Danish Film Institute, 2006.

Touraj, Erik, and Zürcher Atabaki. *Men of Order: Authoritarian Modernization under Atatürk and Reza Shah.* London: I. B. Tauris, 2004.

Trumpbour, John. *Selling Hollywood to the World: U.S. and European Struggles for Mastery of the Global Film Industry, 1920–1950.* Cambridge, UK: Cambridge University Press, 2002.

Tsivian, Yuri. "Between the Old and the New: Soviet Film Culture in 1918–1924." *Griffithiana* 55/56 (1996): 15–63.

———. "The Wise and Wicked Game: Re-Editing and Soviet Film Culture of the 1920s." *Film History* 8.3 (1996): 327–343.

Tsivian, Yuri, and David Mayer. "*Orphans of the Storm.*" In *The Griffith Project,* vol. 10, *Films Produced in 1919–46,* edited by Paolo Cherchi Usai, 116–137. London: British Film Institute; Pordenone, Italy: Le Giornate del Cinema Muto, 2006.

Tsukada Yoshinobu. *Nihon eigashi no kenkyū.* Tokyo: Gendai Shokan, 1980.

Ueda Manabu. "Kankyaku no tomadoi: Eiga sōsōki ni okeru shinamatekku no kōgyō o megutte." *Āto risāchi* 7 (2007): 129–139.

Ullman, Sharon. "'The Twentieth Century Way': Female Impersonation and Sexual Practice in Turn-of-the-Century America." *Journal of the History of Sexuality* 5.4 (1995): 573–600.

U.S. Department of Commerce, Bureau of Foreign and Domestic Commerce. *Motion Pictures in Argentina and Brazil.* Washington, DC: Government Printing Office, 1929.

———. *Motion Pictures in Mexico, Central America, and the Greater Antilles.* Washington, DC: Government Printing Office, 1931.

———. *Trade Information Bulletin No. 601.* Washington, DC: U.S. Department of Commerce, Bureau of Foreign and Domestic Commerce, 1929.

Usabel, Gaizka S. de. *The High Noon of American Films in Latin America.* Ann Arbor, MI: UMI Research Press, 1982.

Václavek, Bedřich. "On the Sociology of Film." In *Cinema All the Time: An Anthology of Czech Film Theory and Criticism, 1908–1939,* edited by Jaroslav Anděl and Petr Szczepanik, translated by Kevin B. Johnson, 155–160. Prague: National Film Archive, 2008.

van Houten, Theodor. *"Eisenstein Was Great Eater": In Memory of Leonid Trauberg.* Buren, Netherlands: A&R/GP, 1991.
Vance, Jeffrey. *Douglas Fairbanks.* Berkeley: University of California Press, 2008.
Vasey, Ruth. *The World According to Hollywood, 1918–1939.* Madison: University of Wisconsin Press, 1997.
Vasudevan, Ravi. "In the Centrifuge of History." *Cinema Journal* 50.1 (Fall 2010): 135–140.
Vertov, Dziga. *Kino-Eye: The Writings of Dziga Vertov.* Edited by Annette Michelson. Berkeley: University of California Press, 1984.
Vertovec, Steven, and Robin Cohen, eds. *Conceiving Cosmopolitanism: Theory, Context, and Practice.* New York: Oxford University Press, 2002.
Viertel, Salka. *The Kindness of Strangers.* New York: Holt, Rinehart and Winston, 1969.
Villard, Henry S. "Film Importers Face Difficulties in Persia." *Commerce Reports* 14 (1931): 37–38.
Vincendeau, Ginette. "Hollywood Babel: The Multiple Language Version." *Screen* 29.2 (1998): 24–39.
Vitali, Valentina, and Paul Willemen. Introduction to *Theorising National Cinema,* 1–14. London: British Film Institute, 2006.
Vonderau, Patrick. *Bilder vom Norden: Schwedisch-deutsche Filmbeziehungen, 1914–1939.* Marburg, Germany: Schüren-Verlag, 2007.
Walker, Alexander. *Garbo: A Portrait.* New York: Macmillan, 1980.
Walkowitz, Rebecca L. *Cosmopolitan Style: Modernism beyond the Nation.* New York: Columbia University Press, 2006.
Wallengren, Ann-Kristin. "Celebrating Swedishness: Swedish-Americans and Cinema." In *Swedish Film: An Introduction and Reader,* edited by Mariah Larsson and Anders Marklund, 134–143. Lund, Sweden: Nordic Academic Press, 2010.
Wang, Yiman. "Anna May Wong: Toward Janus-Faced, Border-Crossing, 'Minor' Stardom." In *Idols of Modernity: Movie Stars of the 1920s,* edited by Patrice Petro, 159–181. New Brunswick, NJ: Rutgers University Press, 2010.
———. "The Art of Screen Passing: Anna May Wong's Yellow Yellowface Performance in the Art Deco Era." *Camera Obscura* 20.3 (2005): 159–191.
Waters, Sarah. "'A Girton Girl on a Throne': Queen Christina and Versions of Lesbianism, 1906–1933." *Feminist Review* 46.1 (1994): 41–60.
Weinbaum, Alys Eve, Lynn M. Thomas, Priti Ramamurthy, Uta G. Poiger, Madeleine Yue Dong, and Tani E. Barlow, eds. *The Modern Girl around the World: Consumption, Modernity, and Globalization.* Durham, NC: Duke University Press, 2008.
Weiss, Andrea. *Vampires and Violets: Lesbians in Film.* New York: Penguin Books, 1993.
Werner, Gösta. *Mauritz Stiller: Ett livsöde.* Stockholm: Prisma, 1991.
Whissel, Kristen. "Guest Editor's Introduction: Genealogical and Archaeological Approaches to 3-D." *Film Criticism* 37/38.3/1 (Spring/Fall 2013): 6–11.
———. *Picturing American Modernity: Traffic, Technology, and the Silent Cinema.* Durham, NC: Duke University Press, 2008.
White, Patricia. "Black and White: Mercedes De Acosta's Glorious Enthusiasms." *Camera Obscura* 15.3 (2000): 227–264.
———. *Uninvited: Classical Hollywood Cinema and Lesbian Representability.* Bloomington: Indiana University Press, 1999.

Williams, Linda. "Of Kisses and Ellipses: The Long Adolescence of American Movies." *Critical Inquiry* 32 (Winter 2006): 288–340.

———. *Playing the Race Card: Melodramas of Black and White from Uncle Tom to O. J. Simpson.* Princeton, NJ: Princeton University Press, 2001.

Wolf, Eric. *Europe and the People without History.* Berkeley: University of California Press, 1982.

Woolf, Virginia. *Orlando: A Biography.* New York: Harcourt Brace Jovanovich, 1973.

Yanai Yoshio. *Katsudō shashin no hogo to torishimari.* Tokyo: Yūhikaku, 1929.

Yoshida Chieo. *Mō hitotsu no eigashi.* Tokyo: Jiji Tsūshinsha, 1978.

Yoshida Yoshishige, Yamaguchi Masao, and Kinoshita Naoyuki, eds. *Eiga denrai: Shinematogurafu to "Meiji no Nihon."* Tokyo: Iwanami Shoten, 1995.

Yoshimura Fuyuhiko [pseud.]. *Zoku Fuyuhiko shū.* Tokyo: Iwanami Shoten, 1932.

Yoshiyama Kyokkō. *Nihon eigakai jibutsu kigen.* Tokyo: Shinema to Engeisha, 1933.

Youngblood, Denise. "'Americanitis': The Amerikanshchina in Soviet Cinema." *Journal of Popular Film & Television* 19.4 (January 1, 1992): 148–156.

———. *Movies for the Masses: Popular Cinema and Soviet Society in the 1920s.* Cambridge, UK: Cambridge University Press, 1992.

Xu Guangping. "Ji Lu Xun xiansheng de yile" [On Mr. Lu Xun's entertainment]. In *Lu Xun de xiezuo yu shenghuo: Xu Guangping yi Lu Xun* [The writing and life of Lu Xun: Xu Guangping remembering Lu Xun (selected essays)]. Shanghai: Shanghai wenhua chubanshe, 2006.

Zhang, Zhen. *An Amorous History of the Silver Screen: Shanghai Cinema, 1896–1937.* Chicago: University of Chicago Press, 2005.

Contributors

KAVEH ASKARI is Associate Professor in the English Department at Western Washington University. He has published articles on the magic lantern, early cinema and art education, and early 16mm color. In 2008, he edited a special issue of *Early Popular Visual Culture* on the Middle East and North Africa. He is currently at work on *Picture Craft: Discourses of Art from the Magic Lantern to Early Hollywood.*

JENNIFER M. BEAN is Director of Cinema and Media Studies and Associate Chair of Comparative Literature at the University of Washington. She is co-editor of *A Feminist Reader in Early Cinema* (2002) and editor of *Flickers of Desire: Movie Stars of the 1910s* (2011). She has published widely on silent era cinema, including recent chapters in *Slapstick Comedy* (ed. Rob King and Tom Paulus, 2010) and *American Cinema of the 1920s* (ed. Lucy Fischer, 2009). She is currently completing a study on the "imagination of mass culture" and multi-media synergy in early-twentieth-century America.

AARON GEROW is Professor of Film Studies and East Asian Languages and Literatures at Yale University. He has published numerous articles in English, Japanese, and other languages on such topics as Japanese early cinema, film theory, contemporary directors, film genre, censorship, Japanese manga, and cinematic representations of minorities. His book on Kitano Takeshi was published in 2007, *A Page of Madness* came out in 2008, and *Visions of Japanese Modernity: Articulations of Cinema, Nation, and Spectatorship, 1895–1925*, was published in 2010. He also co-authored the *Research Guide to Japanese Film Studies* with Abé Mark Nornes (2009). He is currently working on books about the history of Japanese film theory and Japanese cinema after 1980.

LAURA HORAK is a postdoctoral researcher in the Department of Media Studies at Stockholm University. Her writings have appeared in *Camera Obscura, Cinema Journal,* and *Film Quarterly.* She is currently at work on *Girls Will Be Boys: Cross-Dressed Women and American Silent Cinema,* as well as researching a new project on sexuality in early Swedish cinema.

PRIYA JAIKUMAR is Associate Professor of Critical Studies at the University of Southern California's School of Cinematic Arts. Her research has focused on colonial and postcolonial visuality, cinema, and state power in India and Britain. Her book *Cinema at the End of Empire: A Politics of Transition in Britain and*

India (2006) details the intertwined film histories of a declining empire and a nascent nation, conceiving of the colonial in relation to emergent national and proto-global cultural networks. Her current research is on space in cinema, film locations, and theories of film historiography.

ANUPAMA KAPSE is Assistant Professor in the Department of Media Studies, Queens College, CUNY. She is currently completing a book titled *Performing the Body Politic: Melodrama and Early Indian Cinema, 1913–1939*. Her articles have appeared in *Framework*, *Figurations in Indian Film* (ed. Meheli Sen and Anustup Basu, 2013), and *The Routledge Encyclopedia of Film* (forthcoming). Her research focuses on melodrama, transnational film genres, gender, performance and visuality, and film and media histories.

JAN OLSSON is Professor of Cinema Studies at Stockholm University. He has published widely on multiple aspects of film and media studies, most recently as the author of *Los Angeles before Hollywood: Journalism and American Film Culture, 1905–1915* (2008) and as editor of *Media, Popular Culture, and the American Century* (2010). His current research interests include early cinema, television studies, and the global reach of American media.

PATRICE PETRO is Vice Provost for International Education and Professor of English, Film Studies, and Global Studies at the University of Wisconsin–Milwaukee. She is the author and editor of ten books, most recently *Idols of Modernity: Movie Stars of the Twenties* (2010). She is past president of the Society for Cinema and Media Studies (SCMS), the preeminent scholarly association for the study of film, television, and media.

MARK B. SANDBERG is Professor in the Department of Film and Media and the Department of Scandinavian at the University of California, Berkeley. He is the author of *Living Pictures, Missing Persons: Mannequins, Museums, and Modernity* (2003), as well as numerous other publications in the fields of museology, theater history, Scandinavian cinema, and late-nineteenth-century visual culture.

LAURA ISABEL SERNA is Assistant Professor of Critical Studies at the University of Southern California's School of Cinematic Arts, where she teaches courses in international silent cinema, historiography, Mexican cinema, and Latina/o media culture. She is the author of *Making Cinelandia: American Films and Mexican Film Culture before the Golden Age* (2014). She is currently at work on two projects, one a historical investigation of "brownface" in American silent cinema and the other the construction of a cultural geography of Latino cinema culture in Los Angeles from the 1920s to the 1960s.

YURI TSIVIAN is the William Colvin Professor in the Departments of Cinema and Media Studies (Chair), Art History, and Slavic Languages and Literatures at the University of Chicago. His books include *Early Cinema in Russia and Its Cultural Reception* (1994), *Ivan the Terrible* (2002), *Lines of Resistance: Dziga Vertov and the Twenties* (2004), and *Approaches to Carpalistics: Movement and Gesture in Art, Literature and Film* (2010). His CD ROM *Immaterial Bodies: Cultural Anatomy of Early Russian Films* (2000) received the 2001 BAFTA award. His new interest is in digital methods of film studies; see http://www.cinemetrics.lv.

YIMAN WANG is Associate Professor of Film and Digital Media at the University of California, Santa Cruz. She is author of *Remaking Chinese Cinema: Through the Prism of Shanghai, Hong Kong and Hollywood* (2013). Her articles have appeared in the *Quarterly Review of Film and Video, Film Quarterly, Camera Obscura, Journal of Film and Video, Literature/Film Quarterly, Positions: East Asia Cultures Critique, Journal of Chinese Cinemas, Chinese Films in Focus* (ed. Chris Berry, 2003, 2008), *Idols of Modernity: Movie Stars of the 1920s* (ed. Patrice Petro, 2010), *The New Chinese Documentary Film Movement: For the Public Record* (ed. Chris Berry, Lü Xinyu, and Lisa Rofel, 2010), *Cinema at the City's Edge: Film and Urban Networks in East Asia* (ed. Yomi Braester and James Tweedie, 2010), and *Engendering Cinema: Chinese Women Filmmakers Inside and Outside China* (ed. Lingzhen Wang, 2011).

Index

Italic page numbers indicate material in figures.